RENAISSANCE DRAMA
IX ∾ 1966

Renaissance Drama

IX

Edited by S. Schoenbaum

Northwestern University Press

EVANSTON 1966

THE ILLUSTRATION *on the front cover of this volume is from the title page of the 1621 Venice edition of* Il Pastor Fido. *It is reproduced by courtesy of the Charles Deering Library of Northwestern University.*

Editorial Note

RENAISSANCE DRAMA, an annual publication, provides a forum for scholars in various parts of the globe: wherever the drama of the Renaissance is studied. Coverage, so far as subject matter is concerned, is not restricted to any single national theater. The chronological limits of the Renaissance are interpreted liberally, and space is available for essays on precursors, as well as on the utilization of Renaissance themes by later writers. Investigations shedding light on theatrical history and actual stage production are especially welcome, as are comparative studies. Editorial policy favors articles of some scope. Essays that are exploratory in nature, that are concerned with critical or scholarly methodology, that raise new questions or embody fresh approaches to perennial problems are particularly appropriate for a publication which originated out of the proceedings of the Modern Language Association Conference on Research Opportunities in Renaissance Drama. In future numbers the Editor hopes to enlarge the review section.

The 1967 volume will be devoted primarily to masques and entertainments. Contributions offered for publication should be addressed to the Editor, RENAISSANCE DRAMA, Northwestern University, 619 Emerson Street, Evanston, Illinois 60201. Prospective contributors are requested to follow the recommendations of the *MLA Style Sheet* (revised edition) in preparing manuscripts.

v

Contents

RENAISSANCE DRAMA
IX ❧ 1966

Time and Art
in Shakespeare's Romances

L. G. SALINGAR

THE PLAYER WHO SPEAKS as Time, the Chorus at the beginning of
Act IV in *The Winter's Tale,* combines several functions. He is a
Presenter, carrying the story forward like the Chorus in *Henry V.*
As a figure from pageantry,[1] he prepares the ground for the two great
masque-like scenes that distinguish the second part of the play from the
first. He has an emblematic function, bringing out the significance of the
action he foreshadows like Rumour in *2 Henry IV,* but doing so both
more authoritatively and more ambiguously, since he needs to defend
himself against the presumption that he is nothing better than a vandal or
a thief. And with this, Shakespeare gives him another task, recalling
Terence's prologues; he glancingly defends the dramatist's technique
against possible critics:

> Impute it not a crime
> To me or my swift passage that I slide
> O'er sixteen years, and leave the growth untried

1. See *The Winter's Tale,* ed. J. H. Pafford, [New] Arden Shakespeare (London,
1963), Appendix, p. 168. Titles of Jacobean pageants, etc., include *The Time
Triumphant* (London, 1604) and *Time's Complaint* (Oxford, 1608); cf. *The
Triumph of Time* in Beaumont and Fletcher's *Four Plays, or Moral Representations,
in One (c.* 1608–1613).

3

> Of that wide gap, since it is in my pow'r
> To o'erthrow law, and in one self-born hour
> To plant and o'erwhelm custom.
>
> (IV.i.4–9)

This constitutes a bland apology to objections such as those uttered by the Prologue to the revised *Every Man in His Humour,* where Jonson declares that he "justly hates" the "ill customs" of the popular theaters and where he goes on to select Shakespeare's Histories for a particular example. Before Jonson ridicules the staging of "York and Lancaster's long jars" and defines his own standard of realism, he makes it clear that his disdain for "ill customs" refers first of all to breaches of the Unity of Time:

> Though neede make many *Poets,* and some such
> As art, and nature haue not betterd much;
> Yet ours, for want, hath not so lou'd the stage,
> As he dare serue th'ill customes of the age:
> Or purchase your delight at such a rate,
> As, for it, he himselfe must iustly hate.
> To make a child, now swadled, to proceede
> Man, and then shoote vp, in one beard, and weede,
> Past threescore yeeres. . . .
>
> (Prologue, 1–9) [2]

Very likely Jonson's graybeard is an imaginary case for the sake of caricature; it would be hard to name many Elizabethan plays to which his objection applies strictly, even in principle. But among the few known plays of the period where a character grows up from babyhood are *Pericles*—that "mouldy tale," as Jonson was to call it—and the play that Time, the Chorus, is now defending. Even allowing for the possibility that Jonson wrote the Prologue to his revised *Every Man* a year or two later than *The Winter's Tale,*[3] Shakespeare must have been very thoroughly acquainted with Jonson's opinions; in any case, they were well known through such critics as Sidney.

---

2. Jonson citations are from the Herford and Simpson edition.

3. See E. K. Chambers, *Elizabethan Stage* (Oxford, 1923), III, 360; Jonson, *Ode to Himself* (1631), ll. 19–24. Cf. John Tatham's verse letter to Brome (on *A Jovial Crew,* 1640): "There is a Faction (Friend) in Town, that cries, / . . . *Shakespeare the Plebean Driller,* was / Founder'd in's *Pericles*" (*Dramatic Works of Richard Brome* [London, 1873], III, 348).

The attitude Shakespeare's Chorus adopts toward critical "law" in *The Winter's Tale* parallels that of another contemporary, Lope de Vega, expounding "the art of making comedies in Spain, where whatever is written is against art":

> . . . when I have to write a play I lock the rules away with six keys; I remove Terence and Plautus from my study that they may not cry out at me. . . . O! how many in these days cross themselves to see the years that must elapse in a matter which ends in one artificial day; for this, though, they would not allow the mathematical day. But considering that the anger of a seated Spaniard is not calmed unless he sees within two hours a representation from Genesis to the Last Judgment, I consider it most proper here, if our purpose is to please, to arrange all so that it be a success.

Lope claims that he willingly adopts "the barbarous manner" of writing that will please his public;[4] and Shakespeare too seems to be dismissing neoclassical rules from a theater whose "custom" is essentially medieval.

The critical argument Shakespeare puts into the mouth of Time reaches further, however, than claiming a right to please the crowd. Time goes on to suggest a broader and more detached view than Jonson, for instance, was prepared to take of historical changes in dramatic art:

> Let me pass
> The same I am, ere ancient'st order was
> Or what is now receiv'd. I witness to
> The times that brought them in; so shall I do
> To th' freshest things now reigning, and make stale
> The glistering of this present, as my tale
> Now seems to it.
>
> (IV.i.9–15)

On one side, Time concedes that his tale, with its sixteen-year gap in the middle, has an undeniably old-fashioned look about it; on the other, he contends that neither the ancient rules themselves nor modern efforts to restore them can be absolute and everlasting. So far, his plea can be

---

4. Lope de Vega, *The New Art of Making Comedies* (1609), trans. Olga Marx Perlzweig, in *Literary Criticism: Plato to Dryden,* ed. Allan H. Gilbert (New York, 1940), pp. 542–545.

described as "modernist" (like Nashe's defense of freedom in language).[5]
But the Chorus glances further, from the external history of drama to its
inner nature, its aesthetics. Not only, he implies, is drama affected externally by historical time, and not only is it nominally made of the stuff of
time, in the sense that it purports to show successive events in the
characters' lives, but its inmost structure is an experience of time communicated to the minds of the audience. Such experience is imaginative,
subjective. As Rosalind had said in *As You Like It,* "Time travels in
divers paces with divers persons"; here, Time himself implies that the
sixteen-year gap he is bridging is not a void but a subjective experience,
for the audience as well as the characters: something to be compared with
sleep (which may be creative) and, with more emphasis (since it repeats
one of the chief metaphors in the play), something "growing." Moreover,
since the experience of time supplies the continuity of drama, Time in the
theater may be said to govern Place as well:

> Your patience this allowing,
> I turn my glass, and give my scene such growing
> As you had slept between. Leontes leaving—
> Th' effects of his fond jealousies so grieving
> That he shuts up himself—imagine me,
> Gentle spectators, that I now may be
> In fair Bohemia. . . .
>
> (IV.i.15–21)

If Shakespeare was not a proclaimed critic like Jonson, he was clearly far
from working by rule of thumb; what Time hints at in these lines is a
maturely considered theory of drama. But Shakespeare's theory is undog-
matic and flexible. In *The Winter's Tale* he is prepared to repeat and even
to defend the glaring disregard of classical rules he had been guilty of in
Pericles. Yet immediately afterwards, in *The Tempest,* he observes the
Unity of Time, if not other neoclassical precepts, as exactly as even Jonson
could have wished. His treatment of the factor of time in these late plays
shows sensitive experimentation, with an increasing or renewed awareness
of the special nature of romance and of the general problems of dramatic
form.

5. Nashe against Harvey, in *Strange Newes* (1592), in *Elizabethan Critical Essays,*
ed. G. Gregory Smith (London, 1904), II, 242–243.

I

Modern scholars have discussed the background of Shakespeare's romantic plays with an emphasis on the traditions of courtly love and of pastoral tragicomedy.[6] Certainly, these traditions influenced Shakespeare; but they do not lead to the center of his interests as a dramatist in the group of works from *Pericles* to *The Tempest*. Pastoral has nothing directly to do with *Pericles,* for instance, and the notion of tragicomedy as a theatrical genre was still a vague one; there is no need to assume that Shakespeare turned to Fletcher's definition in *The Faithful Shepherdess* (1608–1609) for the planning of *Cymbeline* or *The Winter's Tale*. The courtly tradition, sophisticated by Neoplatonism, counted for a great deal in Shakespeare's love scenes; but it is noticeable that his only dramatic subject taken directly from the literature of courtly love is *Troilus and Cressida* and that his treatment of it there is far from romantic. To understand Shakespeare's approach to his last plays, it is desirable to take account of two other traditions of romance, both of them much older and more closely linked with the history of drama than romances of chivalry. Both are concerned with Shakespeare's subject matter of quarrels and reconciliation, separation, wandering, sea adventures, and reunion. And, from the point of view of an Elizabethan playwright, both raise acutely the problem of the representation of time.

One of them runs back through Italian drama of the sixteenth century and the Hellenistic prose romances that were revived during the same period to classical New Comedy and the antecedents of New Comedy in classical tragedy. The kind of plot in question here can be described as Euripidean romance, for it was chiefly Euripides, through such plays as his *Ion,* who turned the course of New Comedy in this direction and hence the romantic drama of the Renaissance. As the Alexandrian biographer of Euripides pointed out,

quarrels between husband and wife, father and son, servant and master, or situations involving sudden change of fortune [*peripeteia*], substitution of

6. Cf. H. B. Charlton, *Shakespearian Comedy,* 4th ed. (London, 1949), pp. 23–33; E. C. Pettet, *Shakespeare and the Romance Tradition* (London, 1949); Philip Edwards, "Shakespeare's Romances: 1900–1957," *Shakespeare Survey 11* (Cambridge, Eng., 1958), pp. 14–18.

children, violation of girls, and recognition by rings and necklaces; . . . all this is really the mainstay of New Comedy, and it was Euripides who perfected it.[7]

"All this"—though certainly not this alone—is the "mainstay" of New Comedy, not merely in serious and, as we should be inclined to call them, romantic plays like *Andria, Hecyra, Captivi, Rudens,* but in outwardly farcical comedies such as *Menaechmi.* They all depend on an antecedent loss of a child due to misfortune or else on a lovers' quarrel due to a mistake, and they all concentrate upon the phase of the story leading to a scene of recognition and the reestablishment of a divided family. In the sixteenth century Italian playwrights took up the theme, to such an extent that at least one of them, Grazzini, protested. There are so many modern comedies, he says, taken from Terence and Plautus and ending in "rediscoveries" that when the spectators learn from a prologue "that in the capture of a certain City, or the sack of a certain Castle, some little boys or girls went astray or were lost," then they feel sure they know the plot already and would be willing to go away.[8] But a protest like this was hardly enough to dam the stream, which was fed from theatrical episodes incorporated in the Hellenistic novels[9] as well as directly from New Comedy.

Euripidean romance concentrates upon mistakes of identity, misunderstandings, the mutual ignorance of lovers or members of the same family who meet on the stage without knowing each other; it welcomes disguise and heightens coincidence; it dwells for its governing idea on the irony of Fortune. The second tradition of nonchivalric romance deals with the same or similar narrative material but treats it in another spirit. This tradition emerges, from the same literary culture as the Hellenistic novels, in Christianized romances like the *Clementine Recognitions* and *Apollo-*

---

7. Satyrus (*c.* 200 B.C.); see K. J. Dover, "Greek Comedy" in *Fifty Years of Classical Scholarship,* ed. Maurice Platnauer (Oxford, 1954), p. 122.

8. Grazzini, Prologue to *La Gelosia* (1551); see Ireneo Sanesi, *La Commedia* (Milan, 1911), I, 304.

9. S. L. Wolff, *The Greek Romances in Elizabethan Prose Fiction* (New York, 1912); Aristide Calderini, *Le Avventure di Cherea e Calliroe* (Turin, 1913), pp. 159–169, 196–214.

nius of Tyre;[10] it could be described as the tradition of exemplary romance. It also deals with families divided and reunited, but it throws emphasis on the tribulations and wanderings of the principal characters; it preaches the virtues of faith and patience; it illustrates the Christian idea of Providence, as against pagan Fortune. For example, in the Life of St. Clement, as told in *The Golden Legend* (from a much earlier source in the *Clementine Recognitions*), the saint finds his mother, his twin brothers, and eventually his father, all of them unknown to each other on the same island, after an interval of twenty years or more, during which he had supposed them all lost at sea. Not knowing his son Clement (who is in the company of St. Peter), the old man denies the existence of Providence, attributing his own disasters to "that which fortune hath destined"; but it is the story he tells to support his denial that leads to the recognition and hence to his conversion.[11] *Apollonius of Tyre* is based on the same theme of a family scattered and then reassembled by Providence, which is also the theme of the legend of Placidas (St. Eustace) and of metrical romances like *Sir Isumbras* and *Sir Eglamour.* The theme of the man tried by Providence was common throughout Europe, in miracle plays and allied popular drama, from the fourteenth to the seventeenth century.[12] At least eight plays from the fifteenth and sixteenth centuries have, for instance, been recorded on the subject of Robert of Sicily (two of them in England—at Lincoln, *c.* 1450, and Chester, 1529).[13] An *Eglemour and Degrebelle,* one of the few purely secular English plays of the fifteenth century of which the record has survived, was acted at St. Albans in 1444,

10. Calderini, pp. 198–199; A. H. Smyth, *Shakespeare's Pericles and Apollonius of Tyre* (Philadelphia, 1898); J. W. Wells, *A Manual of the Writings in Middle English, 1050–1400* (New Haven, 1916), pp. 112–124.

11. Caxton, *The Golden Legend,* ed. F. S. Ellis, Temple Classics (London, 1900), VI, 260.

12. C. R. Baskervill, "Some Evidence for Early Romantic Plays in England," *MP,* XIV (1916), 229–259, 467–512; Baskervill, "An Elizabethan Eglamour Play," *MP,* XIV (1917), 759–760; J. M. Manly, "The Miracle Play in Mediaeval England," *Trans. Royal Soc. Lit.,* N.S., VII (1927), 133–153; Madeleine Doran, *Endeavors of Art* (Madison, 1954), pp. 102–105; cf. Laura A. Hibbard, *Mediaeval Romance in England: A Study of the Sources and Analogues of the Non-Cyclic Metrical Romances* (New York, 1924).

13. Hibbard, *Mediaeval Romance,* p. 61; cf. Alfred Harbage, rev. S. Schoenbaum, *Annals of English Drama* (London, 1964), *sub* 1623.

a *Placidas, alias St. Eustace* at Braintree in 1534. When Shakespeare used
the ever popular story of Apollonius of Tyre for Ægeon's part in *The
Comedy of Errors,* he was therefore drawing upon what was already an
old tradition of the stage; and probably he had in mind other variants of
the tale of a man tried by Providence, since the ingredients of the
Apollonius story are shared by the legends of St. Clement and St. Eustace,
with the addition of twin brothers.[14] However this may be, the two main
plots he used in *The Comedy of Errors* evidently held a strong fascination
for Shakespeare. He returned to one source, the *Menaechmi,* in *Twelfth
Night.*[15] And in *Pericles* he returned directly to the other, *Apollonius.*
Moreover, the story of Prospero is an extension of the same theme.

   The favorite subject of medieval playwrights wishing to exhibit the
trials of Providence was a sorely tried heroine of the type of Chaucer's
Constance. In a survey of the minor medieval verse romances current in
England, Laura Hibbard mentions stage analogues, English or Continen-
tal, for fifteen of her romances; seven of these relate the misfortunes of a
calumniated wife. Nearly all the medieval romances about a calumniated
wife were dramatized in one variant or another; they account for seven of
the twenty plays more secular than ecclesiastic among the forty *Miracles
de Nostre Dame* in the Parisian collection of the late fourteenth century.[16]
The oldest surviving entirely secular stage romances belong to the same
period—three Dutch plays and the slightly later French *Griseldis* (1395).
The Dutch *Esmoreit* and *Lancelot of Denmark* have maligned heroines;
the French play, dealing with Boccaccio's long-suffering heroine, was the
first of a series that continued as far as Dekker.[17] These secular and quasi-

   14. See Sophie Trenkner, *The Greek Novella* (Cambridge, Eng., 1958), pp.
100–108; *The Comedy of Errors,* ed. R. A. Foakes, [New] Arden Shakespeare
(London, 1962), pp. xxxi–xxxii. Barnabe Riche included a variant of the Placidas
story (*Sapho, Duke of Mantona*) in *Riche His Farewell to Militarie Profession*
(1581), ed. New Shakespeare Society (London, 1846).
   15. See my article on *Twelfth Night* in *SQ,* IX (1958), 127–128, 137–139.
   16. Hibbard, *Mediaeval Romance;* Alexandre Micha, "La Femme injustement
accusée dans les Miracles de Notre-Dame par personnages," *Mélanges d'histoire du
théâtre ... Gustave Cohen* (Paris, 1950), pp. 85–92. On the *Miracles de Nostre-Dame
par personnages,* ed. G. Paris and U. Robert, 8 vols. (Paris, 1876–1893), see also Petit
de Julleville, *Les Mystères* (Paris, 1880), I, 115–179; II, 226–335; Grace Frank, *The
Medieval French Drama* (Oxford, 1954), pp. 114–124.
   17. *An Ingenious Play of Esmoreit,* trans. Harry Morgan Ayres (The Hague,
1924); *A Beautiful Play of Lancelot of Denmark,* trans. Dr. P. Geyl (The Hague,

religious romances have been influenced by the chivalric exaltation of women, but they are basically folk tales,[18] and it is to this factor that the stories owed most of their currency. They enjoyed a striking popularity. The tales of five, at least, of the seven *Miracles* were dramatized repeatedly; it will be convenient to number them. (1) The tale of *La Fille du roi de Hongrie* reappears, for instance, as the fifteenth-century Italian miracle of *Santa Uliva* (printed, in the first of several known editions, as late as 1568).[19] (2) *L'Empereris de Rome* was almost certainly known as an English play in the early fifteenth century; it was repeated in German by the popular Nuremberg dramatist, Hans Sachs (1494-1576), and in Italy both in another *sacra rappresentazione* and in *L'Ammalata* (1555), by the humanist Giovanni Cecchi.[20] (3) *Le Roi Thierry* found analogues in another *sacra rappresentazione,* another play by Hans Sachs,[21] and in Beaumont and Fletcher's tragedy. These three *Miracles,* with their motifs of a father's attempted incest, of self-mutilation, and of slanders about monstrous births, are simply folk tales with a veneer of edification. There is chivalry in *La Marquise de la Gaudine,* and *Oton, Roy d'Espaigne* has a feudal tone; but the story behind *Oton* was also current in folk tales. The plot of (4) *La Marquise* furnished Bandello's story of the Duchess of Savoy; from this source it was dramatized in German (by Hans Sachs

1924); see Theodoor Weevers, *Poetry of the Netherlands* (London, 1960), pp. 48–55; *L'Estoire de Griseldis,* ed. Mario Roques (Geneva and Paris, 1957); for later Griselda plays see Baskervill, *MP,* XIV, 487–488.

18. See Margaret Schlauch, *Chaucer's Constance and Accused Queens* (New York, 1927).

19. *La Fille du roi de Hongrie,* in *Miracles de Nostre-Dame,* IV, analysis in P. de Julleville, II, 300–303; cf. Schlauch, *Chaucer's Constance,* pp. 21–47, 61, 76–94; on dramatic analogues see Hibbard, *Mediaeval Romance,* pp. 23–34; *Santa Uliva,* in *Sacre rappresentazioni,* ed. Alessandro d'Ancona (Florence, 1872), III, 235–315; cf. d'Ancona, *Origini del teatro italiano,* 2nd ed. (Turin, 1891), I, 332, 436–437; further analogues in A. Aarne and Stith Thompson, *Types of the Folktale,* 2nd rev. ed. (Helsinki, 1961), Type 706: "The Maiden Without Hands."

20. *L'Empereris de Rome,* in *Miracles de Nostre-Dame,* IV. M. D. Anderson discusses evidence for an English play in *Drama and Imagery in English Medieval Churches* (Cambridge, Eng., 1963), pp. 188–192. See also Hibbard, *Mediaeval Romance,* pp. 13–14; *Santa Guglielma,* in d'Ancona, *Sac. rapp.,* III, 199–234; d'Ancona, *Origini,* II, 156–157 (on Cecchi); cf. Aarne and Thompson, Type 712: "Crescentia."

21. Hibbard, *Mediaeval Romance,* p. 267; *Stella,* in d'Ancona, *Sac. rapp.,* III, 317–359.

again) and in French (by Jean Behourt, in *La Polyxene, Tragicomedie,* 1597); it was well known to the Elizabethans.[22] (5) *Oton* belongs to the cycle of stories about wagers on a woman's chastity that attracted Boccaccio and then Shakespeare; in the sixteenth century a Spanish play was drawn from this cycle (Lope de Rueda's *Eufemia, c.* 1550), besides three German plays, one of them by the indefatigable Hans Sachs (1548) and another by Jakob Ayrer (*c.* 1600).[23]

In addition to these and the Griselda plays, other variants on the theme of the calumniated wife, such as Greene's *James IV* and the French, Italian, English, German, and Dutch analogues to *Much Ado,*[24] were familiar on sixteenth-century stages. In his study of French tragicomedy contemporary with Shakespeare, H. C. Lancaster emphasized the survival of subject matter from the fourteenth-century *Miracles,* particularly in connection with stories of calumniated heroines.[25] There is less direct evidence for continuity in England. But there is no doubt that Shakespeare was returning to one branch of medieval exemplary romance with Imogen and Hermione, just as with Pericles he was returning to the other. And there can be little doubt that Shakespeare was conscious of reviving subjects that belonged to the theater's past. Artistic self-awareness is one of the distinctive notes in his last plays.

II

When Shakespeare began writing in London, medieval romance was still popular in the theater, but it seems clear from the incomplete records

22. Hibbard, *Mediaeval Romance*, pp. 36–37; H. C. Lancaster, *The French Tragi-Comedy . . . from 1552 to 1628* (Baltimore, 1907), pp. 9, 65–69; René Pruvost, *Matteo Bandello and Elizabethan Fiction* (Paris, 1937), pp. 16–21, 30, 75 n.; George Pettie, *A Petite Pallace of Pettie His Pleasure* (1576), ed. I. Gollancz (London, 1908), I, 35; II, 12, 107.

23. *Oton, Roy d'Espaigne,* in *Miracles de Nostre-Dame,* IV; see Gaston Paris, "Le Cycle de la *Gageure,*" *Romania,* XXXII (1903), 481–551; Baskervill, "Early Romantic Plays in England," 488–489; cf. Aarne and Thompson, Type 882: "The Wager on the Wife's Chastity."

24. See Charles T. Prouty, *The Sources of "Much Ado"* (New Haven, 1950), pp. 11–32; *Narrative and Dramatic Sources of Shakespeare,* ed. Geoffrey Bullough (London, 1958), II, 67–71.

25. Lancaster, *French Tragi-Comedy,* pp. 10–15.

of the period that it was on the way out. *Sir Clyomon and Clamydes* (*c.* 1570–1583) and *Common Conditions* (1576) have plots of knight-errantry and wandering lovers; *The Rare Triumphs of Love and Fortune* (1582) contains the same kind of thing, a little sophisticated; *Mucedorus* (*c.* 1590) provides evidence of its enduring popularity. This evidence can be supplemented from some titles like *The Solitary Knight* from the 1570's and from one or two of a later date, like *Valentine and Orson* (1595 and 1598) and perhaps *Fair Constance of Rome* (1600). But already as early as the 1570's other romantic-sounding titles (such as *Theagenes and Chariclea* or *Perseus and Andromeda*) indicate a shift of taste. And when the debate over the theaters began, it was the medieval tradition that came in for special attack:

> Sometime you shall see nothing but the aduentures of an amorous knight, passing from countrie to countrie for the loue of his lady, encountring many a terible monster made of broune paper, & at his retorne, is so wonderfully changed, that he can not be knowne but by some posie in his tablet, or by a broken ring, or a handkircher, or a piece of a cockle shell. What learne you by that?

This part of Gosson's diatribe of 1582 [26] is humanist rather than puritan; Whetstone had said much the same in his Epistle Dedicatory to *Promos and Cassandra* in 1578. And in this respect Sidney's defense of the theater coincides with Gosson.

These criticisms, which lead on to Ben Jonson, help to fill in the faint outlines of a picture of popular drama about 1580. Gosson's general description could fit *Sir Clyomon*. Sidney's sketch is more detailed, with more specific evidence (which I shall emphasize) of offenses against the Unity of Time:

> . . . you shal haue Asia of the one side, and Affrick of the other, and so many other vnder-kingdoms, that the Player, when he commeth in, must euer begin with telling where he is, or els the tale wil not be conceiued. Now ye shal haue three Ladies walke to gather flowers, and then we must beleeue the stage to be a Garden. By and by, we heare newes of shipwracke in the same place, and then wee are to blame if we accept it not for a Rock. Vpon the backe of that, comes out a hidious Monster, with fire and smoke, and then the miserable beholders are bounde to take it for a Caue. While in the meantime two Armies

26. Gosson, *Playes Confuted* (1582), in Chambers, *Elizabethan Stage*, IV, 215–216.

flye in, represented with foure swords and bucklers, and then what harde heart will not receiue it for a pitched fielde? Now, *of time they are much more liberall, for ordinary it is that two young Princes fall in loue. After many trauerces, she is got with childe, deliuered of a faire boy; he is lost, groweth a man, falls in loue, and is ready to get another child; and all this in two hours space:* which how absurd it is in sence euen sence may imagine, and *Arte hath taught,* and all auncient examples iustified, and, at this day, the ordinary Players in Italie wil not erre in.[27]

Similarly, Whetstone had complained that an English dramatist "runs through the world" in three hours, "marries, gets Children, *makes Children men*" (and also "bringeth Gods from Heaven, and fetcheth Devils from Hell").[28] Now, far from being "ordinary," it is very rare in Elizabethan texts for a child to be born and grow up in the course of the play; this critical charge cannot even be leveled against *Sir Clyomon* or *Common Conditions.* But the features Sidney notes as typical of popular stages about 1580 are also typical of medieval stage romances. The only surviving English miracle play in the form of a romanticized saint's life is *Mary Magdalene* (*c.* 1480–1520), which contains scenes taken from *The Golden Legend;* in the course of these, the King and Queen of Marseilles set out by sea on a pilgrimage, the Queen dies in childbirth and must be left on a rock when the sailors insist on ridding their ship of her corpse, and the King, returning from the Holy Land, finds her with her baby, both miraculously living (scenes 41–44). Scenes wherein the heroine is "delivered of a fair boy" are common in the *Miracles,* and there are two such in *Griseldis* (illustrated by manuscript drawings, one of Griseldis in childbed and the other showing her "obviously pregnant").[29] Similarly, the multiple setting Sidney describes could be a setting for *Oton* or *L'Empereris de Rome* (except that the *mise en scène* of the *Miracles* was more realistic). And the time scheme he outlines would fit such works as *La Fille du roi de Hongrie* or the Dutch romance *Esmoreit.* The action there shifts from Sicily to Damascus and back. The prince of Sicily, Esmoreit, is kidnaped at birth, while his mother is imprisoned on

27. Sidney, *Apology for Poetry* (*c.* 1583; printed 1595), in *Elizabethan Critical Essays,* ed. G. Gregory Smith, I, 197.

28. Whetstone in Bullough, *Sources of Shakespeare,* II, 443.

29. *Griseldis,* ed. Roques, ll. 1260–1281, 1490, 1536–1539; *La Fille du roi de Hongrie,* ll. 990–1072; d'Ancona, *Origini,* I, 454 n.; cf. English Annunciation and Nativity plays, e.g., *Towneley Plays,* ed. George England (EETS, 1897), X, l. 156.

trumped-up charges which the king accepts with the credulity typical of husbands in tales of calumniated wives. After eighteen years Esmoreit finds and frees his mother and marries a Saracen princess.[30] As far as stage construction goes, then, Sidney, Whetstone, and Gosson could be describing miracle plays. It is very likely indeed that the plays they were condemning incorporated many of the traditional plot motifs as well.

III

Insofar as critical ideas were leaning around the 1580's toward classicism, *The Comedy of Errors* can be regarded as a bid for critical approval. In the context of its own time (*c.* 1590–1594) it is a strikingly "classical" piece of work. By choosing *Menaechmi* as his principal model, Shakespeare was imitating the comedy that had been revived for performance in the sixteenth century more frequently than any other Roman play.[31] He observes the Unity of Place as closely as Elizabethan stage conventions would allow and emphasizes the Unity of Time.[32] In "contaminating" his

30. *Esmoreit,* trans. Ayres; see Schlauch, *Chaucer's Constance,* pp. 10–11, 53–59, 87–91, 117–119.

31. Renaissance schoolmasters preferred Terence, but audiences preferred Plautus, especially *Menaechmi*. I have counted references to 69 revivals of Roman comedy at Ferrara, Florence, Mantua, Rome, and Venice between *c.* 1465 and 1526 (d'Ancona, *Origini,* II, 61–162 and Appendix II; V. Rossi, *Il Quattrocento* [Milan, 1933], pp. 529–531; *Enciclopedia dello spettacolo* [Rome, 1954–1962]). Fifty-four of these 69 performances were revivals of Plautus, 15 of Terence; *Menaechmi* was clearly the play most enjoyed, with 15 revivals, while *Andria* had 9. *Menaechmi* was the most favored among Plautus' plays for school use (T. W. Baldwin, *Shakspere's Five-Act Structure* [Urbana, 1947], p. 668), and it was probably the favorite Roman quarry for new sixteenth-century plays (Sanesi, *Commedia;* cf. K. von Reinhardstoettner, *Plautus* [Leipzig, 1886]; Bullough, *Sources of Shakespeare,* I, 4–5). Revivals of Latin comedy began in England with *Menaechmi* and *Phormio,* acted for Wolsey by St. Paul's boys, 1527–1528 (Chambers, *Mediaeval Stage* [Oxford, 1903], II, 215). At Oxford and Cambridge, F. S. Boas records 17 revivals of Plautus, 5 of Terence, and 8 of Seneca, 1549–1592 (*University Drama of the Tudor Age* [Oxford, 1914], pp. 385–390); *Menaechmi* was acted three times, no other Roman comedy more than twice.

32. Harold Brooks, "Theme and Structure in *Comedy of Errors,*" in *Early Shakespeare,* ed. John Russell Brown and Bernard Harris (London, 1961), pp. 63–71; *Comedy of Errors,* ed. Foakes, pp. xxxiv–xxxix.

main plot source, he is following a practice well established among the Italians. His title is virtually a proclamation of classicism, for commentators were agreed that "error" was the hallmark of Roman comedy.[33] Moreover, there is something new about the very nature of Shakespeare's borrowings. The first thoroughly neoclassical comedy in English—that is, the first containing "rediscoveries" as well as farcical tricks—had been Gascoigne's translation from Ariosto, *Supposes,* acted at Gray's Inn in 1566 and printed in 1573. There seem to have been no others before Shakespeare wrote *The Comedy of Errors* (also acted at Gray's Inn, in 1594). There were new comedies copying Roman or Italian models: three or four Latin plays at the Universities [34] and, in the public theaters, Munday's *Fedele and Fortunio* (*c.* 1584) and Lyly's *Mother Bombie* (*c.* 1589). But these plays were farces of trickery, exhibiting what Castelvetro calls "deceits fashioned by men," not comedies of coincidental recognitions—"deceits fashioned by fortune." [35] In contrast, Shakespeare's play is not simply a farce; there is too much serious emotion in it for that. And it turns on genuine mistakes of identity, bringing about ironic reversals of a state of unhappiness and confusion. To this extent, it is a romance in the Euripidean tradition, very probably the first such play written for the London theaters.

At the same time, it carries on the tradition of exemplary romance, too. An audience hearing the play without preliminary knowledge would be led to anticipate something like tragicomedy from the opening scene, with its prolonged exposition of the woes of Ægeon, under sentence of death—

ÆGEON
Thus have you heard me sever'd from my bliss,
That by misfortunes was my life prolong'd,
To tell sad stories of my own mishaps. . . .
DUKE
Hapless Ægeon, whom the fates have mark'd
To bear the extremity of dire mishap!
(I.i.119–121, 140–141)

33. Baldwin, *Five-Act Structure,* pp. 28–52, 691–694.

34. Boas, *University Drama,* pp. 139 ff.; Baldwin, *Five-Act Structure,* pp. 472–492.

35. Castelvetro, *Poetica,* 2nd ed. (Basle, 1576), p. 93: "per insidie altrui, o da caso" (trans. H. B. Charlton, in Barrett H. Clark, *European Theories of the Drama* [New York, 1947], p. 66; cf. Gilbert, *Literary Criticism,* p. 313).

And Shakespeare tries to sustain the sense of Ægeon as a man tried by fate over many years in the final scene, where Antipholus of Ephesus fails to recognize him:

ÆGEON

Why look you strange on me? You know me well.

ANTIPHOLUS OF EPHESUS

I never saw you in my life till now.

ÆGEON

O! grief hath chang'd me since you saw me last;
And careful hours with time's deformed hand
Have written strange defeatures in my face.
But tell me yet, dost thou not know my voice?

. . . .

Not know my voice! O time's extremity,
Hast thou so crack'd and splitted my poor tongue
In seven short years that here my only son
Knows not my feeble key of untun'd cares?

(V.i.295–300, 306–309)

There is nothing corresponding to the father's dismay about his voice in *Menaechmi,* of course, nor in *Apollonius of Tyre.* But there are points of resemblance between this passage and the episode in *The Golden Legend,* where, after Clement and Peter have found Clement's father, Faustinian, Peter's enemy Simon Magus ("Simon the enchanter") puts Faustinian under a spell:

And forthwith came a messenger which said that there was come a minister of the emperor's unto Antioch, and sought all the enchanters for to punish them to death. Then Simon Magus, because he hated the sons of Faustinian, because they forsook him, he imprinted his similitude and likeness in this old man Faustinian, in such wise that of every man he was supposed to be Simon Magus. And this did Simon Magus because he should be taken of the ministers of the emperor, and be slain instead of him, and Simon then departed from those parts. And when this old Faustinian came again to S. Peter and to his sons, the sons were abashed, which saw in him the similitude and likeness of Simon Magus, and understood the voice of their father, but S. Peter saw the natural likeness of him. And his wife and his sons blamed and reproved him, and he said: Wherefore blame ye me and flee from me that am your father? And they said: We flee from thee because the likeness of Simon Magus appeareth in thee.[36]

36. *Golden Legend* (Temple Classics), VI, 261–262; cf. Trenkner, *Greek Novella,* pp. 100–108.

Shakespeare's episode resembles this passage from *The Golden Legend,*
not only by way of the reference to a father's voice in such a context, but
in the presence of a whole family, including twin brothers, on the scene,
in interference by an enchanter (Shakespeare having made Pinch sound
more like a magician than the comic doctor in Plautus), in the imminent
danger of an execution, and also in the biblical and geographical associations of both narratives. This part of Ægeon's story has no connection with
Apollonius. It looks, then, as if Shakespeare took Ægeon from the broad
tradition of exemplary romance, not from one source alone. The biblical
coloring of *The Comedy* and his homiletic treatment of the subject of
marriage [37] reinforce this impression.

The story of Ægeon as a man tried by fate reacts on Shakespeare's
Plautine material too. Shakespeare introduces Antipholus of Syracuse
while his father's distress is still ringing in the audience's ears in Act I,
and with Antipholus the poet almost at once strikes a note of melancholy
and inward restlessness that is not heard in Plautus:

> He that commends me to mine own content
> Commends me to the thing I cannot get.
> I to the world am like a drop of water
> That in the ocean seeks another drop,
> Who, falling there to find his fellow forth,
> Unseen, inquisitive, confounds himself.
> So I, to find a mother and a brother,
> In quest of them, unhappy, lose myself.

> (I.ii.33–40)

We have already heard that Ægeon has "hazarded the loss of whom [he]
lov'd" in the long search for his family (I.i.25–140). Shakespeare has not
only broadened the scope of his Roman source play and brought the
shadowy father from the Roman Prologue into the range of our active
sympathies, but by doing so he has given a new dimension to his plot, the
dimension of "memory and desire." Antipholus' melancholy is reinforced
by his father's distress. He is seeking not only for a brother, or "a mother
and a brother," but for assurance of his own identity, his place in the
world. He has begun to "lose himself" subjectively even before he risks

37. Baldwin, *Five-Act Structure,* pp. 675–683, and "Three Homilies in *The
Comedy of Errors,"* in *Essays on Shakespeare . . . in Honour of Hardin Craig,* ed.
Richard Hosley (London, 1963), pp. 137–147.

becoming a "traitor to himself" through love and to "wander in illusions" conjured up by the plot (III.ii.160; IV.iii.38). But in the course of the action his imagined loss of self enables him to find a wife and rediscover his family. Already in this early play Shakespeare has begun to work out the theme that was to be central to his later comedies and his romances, the theme of emotional changes brought about through the "imaginary wiles" (IV.iii.10) caused by disguise, coincidence, deception, and similar contrivances of the theater. From the soliloquy of Antipholus to Gonzalo's cry at the end of *The Tempest,* there runs a continuous line of development:

> O, rejoice
> Beyond a common joy, and set it down
> With gold on lasting pillars: in one voyage
> Did Claribel her husband find at Tunis;
> And Ferdinand, her brother, found a wife
> Where he himself was lost; Prospero his dukedom
> In a poor isle; and all of us ourselves
> When no man was his own.
>
> (V.i.206–213)

IV

According to many studies of *The Comedy of Errors,* Shakespeare adds material from romance to a plot that had originally been farcical. It is at least possible, however, that he approached his play the other way round; that he set out with the familiar tradition of exemplary romance in his mind and then saw how to modernize it. Clearly, Shakespeare associated the material of romance with deep-seated feelings about family relationships. At the same time, a plot of complicated mistakes of identity would answer to his sense of theater and attract the judicious. There is remarkable self-confidence about the construction of the last scene in *The Comedy of Errors,* which must be as intricate as any denouement spectators had witnessed in a theater before.

Yet the skillful dovetailing of two kinds of dramatic convention left the general problem of representing the passage of time on the stage unsolved. It was important to Shakespeare as a poet to bring this sense to life within his story as a whole; but the two traditions of drama he was dealing with tackle the problem in diametrically opposed ways. As Renaissance theorists

pointed out, New Comedy—Euripidean romance—followed an "artificial order" as opposed to a "natural" one ("the artificial order is when,
contrary to the usual reckoning of time, we very often begin at the end
and then return to earlier events" [38]). Playwrights in this tradition, aiming
at continuous interest, relegate the narration of their characters' past to a
prologue or expository scene or else prepare for it (as in *Andria,* IV.v) at
the moment when it will trigger-off the recognition scene. But plays in
the medieval tradition follow the "natural" order of the events that count
in the story, without paying attention to the psychological effect—or the
effect on audiences aware of a different method—of references to the lapse
of time. In *Mary Magdalene* it comes as a surprising but inert bit of
information when the saint suddenly declares—because it was part of the
legend—that she has been an anchorite in the wilderness "this thirty
winter" (scene 49, l. 2055). In Lyly's *Endimion* we can perhaps accept it
that the hero has been "cast into a dead sleep, almost these twenty years,
waxing old, and ready for the grave," because the whole play is presented
with a stylized unreality. But we cannot believe that Faustus is twenty-
four years older by the end of Marlowe's play (which follows in the wake
of the miracles), although the dramatist does his best to mask the difficulty with the allegorical figure of the Old Man; when in the last act we
hear the clock strike, we realize simply that the pact is over. Neither the
classical convention nor the medieval one, even in its more sophisticated
Elizabethan form, could solve Shakespeare's technical problem directly,
and the two together were liable to cancel each other out. This was the
difficulty Shakespeare accepted when, some fifteen years after *The
Comedy of Errors,* he returned to the Apollonius saga in *Pericles.* Since
each of the late romances deals with the interaction of two generations,
each of them is affected by the problem of giving imaginative reality to
the movement of time.

V

Whether Shakespeare chose the subject of *Pericles,* or whether, as seems
much more likely, he agreed to finish a play that someone else—Wilkins

38. Landinus (1482), quoted in Marvin T. Herrick, *Comic Theory in the
Sixteenth Century* (Urbana, 1964), p. 99.

and Day, perhaps—had begun,[39] it is clear that Gower's story had a strong appeal for him; he follows his narrative source with unusual docility. What interests the poet most in the scenes unquestionably by Shakespeare is the emotional overtone of the story, the sense of awe in face of the storm—

> The seaman's whistle
> Is as a whisper in the ears of death,
> Unheard—
>
> (III.i.8–10)

and the sense of wonder in the father's reunion with his daughter:

> thou dost look
> Like Patience gazing on kings' graves, and smiling
> Extremity out of act.
>
> (V.i.136–138)

Shakespeare leaves such moments here to stand as poetic symbols of a possible phase of experience, without trying to buttress them by means of the character development which had occupied so much of his interest in his tragedies or by complications in the plot. The dramatic scenario closely resembles a biographical miracle play (as F. D. Hoeniger has pointed out), nearly duplicating *Mary Magdalene* in the scenes of Thaisa's apparent death in childbirth at sea and her rediscovery.[40] And Shakespeare supports his unrealistic story with old-fashioned pageantry, including a dumb show, an "inexplicable dumb-show," which he had last used only for a play within the play.[41] All this must have seemed a surprising and possibly lamentable departure at a time of increasing sophistication in the London theaters, when other dramatists—not only Jonson, but Chapman, Fletcher, and Webster as well—were protesting their neoclassical intentions and when Jonson could allude to the recent past, as he does in the Induction to *Bartholomew Fair,* with an air of humorous indulgence: "Hee that will sweare, *Ieronimo,* or *Andronicus* are the best playes, yet, shall passe vnexcepted at, heere, as a man whose Iudgement shewes it is

39. See *Pericles,* ed. F. D. Hoeniger, [New] Arden Shakespeare (London, 1963), pp. lii–lxiii.

40. *Pericles,* ed. Hoeniger, pp. lxxxviii–xci.

41. *Pericles,* III.*Chorus* (see Hoeniger's note on ll. 1–14).

constant, and hath stood still, these fiue and twentie, or thirtie yeeres" (ll. 106–109). From this point of view, *Pericles* was indeed "a mouldy tale."

Shakespeare, or Shakespeare and his coauthors, meet some of this type of criticism by using "the worthy and ancient Poet John Gower" as Chorus.[42] The main action as a whole is thereby distanced, becoming like a play within the play to some extent. There are touches of deliberate archaism in the Chorus, not only in the imitation of the historic Gower's octosyllabic verse, but in the way the stage Gower refers to "our story" (**IV.***Chorus*.19), like a medieval Presenter (in the Digby *Conversion of St. Paul* [*c.* 1480–1520] the Presenter is called Poeta). The stage Gower catches the medieval manner even when he reveals knowledge of Renaissance technicalities:

> I nill relate, action may
> Conveniently the rest convey;
> Which might not what by me is told.
> In your imagination hold
> This stage the ship, upon whose deck
> The sea-toss'd Pericles appears to speak.
>
> (III. *Chorus*.55–60)

Similarly, the way the first lines of the historic Gower's narrative are padded out in the first Chorus of *Pericles* recalls, no doubt deliberately, the introduction to a miracle play:

> To sing a song that old was sung,
> From ashes ancient Gower is come,
> Assuming man's infirmities,
> To glad your ear and please your eyes.
> It hath been sung at festivals,
> On ember-eves and holy-ales;
> And lords and ladies in their lives
> Have read it for restoratives.
> The purchase is to make men glorious;
> Et bonum quo antiquius, eo melius.[43]
>
> (I.*Chorus*.1–10)

42. *Pericles,* ed. Hoeniger, frontispiece, pp. xix–xxiii.

43. Cf. ll. 18–21 of *Griseldis,* ed. Roques: "Si fait bon oÿr exemplaire / Et bonnes vertus raconter, / Dont on puet par raison monter / En l'estat de perfectïon."

For a medieval dramatist, his legend—his "matter" or "story"—was a revered text to be illustrated by visible action, a preexisting truth to be reaffirmed by performance. The authors of *Pericles* catch this medieval note with some subtlety; they not only retell an old story but retell it as an old dramatist would have told it. These consciously antiquarian touches reveal the Jacobean, as distinct from the Elizabethan, theater; Middleton imitated them in *Hengist* (c. 1618) by introducing the Chester chronicler, Raynulph Higden, as Chorus, speaking similar octosyllabics in praise of "ancient stories." In the Shakespearean choruses in *Pericles* this sense of the telescoping of different ages—the ancient story, Gower, the present day—goes with a renewed interest in the general problem of imagining time dramatically:

> The unborn event
> I do commend to your content;
> Only I carry winged time
> Post on the lame feet of my rhyme;
> Which never could I so convey
> Unless your thoughts went on my way.
>
> (IV.*Chorus*.45–50)

> Thus time we waste, and longest leagues make short;
> Sail seas in cockles, have an wish but for't;
> Making, to take our imagination,
> From bourn to bourn, region to region.
> By you being pardon'd, we commit no crime
> To use one language in each several clime
> Where our scenes seem to live. I do beseech you
> To learn of me, who stand i' th' gaps to teach you
> The stages of our story.
>
> (IV.iv.1–9)

These passages read like a first draft for Time, the Chorus in *The Winter's Tale*.

VI

Pericles is a passive hero. A Lear, a Timon, a Coriolanus makes excessive demands for love or respect on his society and suffers excessive retribution. But Pericles undergoes loss and exile without guilt, but without any dramatic starch in his innocence, either; he is merely a receptacle for Providence, suffering and receiving. With Posthumus and Leontes, Shakespeare returns to the sphere of moral cause and effect. But he is not searching for psychological complexity, nor on the other hand for allegory, but rather for a symbolic quality in a semirealistic action. And he treats both fables of calumniated wives with something of the conscious archaism he had adopted in *Pericles;* or rather, in both plays he seems to be aiming at a synthesis of Renaissance and medieval methods of stagecraft.

Cymbeline is an experiment, but hardly a success. Shakespeare could have treated the story of the wager, as he found it in Boccaccio and in the early Tudor tale, *Frederyke of Jennen,*[44] simply as a tragicomedy of marriage or as a serious comedy in the spirit of *Much Ado.* Instead, he surrounds it with larger themes. There are the contrasts between courtliness and savagery, ending in reconciliation; here the play comes near to pastoral. And there are the reconciliations across a gap of time, involving Belarius and the princes. As if to accommodate these surrounding themes, Shakespeare alters Boccaccio's plot considerably. But the play as a whole fails to knit together.

Most of the unsatisfactory quality in the play relates to the king. Holinshed's information about Cymbeline boils down to five statements (which again I shall number for convenience): (1) "This man (as some write) was brought up at Rome, and there made knight by Augustus Caesar, under whom he served in the wars," and (2) "was in such favour with him that he was at libertie to pay his tribute or not." On the next page Holinshed is uncertain whether Cymbeline "or some other prince of the Britains" quarreled with Augustus, but he repeats that Cymbeline, according to "our writers," "ever shewed himselfe a friend to the Romans," so that he might send the youth of Britain to Rome, "whereby they might learne both to behave themselves like civill men, and to atteine to the knowledge of feats of warre." Holinshed adds (3) that an expedition of Augustus was diverted from Britain by a revolt of the Pannonians

---

44. J. M. Nosworthy discusses *Frederyke of Jennen* in his edition of *Cymbeline* [New] Arden Shakespeare (London, 1955), pp. xxi–xxiv, and reprints it, Appendix, pp. 198–211.

and Dalmatians; and, as to Cymbeline himself, (4) "Little other mention is made of his dooings, except that [5] during his reigne, the Saviour of the World our Lord Jesus Christ . . . was borne of a virgin. . . ."[45]

Some allusion to this synchronism can be read, with an effort, into Shakespeare's play;[46] and he notices the Pannonians and Dalmatians in passing (III.i.75). His principal debt to this chapter of Holinshed is item (1), with its contrast between Rome's "civility" and Britain; but he inverts item (2) by making Cymbeline agree to defy the Romans, adding miscellaneous details taken from other chapters in the legend of early British chivalry under Brutus and his descendants.[47] Holinshed has no hint, of course, of any Imogen in his chapter on Cymbeline, nor of any second queen and stepson; and in Holinshed, Guiderius and Arviragus succeed to the throne in the regular way, without having been stolen in childhood by any Belarius. Evidently Shakespeare meant to take full advantage of Holinshed's fourth statement about Cymbeline, that "little other mention is made of his dooings."

Shakespeare embellishes history with romance. "Quarrels between husband and wife, father and son, servant and master, or situations involving sudden change of fortune, substitution of children, violation of girls, and recognition by rings and necklaces"—it is as if he intended to match every article in the Euripidean catalogue.[48] And his echoes from medieval

45. Holinshed, *Chronicles* (ed. 1587), pp. 32–33.

46. J. P. Brockbank, "History and Histrionics in *Cymbeline*," *Shakespeare Survey* *11* (1958), pp. 45–46; Northrop Frye, "Recognition in *The Winter's Tale*," in *Essays . . . in Honour of Hardin Craig,* ed. R. Hosley (London, 1963), p. 240; cf. G. Wilson Knight, *The Crown of Life* (London, 1948), pp. 168–202.

47. Brockbank, pp. 42–49. In the chapter about Brutus that Brockbank discusses (p. 43), Brutus tells the Greek king, Pandrasus, that he and his companions prefer the wild freedom in the woods to the yoke of slavery. Shakespeare may have noted this passage, either in Holinshed (Bk. II, chap. 1, p. 8) or, possibly, in Geoffrey of Monmouth. Another detail suggests the latter; in Geoffrey, but not in Holinshed, Ignoge (Imogen; Brockbank, p. 43) gazes back at her homeland from Brutus' ship: "Ignoge stood on the high poop. . . . She wept and sobbed at being forced to leave her relations and her homeland; and as long as the shore lay there before her eyes, she would not turn her gaze away from it" (*Historia Regum Britanniae* [ed. 1587], Bk. I, chaps. 4, 11; trans. Lewis Thorpe, Penguin Books [London, 1966], p. 64); cf. *Cymbeline*, I.iv.

48. Pp. 7–8, above.

romance are equally obvious, quite apart from his borrowing of the wager story. The vision of Jupiter could have been suggested by *Amphitryon* (the classical *tragico comoedia*) or by late, Elizabethan variants of the common miracle-play scenes of a descent from heaven.[49] The compassionate servant, the wise physician, and the soothsayer could have stepped out of *Pericles*. The lost princes, trained in arms by a hermit, the wicked stepmother, and the boorish prince belong to folk tale. Fantastic geography, with a Roman landing at Milford Haven, ladies gathering flowers, a cave, battle scenes in dumb show—of set purpose or not, Shakespeare is reconstructing the *mise en scène* Sidney had ridiculed more than twenty years previously.[50]

J. M. Nosworthy has suggested that Shakespeare chose his plot badly; romance, he says, "can encompass a half-civilized Britain but not the ordered state of Rome." [51] But there is no difficulty about the interplay between "Roman" and "British" characteristics connected with Iachimo and Lucius, Posthumus, Cloten, and the princes. The real difficulty is to see why Shakespeare has brought Imogen and Cymbeline into the same play. Here the idea of a lost source, which recent studies of *Cymbeline*

49. See *Amphitryon,* III.i (where Jupiter tells the audience that he will save Alcmena from her husband's unjust accusation, as he, Jupiter, would be guilty if he allowed the innocent to suffer) and V.i (where Jupiter is described as appearing in thunder, while Amphitryon lies in a faint); Shakespeare had already used this play in *The Comedy of Errors.* But there were also regular epiphany scenes in miracle plays: e.g., *L'Empereris de Rome* (ll. 1180–1316), where Notre Dame descends and leaves magical herbs of healing with the distressed Empress while the latter sleeps; cf. *Mary Magdalene* (scene 48), where Angels descend and carry Mary up to heaven. An extraordinary passage in *Sir Clyomon* (scene 18) looks like a relic of this stage convention. Neronis finds a hearse in which she imagines Sir Clyomon is buried; she is about to kill herself in despair, when *"Descend* Providence," who tells her to read the comforting inscription on the hearse—"if case thou canst it read." By its very absurdity, this episode suggests that Shakespeare could have known other, and more sensible, postmedieval epiphany scenes. The parallel between *Cymbeline* and *Love and Fortune,* which Nosworthy stresses (p. xxxvi), is not very close, because in *Love and Fortune* Jupiter does not show himself to the mortals at all; he sends Mercury to tell Venus and Fortune to show themselves instead. Shakespeare's "source" for his vision scene is much more likely to be a mixed tradition than this particular play. Cf. Whetstone, p. 14, above.

50. Pp. 13–14, above.

51. Nosworthy, p. 1.

have tended to dismiss,[52] deserves some fresh consideration. Gaston Paris held that the folk versions of the wager story, recorded subsequently, date back to the sixteenth century;[53] and he and others have believed in the existence of some intermediate linkage between *Cymbeline* and the four-teenth-century *Miracle* of *Oton, Roy d'Espaigne*. The main case for this view is that where Shakespeare changes the plot he found in Boccaccio and *Frederyke of Jennen, Oton* contains parallels to several of his altera-tions. In Boccaccio and *Frederyke* the heroine plans her own revenge on the villain and the proof of her innocence to her husband; Posthumus and Imogen are reconciled by remorse and forgiveness, without contrivance on either side. This is characteristically Shakespearean; but, in addition, he sends the heroine into a setting of pure romance (in contrast to the mercantile surroundings provided by Boccaccio and *Frederyke*)[54] and brings husband and wife together by means of a war, with chivalric associations; and these details recall the miracle play. In both *Oton* and *Cymbeline* (and only, it seems, in these two versions of the story) the villain first tries to win the heroine over by telling her that her husband is keeping a mistress;[55] in both plays the heroine, in male disguise, serves her own kinsmen, unrecognized, as a page and carver;[56] and in both plays, the husband, having condemned his wife, takes arms despairingly with the national enemy (with the Saracens in *Oton*), repents (with the help of a divine vision in the miracle play), returns to his own people, is taken prisoner for a time, and fights the villain man to man.[57] These are suggestive parallels; and if Shakespeare knew a version of the wager story related to *Oton*, it might account for his inclusion of the Roman-British war. Some evidence for this possibility comes indirectly from the booklet *Westward for Smelts*, printed in 1620. *Westward for Smelts* consists of

52. See Nosworthy, pp. xx–xxi. Kenneth Muir, *Shakespeare's Sources* (London, 1957), I, 231–240, ignores *Oton* entirely. (Dowden paid attention to it in the first Arden *Cymbeline*, 4th ed. [1903], pp. xxix–xxxiii.)

53. Paris, in *Romania*, XXXII, p. 549.

54. In *Frederyke*, however, the heroine in disguise proves herself a doughty warrior (Nosworthy, pp. 206–207).

55. See *Oton* (*Miracles*, ed. Paris and Robert, IV), ll. 726–741; Paris, pp. 513–515.

56. *Oton*, ll. 1275–1292; *Cymbeline*, IV.ii.49–51.

57. *Oton*, ll. 1195–1224, 1293–1310, 1501–1609, 1662–1709, 1732–1953. After the combat, the heroine, still disguised, makes peace between Oton's uncle, the Emperor Lotaire, and her father, King Alfons of Spain.

old stories, for and against the honor of women. In the wager story there, the main characters are merchants of the time of the Wars of the Roses. When the husband, in despair, orders his wife to be killed, he decides "utterly to forsake his house and lands, and follow the fortunes of king Henry"; [58] the wife in male disguise, starving because of the war, is found near York and taken into favor by Edward IV, "beeing come out of France"; she meets the villain and her husband again as defeated Lancastrians after the Battle of Barnet. It is most unlikely that "Kinde Kit," the writer of *Westward for Smelts,* sought out these circumstantial details from history; they must represent some English version of the story coming from the Yorkist or early Tudor period. Indeed, "Kinde Kit" regards it as an old wives' tale; when one of the fishwives in *Westward for Smelts* has finished telling it, another comments on the heroine:

I like her as a garment out of fashion; shee shewed well in that innocent time, when women had not the wit to know their owne libertie: but if she lived now, she would show as vild as a paire of Yorkshire sleeves in a Goldsmith's shop.

The war episodes associate this version of the story with *Oton* and with *Cymbeline;* and if "Kinde Kit" thought the story dated, Shakespeare could have thought so too.

Shakespeare distorts the time scheme of *Cymbeline* in several ways. He brings a Renaissance Italian to early Britain. He shortens the heroine's period of distress (in Boccaccio she remains in disguise long enough to learn Arabic); but, on the other side, he introduces a recession of time within the action by adding the subplot of the theft of the princes ("Howsoe'er 'tis strange, / Or that the negligence may well be laugh'd at"), so that he needs to give a second and transparently clumsy exposition, virtually an internal prologue, to Belarius in order to account for it (I.i.55–67, III.iii.55–107). This subplot creates a pattern of wrongs, Cymbeline having mistrusted Belarius as Posthumus mistrusts Imogen. And it enables Imogen to escape from the court to a life of sheltered primitivism, where time is measured by the sun and the only occupations are the simple rituals of hunters—a comparatively timeless existence, from which treachery is excluded, but with it, as the young men insist, the possibility

58. *Westward for Smelts* (Trinity College Library copy), C1^{v}.

of real experience. All this suggests a deliberate recall of medieval romance, with an imaginary time scheme, suitable to ideal reconciliations. On the other hand, Shakespeare also advances his main plot by means of devices of the Renaissance theater, including his own. He arrives at his amazing denouement by way of trickery, double bluff and deception practiced in innocence, double and triple disguises, mistakes of identity, and ironies of coincidence. Just as, in *The Comedy of Errors,* the reunion of brothers indirectly serves to cure a wife of jealousy and save a father from execution, so, in *Cymbeline,* by an almost symmetrical inversion, a husband's jealousy causes the wife to find her lost brothers, who rescue their father from invaders. Husband and wife forgive each other by each imagining the other dead, as Friar Francis had recommended in *Much Ado.* And with this repetition of old stage motifs goes an emphasis on acting—acting, as distinct from deception. Shakespeare makes the asides of the Second Lord, the Queen, and Cornelius heavily obvious (I.ii; I.v) before he comes to the scene where Iachimo utters his long pseudo-aside with the intention of being overheard (I.vi.32–50); Posthumus raging against Imogen, and Imogen indignant with Posthumus, speak the language of actors rising to their parts rather than the Shakespearean language of passion. The effect is elusive, especially in a modern performance. But it suggests again that the reconciliation Shakespeare's action is leading to can be found only on the plane of theatrical idealization, not on the plane of drama as an image of reality.

VII

Where *Cymbeline* seems in a limiting way theatrical, *The Winter's Tale* is both symbolic and realistic. Not, of course, that the second play has a more "probable" plot; but in *The Winter's Tale* Shakespeare indicates a natural rhythm of common experience beneath the feelings he had represented ideally and fragmentarily in *Cymbeline* and *Pericles.* Leontes' jealousy is more disturbing than the outcries of Posthumus, partly because Leontes stresses images from common life. Pastoral Bohemia comes nearer to Warwickshire than the Welsh mountains of *Cymbeline.* When Shakespeare makes Hermione postpone her reconciliation with Leontes for sixteen years—although it would have been easy for him to arrange the denouement otherwise—the effect seems natural because we have received a poetic impression of time and natural development during the dramatic interval.

Part of the total subject in *The Winter's Tale,* as in all the late plays, is the relationship, at once likeness and difference, between the experience of real life and the experience of art. In *The Winter's Tale* this theme rises to the surface and advances with the general movement of the play.[59] The first part is filled with fantasy material, as with the first stirrings of a poem: Polixenes' dream of timeless happiness, retained from boyhood; Leontes' neurotic imaginings; his son's nursery tale; the envoys' wonder at the oracle of Apollo; Antigonus' ill-omened dream. After the entry of the pageant-figure of Time in Act IV a new phase begins, wherein the artistry due to the characters is intentional and where their art corresponds to shared experiences in life. Perdita dresses as the goddess Flora in obedience both to custom and to Florizel's wishes. Her play-acting has the ironic effect of suggesting a reality about her that neither she nor Florizel is aware of, and the audience is reminded of this through her debate about gardening with Polixenes; but this effect enriches the scene without hiding its simple naturalism from view. The highest idealization of Perdita comes naturally, from Florizel, as a poetic lover; and the tendency toward artistic idealization in the sheep-shearing episode as a whole is countered by the ballads of Autolycus. Perdita's share in the feast, moreover, is set off, as by a contrasting background, by the Shepherd's recalling her foster mother's activity at similar feasts in the past. The complex of ideas suggested here carries over into the statue scene in Act V, where Perdita kneels before her real mother. Again the disguising is planned, by Paulina instead of Florizel, and again it is appropriate because the time is ripe for it. Although Paulina's time scale is loftier than Florizel's and her intention more elaborate, she nevertheless professes to copy a human being, not a myth. And the wonder aroused by art in the statue scene melts into the realization of Polixenes' earlier statement, that "over that art / Which you say adds to nature, is an art / That nature makes." The pretended creator of Paulina's statue, "that rare Italian master, Julio Romano," was noted for his *trompe-l'œuil* effects; but no sculptor could literally make an image move. The theatrical arts, masques, and

59. See Northrop Frye, *Essays . . . in Honour of Hardin Craig,* pp. 240–245.

pageants can do that (as, for instance, in Jonson's *Masque of Queens* [1609], where the Queen and her ladies descend from their throne on a brightly lit Hall of Fame, after "a loud music" has caused the scene to change, driving off the dark hags of Suspicion and Slander). And in contact with the theatrical arts we can believe that someone truly "is" the character he impersonates—literally so in a Jacobean court masque, if only by metaphor in a stage play. Yet not even a masque can mimic the process of age, still less revive at the same time the emotions of years past, as Hermione's statue does; so that it appears as if only nature, only the fact that the statue is Hermione herself, can produce such an illusion. No art at all can reproduce time lived, duration. Yet dramatic art, whose medium is time, can at least suggest duration. And it is one of the triumphs of art to conceal herself behind nature. In the course of the statue scene, we are not allowed to forget that Paulina has stage-managed the effect of Hermione's return to life.

References to folklore and folk stories are scattered through the dialogue of *The Winter's Tale,* until the action itself, in the recognition scenes, is compared to "an old tale": "A sad tale's best for winter"; "it was told me I should be rich by the fairies"; "Is it true, think you?"—"Very true, and but a month old"; and "I never heard of such another encounter, . . . Like an old tale still, which will have matter to rehearse, though credit be asleep"; "That she is living, / Were it but told you, should be hooted at / Like an old tale." [60] Part of the effect of these references is to play with the suspension of disbelief. But at the same time they suggest, like Gower's Prologue to *Pericles,* but more subtly, that the whole action is like an old song. And in this respect they reinforce Shakespeare's treatment of his source narrative and its title, Greene's *Pandosto, The Triumph of Time.*

First printed in 1588, *Pandosto* was an exceptionally popular novelette, reaching its fourth edition by 1607 and appearing in many later English editions in the course of the century, besides two French translations and two tragicomedies in French by 1631. [61] For Shakespeare in particular, this

60. *Winter's Tale:* II.i.25; III.iii.112–113; IV.iv.260–261; V.ii.54–61; V.iii.115–117.

61. *Winter's Tale,* ed. Pafford, pp. xxvii–xxviii; René Pruvost, *Robert Greene et ses romans* (Paris, 1938), pp. 286–287. Mahelot's setting for *Pandoste* at the Hôtel de Bourgogne, employing *décor simultané,* is illustrated by Allardyce Nicoll, *The Development of the Theatre,* 4th ed. (London, 1958), p. 117.

romance by his former rival must have carried associations with his apprentice days in the theater, the days of *The Comedy of Errors* and Greene's *Groatsworth of Wit;* he must have felt some ironic satisfaction in turning for a subject to *The Triumph of Time.*[62] But the time symbolism of the story, brought out by the pivotal figure of the Chorus, has a broader significance for him. For one thing, *Pandosto* was the first piece of English fiction where "love between the children is made use of by Fortune to wipe out the consequences of errors and crimes that the fathers had been guilty of or had suffered from in the previous generation."[63] Secondly, beneath its trappings of up-to-date pastoral, Greene's plot very nearly follows the outline of those old romances, like *Valentine and Orson* and *The Knight of the Swan,* where, after many years, the child comes to rescue the falsely accused mother from prison; except that Greene makes the accused mother die of grief, he might be following the scenario of the old Dutch play *Esmoreit.* Shakespeare, for his part, keeps Hermione alive until her daughter returns to free her from hiding, as in the old romances.[64] And other details imply that the recall of old plays, as well as stories, was part of his dramatic intention. Hermione's appearance in advanced pregnancy in the first act would be strikingly unusual on a Jacobean stage; it would hark back to the pieces Sidney had derided.[65]

Moreover, a common motif in folk tales, and plays founded on them, had been a father's lust for his daughter (as in the beginning of *Pericles*) or a king's public choice of his daughter as his second consort; in tales like *Catskin* and in miracles like *La Fille du roi de Hongrie* the widower will only marry again if he can find a second wife resembling his first, and it is for this reason that the king chooses his daughter when his nobles press

---

62. It seems that Shakespeare used one of the first three editions of *Pandosto*, 1588–1595 (*Winter's Tale,* ed. Pafford, p. xxviii). Is there an autobiographical joke in Autolycus, the shape-changer, the ballad-seller, the "snapper-up of unconsidered trifles"—the "upstart Crow, beautified with our feathers"?

63. See Pruvost, *Greene,* p. 290.

64. See pp. 14–15, above; Pruvost, *Greene,* pp. 293–294. Shakespeare went behind Greene also to *Daphnis and Chloe* and (for the name Florizel) to *Amadis de Grecia* (*Winter's Tale,* ed. Pafford, pp. xxxvi, 164).

65. Nevill Coghill, "Six Points of Stage-craft in *The Winter's Tale,*" *Shakespeare Survey 11* (1958), p. 33; see p. 14, above. (In Dekker's *Patient Grissil* [1600] the dramatist refrains from showing Grissil "visibly pregnant.")

him to remarry.[66] Greene repeats this motif, clumsily veiled: Pandosto tries to seduce Fawnia when he meets her, then kills himself out of shame when he discovers who she is.[67] But Shakespeare restores the original motif with exquisite appropriateness. Before Perdita reaches Leontes' court in Act V, the noblemen have been urging him to remarry, but Paulina has made him promise not to take another bride unless she can find him one "As like Hermione as is her picture" (V.i.74); and when Perdita appears with Florizel, Leontes is so patently attracted by her that Paulina has to remind him sharply of Hermione—whereupon he replies, "I thought of her / Even in these looks I made" (V.i.227–228). In his outburst of jealousy in Act I Leontes had reiterated that "they say" that his son and himself are "Almost as like as eggs"; the identification of daughter and mother in Act V contributes to the great recognition scenes a feeling of the recovery of time lost. And, like the references to "old tales," and the pastoral scene, rooted in custom, this motif of father and daughter lends a semimythical quality to *The Winter's Tale* as a whole. The play becomes a reenactment, a part of the cycle of time.

VIII

Presumably one reason why the time scheme in *The Tempest* contrasts sharply with *The Winter's Tale,* while otherwise the two plays have so much in common, is that *The Tempest* deals with the last phase of the story, corresponding to Act V in *The Winter's Tale,* the phase of reunion and reconciliation, when old wounds are healed and life can make a fresh beginning. Prospero must seize the moment of his "most auspicious star"; the fictitious duration of the action almost coincides with the real performance. On the other hand, Prospero's exposition scene evokes "the dark backward and abysm of time," and he reminds Ariel, with emphasis, of the latter's "dozen years" of imprisonment—before Prospero and

66. In *La Fille du roi de Hongrie,* ll. 1–253, Pope and Cardinals solemnly permit the incestuous marriage; cf. *La fille d'un roi* in *Miracles de Nostre-Dame.* See Schlauch, *Chaucer's Constance,* pp. 35–47; P. Saintyves, *Les contes de Perrault* (Paris, 1923), pp. 187–193.

67. *Pandosto* (in *Winter's Tale,* ed. Pafford), pp. 218–225.

Miranda had been cast adrift. There are other references, too, to extradramatic time. Alonso's party chat about Aeneas and Dido; Sebastian "remembers" how Antonio supplanted his brother; Gonzalo remarks how nowadays the wildest travelers' tales are differently received from "when we were boys." The present moment absorbs the past, as in the last act of *The Winter's Tale*. Ferdinand has barely time to *imagine* grief for his father, to *rehearse* the hardships he must undergo for Miranda, before he is hurried to the joyful ending.

Because, too, of the storm and shipwreck on the island, it seems natural that the characters should share the same experiences to an unusual degree, so that personalities overlap and the whole of *The Tempest* becomes an extended recognition scene. The shipwrecked party compare their reactions to the island; Ferdinand and Miranda express the same wonder at meeting. By such means as these, Shakespeare again gives a symbolic, a mythical, overtone to his play. Unity of Place contributes to this, but the Unity of Time counts as well. Caliban learns submission, while Ariel gains his freedom; Caliban's plot against Prospero interweaves with Antonio's plot against Alonso, which renews his old treachery against Prospero too.

The strict time scheme in *The Tempest,* marked by reference to the hours, also repeats a technical effect of Renaissance "art" that Shakespeare had not attempted since *The Comedy of Errors*.[68] The end he seems to have in view is not "verisimilitude," which is hardly affected, but that other justification for the Unities in the eyes of Renaissance theorists, the sense of difficulty overcome. Even a stern champion of the Unities like Castelvetro takes it for granted that a varied plot, containing "a number of actions by several persons," has "pleasure and greatness and magnificence"; his decisive argument for a single plot is that, if it comes off, "there is revealed the judgment and industry of the poet." [69] Shakespeare combines the advantages of variety and unity by means of his interwoven plots, guided by a single mind. When Prospero tells Ariel to "bring the rabble" quickly "here to this place," to "incite them to quick motion" for "another trick," his excuse for haste is that he means to adorn the play

---

68. *Comedy of Errors:* I.i.151; I.ii.26; III.ii.172; IV.i.10; V.i.118. *Tempest:* I.ii.36–37, 181–183, 240; V.i.3–4.

69. Castelvetro, trans. in Gilbert, *Literary Criticism,* pp. 318–319; cf. Doran, *Endeavors of Art,* pp. 259–279.

with an additional subplot in the form of the masque: "I must / Bestow upon the eyes of this young couple / Some vanity of mine art" (IV.i.39–41). This is an ingenuity of compression beyond Plautus' scope.

Yet the technical bravura serves a further purpose too. Antonio's reanimation of an old crime seems to Sebastian like a dream. The overlapping of the characters' deeds and feelings and the telescoping of past and present render the action of *The Tempest* dreamlike to the audience. The displays of art created by Ariel—the music, the pageant of harpies, the wedding masque—are also dreamlike; Prospero dwells on this comparison in his discourse to the young couple. But the illusory quality attached to theatrical art did not, for Renaissance poets, mean that drama was inherently false; on the contrary, this quality brought out and, as it were, made visible what was illusory and merely provisional in life itself. A play was like human life—because human life was like a play.[70] Hence the multiplication of disguises on the stage, or the introduction of a play within the play, was not necessarily mere artifice, but, suitably handled, could bring a deeper sense of reality. In Prospero's lecture, "the great globe itself" will ultimately "dissolve," no less than the theater buildings and the masque that has just vanished. The time sense in *The Tempest* contributes to this symbolic dimension of art in the play. In the last scene and in his Epilogue, Prospero touches on the thought of life as a pilgrimage; by throwing our perception of the unity of time into relief, Shakespeare sharpens the impression of the pilgrimage's brevity. He could hardly have achieved this subtle and haunting effect without his prolonged effort to combine the traditions of classical and medieval romance.

70. See Jean Jacquot, " 'Le Théâtre du Monde' de Shakespeare à Calderón," *Revue de litt. comparée,* XXXI (1957), 341–372.

"Of Mighty Opposites":
Stoicism and Machiavellianism

JOSEPH S. M. J. CHANG

W HILE THERE HAVE BEEN many studies of Stoic and Machiavellian
influences on Elizabethan drama,[1] a simple oversight has left obscure what may be their most important contribution. Because critics
have failed to observe how frequently the two manifest themselves
in the same play as contrary forces, they are limited to seeing Stoicism and
Machiavellianism as operating within a conventional dramatic framework, such as *de casibus* or revenge tragedy. Influence is thought of with
respect to characterization rather than situation: dramatists made use of
the Stoic sage and the Machiavel because of their vividness as characters.
Thus *Richard III* is essentially a chronicle history, with the Marlovian

---

1. On Senecan and Stoic influences see John W. Cunliffe, *The Influence of Seneca
on Elizabethan Tragedy* (London, 1893); also his "Introduction," *Early English
Classical Tragedies* (Oxford, 1912), pp. vii–c; F. L. Lucas, *Seneca and Elizabethan
Tragedy* (London, 1922); Allan H. Gilbert, "Seneca and the Criticism of Elizabethan Tragedy," *PQ*, XIII (1934), 370–381; C. F. Beckingham, "Seneca's Fatal-
ism and Elizabethan Tragedy," *MLR*, XXXII (1936), 434–438; Henry W. Wells,
"Senecan Influence on Elizabethan Tragedy: A Re-Estimation," *Shakespeare Association Bulletin*, XIX (1944), 71–84; Michael Higgins, "The Development of the
'Senecal Man': Chapman's *Bussy d'Ambois* and Some Precursors," *RES*, XXIII

emphasis on a single figure, an effect best achieved by means of the Machiavel. There are other plays, however, in which the combined presence of the Stoic hero and the Machiavellian villain influences the nature of the dramatic conflict. In many tragedies heroes and villains are differentiated on the basis of their general alignment with Stoic or Machiavellian doctrines. The coincidence is not accidental, and it indicates that the influence of one can be best understood in terms of the other. Indeed, the distinctiveness of the types is an index of the basic difference between the two. Because the dramatists and their audiences recognized this difference and appreciated all that it indicated, they were able to develop a tragic form significantly different from those generally recognized. Even as medieval Christianity provided early English drama with a situation for dramatic representation, the fall and regeneration of Everyman, and the medieval conception of Fortune formed the basis of *de casibus* tragedy, later modified in the Mirror tradition and adopted by the Elizabethan stage, so, too, Stoicism and Machiavellianism mutually contributed an opposition to Renaissance tragedy that was inherently dramatic and capable of the finest effects.[2] Marlowe used the morality structure in *Faustus* even while he surpassed Mankind in his hero, and Shakespeare used Stoicism and Machiavellianism in *Hamlet* without depicting the Prince as a Clermont or Claudius as a Nick Machiavel.

Although there are incidental points of similarity between Stoicism and Machiavellianism, and it is possible to see elements of each in the Eliz-

---

(1947), 24–33; Jean Jacquot, "Les Tragédies de Sénèque et le théâtre élisabétain," *Études Anglaises,* XIV (1961), 343–344. Studies questioning the extent of Stoic (or Senecan) influence are Howard Baker, *Induction to Tragedy* (University, La., 1939), and Peter Ure, "On Some Differences between Senecan and Elizabethan Tragedy," *Durham University Journal,* N.S., X (1948), 17–23. On Machiavelli's influence see Edward Stockton Meyer, *Machiavelli and the Elizabethan Drama* (Weimar, 1897); Napoleone Orsini, "Elizabethan Manuscript Translations of Machiavelli's *Prince,*" *JWCI,* I (1937), 166–169; also, his " 'Policy' or the Language of Elizabethan Machiavellianism," *JWCI,* IX (1946), 122–134; Mario Praz, " 'The Politic Brain': Machiavelli and the Elizabethans," *The Flaming Heart* (New York, 1958), pp. 90–145 (this essay is an expansion of one first appearing in *The Proceedings of the British Academy* [London, 1928], pp. 49–97).

2. The best discussion of Stoic tragedy is Hardin Craig's essay, "The Shackling of Accidents: A Study of Elizabethan Tragedy," *PQ,* XIX (1940), 1–19.

abethan tyrant or the villain-hero,[3] of greater importance are the fundamental differences between the two approaches to conduct, principally
with respect to man's response to Fortune. They offer boldly contrasting
solutions to the problem of free will and determinism—an enduring
concern to men of all ages, but especially important in the Renaissance.
Dramatists of great and small talents exploited this sharp contrast in
creating a variation of tragedy based on Fortune. As in the medieval
period, Fortune was the central fact in Renaissance tragedy. In *de casibus*
tragedy the fall itself was of sufficient interest to sustain a tale. However,
as Professor Farnham demonstrates, in Elizabethan tragedy the focus
shifted to the reasons for the fall, thereby making tragedy based on
character possible.[4] There is yet another way in which the Elizabethans
made use of the *de casibus* tradition, one which reflected the then current
interests in Machiavelli and the Stoics. Using the fall as a precondition
instead of a consequence, the Elizabethans developed a tragic form based
on the protagonist's ability to prevail in spite of all, a heroic achievement
underscored by the antagonist's futile attempts to withstand change by the
familiar devices of policy and force.

The most obvious instance of this pattern of opposition is in Chapman's
The Revenge of Bussy D'Ambois. Clermont, as master of himself, is
victorious against Fortune:

> In short, this Senecal man is found in him,
> He may with heaven's immortal powers compare,
> To whom the day and fortune equal are;
> Come fair or foul, whatever chance can fall,
> Fix'd in himself, he still is one to all.
>
> (IV.iv.42–46) [5]

---

3. Praz first makes this point. Other studies include W. A. Armstrong, "The
Influence of Seneca and Machiavelli on the Elizabethan Tyrant," *RES*, XXIV
(1948), 19–35; and Clarence Valentine Boyer, *The Villain as Hero in Elizabethan
Tragedy* (New York, 1964).

4. Willard Farnham, *The Medieval Heritage of Elizabethan Tragedy* (New York,
1956).

5. In quoting from Chapman I have used *The Plays and Poems of George
Chapman: The Tragedies*, ed. Thomas Marc Parrott (New York, 1961).

As for his enemies, "These are your Machiavellian villains. . . ." In Shakespeare, variations of this opposition are found in *Titus Andronicus, Hamlet,* and *King Lear.* Indebted as *Titus Andronicus* is to Seneca's *Thyestes,* Aaron and Tamora owe something to the Machiavel. Tamora masters Fortune by her wit, that is, by *prudenzia:*

> Now climbeth Tamora Olympus' top,
> Safe out of Fortune's shot; and sits aloft,
> Secure of thunder's crack or lightning flash,
> Advanc'd above pale envy's threat'ning reach.
> . . . .
> Upon her wit doth earthly honour wait,
> And virtue stoops and trembles at her frown.
>
> (II.i.1–11) [6]

In contrast to this security based on astuteness is the precariousness of Titus, who finds himself in the familiar position of the embattled Stoic, subject to the trials of the gods:

> For now I stand as one upon a rock,
> Environ'd with a wilderness of sea,
> Who marks the waxing tide grow wave by wave,
> Expecting ever when some envious surge
> Will in his brinish bowels swallow him.
>
> (III.i.93–97)

Sejanus' tyranny is countered by Stoic resolution:

> None, but the plaine, and passiue fortitude,
> To suffer, and be silent; neuer to stretch
> These armes, against the torrent; liue at home,
> With my owne thoughts, and innocence about me,
> Not tempting the wolves iawes: these are my artes.
>
> (IV.294–298) [7]

6. Shakespeare citations are to the Alexander edition of the *Complete Works* (London and Glasgow, 1951).

7. In *Ben Jonson,* ed. C. H. Herford and P. and E. Simpson (Oxford, 1925–1952), IV.

Behind this pattern of opposition, which anachronistically ignores the passing of a thousand years to bring together two systems of conduct, is a common concern with the problem of individual liberty in an apparently deterministic or hostile universe. Tamora is beyond Fortune's power and sits among the gods; Clermont is, in another sense, Fortune's master and is also godlike in his autonomy. Both Machiavellianism and Stoicism attempt to deal with the central question of moral philosophy: whether man is free, or whether he is subject to the external compulsions of Fortune, Fate, or Providence. Valla, Pomponazzi, Erasmus, and Luther investigated the problem; but so did Shakespeare and Marston, among other playwrights. Edmund rejects "heavenly compulsion," "planetary influence," and "spherical predominance" (I.ii.111–115); in *Sophonisba* the heroine carefully reconciles human freedom with divine foreknowledge.[8] The ethical dilemma was too important, and the Stoic and Machiavellian positions were too inalterably opposed, to permit what T. S. Eliot suggests, that ". . . the Senecan attitude of Pride, the Montaigne attitude of Scepticism, and the Machiavelli attitude of Cynicism, arrived at a kind of fusion in the Elizabethan individualism."[9]

Syncretists as the Elizabethans were, they were not insensitive to philosophical distinctions. The truth in Eliot's remark lies in its recognition of the appeal to individualism in both Stoicism and Machiavellianism. Modern readers of *The Prince* may well insist, along with Mario Praz,[10] that the work be read as a disinterested, scientific study of politics; few of its original readers, I suspect, were much interested in it as a program designed to solve the plight of the Italian states. Of principal concern here is how the Elizabethans reacted to Machiavelli's most famous work.[11] *The Prince* became notorious for its blatant and cynical advice that the politician should forsake his honor when convenient and that he should rule

8. II.i, p. 23, in *The Plays of John Marston,* ed. H. Harvey Wood (Edinburgh, 1938), II. As lines are not numbered in this edition, I provide page references instead.

9. "Shakespeare and the Stoicism of Seneca," *Selected Essays* (New York, 1950), p. 112.

10. Praz, p. 96.

11. Especially useful is Felix Raab's *The English Face of Machiavelli* (London, 1965).

from fear rather than love. More significantly, it effectively denied the primacy of ethical criteria in public life and defined a novel way for dealing with Fortune. The problem of maintaining self-determination is never far from Machiavelli's mind, and it is the last subject to be treated before the final exhortation to free Italy of the barbarian invaders. In a real sense, *The Prince* is a program for sovereignty, political and personal. The treatise culminates in the patriotic call to arms only after Machiavelli resolves the question of free will and Fortune. The state as a work of art can be asserted only upon some assurance that man has a measure of personal freedom. Machiavelli's answer to the philosophical problem of free will is well known:

And yet least the power of *our* owne freewill shoulde seeme altogether voyde and frustrate, I am of this opinion that one parte of our affaires is disposed att the pleasure of Fortune, and the other parte or little lesse to be lefte att the libertie of *our* owne discreation. . . .[12]

In the context of the traditional ethics of the English Renaissance, the statement is radical, despite its assertion of human freedom, to the extent that it refuses to discuss the matter in philosophical terms. Here, as in the previous chapters, Machiavelli's program for conduct exists in an ethical vacuum, with an eye directed to what is possible rather than to the nature of things. Machiavelli makes no distinction between Fortune and Divine Providence; his concern is not with the nature of that which lies beyond man's power or understanding. Whatever it is, the significant fact to be dealt with is that it impinges on the freedom of the Prince. Similarly, there is no attempt to define human nature; the only standard of reference for human conduct is its own possibilities for effectiveness. The enlarging of the Prince's scope is what matters, and to this end the Prince relies on his *virtù* and *prudenzia*. In effect, the opportunism of *The Prince* amounts to a negation of any rational order in the universe, leaving only the undirected world to be shaped by men willing to apply themselves to that task.[13]

The arbitrary division of initiative between man and Fortune indicates

---

12. *The Prince*, ed. Hardin Craig (Chapel Hill, 1944), pp. 110–111.

13. See my essay, "Machiavellianism in Daniel's *The Civil Wars*," *Tulane Studies in English*, XIV (1965), 5–16.

how far Machiavelli departs from tradition: Fortune represents nothing more than a realist's concession to the fact that no man can control all the variables which influence his life. Machiavellian Fortune is simply a name for those effects which result from causes other than the Prince's own efforts, the direction events will take, under a set of pertinent circumstances, "the sum total of all the elements beyond personal control which accompany an individual in his actions." [14] The Machiavel, always plotting, is but the stage version of the ideal Prince who anticipates the cresting flood waters with channels and dams.[15] In this comparison of the politician to the flood-control expert, Machiavelli's pragmatism and opportunism are evident; despite the measures taken to counter disaster, the river can always rise to unexpected heights or generate pressures beyond the capability of the dikes. Nevertheless, disaster is by no means inevitable and can be averted by foresight and planning. Realist that he was, Machiavelli, knowing that no man can consistently assess every political situation with complete accuracy and react adequately with the twin resources of acumen and power, was content to divide control between man and Fortune. By the same reasoning, however, the division is never absolute, as it tends to be when the question of free will is approached philosophically by an inquiry into the nature of man. For Machiavelli, man is subordinate to Fortune, not by nature but by contingencies, which careful planning can anticipate. The obligation of the Prince is to increase his control over all the variables which may affect his position.

The Stoics rejected Fortune as an actuality, though for entirely different reasons. Insisting on a rational, teleologically oriented pattern encompassing all being, the Stoics found in Fortune a contradiction. In their view the figure of the blind and capricious goddess imposing her will on man belied the orderly universe on which Stoic ethics is predicated. For the Stoics, Nature is not blind, it is providential. Fortune is nothing but man's false understanding of the meaning of events arising from vain desires which have no basis in his rational nature.[16] It is a convenient term to use

14. Vincenzo Cioffari, "The Function of Fortune in Dante, Boccaccio and Machiavelli," *Italica*, XXIV (1947), 8.

15. *Il Principe*, in *Opere*, ed. Mario Bonfantini (Milan, 1954), cap. XXV.

16. See, for example, Cicero, *De Officiis*, trans. Walter Miller, Loeb Classical Library (Cambridge, Mass., 1938), p. 303; Seneca, *Consolation to Helvia*, trans. John W. Basore, Loeb Classical Library (New York, 1928), p. 429; Epictetus, *The*

with respect to the vagaries of life, but it does not describe the nature of life in essential terms. That is, princes do rise and fall for unaccountable reasons, but these events do not call into question human freedom. The practical end of Stoic ethics is to understand how human ends cannot be frustrated by external agencies which are necessarily beyond personal control but, rather, may be achieved through the exercise of one's essential humanity in terms of reason and choice.

This is the fundamental difference between Stoicism and Machiavellianism with respect to Fortune, as I believe it appeared to men of the Renaissance with a commitment to the Christian ethical tradition. The modern student of the Renaissance may wish to keep separate the Machiavellian and Stoic conceptions of Fortune, but he should keep in mind that in the Renaissance, given the ethical premises of the age, the impulse would have been to examine each to find what truth it offered with respect to Fortune, Fate, and Providence. It was an eclectic age, but not one indifferent to philosophical distinctions. Indeed, Renaissance eclecticism is evidence that the principal concern was with the truth of things, not with the preservation of such distinctions as Peripatetic, Platonic, Epicurean, and Stoic. Men would have asked themselves which of the two definitions of Fortune—man's inability to manipulate his circumstances, or man's inability to perceive the operation of Providence—best accounted for the competing realities of free will and external compulsion. And within the context of orthodox Christianity, only one answer was possible, for Machiavellian Fortune implicitly negates Divine Providence, and any act predicated on Machiavelli's premises would have seemed an assertion of man's will over God's. Commenting on Chapter XXV, Innocent Gentillet reminds the Christian that, since all of life is directed by

---

Manual, trans. W. A. Oldfather, Loeb Classical Library (New York, 1938), p. 480; Marcus Aurelius, *The Communings with Himself,* trans. C. R. Haines, Loeb Classical Library (New York, 1961), p. 135. A few examples from the Renaissance are found in Justus Lipsius, *Tvvo Bookes of Constancie,* trans. John Stradling, ed. Rudolf Kirk (New Brunswick, 1939), p. 79; Guillaume du Vair, *The Moral Philosophie of the Stoicks,* trans. Thomas James, ed. Rudolf Kirk (New Brunswick, 1951), p. 61; Joseph Hall, *Heaven vpon Earth and Characters of Vertues and Vices,* ed. Rudolf Kirk (New Brunswick, 1948), p. 146; Girolamo Cardano, *Cardanus Comforte,* trans. Thomas Bedingfeld (London, 1573), A1ᵛ.

Providence, man must yield to apparent misfortunes to serve the will of God:

. . . That nothing fals to us, but by Gods providence, and that such afflictions as are sent us, are for our good, least the slipperie way of prosperitie make us fall, to our destruction: insomuch, as wee praise God for both good and evill; resolving our selves, that that which unto our carnall sences appeareth to bee evill, is not evill to our soules, but very healthfull and good, because there is a Christian Maxime, That no evill can happen to a Christian, from the hand of God our Father. . . .[17]

Though the Elizabethan could refer to Fortune, in all probability he felt as Ralegh did, believing *"Whom the Poets call Fortune, we know to be God."* [18]

Equally clear is Justus Lipsius on man's unwillingness to submit to life's tribulations: "For if it bee so that God doe not only suffer, but send all these things: then ye which thus striue and struggle, what doe you els but (as much as in you lyeth) take the scepter and sway of gouernment from him?" [19] Most assuredly, the Renaissance did not have to turn to Stoicism for a reply to Machiavelli's challenge to orthodoxy; the well-elaborated doctrines of Christian tradition were available. However, Stoicism was uniquely suitable insofar as it could be assimilated into the Christian tradition, even while it satisfied the sense of individualism aroused by Machiavelli. Stoicism invested life with a nobility uncharacteristic of medieval Christianity without forcing a disavowal of its principal doctrines. It had the inestimable value of allowing an orderly transition from one age and culture to another. This statement of Montaigne's might well be taken for one of Machiavelli's, though it is probably Stoic in origin: "A man must be valiant for himself and for the advantage he hath to have his courage placed in a constant and assured seate, to withstand all assaults of fortune." [20]

17. *A Discovrse vpon the Meanes of vvel Governing and Maintaining in Good Peace, a Kingdome, or other Principalitie . . . Against Nicholas Machiavell the Florentine,* trans. Simon Patericke (London, 1608), N4ʳ.

18. *History of the World* (London, 1614), p. 15.

19. Lipsius, pp. 104–105.

20. *The Essayes,* trans. John Florio, introd. Desmond McCarthy (London, 1928), II, 16.

The Stoic seeks complete independence and self-reliance. Like the Machiavellian, he seeks to maintain himself against the vicissitudes of life. The resemblance can also be illustrated by a passage from the French neo-Stoic, Guillaume du Vair:

Will you then rather choose to runne vnto Fortune, and waite at her deceitfull handes for that good, which you may giue vnto yourselfe and if you will? For this is a diuine and inuiolable lawe, which hath been made since the beginning of the world, that if we will haue any good, we must purchase and get it our selues, by our owne labour and industrie.[21]

The Stoic is an egotist for reasons entirely different from those of the Machiavellian. According to Montaigne, "We cannot be tied beyond our strength and meanes. The reason is, because the effects and executions are not any way in our power, and except our will, nothing is truely in our power. . . ."[22] The Stoic's retreat into the citadel of the mind is a retreat into human nature, which is necessarily inviolable so far as external forces are concerned; his passivity is based on the recognition that he is unable to shape the world, this task being reserved for Providence. Unlike the Machiavellian, who directs his energies to the manipulation of circumstances, hoping always to curb the influence of Fortune, the Stoic searches for freedom and autonomy by living within human limitations. *"The greatnesse of the minde,"* Montaigne writes, *"is not so much, to drawe up and hale forward, as to know how to range, direct and circumscribe it self."*[23] The Stoic asserts his will by accepting God's; according to Lipsius, *"Wee are borne in a kingdome, and to obey God is libertie."*[24]

Nevertheless, there does remain between Machiavellian *virtù* and Stoic virtue this similarity: Success or happiness can come only to those who retain the initiative. Girolamo Cardano's statement on how man may best resist misfortune is like Machiavelli's famous dictum, that Fortune "dimostra la sua potenzia dove non è ordinata virtù a resisterle. . . ."[25] For Cardano, "Calamity durst not come nere anye, but such as were of base minde, simple, & subiecte to effeminacy. But among such as were valiant

21. Du Vair, p. 59.
22. Montaigne, I, 7.
23. Montaigne, III, 13.
24. Lipsius, p. 105.
25. Machiavelli, XXV.

and armed with vertue, she durst not come."[26] In a sense, both the Machiavellian and the Stoic are made of the same stuff, and it is possible for Professor Harry Levin to see one of Marlowe's heroes passing from one form of egotism to the other:

> Mortimer has viewed himself, in his heyday, rather as Fortune's successful foe than as her erstwhile favorite. With her triumph and his decline, he still may depend on his virtue; but virtue, at this point, devolves from Machiavelli's conception back to Seneca's. The individual, in a narrowing world, has less room to act and more occasion to suffer. The ethical criterion is the stoical resignation with which he meets inevitable and overwhelming odds.[27]

Inevitable disaster is the basic ingredient of the Elizabethan version of Stoic tragedy, forcing the characters to demonstrate what they are. According to the Seneca created for *The Tragedy of Nero,* "High fortunes like stronge wines do trie their vessels."[28] Adversity as the god's instrument for the testing of men's souls is a constant theme in Stoic tragedy. Even in so unsophisticated a play as *Gismond of Salerne* it is explained, in the prefatory verses,

> So Ioue, as your hye vertues doen deserue,
> geue yow such féres as may yoʳ vertues serue
> wᵗʰ like vertues. . . .[29]

This early play is "Senecan" with its excessive horrors, long speeches, and act divisions, to be sure, but it is Stoic in that it represents on stage the struggle between man and Fate, which in this play assumes the particular identity of Cupid. The real issue is not whether man can resist his passions but whether he can successfully contest the supremacy of the gods:

> But now the world, not seing in these dayes
> such present proues of myne almighty power,

26. Cardano, N6ᵛ.

27. *The Overreacher: A Study of Christopher Marlowe* (Cambridge, Mass., 1952), p. 99.

28. *A Collection of Old English Plays,* ed. A. H. Bullen (New York, 1964), I, 22. First published 1882–1889.

29. In *Early English Classical Tragedies,* ed. John W. Cunliffe (Oxford, 1912), p. 164.

disdaines my name, and seketh sondry wayes
to conquer and deface me euerie houre.
My name supprest to raise againe therfore,
and in this age myne honor and renome
by mighty act intending to restore,
down to the earth in spite now am I come.

(I.i.49–56)

Though these lines seem to bring the play close to the theme of Chaucer's *Troilus and Criseyde* (I.206–210), it should be kept in mind that both Guishard and Gismond are true lovers, never having given the god of love occasion to complain, as did Troilus.

What the lovers must do is indicated by the Chorus. They must resist this god, whose assault cannot touch the citadel of the mind, the essential man, for

weak is his bowe, his quēched brand is cold.
Cupide is but a childe, and can not daunte
the minde that beares him on his vertues bold.

(III.iii.38–40)

Significantly the Chorus proceeds to characterize Love as a deceiver, thereby anticipating the entry of the Machiavel in later years:

But he geues poison so to drink in gold,
and hides vnder such pleasant baite his hoke,
but ye beware it will be hard to hold
your gredy minde. But if yow wisely loke,
what slye snake lurkes vnder those flowers gay,
but ye mistrust some cloudy storme, and fere
a wett showër after so fair a day,
ye may repent, and by yoᵣ pleasure dere.

(III.iii.41–48)

Here the deceiver is Cupid, a god and not a man, whereas in later tragedy he is more often found to be a Machiavel. It is this later incorporation of the Machiavel into the contest between men and gods that distinguishes the Elizabethan version of Stoic tragedy.

The basic situation in such a tragedy involves an antagonist who, in seeking to manipulate his circumstances by policy, forces his protagonist to come to ruin. Fortune for one is the barrier to ambition; for the other it is disaster wrought by policy and allowed by the gods. The conflict is therefore triangular, bringing together the Stoic hero, the Machiavellian villain, and the gods. The villain is usually indifferent to moral precepts, and while his victims may accuse him of challenging the authority of the gods, his consciousness is generally limited to the achieving of specific objectives. For the Stoic hero the conflict is twofold: he must contend with his adversary, and he must also reconcile his experience of evil with his ethical presupposition that the world is rational and subject to the dominion of benevolent gods. In confronting his antagonist, the hero is at a considerable disadvantage, as are all honest men in coping with deceit, fraud, and intrigue. All that remains for the hero is to appeal to the gods in the hope that, providentially, evil will be made to recoil upon itself. So it is that the villain, though momentarily successful, eventually falls, not through the activities of his victims, but for the reason that his thrust for power is ultimately aimed at the gods. The hero in turn achieves a greater nobility in having successfully preserved the integrity of his character. The principle is that

> The gods inflict on men diseases never,
> Or other outward maims, but to decipher,
> Correct, and order some rude vice within them:
> And why decipher they it, but to make
> Men note, and shun, and tax it to th' extreme?
> (*Caesar and Pompey,* I.ii.260–264)

Depending on the artistry of the dramatist, the dilemma of free man faced with inevitable disaster could be presented with facile solutions in sententious maxims, or it could be offered as the agonizing experience of man caught in a situation which threatens his very humanity. Seldom was Chapman able to do more than define the kind of response one should bring to adversity; in defeat, Pompey gives the formula,

> nor desire to be
> (Do Fortune to exceed it what she can)
> A Pompey, or a Caesar, but a man.
> (IV.iii.90–92)

In King Lear's progressive descent from lord of all to unaccommodated man stripped of all lendings not essentially his, there is the same paradoxical destruction of identity combined with the dis-covering of humanity.

The difference between Pompey and Lear, between Clermont and Hamlet, indicates the two uses dramatists made of Stoicism. For Chapman, Stoicism represented an admirable code of ethics, one worthy of representation on stage for the edification of his audiences. For Shakespeare, Stoicism focused on an ethical problem eminently suited to tragedy. By concentrating on a dramatically viable representation of the classic problem of Stoicism—the preservation of self against the incursions of life and death—Shakespeare succeeds in creating human beings instead of Stoic sages.[30] In *King Lear* Shakespeare takes a man who is capricious and entirely lacking in self-knowledge, patience, and constancy and plunges him into the furnace of tragedy, where the dross of his peccant humanity is burned away. The point almost seems to be that this least of men, in spite of all his inadequacies, is capable of heroic endurance. Lear is more sinned against than sinning, and the view that tragedy represents the consequence of sin or personal flaw of character can be maintained in this play only if one is callously indifferent to the gross disproportion between his folly and his retribution. Neither is it necessary to conclude gloomily that the tragedy is utterly dark with pessimism, for here the important thing is not how massively powerful gods and men are but how well one draws on the resources of one's humanity. In fact, the measure of Lear's greatness lies in the extent of his persecution.

In the closing moments of the play, Kent says with reference to his master,

> If fortune brag of two she lov'd and hated,
> One of them we behold.
>
> (V.iii.280–281)

There is no difficulty in finding Lear as one hated by Fortune; there is a surplus of evidence. How that evidence may be construed as an indication of his being Fortune's minion depends on our being mindful of the Senecan proposition that God "does not make a spoiled pet of a good man; he tests him, hardens him, and fits him for his own service."[31] In

---

30. The notable exceptions are in *Julius Caesar,* in which all the major characters are to some degree Stoic as a consequence of their being Romans.

31. *On Providence,* p. 7.

the theater of the world, ". . . the gods are moved by the desire to behold great men wrestle with some calamity." [32]

Lear can only respond to the enormous pressure generated by Edmund, Goneril, Regan, and the gods, acting in concert, by finding his humanity, that part of him which is essentially his own. Paradoxically the discovery of self comes only with the discovery of others, and Lear experiences the relief which Edgar feels in witnessing his king's misfortunes:

> When we our betters see bearing our woes,
> We scarcely think our miseries our foes.
> Who alone suffers suffers most i' the mind,
> Leaving free things and happy shows behind;
> But then the mind much sufferance doth o'erskip
> When grief hath mates, and bearing fellowship.
> How light and portable my pain seems now,
> When that which makes me bend makes the king bow. . . .
>
> (III.vi.102–109)

Lear is exposed to feel what wretches feel; he can face the prospect of incarceration supported by the love of Cordelia. In the play's single moment of lyrical rhapsody, Lear gives voice to what appears to be the equivalent of the Stoic's ability to transcend the vagaries of time and the fluctuations of court life and to enter into the heart of life where constancy prevails:

> No, no, no, no! Come, let's away to prison.
> We two alone will sing like birds i' th' cage;
> When thou dost ask me blessing, I'll kneel down
> And ask of thee forgiveness; so we'll live,
> And pray, and sing, and tell old tales, and laugh
> At gilded butterflies, and hear poor rogues
> Talk of court news; and we'll talk with them too—
> Who loses and who wins; who's in, who's out—
> And take upon's the mystery of things
> As if we were God's spies; and we'll wear out,
> In a wall'd prison, packs and sets of great ones
> That ebb and flow by th' moon.
>
> (V.iii.8–19)

32. *Ibid.,* p. 11.

Where Lear expects the servitude of life to dissolve in the love he shares with Cordelia, Edmund meets the challenge of Fortune by denying its existence. There is no necessity, compulsion, or inevitability; there is nothing but "the plague of custom" and the "curiosity of nations" (I.ii.3–4) to account for his being denied station. The conditions of his birth, as the second son and as a bastard, are as irrelevant to his nature qua man as the torments Lear suffers are to his sins. Edmund chooses not to follow Lear's course; he will not be patient, he will not endure, he will not, as Gloucester will,

> . . . bear
> Affliction till it do cry out itself
> 'Enough, enough' and die.
>
> (IV.vi.75–77)

Edmund is arrogant, and he deceives himself in thinking that he can fashion the world as he pleases; but in his distorted individualism, he hits upon a truth which remains obscure to Lear even at the moment of reconciliation with Cordelia, in whose company he hopes to find constancy in a changeable world. The irony of that blissful interim is that it would have been more accurate for Lear to have said, "We two together," rather than "We two alone," for, with Cordelia, he is not alone. Fortune does not concede to man the right to live out his days in the comforting shadow of love. The contest with change must be waged individually, in the mind, if man is to have hope of winning. If the principal challenge is to find order and value, to escape mutability, to enter "the mystery of things," then the challenge must be faced alone, for the capricious goddess controls all else, including whether Cordelia is to live or die. Subject herself to mutability, she is no weapon against it.

In *King Lear* Fortune is transmuted from a tired and ancient convention to the immense reality all men confront beyond the palpable trivialities of life. Far more than a label for the unexpected in life, Fortune indicates the irrationality and incomprehensibility of life. In his madness Lear sees that there is no measuring of life in reasonable terms so long as the beadle lashes the whore after whom he lusts. His personal anguish, though intense, is but a detail in a chaotic world not to be accounted for by simple norms of justice.

In *Hamlet* the dramatic issue is essentially the same, though its presentation is far more subtle. Claudius is so finely wrought that he has won the sympathy of some critics, and Hamlet finds himself deficient in the Stoic virtues exemplified by Horatio. Neither character seems suitable to the hypothesis sketched in this essay. The difficulty arises when we try to find commonplace attitudes and stock responses in fully realized characters. If we can divert our attention to the basic situation of the play, we can see that, again, the characters are pitted not only against each other but against some large, superhuman agency as well. Hamlet must deal with the Ghost, with the heaven which has apparently appointed him scourge and minister, with the divinity shaping his end. By implication, Claudius is as much victim of special providence as he is of Hamlet. The dynamic presence of this third force, which is variously referred to, is confirmed by the Player's speech describing the encounter of Pyrrhus and Priam. The issue between these two reverberates in the tower's falling, and the Player apostrophizes:

> Out, out, thou strumpet, Fortune! All you gods,
> In general synod, take away her power;
> Break all the spokes and fellies from her wheel,
> And bowl the round nave down the hill of heaven,
> As low as to the fiends.

(II.ii.486–491)

The appeal to the gods for relief from Fortune presupposes sympathy to human needs, in contrast to Fortune's hostility. In these two attitudes are the two extreme positions taken by Hamlet. Fortune for him is manifest in all experiences which do not conform to reason, order, and justice, that part of life which imposes itself on human awareness even as it escapes understanding. Though the events of the play are limited to the physical scene of Elsinore, Hamlet is always conscious of the realities beyond time and death, of heaven and hell, of that undiscovered country. These mysterious realities impinge on his consciousness, along with his mother's unfeeling indiscretion, his unworthy uncle's ascent to the throne, and his father's death. Even before the Ghost's appearance, then, Hamlet finds his world to be disorderly and deprived of meaning. With the Ghost's revelations, Hamlet's disillusionment is extended to include life as a whole; moreover, there is added the burden of revenge. In a profound sense Hamlet is a victim of Fortune in that both reason and will, the essential constituents of his being, are jeopardized by an incomprehensible world not of his own making but for which he finds himself responsible.

In the reaction against the charge that Hamlet is constitutionally unable to act, being contemplative by nature, there has been a tendency to disregard the character's own preoccupation with the problem. Actually there need be no embarrassment over the matter if it can be understood that Hamlet is not handicapped in an extraordinary way but is groping toward the awareness that much of man's life is beyond his power. Unless we share his concern over personal freedom in a world which offers so little opportunity for its exercise, we will necessarily see his tragedy as the consequence of his idiosyncrasies rather than what it is, a realistic depiction of man's struggle to save some part of his identity. External compulsion weighs heavily on Hamlet: he is obligated as an obedient son to his mother, as subject to nature, which imposes on him the burden to mourn his father, as one born to set the world right, as scourge and minister to heaven. In the "dram of eale" speech he muses on how a man's reputation may suffer through no fault of his own. The theme is reaffirmed in Polonius' and Laertes' warnings to Ophelia, reminding her that the Prince is not his own man, free to marry whomever he pleases. In all these obligations and duties, there is a mixture of the trivial and the important, those externally imposed and those derived from human nature. At first Hamlet is only aware of their weight; by the play's end, he will establish a basis for action which fulfills his nature and, as a result, meets his obligations.

Contrasting with Hamlet's preoccupation with freedom and his self-denigration as a "peasant slave," Claudius and his allies are apparently unimpeded in the pursuit of their ends. Pompously self-assured, Polonius is a comic version of his master, Claudius, a man entirely confident of his ability to survive the threats posed by Fortinbras, Laertes, or Hamlet. Though the King may employ the agency of one or another subordinate, we are never in doubt that he is self-possessed. In his creature Guildenstern's words, "We will ourselves provide" (III.iii.7), we have a perfect expression of Claudius' independence, an independence which contrasts effectively with Hamlet's eventual reliance on special providence. Unlike Hamlet, Claudius seems to be completely unfettered, free to manipulate his own destiny. He is the spiritual brother of Jonson's Catiline, who says to his henchmen,

> Then, let me worke out
> Your fortunes, and mine owne.
>
> (I.517-518)

Just as the Ghost incites Hamlet to just revenge, Claudius adeptly works Laertes to his will.

Laertes, who has the same specific duty as Hamlet, can adopt the Machiavel's devices only after attempting to disengage himself from those bonds which define humanity:

> To hell, allegiance! vows, to the blackest devil!
> Conscience and grace, to the profoundest pit!
> I dare damnation.
>
> (IV.v.128-130)

With these words Laertes is free to harvest his revenge, but he, like Claudius, is bound fast by a guilty conscience. Ironically, where Hamlet is cautious in dealing with the Ghost, fearing that it might be a devil, where he pondered revenge in terms of conscience, where he balanced suicide against damnation, Laertes is indifferent to all so long as he realizes his intent. It is on this point that the issue between free will and determinism turns. In respect to the ultimate arbiter of human conduct, conscience, Hamlet preserves his freedom, either attributing the deaths he causes to higher purposes than his own or finding his intentions consistent with "perfect conscience." [33] Underscoring the importance of conscience in *Hamlet* is the closet scene, wherein Gertrude is finally persuaded by her own sense of guilt, rather than the threat of violence posed by her son, to pledge,

> Be thou assur'd, if words be made of breath
> And breath of life, I have no life to breathe
> What thou hast said to me.
>
> (III.iv.197-199)

A clear conscience is the Stoic's refuge in a world with purposes of its own. It is the implementation of Cardano's maxim, "A man is but his minde," insofar as it prescribes the manner in which man's essential

---

33. V.ii.67; cf. III.ii.274-277 and V.ii.58.

nature may be preserved, both with respect to itself and to the external world. As with Jonson's Cicero, at the mercy of Catiline, there is comfort in an unassailable conscience,

> . . . a firme conscience, which shall arme each step
> Tane for the state: and teach me slacke no pace
> For feare of malice.
>
> (III.782–785)

The successful encounter with life is not simply a matter of petulantly shrinking from it, turning within to a vacuum. There must be something within, nothing less than the human spirit, conscious of its own worth and essential inviolability at the hands of any agent other than itself. In coping with his human adversary, the hero is forced to come to terms with himself, and thus the conflict is enlarged to philosophic dimensions. Pompey's declaration,

> I will stand no more
> On others' legs, nor build one joy without me.
> If ever I be worth a house again
> I'll build all inward . . .
>
> (V.i.203–206)

is a recognition of man's limits. In contrast, the Machiavellian who accepts no teleologically ordained limits sacrifices his humanity; as Marston observes in *Sophonisba*, ". . . a statist must not be a man" (II.ii, p. 25). And the lesson in this play applies equally well to *Hamlet:*

> The Gods assist just hearts, & states that trust
> Plots before *Providence* are tost like dust.
>
> (II.ii, p. 25)

In *Hamlet* there is a reconciliation between free will and Providence that is not dependent on the assumption that God is benevolent and so man can submit. To be sure, in Act V there are indications that God does indeed provide, but this truth is balanced by Hamlet's own tranquillity based on conscience. In his speech, "We defy augury," Hamlet demonstrates the attitude which Bishop Hall speaks of as characteristic of the Honest Man:

His conscience over-rules his providence; so as in all things good or ill, he respects the nature of the actions, not the sequell. If he see what he must doe, let God see what shall follow. He never loadeth himselfe with burdens above his strength, beyond his will; and once bound, what he can he will doe, neither doth he will but what he can doe.[34]

Hamlet goes forth to the duel not with unbounded confidence that God is at his side, for in truth he is full of dread. Of his skill he has no doubts, yet there are misgivings: "I shall win at the odds. But thou wouldst not think how ill all's here about my heart; but it is no matter" (V.ii.211–213). What does matter is that now Hamlet knows guilt to be the only fardel man must bear, and conscience is a mark untouched by the slings and arrows of outrageous fortune. In order to fulfill Hall's precept—"what he can he will doe, neither doth he will but what he can doe"—"The readiness is all."

34. Hall, pp. 149–150.

Formalism and Realism
in Elizabethan Drama:
The Miracles in King Lear

ALVIN B. KERNAN

IN THE GREATEST ELIZABETHAN DRAMA the tension between formalism
and realism is at a maximum. Even in the most "realistic" plays the
characters will often be grouped in the stiff configurations of the
morality play: the good lieutenant (Cassio) is balanced by an evil lieutenant (Iago), and the father with three daughters (one good and two
wicked) is paired with the father with two sons (one good and one evil).
At the same time, these characters, who group so nicely into moral
schemes and seem destined to march neatly down some such pattern as
"murder will out" or "disorder will ultimately be brought back to order,"
have such vital energy, are so uniquely themselves, that they seem to be
driving into unknown areas where no previously known forms can
contain them. The known and the unknown, the general scheme and the
particular individual, these elements compose the great counterpoint of
Elizabethan drama, and much of the delight of reading the plays comes
from noting how in a given speech a character will speak in a peculiarly
individualistic way, seeming to be himself only and like no other; and yet,
as he speaks, rhythms and words and gestures link up with what has gone

before and after to join him to the great patterns which are developing.

The Elizabethan dramatist was apparently poised between a belief in the traditional patterns which his culture had developed to represent and order life—expressed by formal schemes—and a new experimentalism which led him to imitate actual life and follow it wherever it went. The weaker dramatists—a Lyly or a Dekker, to suggest the range—reduced the tension, which they may never have felt very strongly, by ruthlessly following the patterns and suppressing the individuality of the characters. The greater dramatists seem to have accepted the tension and made it the very subject of their drama. Even the gigantic individuals created by the iconoclastic Marlowe are pulled inevitably into the circling of Fortune's Wheel; and in the end Doctor Faustus, who tried by magic to make the world take the forms of *his* mind, is forced to trudge drearily down that ancient path from a bargain with Satan, past devils with firecrackers, into a papier-mâché hell-mouth.

For Shakespeare, at once more conservative and more daring of mind than Marlowe, the opposing tugs of old ideas and the desire to follow nature where it led are most powerful. His characters are frequently masterpieces of realism, and yet they operate very close to such overwhelming schemes as the subject's absolute duty to his king or the individual's subservience to the comic plot, which dictates that Jack shall always have Jill. Shakespeare appears to have been acutely aware of the divisive tendencies in his art, for he openly dramatizes them again and again, nowhere more clearly than in Act IV of *King Lear*.

In *King Lear* we seem to be present at the birth of now familiar philosophical and theological concepts, generated under the pressure of suffering and formulated by the characters in a desperate attempt to understand what they have endured. We are, despite intensely formal elements in the play, seldom aware of a poet who has thought his characters' thoughts before them or has forced words and actions on them to illustrate his conceptual scheme. But when Edgar, in IV.vi, places his old blind father on some sort of low step and informs him that he is on the edge of Dover Cliff, allows him to assume a heroic stance and jump off, and then picks him up, after he has tumbled a foot or so, and persuades him that he has miraculously survived, we seem to be back in a morality or miracle play—with grotesque, absurd overtones—in which the poet has used his characters to set up a dramatic demonstration of an abstract idea. But then, this is not quite correct; for it is one of the characters, Edgar, not the poet Shakespeare, who has set up this formal demonstration of the miracle of life. In turn, it is perfectly appropriate and realistic that Edgar should use this dramatic mode, for until his last lines—"speak what we feel, not what we ought to say"—he has a pronounced tendency to the conventional, the sententious, the formal and theological. Even in his "madness" he explains evil in terms of conventional theories of morality and the devils of folk tale.

The point of Edgar's brief morality play is clear. The last sight that Gloucester *saw* was the diabolic face and the hands of a man reaching to tear out his eyes, and he staggered away from this total denial of humankind, away from the heath and toward the sea, despairing of any value in life. He still believes in the power of the gods, but because of what he has experienced he can no longer believe in their goodness. Suicide seems his only recourse. He engages his son Edgar, still in disguise, to lead him to the cliff at Dover; but Edgar, who despite all he has endured continues to believe in a childlike way, arranges a lesson to persuade his father that life itself, under any conditions, is a miracle to be valued and cherished so long as we still breathe, have heavy substance, speak, and bleed not. Gloucester learns his lesson well—though he forgets it soon afterward when new misfortune comes—and he sums up neatly the moral idea of the scene:

> Henceforth I'll bear
> Affliction till it do cry out itself,
> 'Enough, enough' and die.
>
> (IV.vi.75–77) [1]

No doubt we should applaud Edgar for teaching and Gloucester for learning such sound doctrine, but *Lear* itself has already shown so many scenes of loss and emptiness and human degradation that by this point it requires more than saying that life is a miracle because the heart still beats to make us believe it. And while Gloucester may be taken in by Edgar's miracle, the grotesque awkwardness on stage of that "miracle" emphasizes the fact that it is only a shabby theatrical device, imposed on a man of less than first-rate intellect to make him go on living some dream

1. Citations are to the Alexander edition (London and Glasgow, 1951).

of the gods' care for human life which is at odds with what has happened and will happen.[2]

The relevant literary gloss for this scene is the story of the Grand Inquisitor in *The Brothers Karamazov*. There, the Grand Inquisitor berates Christ for leaving the mass of simple mankind, men much like Gloucester, so completely free to choose or not to choose God. The great number of men, says the Grand Inquisitor, cannot bear to be without the miraculous; they "would see a sign," and Christ by his refusal of the Devil's temptations, by his refusal to hurl himself down from the Temple or to come down from the Cross, has denied them the miracles, the mystery, the authority—in short, the proof—that they need in order to endure the hardships of life and continue to believe in a just and caring God. The church has supplied these solid proofs, requiring of man only the awful freedom that he never wanted anyway. But the Grand Inquisitor, who knows that freedom and certainty are incompatible, regards the miracles his church has engineered as mere tricks designed to ease the minds of the frightened and block the sight of that fearsome emptiness in which true faith must operate.

Edgar, though lacking the Grand Inquisitor's subtle mind, would seem to be supplying his father with the same kind of miracle, at the same expense, and for the same reason. But while Edgar's miracle may be a trick, it is a trick devised to stage and state a truth in such a powerful way that Gloucester can understand that truth *feelingly,* though unable to reason it out for himself. The scene centers around two opposing perspectives, looking down and looking up. By using specific details, Edgar creates both perspectives for his blind father. As the two stand supposedly at the edge of the cliff, the imagination is directed downward and yet farther downward. At first we focus on some birds part way down which

2. Harry Levin, "The Heights and the Depths: A Scene from *King Lear,*" in *More Talking of Shakspeare,* ed. John Garrett (London, 1959), was the first to see that Edgar's "miracle" is a reenactment of the descent from on high which the play as a whole dramatizes. He shows also that Edgar, whose misery on the heath brought Lear to a sense of fellow-feeling, is the appropriate instrument for saving Gloucester from despair. But Levin does not see that the "miracle" also is a dramatization of what has previously happened and is forced to call it a "pious fraud," and he concludes that staging it would have been "difficult" on Shakespeare's nonrepresentational stage and "impossible" on a proscenium stage. I would suppose that the awkwardness, i.e., the stylization, would be part of the point.

"show scarce so gross as beetles"; then we descend halfway to a man clinging to the cliff, a samphire-gatherer who "seems no bigger than his head." Then we plunge to the bottom to look at fishermen who seem no larger than mice, at a ship become as small as her boat, and at last to the idle pebbles of the beach, washed soundlessly and meaninglessly back and forth by the surge of ocean. We have moved by means of details, each of which suggests in several ways the diminution of life, to the point where life vanishes into nothingness and meaninglessness.

This precipitous movement parallels and summarizes the experiences of Lear and Gloucester and Edgar to this point in the play. They have begun on high, certain of their own power and titles, assured of the value of human life, and trusting in the goodness and richness of the world. But as the play proceeds, the world narrows from "champains rich'd, / With plenteous rivers and wide-skirted meads" to the storm-tortured heath. And as the world constricts, man diminishes in size and importance from King and Father to "the thing itself . . . a poor, bare, forked animal."

In the vision from the cliff, Edgar recreates in visual terms the journey that has reduced Gloucester and his fellows from a condition of prosperity and importance, through a series of diminutions, to a condition of animality. In his supposed plunge from the cliff, Gloucester reenacts the downward movement, precipitated by his own act in begetting Edmund out of wedlock, which has brought him from being the great Duke of Gloucester to a blind, ragged beggar seeking his own death.

The leap into the void is a truthful dramatization of what has happened; but what about Gloucester's miraculous survival? It would seem that if Edgar's little morality play is to be accurate, it would have to allow Gloucester to be dashed into nothing—the word that rings through the play as a dreadful threat. But is there not something miraculous in what has happened to Gloucester and Lear? Obviously enough, as one lost his sight he *saw* for the first time, and as the other lost his senses he gained his sanity. But even beyond these ironies, on the heath in the center of the storm, when it looked as if man could be reduced infinitely downward into nothing, man discovered feelingly—not consciously—a basis for his humanity in his concern for other sufferers, both those present and those only imagined: "Poor naked wretches, whereso'er you are." Man is, they find under pressure, more than a "worm" or a "forked animal." He is a creature capable of pity and therefore cannot be reduced to nothing. The

gesture, discovered on the heath, expressing this feeling of shared humanity, "Give me your hand," is picked up and repeated here on the edge of
Dover Cliff. Edgar, who has led his blind father by the hand from the
heath, repeats the formula of fellowship on the very edge of the void by
requesting his father's hand, lest he fall from this fearsome place. In
Gloucester's reply, "Let go my hand," we hear his renunciation of any
belief in the possibility of kindness.

But the fall from the cliff ends in miraculous survival and thus dramatizes the truly miraculous salvation found by the wanderers and outcasts
on the heath. All their lives *are* miracles in the sense that, just as they
thought their humanity was about to disappear into bestiality and nothingness, they discovered their human reality in a way they had never
expected. Edgar's exhortation,

> Look up a-height; the shrill-gorg'd lark so far
> Cannot be seen or heard. Do but look up.
>
> (ll. 58–59)

is based not merely on hope but on experienced truth.

True in the same way is his description of the fiend, eyes like moons,
twisted and waved horns, whom Edgar says stood beside Gloucester at the
top of the cliff describing life and the world as diminishing to meaningless nothingness. Such a view of things is in *King Lear* not entirely true;
it is rather a fiendish view of life imposed on man by the "realists" of the
play, Edmund, Cornwall, Goneril, and Regan; it is a "miraculous" dramatization of what Cornwall "told" Gloucester life is when he tore out
his eyes.

It has often been noted that Gloucester is a man of the senses, Lear a
man of the mind, and that they suffer appropriately by the loss of sight in
the first case, the loss of mind in the second. Their regenerative experiences in Act IV follow the same pattern. Since Gloucester is not a thinker,
it is necessary that his remarkable survival be translated for him into the
solid, sensible terms of miracle. But Lear can experience both his loss and
his marvelous recuperation in less miraculous terms. Where Gloucester is
"shown" the diminution of life he has endured in terms of a fictional
perspective from the cliff, Lear faces unflinchingly what the loss means in
more immediate, though less visible, terms. All of society is, he now
believes in his madness, corrupt: the great lady is as lustful as the gilded

fly, the gods inherit but to a woman's waist, the justice is but a thief dressed in robes of office, the beadle longs for the whore he whips, and the "usurer hangs the cozener."

> Through tatter'd clothes small vices do appear;
> Robes and furr'd gowns hide all. Plate sin with gold,
> And the strong lance of justice hurtless breaks;
> Arm it in rags, a pygmy's straw does pierce it.
>
> (ll. 164–167)

This view of all life as bestiality masked by clothes and money, shouted by the old king, presents in social terms the same perspective on life as that which looks downward from the cliff. Again the matter of hands comes up: when Gloucester asks the mad Lear to allow him to kiss his hand, Lear too rejects the saving clasp of fellowship ("Let me wipe it first; it smells of mortality") and runs wild in the fields like a hunted animal—his parallel to Gloucester's suicidal leap.

Lear's regeneration, his miracle, also drives home the meaning of his as yet unrecognized salvation on the heath. But where Gloucester's miraculous survival was put to him in the "realistic" terms of the harmless fall from the cliff, Lear's is manifested in the less realistic but more "real" terms of sleep, a change of garments, music, and Cordelia. Each of these speaks to Lear of some healing power in nature which he has already experienced, without knowing, on the heath. Cordelia is the fully realized and humanized form of that ability to care for the suffering of others which all the members of that band of ragged outcasts found in themselves in the storm and, in finding, found the basis of their humanity. When Cordelia bends to kiss Lear and says,

> O my dear father! Restoration hang
> Thy medicine on my lips, and let this kiss
> Repair those violent harms that my two sisters
> Have in thy reverence made,
>
> (IV.vii.26–28)

the gesture and the sentiments are a pure distillation of all those feelings of compassion which found such rough and abbreviated expression in the night on the heath.

Act IV of *King Lear* is built around these two parallel scenes of regeneration. In both a child arranges for his despairing father to see once again, in terms appropriate to the characters, that man is finally something more than a worm or a poor, bare, forked animal and, because he is so, that life is worth living, sanity is bearable. In both cases this new faith is not merely imposed on men too broken and exhausted to resist it but is rather a demonstration, an extension into dramatic form, of a saving reality which Lear and Gloucester have already discovered feelingly at the very point when their humanity seemed to be disintegrating into nothingness.

These two interludes—one in the allegorical, the other in the symbolic mode—reconfirm, in surprising and unexpected ways, orthodox traditional views of the values and meaning of life. But true though they may be, they are not finally in *King Lear* adequate realizations of experience. They sum up life too neatly, round it off too perfectly; and so, in Act V, Shakespeare subjects these visions to the savage test of life as individual man truly experiences it. The right side loses the battle, Gloucester dies, Cordelia dies, and Lear dies. True, the wicked die too, but in the midst of other sorrow their deaths, as Albany says of Edmund's death, seem "but a trifle here." Generations of readers have testified to their pained doubt as to how to take or sum up this ending. Is it the "promised end" or "image of that horror"? It allows some truth still to the "miracles" staged by Edgar and Cordelia—after all, some basis of humanity was discovered, though too late to change events—but it qualifies such optimism severely. In the end the actual experience of life escapes any summation. It can only be presented in a play like *Lear,* not in a morality play like Edgar's.

From Lelia to Viola

ROBERT C. MELZI

A<small>N</small> E<small>NGLISH</small> <small>BARRISTER</small>, John Manningham, while a student in the Middle Temple, kept a diary and on 2 February 1602 wrote: "At our feast wee had a play called 'Twelue Night, or What you will,' much like the Commedy of Errores, or Menechmi in Plautus, but most like and neere to that in Italian called *Inganni*."[1] This entry has been cited by most investigators of Shakespeare's sources,[2] and, beginning with Hunter, the conclusion has been reached that the play to which Manningham alluded was not *Gl'Inganni* but *Gl'Ingannati*.[3] Because Professor Bullough's study of Shakespeare's sources has been hailed as the definitive work on the subject, it might seem at first superfluous to reexamine this matter. The problem is, however, much more complex than most

1. *Diary of John Manningham,* ed. John Bruce (Westminster, 1868), p. 18.

2. See *A New Variorum Edition of Shakespeare,* ed. H. H. Furness (Philadelphia, 1901), XIII, 321–326; Kenneth Muir, *Shakespeare's Sources* (London, 1957), p. 67; Geoffrey Bullough, *Narrative and Dramatic Sources of Shakespeare* (London, 1958), II, 269, with ample bibliography.

3. Joseph Hunter, *New Illustrations of Shakespeare* (London, 1845), I, 391, as quoted by Bruce, *op. cit.,* p. 18.

67

investigators have suspected, and, as Luce aptly put it, "in the matter of Shakespearian investigation, every little helps; nay rather, is invaluable." [4] The path that leads from *Gl'Ingannati* to *Twelfth Night* is long and tortuous and perhaps has not been examined with the attention it deserves. The purpose of this paper is to investigate some of the plays and novels that derive from *Gl'Ingannati,* with special attention to the female protagonist. In doing so, I hope to analyze further the psychological complexity of this character as it evolves from the original Italian play down to Shakespeare's *Twelfth Night*. Such an analysis will hopefully shed new light on the creation of Shakespeare's Viola and also provide additional guidelines in the never ending task of studying Shakespeare's sources.

It is well known that the Italian play *Gl'Ingannati* was referred to as *Comedia del sacrificio,* from the festive production by which the main comedy was preceded.[5] This misnomer appears not only in the early editions, such as those printed by Curzio Navo and by Giovanne Padovano, but is continued in later editions up to the turn of the century. If it is true that the 1554 Venice edition by Plinio Pietrasanta mentions both *Il Sacrificio* and *Gl'Ingannati* on the title page, the 1585 Cavalcalupo, also printed in Venice, makes no mention of the main play, specifying only *Il Sacrificio*.[6]

Bibliographical errors concerning *Gl'Ingannati* are by no means the prerogative of the Renaissance but continue up to the present time in a

---

4. *Rich's "Apolonius & Silla," an Original of Shakespeare's "Twelfth Night,"* ed. M. Luce (London, 1912), p. x.

5. Bruce, *op. cit.,* p. 18. See also Edmund V. de Chasca, "Early Editions of *Gl'Ingannati*," *MP,* L (1952), 79–87. I wish to thank Professor de Chasca for having lent me his personal microfilm of the early editions of *Gl'Ingannati;* for further bibliography and a study of the authorship see R. C. Melzi, "*Gl'Ingannati* and Its French Renaissance Translation," *KFLQ,* XII (1965), 180–190.

6. *Il Sacrificio / comedia / de gli Intronati / celebrato ne i giuochi di uno carnovale in Siena / Di nuovo corretta e ristampata / in Venezia / Presso Domenico Cavalcalupo MDLXXV.* As a further proof that *Gl'Ingannati* is the work of Castelvetro it should be pointed out that at the end of the fifth act there is a "Canzone nella morte di una civetta" (Canzone on the death of an owl). The owl is the identification mark of Castelvetro that appears in most of his printed books. See R. C. Melzi, *Castelvetro's Annotations to the Inferno: A New Perspective in Sixteenth Century Criticism* (The Hague, 1966), p. 11.

confusion that involves not only the plays I have mentioned but also others derived from *Gl'Ingannati,* which were generally known under the name of *Gl'Inganni.*[7] This profusion of errors, both ancient and contemporary, should make us wary when we try to read between the lines of Manningham's diary. Would he, in the year 1602, be familiar with the distinction between the original *Gl'Ingannati* and the plays derived from it under the name of *Gl'Inganni,* or would this last designation merely bring to his mind a particular situation, that of the girl who dons men's clothing in order to be near her lover? A similar confusion might have arisen in Shakespeare's mind between the original play and the many others that stemmed from *Gl'Ingannati.* There is consequently no reason to limit our investigation to plays that bear either name, but we should take into consideration every play belonging to the *Ingannati* family; the results will be quite rewarding.

It is common knowledge that the situation of mistaken identity and eventual recognition between two brothers is typical of the Latin comedy and occurs in Plautus' *Menaechmi.*[8] It is equally well known that Cardinal Dovizi da Bibbiena transferred the Latin situation onto the Italian stage in the *Calandria,* a rather unchaste play that nevertheless pleased Pope Leo X at the wedding of Isabella d'Este with Marquis Gianfrancesco Gonzaga.[9] The complete departure of *Gl'Ingannati* from either Plautus or Cardinal da Bibbiena is significant not only in the fact that it creates a new realism in the figures of the servant and the hotel-keeper, but much more in the creation of the type of the woman in love who dons masculine clothing in order to be closer to her lover. From this prototype

7. Among many other errors we may cite the most recent in the generally excellent *Enciclopedia dello spettacolo* (Roma, 1961), VIII, 1797–1798, where Secchi's *Inganni* is mistaken for *Gl'Ingannati;* the French *Dictionnaire des lettres françaises, Le seizième siècle* (Paris, 1951), p. 311, in which *Les Abusez* by Charles Estienne is attributed to Alessandro Piccolomini; and Heinz Kindermann, *Theatergeschichte Europas,* Vol. II: "Das Theater der Renaissance" (Salzburg, 1959), who quite correctly identifies *Les Abusez* as the translation of *Gl'Ingannati* (p. 170), only to call *Les Esbahis* by Grévin an imitation of the *Comédie du sacrifice* (p. 174).

8. See Vincenzo de Amicis, *L'Imitazione latina nella commedia italiana del XVI secolo* (Firenze, 1897).

9. Bernardo Dovizi, *La Calandra,* a cura di A. Racheli, in *Il Teatro classico del secolo XVI* (Milano, n.d.), p. 6.

a new figure is to be born that will spread throughout the Italian and, subsequently, the European stage: the demure, sweet, sometimes self-effacing woman who is ready to sacrifice herself for love. No other play of the time had such a success, which is indicated not only in the number of editions printed between 1537 and 1611 but in the profusion of translations, adaptations, and imitations that pervaded the European stage for almost two centuries. Some of these plays are very similar to the parent play; some only vaguely resemble it; but they all have one element in common: a female character who no longer reacts like the puppet of the *commedia erudita* but who has become a female who loves and suffers, a woman who schemes and plots, a creature endowed with psychological qualities heretofore unknown.[10]

The great majority of those who have investigated Shakespeare's *Twelfth Night* have considered the following to be possible sources: (a) *Gl'Ingannati;* (b) *Gl'Inganni* and *L'Interesse* by N. Secchi; (c) *Gl'Inganni* by Curzio Gonzaga; (d) Bandello's "Novella di Nicuola" (II.xxxvi), from *Novelle;* (e) Belleforest's *Histoires tragiques,* IV.lxi; (f) Giraldi Cinthio's *Hecatommithi,* I.v.8; (g) Lope de Rueda's translation of *Gl'Ingannati,* known under the name of *Comedia de los engañados;* (h) Charles Estienne's translation of the original Italian play, called *Les Abusez;* (i) a Latin translation of the French play, never printed, but apparently performed at Queens' College in Cambridge in 1595, known under the name of *Laelia;* (j) Barnaby Riche's novel of "Apolonius and Silla" from *Riche His Farewell to Military Profession.* Some other possible sources that have been cited should be discounted because their dates of composition place them outside the scope of Shakespearean investigation; an example is afforded by Luce, who mentions Domenico Cornacchini's *Inganni,* first printed in Venice in 1605.[11]

Between *Gl'Ingannati,* the source of all these plays, and *Twelfth Night,* the great Shakespearean crucible in which pewter will miraculously turn into silver, there are many intermediate plays that should not be overlooked, for they all converge upon the *commedia dell'arte.* As Miss K. M.

10. See David Orr, "The Influence of Learned Italian Drama of the XVI Century on English Drama before 1623" (unpub. diss.; North Carolina, 1960). Dr. Orr denies any influence of the *commedia dell'arte,* minimizes the Italian influence on English drama, and sees the impact concentrated mainly on comedy.

11. See *Laelia,* ed. G. C. Moore Smith (Cambridge, Eng., 1910), p. xx.

Lea has shown,[12] the boy-girl convention of *Gl'Ingannati* was amply exploited by the scenario writers, so that it seems only logical that Shakespeare might have been familiar with all its ramifications.[13]

Thus it is important to examine links which up to now have not been deemed essential. Indeed, if Helen Kaufman tried to bring out the importance of *Gl'Inganni* and *L'Interesse* as possible origins of *Twelfth Night*,[14] why should not plays such as Cecchi's *Il Donzello* or Della Porta's *Cintia* be examined, since they represent sources at least equally available to Shakespeare? The offshoots from *Gl'Ingannati* can, for the sake of clarity, be divided into three main groups: the Italian, the French, and the Spanish. In the first collection (the only one that will be examined) there are a few plays that deserve our attention, and since those written by Cecchi are the oldest ones, at least from the point of view of publication date, it seems proper to begin with him.

In spite of his assertion that his plays are mainly derived from Plautus, the influence of *Gl'Ingannati* is obvious in several of Cecchi's comedies, especially in *Il Donzello* and *L'Assiuolo*. *Il Donzello*[15] proves to be a direct outgrowth of *Gl'Ingannati* in the figure of Lapo, who has lost all his belongings in the sack of Rome and has promised his daughter Faustina to an old man, Forese. The latter, in turn, reminds us of Gherardo in *Gl'Ingannati* when he boasts about his virility despite his age. A line in this comedy should attract our special attention because the

12. K. M. Lea, *Italian Popular Comedy* (Oxford, 1934), I, 180–181.

13. On the *commedia dell'arte* see Vito Pandolfi, *La commedia dell'arte* (Firenze, 1957–1961), 6 vols., with both history and texts; John W. Cunliffe, "The Influence of Italian on Early English Drama," *MP*, IV (1907), 597–604; Winifred Smith, "Italian and Elizabethan Comedy," *MP*, V (1908), 555–567; Max J. Wolff, "Shakespeare und die Commedia dell'arte," *Jahrbuch der deutschen Shakespeare-Gesellschaft*, XLVI (1910), 1–20; Benedetto Croce, "Shakespeare, Napoli e la commedia dell'arte," *Nuove curiosità storiche* (Napoli, 1922), pp. 107–122; V. Capocci, *Shakespeare e la commedia dell'arte* (Bari, 1953); Winifred Smith, "Two Commedie dell'arte on the *Measure for Measure* Story," *RR*, XIII (1922), 263–275; P. Rebora, "La *Tempesta* di Shakespeare e la seconda commedia popolare italiana," *Boll. dell'Università italiana per stranieri* (Perugia; 22 agosto 1931).

14. Helen A. Kaufman, "Nicolò Secchi as a Source of *Twelfth Night*," *SQ*, V (1954), 271–280.

15. *Il Donzello / Comedia di M. Gianmaria Cecchi / Fiorentino / con privilegio / in Venezia, Appresso Bernardo Giunti, MCLXXXV* [for *MDLXXXV*], [Allacci, p. 253].

night of the Epiphany, which is Twelfth Night, is described as the night
when the animals speak, "che le bestie favellano."[16] If we keep in mind
that most scholars attribute the title *Twelfth Night* to a line in the Prologue of *Gl'Ingannati* where the words "Notte di Beffana" are found,[17]
this line acquires a special significance.

It would, however, be erroneous to create a connection between this
play and *Twelfth Night* on the basis of such a tenuous link, especially
since Cecchi's plays are not generally considered among Shakespeare's
sources. Two of Secchi's plays, on the other hand, *Gl'Inganni* and *L'Interesse,* should be reexamined, in spite of the scrutiny they have received
from Miss Kaufman,[18] since a few interesting observations can, I believe,
still be offered on the subject.

Miss Kaufman has shown many identities in dialogue between *L'Interesse* and *Twelfth Night,* and her thesis is quite plausible; it should be
brought out, however, that what is known by the name *L'Interesse* is
really *Gl'Inganni* because of an editorial error which has already been
pointed out by Gillet.[19] The 1562 edition of *Gl'Inganni* (the one perused
by Miss Kaufman) does indeed carry on the title page the indication that
the play had been performed in Milan in 1547 in front of King Philip:
"Recitata in Milano l'anno 1547 dinanzi alla maestà del Re Filippo."[20]
A closer examination of the work will show that it was probably written
in 1551, a fact that tends to corroborate Gillet's theory that it could not
possibly have been performed before Philip of Spain in 1547. In the play a
legal document is drafted by which the *Ruffiana* obligates herself to
guarantee for one year the services of her daughter to Gostanzo; in
composing the document, the notary intones, "In Christi nomine amen.

16. *Il Donzello,* p. 9ᵛ.

17. *Il Sacrificio (Gl'Ingannati),* ed. Cavalcalupo, p. 15ᵛ: "La favola è nuova: non
più per altri tempi vista nè letta, nè meno altronde cavata che della lor industriosa
zucca, onde si cavorno anche la notte di Beffana le sorti vostre...."

18. See Kaufman, *op. cit.;* see also *Self Interest by Nicolò Secchi, Translated by
William Reymes,* ed. Helen Andrews Kaufman (Seattle, 1953).

19. Joseph E. Gillet, "Was Secchi's *Gl'Inganni* Performed before Philip of Spain?"
MLN, XXXV (1920), 395–401.

20. *Gl'Inganni, / comedia del signor N. S. / Recitata in Milano l'anno 1547,
dinanzi alla maestà del Re Filippo, / Nuovamente posta in luce / con Licenza e
Privilegio. / In Fiorenza appresso i Giunti, MDLXII.*

Millesimo quingentesimo quinquagesimo primo." [21] Since in the Prologue another play is mentioned, of which Lelio is the protagonist, we have further proof that Gillet was correct when he assumed that in 1581 the editor of the Ziletti edition, Evangelista Ortense, labeled this play (which had come into his possession without a title) *Gl'Inganni* merely because of the general tone of the play itself. In other words, the editor sensed that the play belonged to the *Ingannati* family and possibly remembered that, some thirty years before, a drama of that name, in which a girl dressed as a boy had an important role, had been performed. Miss Kaufman's claim that *L'Interesse* possibly predates *Gl'Ingannati* should therefore be rejected outright, and a further observation should be made: that both of Secchi's plays bring something new onto the stage, the pregnancy of the female protagonist, an element that will be present in Barnaby Riche's tale of "Apolonius and Silla" in his *Farewell*. Since this aspect has not been explored by previous investigators, it is, I believe, appropriate to examine the problem more closely.

In *Gl'Ingannati* the consummation of the marriage between Fabrizio, Lelia's brother, and Isabella, Gherardo's daughter, occurs when the two young people are mistakenly locked in the same room; the legal ceremony follows on the same day. Now, Bandello's tale of Nicuola (II.36),[22] which stems directly from *Gl'Ingannati,* portrays a rather realistic scene of intimacy between Paolo (Nicuola's brother) and Catella (Gherardo's daughter), which is followed by the regular marriage that very same day. Since Belleforest's translation of the tale of Nicuola (under the title "Comme une fille Romaine se vestant en page servist longtemps un sien amy sans estre cogneue, & depuis l'eust a mary avec autres discours," [23]) approximates the original very closely, the marriage also follows, almost

21. *Gl'Inganni*, III, ix, p. 56.

22. Matteo Bandello, *Novelle*, Pt. 2 (Lucca, 1554), p. 36: "Nicuola innamorata di Lattanzio va a servirlo vestita da paggio e dopo molti casi seco si marita, e di ciò che ad un suo fratello avvenne."

23. Le / *Quatriesme / Tome des Histoires / Tragiques, partie extraites des oeuvres Italiennes / du Bandel & partie de l'in- / vention de l'autheur / François Contenant vingt-six Histoires enrichies & ornees avec plus de diligence que / les precedentes: / Par François de Belle-forest Comingeois A Lyon, / Par Jerosme Farine MDLXXVIII*, p. 201.

immediately, the love-making scene. Barnaby Riche,[24] on the other hand, presents a Julina who, believing she is making advances to Silla, enters Silvio's bed and, after a night of love-making, is placed in a condition "whereof she could not bee cured in fourtie wekes after." [25] Her condition becomes such that, "findyng in her self, an unwonted swellyng in her beallie, assuryng her self to bee with child," [26] she hastens to the duke's palace in order to obtain Silvio's release from prison. The prisoner, though, is Silla, who is ignorant of her brother's visit to Julina and therefore severely rebukes the poor pregnant girl, thus causing the duke's anger. Only the true Silvio's timely return saves Julina's reputation and allows the tale to be concluded with a double wedding. Mr. Cranfill's opinion notwithstanding,[27] I believe one can unequivocally state that "Apolonius and Silla" owes much more to Cinthio's novella of Messer Cesare Gravina,[28] in which Messer Pino's daughter becomes pregnant, than to the tale of Nicole in Belleforest's *Histoires tragiques,* in which love is immediately followed by marriage. Since Riche's *Farewell* appeared in 1581, the possibility of an influence of Secchi's *Inganni* or of the *Interesse* should be kept in mind, although it is quite unlikely that Riche would have consulted these Italian plays in that Ireland where "there is no great choyce of bookes to be had." [29]

When the possibilities of a plot are nearly exhausted, playwrights, rather than repeat themselves, often have recourse to further weaving upon the original fabric. As Miss Lea observed some thirty years ago,[30] the resources

24. Luce, *Rich's "Apolonius and Silla";* also *Rich's Farewell to Military Profession 1581,* ed. Thomas Mabry Cranfill (Austin, 1959).

25. *Rich's Farewell,* ed. Cranfill, p. 78.

26. *Ibid.,* p. 80.

27. *Ibid.,* p. xix.

28. *De Gli / Hecatommithi / di M. Giovanbattista / Gyraldi Cintio / Nobile ferrarese / Parte prima / Nel Monte Regale / Appresso Lionardo Torrentino / MDLXV,* viii, 836: "Messer Cesare Gravina temendo l'ira del suo Re, con un figliuol maschio, & una femina, nati ad un parto, si fugge da Napoli, sono assaliti dalla tempesta, cade il Marito & la Moglie nel mare, i figliuoli rimangono nella nave, & ciascuno di essi tien che l'altro sia morto, si ritruovano tutti in buona fortuna &, rihavuta la gratia del Re loro, se ne ritornano a Napoli."

29. *Farewell,* p. xvii.

30. K. M. Lea, *Italian Popular Comedy* (Oxford, 1934), I, 180.

of the girl-into-boy disguise were almost used up by the end of the century. A new plot was evolved by Della Porta,[31] who in *La Cintia* brings to the stage a double deception that will eventually culminate in a double wedding. The importance of this play, which derives from both Secchi's *L'Interesse* and Piccolomini's *Alessandro,* would be very slight were it not for some curious similarities in dialogue between it and *Twelfth Night.* The significance of these resemblances might at first be dismissed because of the closeness between *La Cintia* and *L'Interesse.* If, however, one compares the similarities in the two plays, one discovers that the number of parallels between *La Cintia* and *Twelfth Night* is greater than Miss Lea realized. Keeping in mind the fact that *La Cintia* was first performed prior to 1591 and was printed in 1601,[32] one should not discount the possibility that Shakespeare knew it, either directly or indirectly.

The plot of *La Cintia* is very simple, despite its author's attempt to make it complicated and involved: Cintia's mother has been the mistress of Arreotimo, who has promised to legalize their relationship should she give birth to a boy. When a girl is born, the unsuspecting father is shown a boy borrowed for the occasion, whereupon the wedding is performed. The girl is baptized "Cintio" instead of "Cintia" and grows up, dressed as a boy, in the strictest company of a boy named Erasto, the son of a close friend of Arreotimo. Erasto, unaware of the true sex of his friend and not even remotely suspecting the secret passion that daily grows in the heart of Cintia, falls in love with Cintia's neighbor, Amasia. Blinded by love, Cintia plots with her nurse and, donning Amasia's clothes, has a nocturnal meeting with her Erasto, who marries her, *de jure* and *de facto,* believing that he is taking Amasia as a spouse. The parallel plot occurs when Lidia, Erasto's sister, falls in love with Cintia, thinking her to be a boy, and is quite outspoken in her advances. She falls prey to the desire of Amasio, who for political reasons has been disguised as a girl by his father, Pedofilo, and wears female clothes. When Erasto learns "Amasia's" true sex he blames "Cintio" for having foisted a prostitute upon him; on

31. Giovan Battista Della Porta was born in Naples in 1535 and died there in 1615. In addition to being a brilliant scientist, Della Porta was a prolific playwright who wrote some twenty-nine plays, fourteen of which are extant. See Louise George Clubb, *Giambattista Della Porta, Dramatist* (Princeton, 1965).

32. Clubb, pp. 60–63, 317.

his part, Lidia's father charges "Cintio" with rape. Unable to face a life of disgrace, Cintia decides to die at Erasto's hands. When the nurse reveals her secret, Pedofilo reveals his; the wedding is doubly happy because Cintia has given birth, thus more than sufficiently proving her true sex.

It is easy to see that the situation lends itself to the same puns on the inability of the female to act as a male that we find in *Twelfth Night*. Thus Cintia, before explaining her plight to her father's old and faithful servant, exclaims: "By marrying me off, my father should never expect me to beget any children" (I.i).[33] When confronted by Lidia's nurse, who is coming to her to offer her mistress' hand, our heroine blurts out that Lidia should curtail her futile love, because "to love me is the same as loving a woman" (I.ii),[34] and she adds: "Nurse, all that glitters is not gold; if she only knew who I am . . . well, enough said" (I.ii).[35] The *double entendre* becomes (if possible) more blatant when Cintia continues: "The truth is that I don't have the willingness, nor do I possess the ability" (I.ii),[36] and she further emphasizes that what she lacks is the same thing that the nurse and Lidia are lacking themselves.[37] To the nurse, who in her innocence has asked, "Aren't you a man?" Cintia replies: "You said it. . . . If the world's survival would depend upon sons and daughters from our marriage, it would soon come to an end" (I.ii).[38] Compare the dialogue of Olivia with Viola:

OLIVIA
Stay.
I prithee tell me what thou think'st of me.
VIOLA
That you do think you are not what you are.

33. *La Cintia di GianBattista della Porta napolitano, in Venezia per Giacom'Antonio Somasco, 1601* [Allacci, p. 191]: "Non vedrà mai mio padre, dandomi moglie, da me generar figliuoli."
34. Dille da mia parte che lasci d'amar me, che tanto è amar me quanto una femina."
35. "Balia, non è tutt'oro quello che luce: s'ella sapesse chi sono e,... basta."
36. "Ti dico che non voglio nè posso; e ancorchè intrinsecamente ci fusse il buon volere, ci mancherebbe il potere."
37. CINTIA Anzi mi manca il meglio e quello che più l'importa.
BALIA O Dio, e che ti manca?
CINTIA Quello che manca a te e a lei.
38. "Proprio come hai detto.... Se il mondo non aspettasse altri figli che da noi, tosto verrebbe meno."

OLIVIA

If I think so, I think the same of you.

VIOLA

Then think you right: I am not what I am.

OLIVIA

I would you were as I would have you be!

VIOLA

Would it be better, madam, than I am?

(III.i.134–140)

and Viola's pun: "Pray God defend me! A little thing would make me tell them how much I lack of a man" (III.iv.286–287).

The counterpart of the Cintia-Erasto affair in the Italian play is, of course, the wooing of Lidia by the disguised Amasio. The latter, still dressed as a woman, reveals to Lidia that there is another man who loves her with the same intensity with which she loves Cintio. Not only is this youth of noble birth, but his looks equal his wealth. Asked by Lidia where this young man lives, Amasio replies: "Not far from your own house" (I.v).[39] Queried by Lidia how he knows of this man's love, he replies: "We often talk about you."[40] The dialogue continues:

LIDIA

Did I ever see him?

AMASIO

As you have seen me.

LIDIA

Did he ever speak to me?

AMASIO

Like you spoke to me.

LIDIA

How old is he?

AMASIO

My own age.

(I.v)[41]

39. "Poco lungi da vostra casa."
40. "Ragioniamo spesso de' vostri amori."
41. LIDIA   L'ho veduto io mai?
    AMASIO   Come avete veduto me.
    LIDIA   Ha ragionato meco mai?
    AMASIO   Come avete ragionato con me.
    LIDIA   Di che età egli è?
    AMASIO   Della mia.

Amasio goes on to state that this man's love is such that "he is burning for her more than a burning pile does";[42] this secret lover is such a good friend of Amasio that "he is just like myself";[43] and were it only possible that "you'd love me as much as he loves you" (I.v).[44]

Compare this long dialogue with that between Viola and the Duke:

> DUKE
> Thou dost speak masterly.
> My life upon't, young though thou art, thine eye
> Hath stay'd upon some favour that it loves;
> Hath it not, boy?
> VIOLA
> A little, by your favour.
> DUKE
> What kind of woman is't?
> VIOLA
> Of your complexion.
> DUKE
> She is not worth thee, then. What years, i'faith?
> VIOLA
> About your years, my lord.
>
> (II.iv.21–27)

And to the duke, who questions her on woman's love, Viola replies that her father's daughter loved a man "As it might be perhaps, were I a woman, / I should your lordship" (II.iv.107–108). Olivia's unbending attitude in refusing to acquiesce to Viola's embassy is reminiscent of Lidia, who, pressed by Amasia to relinquish her love for Cintio, replies: "The world would rather change than I change my love. I shall belong to Cintio or to death" (I.v).[45] Viola's desire to die, so tenderly expressed in the lines, "If I do feign, you witnesses above / Punish my life for tainting of my love" (V.i.131–132), echoes Cintia, who, unable to live any longer without the man she loves, decides to seek death at his own hands (IV.vi).

Another parallel episode in the two plays is that of the fight. One of the

42. "Anzi arde; nè ardentissima fornace nodrisce tante fiamme nel suo seno quante egli ne nudre nel cuor suo per amor vostro."

43. "Tanto amico, che son come egli stesso."

44. "Così amaste voi me!"

45. "Si cangiarà più tosto il mondo che cangi io voglia o pensiero, o Amasia. Lasciar io di amar Cintio? sarebbe più possibile lasciar la vita: sarò di Cintio o della morte!"

most comical situations in *Twelfth Night* occurs when Sir Andrew, having had a sword fight with Viola, is suddenly confronted by Sebastian, who not only breaks his head but gives Sir Toby "a bloody coxcomb too" (V.i.169). In *La Cintia* the Capitano, who thinks he is fighting with Cintio, is confronted in reality by Cintia's male counterpart, namely Amasio, who challenges him to a duel and, prior to the challenge, uses a thick stick on the Capitano's back (III.v). Although Sir Andrew and Il Capitano are completely unrelated characters, it is hard to deny at least a fortuitous similarity between the two occurrences.

The direct derivation of *La Cintia* from *Gl'Ingannati* is so obvious that Miss Lea's testimony hardly seems necessary.[46] If further proof were needed, no better evidence could be presented than the comparison of Cintia's soliloquy with Lelia's monologue. Cintia, having heard from Erasto's mouth his determination never to forget her rival, cries out: "Oh, how wretched is my life, ever since I heard with my own ears Erasto pronounce my death warrant. . . . Oh, how implacable fortune is with me" (II.iv).[47] In *Gl'Ingannati* Lelia, having realized that her lover is lost forever, utters in anguish: "Now you have heard, miserable wretch, with your own ears, and from the very mouth of this ungrateful Flamminio, how much he loves you! Wretched, unhappy Lelia . . ." (II.vii).[48]

The same pathos, the same anguish, is found on the lips of Lelia in *Les Abusez* (II.vi) and even in the mouth of the very reserved Lelia in *La comedia de los engañados* (scena iv.48–49). This pathos is still present in plays as remote from the original as *Les Esbahis* and could be corroborated by examining Madeleine's soliloquy in the French play by Grévin (II.vi). It is this very romantic attitude of all heroines whose origin can be traced to *Gl'Ingannati* that makes them unmistakable and creates what can truly be called the *Ingannati* family.

Most critics dealing with the sources of *Twelfth Night* have been

---

46. K. M. Lea, *op. cit.,* I, p. 180. Professor Clubb neglects to bring out this point.

47. "O quanto è misera e infelice la mia vita, posciach'io, io, oimè! io con le mie orecchie ho inteso da Erasto la crudel sentenza della mia morte...; Oh contro me implacabil contumacia di fortuna."

48. "Or hai pur, misera, con le tue proprie orecchie, dall'istessa bocca di questo ingrato di Flamminio, inteso quanto egli t'ami. Misera, scontenta Lelia!" The translation is Bullough's, as found in *Narrative and Dramatic Sources of Shakespeare,* II, 286 ff.

unduly harsh with Lelia. From *Twelfth Night* they have looked backward, and naturally every other character, when compared with the perfection of her who "sat like Patience on a monument," seems pale and faded. No wonder, then, that Bullough finds the exposition of *Gl'Ingannati* "cumbrous and unreal" [49] and the play itself lacking in sentiment and poetic feeling, epithets so questionable that Bullough himself seems to dispute them in another page of the same work. [50] Of course, Shakespeare's sensitivity and refinement are of a uniquely high order, but the author of *Gl'Ingannati* certainly possesses the same qualities in abundance when compared with, for instance, Cardinal da Bibbiena. It is only by proceeding on the road that leads from *Gl'Ingannati* to *Twelfth Night,* rather than by tracing it in reverse, that we realize what a "first" this play was in the history of European drama.

That Shakespeare knew Riche's "Apolonius and Silla" there is no doubt. The question remains whether he knew *Gl'Ingannati* directly or through the French translation or through any of the adaptations that have thus far been examined.

Miss Kaufman has demonstrated quite convincingly the debt that *Twelfth Night* owes to both *Gl'Inganni* and *L'Interesse;* and if we agree on the year 1601 for the date of composition of *Twelfth Night,* the arguments in favor of a direct acquaintance with Della Porta's *Cintia* are rather strong. Without entering into the controversy about Shakespeare's knowledge of Italian, it seems quite unlikely that he would have consulted all these Italian plays, lifting a few lines here and there, while taking the bulk of his ideas from the novelists. Bullough remarks that "in a theatre which depended so much on quick adaptations it is probable that the companies and their writers had access to popular Italian plays of the past half-century." [51] This statement can be true only if we assume the knowledge of Italian to be oral rather than written. In other words, rather than to the *commedia erudita* we should look to the *commedia dell'arte* for an answer. That Shakespeare was acquainted with this form of dramatic art is beyond doubt, since he mentions the Zanies in *Twelfth Night* (I.v.84)

49. Bullough, II, 278.
50. *Ibid.,* p. 280.
51. *Ibid.,* p. 274.

and refers in *As You Like It* to Pantaloon (II.vii.158).[52] We also know that the actor-authors of the *commedia dell'arte* drew quite extensively from the *commedia erudita* for their material.[53] It also seems quite plausible that whenever the actors of the *commedia dell'arte* would present on the stage a version of plays which derived from the *commedia erudita,* they would tend to use puns, wordplays, and comical situations as they had appeared in the original printed text.[54] It is therefore equally probable that an incomparable professional like Shakespeare would have immediately seized upon the dramatic possibilities of some of the situations he must have witnessed.[55] This is the only logical explanation for some of the apparent sources that have come to light thus far and that undoubtedly will emerge in the future, as we deepen our study of Italian Renaissance comedy. Therefore, while we are assured that Shakespeare knew Riche's tale of "Apolonius and Silla," we might theorize that the elements deriving from *Gl'Ingannati* came to him not through direct reading of the Italian plays but through the intermediary of the *commedia dell'arte.* The journey from Lelia to Viola has been a long one, lasting more than seventy years, but during this time she is the only female character who, rather than degenerating into a farcical type, has kept her own gentle character. The first modern female of the Italian Renaissance was not born in vain.

52. See Daniel C. Boughner, "Traditional Elements in Falstaff," *JEGP,* XLIII (1944), 417–428. Professor Boughner states that "if there is a chain of affinity reaching from Ruzzante to Falstaff, Della Porta and the *commedia dell'arte* may have forged the necessary links" (p. 427).

53. In addition to Boughner, see Tina Beltrame, "Giovanni Battista Della Porta e la commedia dell'arte," *Giornale storico della letteratura italiana,* CI (1933), 277–289.

54. The following scenari of the *commedia dell'arte* derive from *Gl'Ingannati: L'Intronati* (Pandolfi, V, 236); *L'Intronati* (V, 267–268); *Intronati* (V, 318). The following scenari derive from Della Porta's comedies: *La Fantesca* (V, 228); *Horatio Burlato* (V, 229); *Il Finto Schiavo* (V, 231); *La Trappolaria* (V, 240); *Il Furbo* (V, 254); *Li dui fratelli rivali* (V, 256); *Horatio Burlato* (V, 263); *La Trapolaria* (V, 300); *Trapolaria* (V, 317); *Le Trappole* (V, 347); *La Trapola* (V, 350); *Li dui simili* (V, 368).

55. For evidence of the Italian actor Drusiano Martinelli's visit to London see Winifred Smith, *Italian Actors of the Renaissance* (New York, 1930), p. 64; also Pandolfi, II, 250.

The Comedy of Timon:
A Reveling Play of the Inner Temple

M. C. BRADBROOK

I. The Manuscript of *Timon*

AMONG THE DYCE MANUSCRIPTS at the Victoria and Albert Museum
is the untitled anonymous play on Timon of Athens (Dyce
52.25F) which Dyce edited for the Shakespeare Society in 1842. Any
attention that the work has received has been due to its relation with
Shakespeare's *Timon of Athens;* it has been debated whether Shakespeare
copied Anonymous, or Anonymous copied Shakespeare, or both are indebted to a common source; [1] no one dissents from the verdict of Steevens,
which has been copied into the MS: "The piece itself (though it appears
to be the work of an academick) is a wretched one."

I venture to affirm that the little piece reveals not only some interest but
some merit if read as a law students' burlesque of Shakespeare's *Timon,*
presented probably at the Christmas revels and almost certainly at the
Inner Temple. It would follow that Shakespeare's play must have been

1. C. F. T. Brooke, *Tudor Drama* (Boston, 1911), p. 411 n.; G. A. Bonnard, "Note
sur les sources de *Timon of Athens,*" *Études Anglaises,* VII (1954), 63–64.

given on the stage, since burlesque would be pointless unless the original were generally familiar; and *Timon of Athens,* which did not reach print till the First Folio of 1623, has often been considered an unfinished draft.[2]

I have already put forward the view that, on the contrary, it represents a novel experiment: a spectacular pageant or show, evoking old forms for a new setting. Beginning with a group of characters who are treated sometimes morally and sometimes satirically, developing through a series of tableaux, it finally is dominated by the figure of the hero, who reaches cosmic and symbolic dimensions, such as the Child of the Sun in Dekker and Ford's masque *The Sun's Darling.* The turning point of the mock banquet shows Timon in judgment, playing the part of an angry Jupiter, hurling stones of vengeance upon his false friends.[3]

This play evoked a pageant burlesque, *The Comedy of Timon,* that incorporates a number of striking features unparalleled elsewhere: the faithful steward, the crew of flatterers, the mock banquet, the miserly old man with a marriageable daughter, and the unrewarded soldier—here a disguise assumed by Laches the Steward, after he is banished by Timon for his salutary counsel.

Nothing is known of the manuscript's origins; it is written on folio

2. Recent views will be found summarized in two editions of *Timon of Athens,* that of J. C. Maxwell for the New Cambridge Shakespeare (Cambridge, 1957), and that of H. J. Oliver for the New Arden (London, 1959). I have discussed the problem recently (see next note).

3. M. C. Bradbrook, *The Tragic Pageant of Timon of Athens* (Cambridge, 1966). This lecture suggests that Shakespeare's play was not incomplete but, rather, was an experimental reshaping of the Elizabethan "show," a different *kind* of performance. It depended not on plot or character but on a number of contrasted scenes written on a central theme. These scenes, written in contrasted styles, include reminiscences of the moral play, a masque, sketches in the satiric style, and, in the second half of the play, a solo tragic part for Burbage. This is essentially an elaborate indoor spectacle and was perhaps designed for the opening of the Blackfriars. In Jacobean terms it might be titled: *A Dramatick Shew of the Life of Timon of Athens, wherein his Progress through the Four Seasons, as also through the Four Humours in an Earthly Zodiack is set forth, together with the City Vice of Usury in Divers Senators, the snarling Asperity of Prideful Scholars, and the mercenary decline of Poetry and Painting in this latter Age. All displayed in Sundry Variety of Dramatic Utterance chiefly by way of Paradoxes.* Variety is essential, within a unified scheme; the development is shown largely in spectacular terms and through iconographical interpretation of the dramatic spectacle.

sheets in two distinct hands but not, perhaps, by two transcribers. Act I and the first part of Act V are in an English hand, Acts II, III, IV in an Italian hand, and the last two pages change to Italian, then back to English for 26 lines, ending with the Italian character. (See Figure 1.) These changes, which come in midpage, suggest, with the weariness and haste that is evident, that originally the writer intended to facilitate reference by varying the hands but grew careless at the end. Except for some insertions and corrections in the Italian hand on page 43, this is a fair copy which could have been used as prompt-book. Stage directions imply performance, especially "Enter Timon and Laches with either a spade in their hands," which has been corrected to "3 spades" since one is needed later for a third character who joins them. "The sign of the 7 starres," evidently an inn sign to be hung out, and "two sprats or the like" for the miser's meal, with an occasional brief direction for music or a dance, confirm this; the list of characters which precedes the play is numbered off (there are twenty in all), and the epilogue presents it as a comedy:

> If our Comedie
> And merry Scene deserve a Plaudite
> Let loving hands loude sounding in the Ayre
> Cause Timon to the Citty to repaire.

The hero—who begins as Timon the Tosspot, goes on to figure as Timon in Love, and ends as Lucianic man-hater—gets rather lost among a crowd of Jonsonian caricatures; but the part was designed for a star, as his capacity for facial expression is often remarked: "His countenance bewraies his vexed soul," says Laches; and later, "How full of fury is his countenance"; while the old nurse observes, less tragically,

> He hath a face like ones that is at cack
> He looks soe sowerlie.

The minor characters depend rather on their variety of rhetoric for effect: the city is well mocked by a foolish city heir; a miser with a mercenary daughter and clownish son; a usurer; a fiddler; a young prodigal; a city cheat, who poses as a traveler to rob the gull. Two

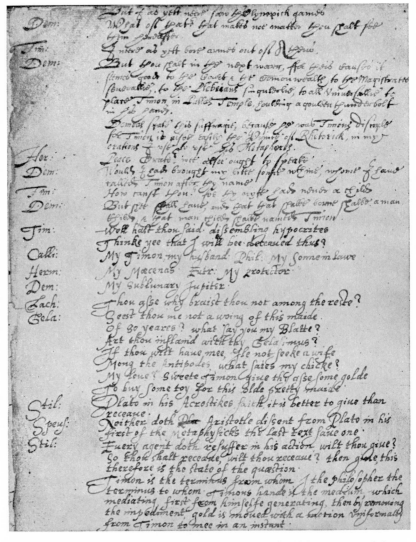

FIGURE I. Part of Folio 23ᵛ. MS Dyce 52.25F. Reproduced by courtesy of the Victoria and Albert Museum, London.

philosophers and an orator satirize academic disputes and pleader's rhetoric.

On his first appearance the orator is being arrested for debt by two sergeants, and his plea burlesques the Ciceronian style:

By what fault or fate of mine (luculent not lutulent Sergeants) shall I say it is come to passe that I an orator not an arator florride not horride should be cast into prison by stolidde not by solidde persons? What have I done? What have I not done? Whom may I invocate? Whom may I not invocate? Etc.[4]

After redeeming him, Timon is later cast off in his poverty ("Thou brazen face I ne'er sawe thee before"), mocked for his rage ("Ha ha he, how tragicall hee is"), and finally given one groat in alms ("But thou must publish my munificence"); later, in Lucianic style, the orator offers to publish Timon's great virtues and plead for his public requital.

It may be well to summarize the action before considering *The Comedy of Timon*, first as a reveling play of the Inner Temple and secondly in its relation to Shakespeare and the professional stage.

Act I   Shows Timon set on a course of munificence—paying a friend's debt but consorting with a fiddler and banishing his faithful steward. Gelasimus of the Golden Hill makes the acquaintance of the false traveler Pseudocheus, parting with a gemmed ring in exchange for a brass one.

Act II   Shows Gelasimus wooing Callimela, the miser's daughter, and Laches reentering Timon's service disguised as a soldier, after he has beaten the fiddler. Timon redeems the orator and leads a drinking party, of which Callimela's clownish brother Lollio is elected prince; in this elevation he sees himself as Achilles leading the Myrmidons.

Act III The drinking party storms the miser's house, where Timon falls in love with Callimela. As he asks no dowry, he wins her from Gelasimus, who decides to challenge not his rival but the lady to a fight. The wedding feast is broken up by the news of shipwreck, which ruins Timon.

Act IV   As all his friends deny Timon relief, Gelasimus is selling his lands to the usurer, in order to seek in marriage the daughter of the King

4. "An orator not an arator" echoes a pun from the Cambridge play of *Pedantius, c.* 1581, which satirized Gabriel Harvey: "Sciebam me Oratorem, non Aratorem . . . esse." On the strength of this single academic "chestnut," G. C. Moore Smith dated *Timon* as mid-Elizabethan (*MLR*, III [1907], 143).

of the Antipodes, promised by Pseudocheus. Two philosophers counsel stoic patience to Timon, who instead stages the mock banquet from which he beats them all away; he quits Athens in company with Laches.

Act V　Gelasimus awaits Pegasus, the winged steed which is to bear him to the Antipodes, but finds Pseudocheus has absconded with all his wealth. He joins Timon and Laches in a digging party, wearing the fool's cap with ass's ears which he had been sent. After Timon strikes the golden hoard, all the city comes to court him; they are denounced and driven off with a beating. In the Epilogue, however, Timon suffers a change of heart as he "doffs Timon."

II. The Legal Connections

There are legal metaphors in the opening lines. Laches wants to cast Timon's treasure "into prison," that is, to put it under lock and key, reminding Timon that "who bears a princely mind needs princely wealth." Timon retorts "Is't even soe, my learned counsaylor?" To which Laches replies

> I'le as silent bee
> As any counsaylor without his ffee.

As lord of the revels, Timon abdicates in favor of the foolish Lollio but himself makes certain laws which are received with general acclaim:

TIMON

That this our compotation may have
A prosp'rous evente wee will and commaunde
Whole hogsheades to be emptied, platters fill'd
None to depart, unles hee first obtayne
Leave of the prince wee also do enacte
That all holde up their heades and laughe aloude
Drinke much at one draughte, breathe not in their drinke
That none goe out to pisse, that none doe spew
In any corner. Hee that shall offende
In any one of these shall weare infixt
Upon his hatte an asses' eares and drinke
Nothing but sowre wine lees for three daies space.

ALL

This Acte wee ratifie confirme allow.

Such laws were commonly enacted at Christmas Revels. When Gray's Inn elected Henry Prince of Purpoole for the Christmas sports of 1594 and he instituted his Honourable Order of the Helmet, the knights were forbidden to wear toothpicks, to carry books in their pockets (or put their hands in except for warmth or to defend their loose cash), or to practice "shrug, nod, or other familiar motion or gesture." The actual rules of governance for the Inns provided, for example, that "Gentlemen should reform themselves in their cut or disguised apparel and not to have long Beards" (Dugdale, *Origines Juridiciales,* 3rd ed. [1680], p. 148). This rule was quoted at the Inner Temple, to prohibit Beatle haircuts, and drinking rules of a not dissimilar kind were observed in Cambridge till this year in a pubcrawl known as "the King Street Run."

Gesta Grayorum [5] records the mock court of the Prince of Purpoole, which was kept in full state; all his officers were given titles, arms, and precedence, in a complete replica of the royal court. It also parodies lawyers in the counselors' speeches and the mock trials. At the end of his reign the Prince was summoned to court by "the Empress of the Fortunate Islands," Elizabeth herself, for a Shrovetide masque, performed in presence of the Queen "with the Nobles of both Courts." The Christmas Prince usually defrayed a large part of the charges himself and therefore needed princely wealth indeed. Henry collected from Gray's Inn by extracting "benevolences," but the actual treasury of the Inn was not called upon.

The parody in *Gesta Grayorum* is played straight; *The Comedy of Timon* varies from high-spirited horseplay to "the dry mock." Legal pretensions are mocked exuberantly by the speech of the orator and the philosophers; but munificence is burlesqued more satirically in the behavior of Timon's absurd rival, Gelasimus of the Golden Hill, son of Rubiconde of the Isles.

Here is the familiar figure of the city gull; he belongs to the tribe of Sir Andrew Aguecheek and of Master Matthew of *Every Man in His Humour;* he is contrasted with Lollio, the country clown, as Matthew is with Stephen. On his first appearance Gelasimus aspires to the Bench ("a severe Areopagite with his contracted eyebrows"), but his page advises him to wait awhile—"otherwise old men will be ashamed to be overcome

5. Ed. W. W. Greg for the Malone Society Reprints (Oxford, 1914).

in counsel and understanding by one that is barbitulous." His greatest adventure is the preparation for a ride on Pegasus, to seek the hand of the daughter of the King of the Antipodes; in the last act he enters booted and spurred, with a riding switch in one hand and a watch in the other. This may recall Don Quixote's imaginary ride and Sancho Panza's desire to be governor of a distant island, or the kind of journeys that wandering knights undergo on the early Elizabethan stage; but Pegasus, who is so much insisted on as almost to become one of the dramatis personae, constitutes the arms of the Inner Temple.

Heraldry, as has been said, played a great part in Christmas sports; and in 1561, at the Grand Christmas held at the Inner Temple, when Lord Robert Dudley was installed as Constable-Marshall, an Order of Pegasus was established. The herald proclaimed the Christmas Prince as "The mighty Palaphilos, Prince of Sophie, high Constable-Marshall of the Knights Templars, Patron of the Honourable Order of Pegasus"—which order, instituted at the command of "Pallas" herself, consisted of twenty-four knights, who may have been really knighted by Dudley (Dugdale, pp. 150–153).[6]

In *Gesta Grayorum* the arms of the Prince of Purpoole are blazoned by his king-at-arms:

> . . . *beareth his Shield of the highest* Jupiter. *In Point, a Sacred Imperial Diadem, safely guarded by the Helmet of the great Goddess* Pallas, *from the Violence of Darts, Bullets and Bolts of* Saturn, Momus *and the* Idiot; *all environed with the Ribband of Loyalty, having a Pendant of the most heroical Order of Knighthood of the Helmet; the Word hereunto,* Sic virtus honorem. *For his Highness's Crest, the glorious Planet* Sol, *coursing through the twelve Signs of the* Zodiack, *on a Celestial Globe . . . supported by two anciently renowned and glorious Griffyns, which have been always in League with the honourable* Pegasus.[7]
>
> (p. 10, ll. 1–13)

6. For instance, Leicester knighted a Lord Mayor in 1566 (William Shaw, *Knights of England* [London, 1906], II, 73).

7. Pegasus had been a badge of the Templars, whose poverty was symbolized by the figure of two knights riding on one horse; the two knights were mistaken for two wings, and so the winged horse became a badge. On such uses of heraldry see Leslie Hotson, "Taking Shakespeare at His Word," *Shakespeare Studies,* ed. J. L. Barroll, I (1965), 137–141.

These are canting arms, for the Prince's real name was Henry Helmes; the Griffin is the device of Gray's Inn (see Figure 2), which was in league with the Inner Temple (Pegasus); this was dramatized in a special Masque of Amity.

Such a burlesque of the arms of the Inn as Gelasimus shows in his proposed ride on Pegasus would have point and be tolerable only at the Inner Temple. It could not have been played elsewhere. Gelasimus actually is very proud of his own arms, which are blazoned by his page in the opening scene:

Three gilded thistles. Three fatt asses drawn out of the deserts of Arabia. Two boares with gilded stones in a feild.

"Bloody," interjects Gelasimus, to which the page responds "Nay rather turdy." But when the cap with ass's ears is sent, Gelasimus recalls these arms sadly as he puts it on: "These were the true arms of my grandfather."

In mumming sports it had been usual for the masquers to claim that they had suddenly arrived from distant parts; in *Gesta Grayorum* the Prince took a voyage to Russia, whence at Candlemas he returned to start up the sports anew. None the less, his Knights were strictly forbidden by their Order to indulge in travelers' tales:

as that he hath ridden through *Venice* on Horse-Back Post, or that in December he hath sailed by the Cape of *Norway,* or that he hath travelled over the most part of the Countries of *Geneva.*

Pseudocheus begins with some talk of a wooden horse (meaning a ship), but Gelasimus says at once, "Ile buye this flying horse"; and when he accosts the traveler, "On ffoote or horse wents't thou this greate voyage," Pegasus is launched in flight by Pseudocheus:

Up to the ffieldes Gurgustidonian
I rode on horse back; the Antipodes
Were distant thence about an hundred myles
There I being seene the Pigmies fearefully
Fledd all awaye.

FIGURE 2. The arms of the Inns of Court and Chancery. From William Dugdale, *Origines Juridiciales,* 3d edition enlarged (London, 1680). Reproduced by courtesy of Girton College Library, Cambridge.

Soon, however, he is discoursing of Proserpina and islands in the moon. The two philosophers debate on the possibility of a man in the moon and whether he be there

really and intrinsically an entitative acte and essence besides a formall existence, or whether that be Platoes Idea abstracted from the humane species, which they affirme to be under the concave of the Moone.

Such had been the fashion of masquing from early Tudor times, and with such "gracious fooling" Feste pleased Sir Andrew Aguecheek: "when thou spok'st of Pigrogromitus, of the Vapians passing the equinoctial of Queubus; 'twas very good, i'faith. I sent thee sixpence for thy leman" (*Twelfth Night,* II.iii.21–24).

Gelasimus is a city heir (and therefore probably not a true "Areopagite"); the deed by which he conveys all his possessions to the usurer is set out in full and with considerable relish. The decree honoring Timon, later set out by the orator, is designed to satirize the honors that in *Gesta Grayorum* are accorded with gravity. The usurer was evidently heavily made up, for in the opening sequence his victim swears "by the glistening jemms of thy red nose." So was Gelasimus, a true son of Rubiconde: "Lord what golden teeth have I! what a purple coloured face," he comments as he views himself in the glass, which suggests that he was vizarded. Timon himself joins in a bawdy song with Gelasimus and the fiddler:

HERMOGENES

There lives a lasse in the nexte towne
Call'd Sophrony, call'd Sophrony

TIMON

Smiles sweetly when I lay her downe
Blithe and bonny, blithe and bonny.

GELASIMUS

Shee is not like some foolishe elfe
She will take up her clothes herselfe

ALL

Ha ha he ha ha he
Ha ha ha ha ha ha he

With his gilt rapier and new cloak, the fiddler is the basest of the upstarts; to pinion Laches and incite the fiddler to hit him is the first and wildest of

Timon's sports. Laches, driven away, returns in heavy disguise to beat the
fiddler:

> A resolute hackster with his scarrs and sword
> My wiskers hanging o'er the overlipp.

When Timon and his drinking party encounter the country clown, he
wonders, "Are they philosophers or brabbling lawyers?" and is told

> Seest thou these young men?
> They are the prime men of this same cittie—

a claim which the Templars might feel disposed to put forward, but
which the Lord Mayor and Aldermen were not likely to "ratify, confirm,
allow." From the quantity of feathers in their hats, Lollio next mistakes
them for fowls (Timon's friend Eutrepalus had been given his by a whore
"as a conspicuous symbol of her love"). In the Grand Christmas of the
Inner Temple the Constable-Marshall and the Lieutenant of the Tower
are both enjoined to wear "a Nest of feather of all colours upon his Crest
or Helm" (Dugdale, p. 155) for the sports of St. Stephen's Day.

Seeing also the inn sign of the Seven Stars, Lollio mistakes it for the
heavenly Plough; later Gelasimus is to be told that the zodiacal signs
represent heavenly inns;

> That cittie hath twelve inns for traveylours:
> Taurus, or Gemini, Cancer, Leo,
> Or Virgo, yf you please, chouse which thou wilt:
> But dost thou hear me, Gelasimus?
> By noe meanes lodge thou in Aquarius. . . .
>
> GELASIMUS
> That's well Ile inn at the Virgine.

Christmas revels naturally included a good deal of sport about times and
seasons, the hours of the clock, or the days of the week. The conceit of the
inns perhaps had a special attraction for the lawyers; and the signs of the
zodiac seem to me to be suggested in Shakespeare's *Timon,* implicitly, in
the progress of the hero through a solar year. Gelasimus' bawdy pun, like
some unabashed references to the female anatomy (expunged by Dyce),
cannot be paralleled in the earlier sports, such as *Gesta Grayorum;* they

could be found in Beaumont's *Knight of the Burning Pestle,* which also suggests the adventures of Gelasimus. This Blackfriars play is broad enough, in the tradition of coterie theater; but I cannot think that any ordinary schoolmaster would have been permitted to teach his charges to utter such things in the presence of their parents and governors, so that the theory that *The Comedy of Timon* is a school play seems unlikely, even if other evidence did not so strongly point to the lawyers. City dignitaries are mocked throughout, not to speak of the morals of city women; in his opening scene Timon cynically describes the mercenary habits of his mistress. Revelry and beatings seem to alternate throughout the middle section of the play. Christmas shows like "The Seven Days of the Week," in *The Christmas Prince,*[8] are dependent on the succession of characters coming "out" and then beating one another "in"; an element of this combines with an attempt at sophistication in *The Comedy of Timon.*

In Christmas sports, also, the whole household had to be included; for example, the show of *Narcissus,* from St. John's College, Oxford, has an epilogue for the College Porter. At the Inns of Court, under the Steward the most important servant is the Chief Butler; in the Grand Christmas of the Inner Temple he was one of the five most eminent officers, elected in the Trinity Term preceding. For Robert Dudley's Grand Christmas of 1561 Mr. Paten was Chief Butler and immediately preceded Christopher Hatton, Master of the Game, and four Masters of the Revels in the Order of Precedence; in the ordering of a Grand Christmas, the special Christmas Butlers, in addition to the ordinary Butlers of the House, are given their duties (Dugdale, pp. 153-154).

In *The Comedy of Timon,* when Lollio is elected prince of the drinking party, he creates all the rest his butlers. Timon's butler, Obba, appears in a couple of scenes, and he is contrasted with the lean "macilente" Grunnio, servant of the miser, who creeps into a hole to enjoy at least the smell of the feast. Grunnio looks like "the son of Famine," and he complains that the miser counts up

> How many spiders are about the house
> Lest any one of us steal one of them.

8. Ed. F. S. Boas for the Malone Society Reprints (Oxford, 1922), pp. 136-151; a little play designed "for those that could do nothing well," which proved a great success.

This "spider-catcher" is a city servant, and the contrast between Obba and Grunnio forms part of the general mockery of the City, which helps to place this comedy in the Inns rather than any one of the City schools, such as St. Paul's, St. Antony's, or Merchant Taylors'.

In a play based on Lucian's *Dialogue of Timon* the Lucianic tone of ironic deflation naturally predominates; though this description of Grunnio, as Dyce points out, depends on Plautus, *Aulularia,* I.ii.9, II.iv.23. The author of the *Comedy* has been corrected by editors for misquoting the opening lines of the *Iliad* (by the drunken clown), but learning is mocked quite openly, when the fiddler tries to buy long words of the philosophers for the exorbitant sum of £20 and then attempts to join in their disputes:

STILPE

Aristotle in his Meterologickes and the XV° page as I remember defendeth Paradox and Atropos.

HERMOGENES

Neither canst thou disprove him, ffor the Lord Paradox and the Lord Atropos perchance were Aristotle's friends.

Hermogenes is taking "defend" in the legal sense of defending a client (instead of a proposition); but one philosopher, seeking fresh gold of Timon, observes "Plato in his Acrostikes saith, it is better to give then receaue," which is confirmed by his fellow in the unctuous tones of the pulpit: "Neither doth Aristotle dissent from Plato, in his first of the Metaphysicks, the last text save one."

Two Elizabethan plays that have special associations with the Inns of Court are recalled in *The Comedy of Timon.* Gelasimus, as has been mentioned, seems to show traits of Sir Andrew Aguecheek; his challenge to a woman, his learning of wooing terms from Pseudocheus, who "coaches" him in compliment, also recall Sir Andrew; and, of course, the way in which he is fleeced of his wealth puts him, together with Sir Andrew, in the general class of the foolish "gull." Shakespeare's *Twelfth Night,* which was acted at the Middle Temple on 2 February 1602 (Candlemas), was not published till 1623; so these are recollections of performance, as the text was not available. Another play which is directly recalled is Ben Jonson's *Every Man out of His Humour,* as Herford and

Simpson note in a special appendix to their edition of Ben Jonson.[9] Pseudocheus is modeled on Puntarvolo, the clown on both Sogliardo and Sordido, the fiddler suggests Shift, and the final transformation of Timon recalls that of Macilente, in the epilogue for the Court. The rare term "macilente" is used in this very play to describe the City servant, enviously lingering at Timon's feast.

In the Folio of 1616 Jonson's play is dedicated to "the noblest novrceries of hvmanity, and liberty, in the kingdome: the Innes of Court" and is recommended for the Christmas season of the Lord of Misrule:

When I wrote this Poeme,[10] *I had friendship with diuers in your societies; who, as they were great Names in learning, so they were no lesse Examples of liuing. Of them, and then (that I say no more) it was not despis'd. . . . when the gowne and cap is off, and the Lord of liberty raignes; then, to take it in your hands, perhaps may make some Bencher, tincted with humanity, reade: and not repent him.*

It is surely another pointer that two plays which had been favorites of the lawyers are recalled in this comedy.

III. The Shakespearean Connections

The connections with *Timon of Athens* and *Twelfth Night* are not the comedy's only links with Shakespeare. Timon is ruined not at all by his prodigality but by sudden shipwreck of all his ventures; this might suggest *The Merchant of Venice*. There is also a comic usurer, who is apparently a Jew. Faint echoes of *King Lear* may be illusory: Laches serves his master in disguise after being turned away; Timon threatens to pull his servant's eyes out, and Laches, after threatening Hermogenes with this, hoodwinks him; later, Timon offers to lead Gelasimus to a cliff top

---

9. *Ben Jonson,* ed. C. H. Herford and P. and E. Simpson (Oxford, 1950), Appendix X, pp. 482–485. Even such eminent scholars have read *The Comedy of Timon* so carelessly as to imagine that Gelasimus as well as Lollio was the son of the miser.

10. *Every Man out of His Humour* was published in three quarto editions in 1600, but this Preface did not appear before the folio.

and "help thee at a push." When Timon is ruined, he reverts to the old-fashioned style of revenge plays, such as Shakespeare himself might have parodied; he spends a long time lying prostrate on the earth—"like an ox," as one of his former friends observes—and he appeals to the gods and furies:

> Tysiphone,
> Bring here thy flames, ...
> Thou Goddes Nemesis revenge my wronge . . .
> O, thou revenge come wholy to my hands.

But in the scene where he hoodwinks and beats the fiddler, Laches has already burlesqued this tragic effect and made it nugatory:

LACHES
My name is Nemesis.
HERMOGENES
O sweete sweete Nemesis, what wouldst thou haue?
LACHES
I am thy evill spiritt
HERMOGENES
What, two of yee oh, spare me good evill spyritt.
LACHES
No no,
Thou shalt be beate because thou art a knave
HERMOGENES
Oh, oh, sweete Nemesis
LACHES
I'le pluck thie eyes out
HERMOGENES
O good ill spiritt, do not soe torment mee
Oh, oh
LACHES
Farewell ffiddler, ffarewell Hermogenes.

Laches' part is the most vigorous in the play; in the final scene he makes an assault on the assembled Athenians with his spade and drives them off with carter's cries: "I am your driver hoi gee hence away." The ridiculous scene in which three outcasts are seen digging in different parts of the stage parodies the great last scenes of Shakespeare's *Timon;* Gelasimus, wearing his cap with ass's ears, invokes the tragic muse in a mournful song, after the other two have left him:

Come, come, O come, Melpomene
Sing doleful Elegies with me
Bewayle my heavy destinie
    Most detestable. . . .

The imagery of Timon as an earthly Jove is mocked very extensively, and this implies, I would think, that Shakespeare's *Timon* had been seen, since it is in Shakespeare's scene of the mock banquet that the image of Jove is most powerfully presented, as a spectacle. In the *Comedy,* just before that mock banquet, Timon ironically exclaims:

O happy mee, equall to Jove himselfe
I going touche the starres, Break out O Joy
And smother not thyself within my breast
Soe many friends, soe many friends I see
Not one hathe falsifi'de his faith to mee.

Again before the banquet the philosophers discuss the question "whether the heaven be made of stones," but after being pelted with the hail of stones from Timon, they reflect ruefully: "Stones sublunary have the same matter with the heavenly"—to which Timon retorts:

If I Jove's horridde thunderbolt did hold
Within my hande, thus, thus would I darte it
                Hee hitts Hermogenes.

The "horrid thunderbolt" he is actually darting had been on the table, disguised as part of the feast:

TIMON
These Artichokes do noe mans pallat please.
DEMAS
I love them well by Joue.
TIMON
                    Here take them then.
Stones painted like to them and throwes them at them.

To the irreverent, Jove's thunderbolt, as depicted by such iconographers as G. Cartari, resembles nothing so much as an elongated artichoke; the whole scene depends on evoking a visual memory, in the audience, of Shakespeare's Timon as Jove.

In the opening scene the comic Timon is already termed "my human Jupiter" (I.ii), "my Jupiter my Jupiter" (II.iv), and, when he has found the new hoard of wealth, the miser and the orator again address him as "another Jove" and "a sublunary Jupiter"; but here again there had already been the parody when Lollio the clown imagined himself to be Achilles leading the Myrmidons to the sack of Troy.

Given all these scrappy, pervasive, broken echoes of Shakespeare's play, it seems that the author of the *Comedy* must have seen that play; even if some of the echoes are not very strong, it is the cumulative effect of them that tells. An additional argument is that Shakespeare presents the ruin of Timon as the result of his riots, whereas in the comedy this causal connection is lost, and the ruin is the result of shipwreck. The *Comedy* represents a breakdown of what had originally been lucid. But as the riotous Timon is not depicted outside Shakespeare and this *Comedy*, it follows that the author of the *Comedy* was the copyist, not vice versa. To depict ruin as the result of riotous living would not have been very much in key with Christmas revels, and so this cautionary warning is simply left out.

Here in fact may be the reason why, at one of their lavish feasts, the young lawyers chose this particular play for parody. The virtuosity of Timon's part suggests a parody of the great Burbage; his variety of face-making has been already noted. At one point he runs mad, at another he speaks with stoic conciseness (he is lying prostrate on the earth):

GELASIMUS
The ground's to colde a bed to lie uppon.
TIMON
Nothing.
GELASIMUS
Thy hearing therefore is not good.
TIMON
And yet I am not deafe.
GELASIMUS
What's this?
TIMON
Somethinge
GELASIMUS
What's this something?

TIMON

Nothing (I say) nothing
All things are made nothing.

This is an echo of Timon's great line in Shakespeare: "And nothing brings me all things" (V.i.186).

In the Epilogue, the last lines of the comedy—

Let loving hands loude sounding in the Ayre
Cause Timon to the Citty to repaire—

might be taken as recollection of a performance that had already taken place within the city. If Shakespeare's *Timon* had been given at Black-friars (the nearest playhouse to the Inner Temple, just within the city walls), perhaps, as Honigmann conjectures, it had been originally de-signed for the Inns of Court; [11] but if it was moved to Blackfriars later, the Epilogue may suggest the transfer of a private show to a public audience and mockingly predict that the comic *Timon* would be trans-ferred as the tragic one had been. It certainly seems probable that there would be a lot of private jokes in *The Comedy of Timon,* which cannot now be recovered.

IV. The Date of *The Comedy of Timon*

When it is placed in the sequence of reveling plays, *The Comedy of Timon* becomes a little easier to place chronologically, and this in turn reflects on the date of Shakespeare's play. I have dealt in my book *The Rise of the Common Player* with the evolution and decline of such revels; [12] whereas the old Lords of Misrule had been purely comic, the mock state of the lawyers at Gray's Inn, when they played their Christmas

11. E. A. J. Honigmann, *SQ,* XII (1961), 3–20; this is one of the best studies of dating. Honigmann argues that *Timon of Athens* was intended for the Inns of Court and links it with *Antony and Cleopatra.*

12. In Chapters XI and XII. The whole subject of the drama at the Inns of Court has recently been studied by Mrs. Marie Axton of Girton College (to whom I am indebted for the reference to Dugdale) in a doctoral thesis presented to the University of Cambridge.

games of 1594, was by no means mere buffoonery. Here the buffoonery
has returned, but it is kept within the bounds of a regular comedy,
founded on classical and contemporary dramas, and is not part of a
"game." The interest in different kinds of rhetoric is more sophisticated
than in *Gesta Grayorum* or in *The Christmas Prince* (which was the
festivity of St. John's College, Oxford, in 1607/8). At Oxford the students
were shy of performing in English; *The Comedy of Timon* presupposes
considerable "audacity" in the players.

The story offers a satiric reflection of the sports of a Christmas Lord,
who often overspent his wealth and at the end of his "reign" became an
ordinary student once more. Yet this Timon is not allowed to have his
ruin directly attributed to his spendthrift ways. Self-mockery is included
in the play, whose main theme is the absurdity of the small aping the
great; this can be traced right down to the details of the staging. Timon's
two rivals, Gelasimus and Lollio, both play the Merrygreek, as when
Lollio leads his Myrmidons to Troy with a flagon for a banner. The satiric
intentions of the first part of Shakespeare's tragic pageant might have
been within this author's grasp, but the lyric ending was quite beyond
him; he turned therefore to Lucian at this point. *The Comedy of Timon*
wavers uncertainly between, on the one hand, exuberant revelry, farcical
action, and private jokes, which belong to the old tradition of the Revels;
and literary satire, sophisticated mockery of the City, the Players, and
their plays, on the other. The mixture of simple high spirits and a rather
strenuous assertion of mental superiority will not be unfamiliar to those
who know the modern university. The tone is noticeably different from
Gerard Leigh's account of the reign of the Earl of Leicester at the Inner
Temple in 1561 or from the sports of 1594, where Shakespeare's play *The
Comedy of Errors* was perhaps given its first performance. This little
Comedy of Timon burlesques such regal traditions, whether because the
development of court masques under James made mock royalty at the
Inns too inadequate or because less glory and less validity by now attached
to the symbolism of monarchy itself. The mixture is most nearly like the
blend of nostalgia and mockery of old forms that can be found in
Beaumont's *Knight of the Burning Pestle* (1608), where the history of
drama is suggested in perspective. May Lords and wandering knights are
shown as belonging to a simpler world, a world that is passing; Beaumont, the son of a judge and himself trained at the Inner Temple, gives

the best guide to the temper of this Inner Temple play, with its mixture of the farcical and satiric. It is an amateur show in which the writer, conscious enough that the days of the Christmas Prince were over and that amateurs should not vie with the splendors of Blackfriars or of Whitehall, reflected a recent spectacular triumph of the Common Players, in a mixture of admiration and superiority.

Although the full reveling games were no longer popular (and even at Oxford where the students were younger and less sophisticated, *The Christmas Prince* had not been an unmixed success), the Inns of Court were still performing plays at the end of the first decade of the seventeenth century. The Registers of the Inner Temple note:

In Feb. 8 Jac. [i.e., 1611] that for further prevention of disorder and scurrility, no more Plays should be in this House upon the feast of *All Saints,* or *Candelmas Day* but this Order was repealed the 4th of November following.
(Dugdale, p. 149)

If Shakespeare's *Timon of Athens* was designed for the new Blackfriars Theater (1609) or was moved there after a performance at the Inns, this reference of 1611 would give a suitable date for *The Comedy of Timon,* which burlesques Shakespeare.[13] It is not without some "scurrility" and "disorder," though these derived not from the declining tradition of *Gesta Grayorum* but from those more popular sports, of which *The Comedy of Timon* also gives a last diminishing echo.

13. The music for the Masque of Amazons in Shakespeare's play, which survives in British Museum MS. Add. 10444, has been dated as written down about 1610.

Drama and Polemics under Queen Mary

DAVID M. BEVINGTON

T HE GOVERNMENT OF QUEEN MARY, coming to power after a reign of increasingly headstrong Protestantism, was faced with a propaganda crisis. To what extent did the situation reflect itself in drama written for her court? Mary's assumption of power found a great deal of popular emotional support, but it naturally antagonized the more zealous Protestants both in and out of government who, tutored in large part by Cromwell's propagandistic techniques, were organized and experienced in the art of mass persuasion. In the summer months of 1553, spontaneous demonstrations of affection for Mary gave way in London to angry Protestant demonstrations at St. Paul's Cross, directed chiefly at the Catholic mass.[1] In these tense months, drama was certain to be viewed apprehensively by the government as a two-edged weapon. Old cycle plays were resuscitated for public performance. Conversely, Protestant drama continued surreptitiously, necessitating on 18 August 1553 a governmental warning against all plays and books of a factional nature.[2] In 1556, after the

---

1. H. F. M. Prescott, *Mary Tudor,* Macmillan paperbacks (New York, 1962), p. 196.

2. Glynne Wickham, *Early English Stages, 1300 to 1660* (London, 1959———), Vol. II, Pt. I, pp. 71–72.

queen's marriage to the hated Philip of Spain, a touring company wearing the livery of Sir Francis Leke uttered "very naughty and seditious matter touching the King and Queens Majesties." [3] Mary found that she had to continue and augment the policy of control begun under her younger brother.

Apart from simple revival of older dramatic forms, new explanations were needed to meet the country's uneasy mood. How far did Mary intend to go in restoring the ancient faith? Was the English service to be replaced compulsorily by the mass throughout England? How would Protestants be treated, both nobles and commoners? What offenses would be punished, what pardoned? Perhaps most crucially, what sort of restitution of seized property and wealth would be required? Would this restitution extend as far as the enormously wealthy lands of abbey and monastery? Most of these lands had been taken by Cromwell in the late 1530's, almost twenty years since.

Mary was subject to intense pressure on the subject of restitution of church lands, and her own feelings were equally strong. Her simple wish was to restore the church to its former splendor and wealth. Few of her most loyal counselors agreed. The nation's newly wealthy men had prospered chiefly at the expense of church property. Mary could hardly have purged all of them without jettisoning the English ruling class. Many who accepted or even welcomed Mary's Catholicism could not tolerate the prospect of losing landed property. Among the commons, traditions of anticlericalism militated against anything approaching a complete return to the ecclesiastical wealth of Henry VII's era. Too much time had elapsed since the dissolution of the monasteries. Yet Mary, deeply pious, emotional, impractical, was determined to do what she could.

It is in such an uneasy situation that the anonymous author of *Respublica* has to make his tactful way. The play is intended for performance at court, during the Christmas season of 1553. Boys are the actors, and many of their roles are feminine. The play could therefore not be toured before the populace, seemingly a curious oversight in view of the need for propagandistic rejoinder to such playwrights as Bale and Weever. More-

3. *Historical Memorials, Ecclesiastical and Civil, of Events under the Reign of Queen Mary I,* ed. John Strype (London, 1721), III, 297, Chapter XXXVIII, 30 April 1556. Quoted by Edith Rickert, "Political Propaganda and Satire in *A Midsummer Night's Dream.* II," *MP,* XXI (1923), 137.

over, *Respublica* does not deal with the theological and ritual aspects of England's return to Catholic status; it spends little time in answering Bale's satire of bell-ringing, ducking and censing, relics, pilgrimages, transubstantiation, saint-worship, and the like. Monasticism, simony, ignorance in the clergy, and pluralism are of concern to this playwright since they bear on the question of fiscal and administrative corruption, but he makes no attempt to defend the beauty of the Catholic service. Nor, surprisingly, is there a single mention of the pope or of the age-old conflict between ecclesiastical and temporal power.

This narrowness of scope is best understood in terms of the play's courtly auspices. The playwright's foremost delicate task is to reconcile Mary's courtiers to her program of restitution and at the same time to caution the queen gently about extremism in punishing or disenfranchising minor offenders. He wishes also to assert Mary's right to rule her council, not be ruled by it as Edward had been. These issues are of concern to England's ruling class, not to the average churchgoer. In doctrinal and ritual matters, the author's cue is to avoid inflammatory recriminations. Mary herself, for all her religious zeal, was sensible of the explosive emotional issue involved and agreed to a plan of discreet restorations of rite where this was possible without public notice. Protestantism as such is called no names in *Respublica,* in fact is hardly seen to exist other than as a rationale for a few greedy men. By implying that there is only one church, the playwright avoids the danger of labels and predetermined attitudes. One of his chief intellectual concerns, in fact, is to suggest the subtlety of definition inherent in words like "reformation." *Respublica* is thus not a comprehensive rejoinder to Bale but a disquisition for the elite on Mary's most acute problems of restitution and royal dominance, problems she never solved and on which she ultimately lost political support. Yet the conciliatory tone of the play, and the avoidance of doctrinal issues, provided a model for Elizabeth's brilliantly successful church compromise and her suppression of polemical feuding in the drama after 1558.

Reference to an exact period of English history is more obvious in *Respublica* than in any political allegory before its time. Although the author speaks "as it were in figure by an allegory" (l. 18), he is at pains to specify the years 1547 to 1553. The play's official status obviates the necessity for disclaimer of exact correspondence. Queen Mary appears among the cast. "She is our most wise / *and* most worthie Nemesis" whom Heaven has sent "to reform thabuses which hithertoo hath been" (ll. 53, 50). She appears at the play's end to restore England, or Respublica, "from hir late decay" (l. 46). England's tribulations have been precisely of five to six years' duration. The Cotswold rustic, People, complains that "vive or zix year ago chad vowre kine to my pail" (l. 1021), reminiscing about his relative prosperity at the end of Henry VIII's reign. His newly restored wealth is in silver coin; "I wis ich cowld not zo zai these zix yeares afore" (l. 1601). Respublica sighs, "O lord, how have I be used these five yeres past" (l. 1777). The entire play is a representation of Edward's reign and the first few months of Mary's reign, ending at the very moment the play is presented. No idealized vision of the future is necessary.

Yet People also looks back to a more distant golden age. Rejoicing in the prosperity at hand, he exclaims, "Whough, than; chil warte [warrant] all within twoo years as plenty / as twas eny time these yeres twise twenty" (ll. 722–723).[4] Although allowances must be made here for exigencies of rhyme, the figure of forty years does carry back to the very beginning of Henry VIII's reign. *Respublica* everywhere expresses Mary's longing for the pre-Reformation years of her orthodox and financially solvent grandfather. The play's chronological exactitude implies the existence of serious disorder by the year 1547. Although the beleagured heroine representing England recalls a time "of late" when she prospered mightily, such a time must have been long ago; for at the moment of the evil counselors' arrival (plainly in 1547) she is already "sore Decayed through defalte of policy," and wealth has "been bard from me a great while" (ll. 484, 490). The Vices realize they are victimizing a lady who "is left almost desolate. Hir wealth is decayed" (ll. 238–239). She willingly accepts the newly proffered administration because she is already in dire straits.

Despite the chronological exactitude of the allegory and the actual presence of Mary as Nemesis, however, characterization in *Respublica* is abstract. A Marian audience, witnessing the arrival of evil counselors some six years prior to 1553, would not hesitate to think of Somerset and Northumberland. The author has license to speak freely, for the Protector-

---

4. Leonard A. Magnus, ed., *Respublica,* EETS Extra Series No. 94 (London, 1905), p. xxv. Textual references are to this edition.

ate ministers were no favorites of Mary's. The historical identification of the evil counselors would seem as obvious as Tudor drama can hope to produce. Yet personal similarities are nonexistent. Leonard Magnus has searched, confessedly in vain, for four historical individuals who might correspond one-to-one with Avarice, Adulation, Insolence, and Oppression.[5] He gingerly proposes that Adulation may represent Sir William Paget or Sir William Cecil, or both, since they (like Adulation) were forgiven their relatively minor crimes of acquiescing to Protestant rule. The hypothesis is unrewarding because it is circular in reasoning. No doubt the Marian courtly audience would have drawn its private conclusions as to which courtiers deserved pardon according to the play's view of justice. Perhaps they would have concurred in a verdict. Artistically, however, Adulation draws his inspiration from morality convention. Sir William Cecil might be appropriate insofar as he met the specifications of a type, no more. The author withholds any particularizing hints because he is interested in the general application:

> To shew that all commen weales Ruin *and* decay
> from time to time hath been, is, and shalbe alwaie,
> whan Insolence, Flaterie, Opression,
> and Avarice have the Rewle in their possession.
>
> (ll. 19–22)

As with Wolsey in Skelton's *Magnificence,* the Protectorate ministers here provide the motive and occasion but not the dramatic materials for the satiric chracterization of the four evil counselors. Conventional abstractions of type are employed even when the author might have been more cutting.

Tact was nevertheless required in alluding to England's distress before 1547 and in assessing King Edward's role as nominal head of state for six bad years. Here the author's avoidance of a separate historical identity for each abstraction becomes completely understandable. There is no ingenuous or neglectful king-figure analogous to Henry. It is enough to say that England fell into serious disrepair "of late," for "a great while"—even longer ago than six years; for exactly how long, or at whose instigation, is left deliberately vague. Mary's attitude toward Henry was naturally

5. *Ibid.,* p. xxvi.

tempestuous and complex after her mother's disgrace. She sided with her mother, whom she more closely resembled than her father, but after Katharine's death she accepted some measure of reconciliation. A playwright could only hint that Henry's later reign fell short of the ideal.

Equally touchy was Mary's relationship with Edward VI, a sickly half-brother, much younger than she, born of a stepmother whom Mary regarded as an adulteress, and, worst of all, acquiescent to the Protestant faith if not instrumental in its alarming spread. Still, he was Mary's blood relative. Rather than dramatize the young king's role in his own administration, the author of *Respublica* exploits the generic character of his allegory to avoid the embarrassing "plain story" (1. 17). The heroine Respublica is no ruler but is rather the timeless spirit of her country, who, suffering indignities, needs a champion to defend her. That a champion is not forthcoming for six years is only an indirect rebuke of Edward. His failures of leadership, or the circumstances of his minority rule, are scarcely hinted at in such moralizations as these:

> Yet by all experience, thus much is well seen,
> That in Comon weales while good governors have been,
> All thing hath prospered; and where such men doo lack,
> Comonweales decay and all thinges do go back.
>
> (ll. 453–456)

The total absence of king-figures in the first four acts suggests that there was no real monarch, after all, from 1547 to 1553. *Respublica* ponders the evils of a power vacuum created by the historical accident of a minority kingship. Its conclusions are that the counselors of the realm cannot be trusted to rule dispassionately. Coming forward at a time when England needed most to rely on her ruling elite, since a form of regency or protectorate was mandatory, Edward's counselors reverted (in the dramatist's view) to the darkest days of the Wars of the Roses. The villains, who may "throughout the whole land rewle all the Roste" (1. 136), determine selfishly to exploit their high offices. No one can stop them. This stark prospect of takeover, and the implicit assault on all royal prerogative, were still crucial in 1553 and afterwards. For if Mary was no minor like Edward, she was a woman whose presumed weaknesses as such encouraged more assertions of upper-class power (both of aristocracy and gentry). Religious debate gave added incentive to the challenge of her authority. Elizabeth, as a young Protestant woman, inherited this struggle between throne and ruling class and had to do battle with domineering advice in a play like *Gorboduc*. Throughout the mid-century period the English monarchy was fighting for ascendancy, and the outcome was by no means assured. Thus *Respublica*'s attack on the corrupt advisers of Edward's reign concerns not only the religious establishment but also the theory of divine right of kings.

Respublica views the so-called "Reformation" as nothing more than one manifestation of lust for power by the ambitious elite. The author avoids theological issues and thereby implies that doctrine and rite were not central to the break with Rome. The devout People never asks for simplified service or an English Bible. The monasteries have been seized for their wealth, not because of decayed charity. Protestantism (never named) is not even heresy in this play; it is a recrudescence of man's innate corruption, prompting him to seek power, wealth, and fleshly dominance. Simony and ignorance no doubt existed in the Catholic Church, but they have not been eradicated by the self-proclaimed reformers; instead, age-old corruption has taken the guise of revolutionary zeal. To the author of *Respublica* the reformers are virtually indistinguishable from one another or from the occasional corrupted ecclesiastic of the pre-Reformation church. They are above all else worldlings.

The generic quality of the satire emphasizes the essentially timeless pattern of what happened from 1547 to 1553. If the four evil counselors correspond with the Protectorate ministers, they also recall World, Flesh, and Devil. Avarice is chief among the evil counselors, not because he most nearly resembles the historical figure of the Protector but because avarice is the root evil, the source of corrupted power. Nor are his struggles to obtain mastery over his peers (I.iii) biographically significant; Vices always behave so in morality drama. Seizure of the monasteries is an instance of covetousness, no different in kind from enclosure of land. Avarice embraces all the shystering tricks of escheats, forfeitures, petty fees (ll. 99–102). The evil courtiers aim to have "good*es,* land*es* & plate" of all the properties they encroach upon, "castels & Townes in every shier," "pastures for shepe" (ll. 295–309). Their monopolistic practices run up the price of "corn & cattall, / wull, shepe, / wood, lead, tinne, Iron, & other metall," even though these commodities are in abundant supply (ll. 667–672). Oppression boasts of his numerous livings: "Feith, if I lust, I maie were miters fowr or five: / I have so many haulf bisshoprikes at the least" (ll. 781–782). Avarice applies his expertise in usury and perjury to ecclesiastical court, to bribes in the awarding of church offices, and to "selling of benefices" (l. 861). He has embezzled chantries and charities and has otherwise accumulated "Church good*es*, scraped upp w*i*thout a law" (l. 868). He takes a wealthy benefice to himself and appoints as curate "a bare clerk" named "Sir John Lack Latten," a personal friend who is obviously unqualified (l. 960). Supposed moral indignation against tolls such as annates and Peter's Pence are no more than a rationalization for appropriation. All the familiar Protestant cries of simony, usury, and absenteeism explain, not the need for true reform, but the excuse for revolution.

Some of the evil counselors' abuses refer more explicitly to the reign of Edward VI. The Vices connive in fraudulent exporting of strategic materials like "grain, bell meatall, tinne and lead / Conveighd owt by crekes whan Respublica was in bed," thus defrauding the king of his customs rights (ll. 878–879). Several acts under Edward VI expressly forbade export or import "in small crekes" of merchandise, including bell metal, "the subsidy aforesaid not payed." [6] People complains bitterly about devaluation of money and coinage in brass rather than silver (ll. 1081–1084); Henry VIII had seriously debased the coinage before, and Northumberland's government was forced to resort in June 1551 to calling in the coinage and setting its own advantageous value on the new specie. In the same year the government cut down the woods of the see of London and appropriated the demesnes of Winchester and Durham; People laments, "Thei have all the woodes throughout the realm destroyed" (l. 1093). [7]

Even here, however, the generic allegory usefully avoids too close an identification with Somerset and Northumberland. The Protectorate ministers were behind the laws to curtail export smuggling and were not themselves involved in the operations, and all English administrations had been officially opposed to enclosure since Henry VIII's time. [8] Famine was more responsible for rising food prices than the disgruntled People will admit. Protected by allegory, the author can safely inveigh against enclo-

6. *Ibid.*, p. 67, n. 837.
7. *Ibid.*, p. xxv.
8. Kate L. Gregg, *Thomas Dekker: A Study in Economic and Social Backgrounds* (Univ. of Washington, 1924), pp. 75–77.

sure or smuggling under the labels of Avarice and Oppression. The administration is blamed by implication for what it could scarcely prevent, together with what it may have mismanaged or deliberately abused.

The author's definition of true reform offers nothing new, except in its view of what Protestantism is. He would restore to the church its wealth and position and allow it to clean house in orderly fashion. Respublica can unabashedly endorse "Reformacion, good holsome lawes to make" (l. 528), both in church and state. The author rejects out of hand the Protestant argument that a wealthy church is subject to great temptations and that the enormities of the pre-Reformation church demanded a systematic alteration of structure. He does not argue merely that Protestants are equally guilty with some worldly Catholics but that the power-seeking impulse is the essence of Protestantism. He wants to see the monasteries restored. By not discussing orders of friars, pardoners, and the like, the author refuses to concede any substantive defects in the church of Henry VII. His appeal for return is considerably more conservative than that of Heywood or other Catholic humanists. This deepening conservatism in a time of defensive action is understandable enough, and it mirrors the change in Thomas More's own attitude toward the Protestant "menace." The author of *Respublica* is unwilling to attempt Heywood's rare balance of mind in the late *Spider and the Fly* (1556), where it is insisted that Catholics have to share the blame for the fallen state of the church.

Politically, then, *Respublica* is an attack not only on the counselors of Edward's reign but also on the very system of yielding power to men of their class. Even their advice is dangerous. Strong, unquestioned single rule can provide the only safeguard. The queen-figure of Act V of *Respublica* is no mere umpire who listens to all estates and decides impartially on the basis of this information. The nobility or merchants are represented by no abstractions in the closing scenes. Nemesis (Mary), who is herself a goddess, listens only to the voice of divine guidance. The insistence on the divine right of kings is thus a political deterrent to the theory of rule by human counsel. In more tactful times, Mary's sister Elizabeth was to cultivate this myth as a weapon in her struggle against powerful advisers.

Respublica does of course have one virtuous friend representing humanity during her tribulations and eventual triumph, but People does not qualify as an adviser. His numerous complaints reach Mary's ears, and in the final scene he is awarded custody of Insolence and Oppression. Nevertheless, he is no lower-class spokesman invited to participate in a thorough redistribution of political responsibility. People is as powerless as Respublica herself. Decisions must be made for him. The humor directed toward him is condescending; he speaks in homely fashion for "we ignoram people," splitting his tongue on highfalutin words like *imagination* ("madge mason," l. 656). He has the countryman's dislike of courtly behavior, and it is his ingenuous viewpoint that the author usually employs for satire of social climbing. The evil counselors appear especially unattractive in their contempt for People. By contrast, his simple, gnomic wisdom commands respect. The dramatic portrait skillfully catches Mary's own attitude toward the commons, of paternalistic (or maternalistic) fondness, of desire for popularity achieved through good works of charity like those of her mother Katharine, of endearing concern for a populace that is supposed to know its place and respond with affectionate loyalty to a strong, compassionate leadership. The author clearly blames the peasant uprising of 1549 on what he takes to be the Protector's vindictive approach to rural problems (l. 744) and predicts agricultural peace under Mary's benevolent single rule. For all Respublica's repeated insistence on listening to People (ll. 1105–1108), however, the author is less democratic than the earlier Catholic humanists. Nemesis' insistence that People stand close by her side (ll. 1819–1924) in equal status with the counselors (which comically embarrasses People, like a menial servant invited to a banquet) signifies not the elevation of commons to political power but the demotion of the counselors.

In chastising "these your late governoures" (l. 1825) who have betrayed Respublica, Nemesis does not bid Respublica to find new counsel. Instead, Nemesis herself undertakes the correction of abuses with the advice of four sisters, Mercy, Truth, Justice, and Peace. These abstractions are spiritual entities, unlike the four debased social types whom they have replaced and to whom they correspond in balanced antithesis of good versus evil. A divine government replaces an earthly one, and Nemesis or Mary is its new head. All five figures are aspects of Mary, for the debate between the sisters urging rigor and those urging clemency has as its source the Parliament of Heaven of early moralities like *The Castle of Perseverance*. With attributes of God himself, Mary exhibits a duality of punishment and forgiveness (a commonplace for Elizabeth in later years). All of the abstractions here are female, in contrast with the male villains of Edward's reign. As a woman, Mary is slow to punish; Mercy appears first, urging infinite compassion but warning that vengeance is in store for the recalcitrant. The author is intent upon justifying the queen's belated moves against her more dangerous enemies. Yet his presentation of the debate is not only a justification; it is also a plea for temperance. Adulation is spared, since he has taken less booty than his fellows. Peace urges accommodation so that brother can live once again with brother.

All agree, however, that no accommodation can be allowed on the question of restitution. Avarice must pay back all: "There is no remedie, powre itt owt in my Lappe" (l. 1737). Since "only Avarice made us all to fall" (l. 1837), it is only just that each sinner return all that he has illegally obtained:

> NEMESIS
> . . . People, take this felowe . . .
> That he maie be pressed as men doo press a spounge.
> that he maie droppe ought, tevery man his lotte,
> to the utmoost ferthing that he hath falslie gotte.
>   (ll. 1903–1906)

Nemesis' divine commission authorizes her, furthermore, to exact penance "in all eastates" (l. 1791), not merely in the corrupted governors of the realm. This sweeping promise, together with a specific endorsement of the hospitable mission of the older religion—when "they had their Liv*inges,* men were both fedde and cladde" (l. 1070)—points to a sizable renovation of religious houses. Mary did in fact attempt such renovation among the friars of Greenwich and in other places, willingly foregoing the profits of many revenues that her father had enjoyed and spent. Doing so cost more than her government could afford; her dream of renewed wealth for the church was as financially impossible as it was emotionally unacceptable to the majority of her people. And although Mary stood ready to impoverish herself for the church, her courtiers who held church lands were not. What seemed so easy and so just in the concluding scenes of *Respublica* proved out of the question.

Queen Mary's reign naturally witnessed a number of other pro-Catholic plays. An adapted revival was the old morality *Impatient Poverty,* with its emphasis on the virtues of a properly administered penance. Others are

now lost, such as *Anglia Deformata and Anglia Restituta,* performed at
Trinity College, Cambridge, and probably the morality *Genus Huma-
num,* performed at court in 1553 or 1554.[9] For the most part, however, the
queen preferred not to confront her problems too intensely in dramatic
form. Increasingly the revels at court turned to entertainments and elaborate masques, as in the latter part of Henry VIII's reign. When an actual
play was chosen, it was apt to be Plautine comedy.

The fact that Nicholas Udall's *Ralph Roister Doister* stresses in its
Prologue the value of mirthful recreation may be no political coincidence.
Formerly assigned to Udall's Eton period around 1538,[10] the play is now
generally thought to have been composed shortly before the appearance in
January 1554 (or perhaps 1553) of the third edition of Thomas Wilson's
The Rule of Reason, containing *The Art of Logic,* which quotes the
mistakenly pointed letter of III.iv as Udall's.[11] Wilson, an old pupil of
Udall's and likely to have been in touch with Udall's latest work, does not
use the letter in earlier editions of 1550–1552. The closing prayer in *Roister
Doister* to the queen is probably not much help in dating the play, since

9. Gertrude Sibley, *The Lost Plays and Masques: 1500–1642* (Ithaca, 1933), p. 8;
G. C. Moore Smith, *College Plays Performed in the University of Cambridge*
(Cambridge, Eng., 1923), p. 107. See also Albert Feuillerat, "Performance of a
Tragedy at New College, Oxford, in the Time of Queen Mary," *MLR,* IX (1914),
96–97.

10. See, for example, Ewald Flügel, "Nicholas Udall: Critical Essay," in *Representative English Comedies,* ed. C. M. Gayley (New York, 1903), I, 89–104; and
Muriel C. Bradbrook, *The Growth and Structure of Elizabethan Comedy* (London,
1955), p. 37.

11. John W. Hales, "The Date of the First English Comedy," *Englische Studien,*
XVIII (1893), 408–421; E. K. Chambers, *The Mediaeval Stage* (Oxford, 1903), II,
215–216; and A. W. Reed, "Nicholas Udall and Thomas Wilson," *RES,* I (1925),
275–283. The date of the third edition of *The Rule of Reason* is January "1553"; the
new style of dating (which would indicate 1553 instead of 1554) is conceivable here,
especially in a printed book, despite the custom of employing the legal calendar in
legal and religious documents. See William L. Edgerton, "The Date of *Roister
Doister,*" *PQ,* XLIV (1965), 555–560, who argues for a date of composition in late
1552. *A Pore Helpe* has been shown to be of little value in dating Udall's play; see
Cathleen H. Wheat, "*A Pore Helpe, Ralph Roister Doister,* and *Thre Lawes,*" *PQ,*
XXVIII (1949), 312–319, who confutes T. W. Baldwin and M. Channing Linthicum,
"The Date of *Ralph Roister Doister,*" *PQ,* VI (1927), 379–395, and M. Channing
Linthicum, "*A Pore Helpe* and Its Printers," *The Library,* 4th ser., IX (1928),
169–183.

epilogues of this sort were frequently updated for printing.[12] Queen Mary's fondness for Udall is well established, despite his earlier occasional service to Protestantism. He has been suggested as the author of *Respublica*. He composed a court masque for Mary in 1555, now lost. Mary took part with Udall in a translation of a paraphrase of the Gospel of St. John in 1549.[13] In any case he had been close to the court ever since 1541, writing under the patronage of various noblemen after his dismissal from Eton. Under these circumstances it appears most likely that Udall wrote *Roister Doister* for the entertainment of Mary, shortly before or after her coronation, to be performed by choristers rather than public-school boys. The actors may have been the boys of Bishop Gardiner's school at Southwark, engaging in a full ecclesiastical revel celebrating the Lord of Misrule.[14] Appropriately, Christian Custance's story of feminine courage, charity, and firm maternalism is calculated to warm Mary's heart. Although Christian Custance is no allegorized alter ego for Mary, she defends a system of values that Mary had cherished from the beginning of her Catholic and conservative childhood.

Roister Doister's Prologue promotes "mirth with modestie" (l. 2),[15] defending the restorative function of recreation and pointing to classical authority for proof of this truism. The reference to "mysteries and forewarnings" (l. 18) in Plautus and Terence does suggest, moreover, a typical Renaissance desire to find something didactic in comic writing. Part of that useful lesson is a satire against boasting. Equally valuable is

12. Cf. William Peery, "The Prayer for the Queen in *Roister Doister*," *UTSE*, XXVII (1948), 222–233.

13. Prescott, *Mary Tudor*, p. 98.

14. A. W. Plumstead, "Satirical Parody in *Roister Doister*: A Reinterpretation," *SP*, LX (1963), 141–154. Edgerton, "The Date of *Roister Doister*," *PQ*, XLIV (1965), 555–560, overstresses the Protestant aspect of Udall's career, especially around 1552–1553. Even if written in 1552, *Roister Doister* could scarcely have been presented before Edward VI's Protestant court. The burlesque of the Burial for the Dead is too loving and familiar, not satirical enough for Edwardian drama.

15. Act, scene, and line references in *Roister Doister* are to *Elizabethan and Stuart Plays*, ed. C. R. Baskervill *et al.* (New York, 1934). In the interests of textual consistency, however, I have used old spelling for all quotations in this paper. In using old spelling I have silently substituted *i* for *j*, *v* for *w*, *i* for *y*, and similar purely scribal vagaries. I have also suppressed some final *e*'s that appear to be little more than scribal flourishes.

the positive image of Christian Custance, compared point by point with Roister Doister throughout the play. This positive ideal heroine has no Plautine counterpart in the *Eunuchus* or elsewhere. Christian Custance is Udall's most significant "English" contribution to his neoclassic sources, although she is usually overshadowed by the composite vice-parasite figure of Matthew Merrygreek.

The climactic battle between Christian Custance and Ralph Roister is essentially a battle of the sexes, reminiscent of the division between female virtue and male vice in *Respublica*. Although Christian is assisted by one boy servant, Tom Truepenny, her household is predominantly female: Madge Mumblecrust, Tibet Talkapace, Annot Alyface. Ralph Roister's forces, on the other hand, include Dobinet Doughty, Harpax, "two drummes with their ensignes," the two-faced Merrygreek, and at various times musicians and a Scrivener. The caricatured names emphasize the distinction between pert "talkapace" maidservants and "daughty," brusque young men. Ralph Roister is himself a lampoon of male roistering, engaging in all the noisy bravado that so annoyed the ladies in *Respublica*. He is a ruffler, a disturber of the peace, divisive and importunate, crass. The maids live in quiet, gay harmony, love their mistress, and are inspired by her bravery, which is so lacking in flamboyance.

The basic contrast between Christian and Roister Doister is in the management of their respective households. Roister Doister bullies his servants, sends them on endless rounds of senseless errands, issues conflicting orders. As Dobinet Doughty mimics his master in exasperation,

> "Go bear me this token!" "Carrie me this letter!"
> Now, "This is the best way"; now, "That way is better!"
> (II.i.9–10)

He is a bad disciplinarian and earns as reward the scarcely concealed contempt of his servants. They scoff at his wooing and complain of the long, late hours so potentially injurious to the health of a schoolboy chorister: " 'Up before day, sirs, I charge you, an hour or twain!' " Later, "Then up to our lute at midnight, twangledom twang" (II.i.11–20). They object to his use of profanity and characterize him as setting the servants to spy on one another in constant fear of treachery: " 'Nay, see, I beseech you, if my most trustie page / Go not now about to hinder my mariage' " (II.i.15–16). Roister Doister manages to create dissension even in Christian's household. He talks Madge into arguing his case before her mistress, for which Madge is enjoined to bring no more letters (I.v), and he soon has Tibet, Annot, and Tom bickering among themselves for the privilege of bearing a token and a ring to Christian (II.iv). These shallow ruses merely give Christian an opportunity to display a patient, warm, and somewhat condescending control over her innocent helpers.

Tibet and the rest are indeed much like the ingenuous People of *Respublica*. They want to please their mistress, but they require detailed, repeated instructions and a good deal of forbearance. The mistress is the wary one, sensing an intruder in Roister Doister when the servants fall for his schemes. To the pathetic Madge, who professes she would take a gay, rich husband "and I were you," Christian good-humoredly replies, "In good sooth, Madge, e'en so would I, if I were thou" (I.v.18). The touch is both superior and affectionate. Christian is not fazed by promises of wealth; anyway, she knows Roister Doister's splendor to be all show: "Perchance, lack of a pint when it shall be all told" (I.v.16). Her warnings about the token and ring of Roister Doister are kindly yet stern; she questions her childlike helpers and comes to the sensible conclusion that they erred through simpleness rather than malice. She dismisses the offense with a warning and a moral tag: "I shall make all girles by you twain to beware. . . . Good wenches would not so ramp abrode idelly, / But keep within doores, and plie their work earnestly" (II.iv.23–30). In its positive aspect the play is a courtesy book for young women rather than for scholars.

Udall's careful attention to the disciplinary relationships of this feminine household seems more apt for Mary's entourage than for the juvenile monasticism of Eton. Christian is thoroughly complex and admirable as a character. She is blessed with a sanity that dismisses Roister Doister's pranks lightly: "This will prove some foolish matter in the end" (II.iv.44). Her view of love is a sane one that allows her to sleep at night (III.ii.37). She has so little curiosity about Roister Doister's importunate letter that she doesn't even bother to open it. She even welcomes the reading of it as amusing "sport," and she returns honest answers to his bluster with no attempt to humiliate. She dismisses Roister Doister and Merrygreek with the forbearing "No, God be with you both, and seek no more to me" (III.iv.85). She wishes only to avoid strife.

At the same time she is very much a woman, loyal to her betrothed

Gawin Goodluck, and on the verge of tears when the seemingly minor irritation of Roister Doister's courtship threatens to blacken her reputation before the world and Gawin. The lesson of prudence in maintaining appearances becomes a serious Christian duty:

> O Lord! how necessarie it is now of dayes
> That eche bodie live uprightly all maner wayes;
> For lette never so little a gappe be open,
> And be sure of this—the worst shall be spoken.
>
> (V.iii.1–4)

Christian is a heroine protected by the same Providence that guarded Mary Magdalene, Susanna, and Queen Hester—a figure associated in court drama with Mary's mother, Katharine. The daily world, dominated by men who go "jetting up and down" with their "lustie bragge" (III.iii.121, 123), is a world of slander and treachery, in which women must move cautiously. Yet God will protect them. Christian's victory over Roister Doister is therefore not one of Amazonian "maistry"—for Christian is loyally subservient to Gawin's proper masculine authority—but an assertion of the feminine values of concord, domesticity, and forbearance. The play argues for precisely the sort of firm maternalism advocated in *Respublica*. The harmless ending of a banquet suggests the social reconciliation that Mary so earnestly desired.

Religious motifs in *Roister Doister* reinforce the hypothesis of courtly auspices under Mary. The celebrated parody of the Catholic service for the dead (III.iii) would have sat strangely with the Protestant advisers of Edward VI who saw *Jacob and Esau*. The tone is light and friendly; the satire is directed not at the service itself but at the comic discrepancy between Roister Doister's ineffectual melancholy and the seriousness of *"Requiem aeternam."* The technique is that of Skelton's "Philip Sparrow," with its tradition of the medieval Venus mass or mass of the birds. The voices of the choristers are lovingly familiar. The mock-heroic rite follows Catholic liturgy rather closely, progressing from the visitation of the sick to the vespers for the dead (*"Placebo dilexi"*), matins (*"Dirige"*), mass (*"Requiem aeternam"*), and burial service (*"In Paradisum"*).[16] There are

---

16. Edwin S. Miller, "Roister Doister's 'Funeralls,'" *SP*, XLIII (1946), 42–58, and William L. Edgerton, "The Apostasy of Nicholas Udall," *N&Q*, CXCV (1950), 223–226.

no malapropisms, as in John Bale's savage lampoon of excommunication in *King John,* no duckings and crossings, no blasphemies or references to the pope.

Neoclassicism, necessarily unexplored in this analysis, explains much of what is brilliant in *Roister Doister.* The English elements of the play do not deal with political questions as such. Nevertheless, there is reason to suppose that the play was considerably influenced by Udall's relationship to Queen Mary. With monarchs looking more and more sharply at the activities of their dramatists, royal taste (conditioned by royal political views) was bound to affect the course of dramatic history. This hypothesis perhaps strengthens the argument that Udall also wrote *Respublica* and *Jack Juggler,* as has been proposed.[17]

No play expresses better than *Jack Juggler* (*c.* 1554)[18] the sense in which Plautine comedy could attempt escape from the weight of responsibility. The playwright, aware that his innocent fun may be forced into topical meaning and his disclaimers cynically ignored, nevertheless offers an antidote to fear and the divisive emotions of politics. He has consciously avoided hidden, serious meaning:

> for higher things endite
> In no wise he wold, for yet the time is so quesie
> That he that speakith best, is lest thank worthie.
>
> (ll. 66–68)[19]

The old comedy can be enjoyed for its own sake. Of course no author in the Tudor period can refuse to pay lip service to the dogma of moral usefulness, and the ancient writers accordingly furnish "mutch wisdom & teach prudent pollecie" (l. 54). Still, this wisdom is not "worth an oyster

17. W. H. Williams, "The Date and Authorship of *Jacke Jugeler,*" *MLR,* VII (1912), 289–295; W. H. Williams, ed., *Jacke Jugeler* (Cambridge, Eng., 1914), pp. vii–xvii; and Leonard A. Magnus, ed., *Respublica,* EETS Extra Series No. 94 (London, 1905), pp. xii–xxii.

18. On date, see Alois L. Brandl, ed., *Quellen des weltlichen Dramas in England vor Shakespeare* (Strassburg, 1898), p. lxxi, and Chambers, *Mediaeval Stage,* II, 457–458. The printed book of *Jack Juggler* was evidently in existence before the S. R. entry of 1562; see W. W. Greg, "Some Notes on the Stationers' Registers," *The Library,* 4th ser., VII (1926), 376–386.

19. Line references and text of *Jack Juggler* are from the Malone Society Reprints edition, prepared by Eunice L. Smart and W. W. Greg (Oxford, 1933).

shel / Except percace it shall fortune too make you laugh well" (ll. 62–63). The essence of *Jack Juggler* is a trifle:

> Therfore, sith nothing but trifles may be had
> You shall hear a thing that onlie shal make you merie and glad
> And such a trifling matter as when it shalbe done
> You may report and say ye have heard nothing at all.
>
> (ll. 69–72)

Comedy of relaxation had precedents both in Old Comedy and in English drama, especially in *Thersites* and *Gammer Gurton's Needle* (perhaps as early as 1550). Yet these plays were intended for public school or university, where they could take advantage of the ivory tower. The defense of pleasure is unusually vociferous in *Jack Juggler* because it appears against a political background in which "the time is so quesie." The playwright looks upon boys' drama as the last refuge of innocence, in which political considerations are both a comfort-killing intrusion and an artistic indecorum: "For this maker shewed us that such maner things / Doo never well besime litle boyes handelings" (ll. 76–77). Plays like *Jacob and Esau,* the Prologue implies, force upon the boys a political maturity ill-suited to their specialized talents. Why should choristers plead like Calvinists? The tradition of "pure" boys' drama has been all but forgotten in the grimness of a Reformation court.

The attitude of courtly irresponsibility, akin to the spirit of the "Cavalier," appears throughout the play of *Jack Juggler.* The plot is one of mistaken identities, engineered by the fun-loving Jack Juggler in "as mad a pastime this night / As you saw this seven yers" (a span of time comparable to the five or six years of Protestant corruption bewailed in *Respublica*), "as propre a toy / As ever you saw played of a boy" (ll. 105–107). Jack's victim is Jenkin Careaway, whose name connotes his comic irresponsibility. Jenkin has dawdled in conveying a message to his mistress in order that he might play at dice with the "bucklers" of London; he has lost all his money and stolen the apples of a street vendor. For these acts, treated as heinous social problems in the moral drama of the period (such as *Impatient Poverty* or *Lusty Juventus*), Jenkin is never punished. His master reprimands him for dilatoriness, not for theft, and Jack's viewpoint is one of amusement at Jenkin's discomfiture.

If the play suggests any relevance to current social norms, the suggestion is of a modest courtly hedonism. Some details are not evident in the source play, Plautus' *Amphitruo*. Jenkin's master and mistress enjoy a life of idle pleasure, dining and dancing, kissing "gentilwomen tow or three" (l. 261). In a tale to beguile his mistress that Jenkin concocts out of the events of his daily life, he speaks of "Gorges damies of the corte and galaunts also / With doctours' and other rufflers mo" (ll. 272–273). Later, Jenkin reconstructs the day's activities of himself and master:

> For went not I with my maister to day
> Erelie in the morning to the Tenis play?
> At noon while my maister at his dinner sate
> Played not I at Dice at the gentilmans gate
> Did not I wait on my maister too supperward
>
> (ll. 573–577)

The mistress, who is "As denty and nice as an halpeny worth of silver spoons / but vengable melancolie in the aftir noons" (ll. 221–222), longs for more social activity. Jenkin supposes she will not be unwilling to hear of a would-be gentleman caller who desires to send love tokens and make a visit in the master's absence. None of these dissipations is viewed with moral revulsion in the play nor merits retribution.

Jack Juggler, named for his protean skill in intrigue, is the moving spirit of harmless disrespect for authority. He sets servant against master, antagonizes husband and wife, and delays the evening meal, all for the pleasure of viewing "this sport" (l. 873) that leads ultimately to a restoration of harmony. All sympathy rests with the irresponsible youth of both Jack and Jenkin. Much of this is of course Plautine; but the applicability to Catholic courtly society, wearied of Protestant sobriety, is explicit and new.

Protestant morality in its turn found this view intolerable and asserted its opinion in a later postscript to *Jack Juggler*. An unidentified spokesman follows Jenkin Careaway on stage (l. 1143) to deliver a conventional moral ending at once so jarring in tone and so simply irrelevant that it is surely an Elizabethan addition for publication in 1564. The Epilogue could not be the work of the playwright who has so heatedly denied topical meaning, for the Epilogue openly indulges in allegorical sleuthing. Rejoicing that "no tale can be told / But that sum English may be piked therof out" (ll. 1145–1146), the Epilogue deplores "the fashion of the world now a dayes" in which innocents are deluded and "shamefullie abused" to their "gret harm"—as if Jenkin were innocent or had suffered any serious punishment. The most outrageous abuse is that men are made "To belive and say the moune is made of agrene chese" (l. 1155), presumably allegorizing Jenkin's hapless loss of identity into Catholic thought-control. As B. J. Whiting observes, the reader is alarmed to discover that *Jack Juggler* has suddenly become a satire on transubstantiation.[20] "Darest thou affirm to me / That which was never syne nor hereafter shalbe / That on man may have too bodies & two faces / And that one man at on time may be in two placis" (ll. 899–902). Ironically, an Elizabethan publisher has foisted this retrospective interpretation on a play that urgently pleads for a courtly drama innocent of political motive. Catholic entertainment becomes Calvinist polemic. By the early 1560's English society had sufficiently recovered its senses to know that plays must omit no opportunity, however strained, to castigate "Force, strength, power, & colorable subtlete" which "Doth oppress, debare, overcum and defeat right" (ll. 1158–1159). Jenkin Careaway has been somehow transformed into a hero from Foxe's *Book of Martyrs*. The struggle for political control of drama as an organ of religious settlement had not yet ended.

20. Bartlett J. Whiting, *Proverbs in the Earlier English Drama* (Cambridge, Mass., 1938), pp. 198–201. For an untenable autobiographical interpretation see Williams, "Authorship of *Jacke Jugeler*," *MLR*, VII, 289–295, and Williams, ed., *Jacke Jugeler*, pp. x–xvi. Williams proposes that Udall alludes to his alleged robbing of silver plate in 1542 and here insinuates that he was forced to confess a crime not committed.

The Comic Accomplice in Elizabethan Revenge Tragedy

DOUGLAS COLE

THE ELIZABETHAN PLAYWRIGHTS, like their medieval forebears, characteristically wove into the texture of their work both the sublime and the ridiculous, the awesome and the ludicrous, the tragic and the comic. Elizabethan audiences seem not only to have tolerated such extremes within a given play but to have expected them; hence, even Polonius' descriptive category of "tragical-comical-historical-pastoral" is far less a caricature than it sounds. In the case of revenge tragedy, a form so closely related to Senecan models of relentless solemnity and gore, one is perhaps surprised but ultimately not shocked to find that here, too, the Elizabethan dramatist, particularly if he were writing for the public stage, did not hesitate to introduce a decidedly un-Senecan note of comedy. Such comic elements may take several shapes: in some instances a conventional stock figure will be borrowed from the comic genre itself—a braggart warrior, a jealous husband, a foppish would-be lover; in others such figures may be joined in a subordinate line of farcical action to counterpoint the more grimly sensational revenge plot; in still others the comedy may inhere only in the curiously disarming effects of posing a villain in the theatrical stance of the old morality Vice—making him an artful gamester whose double-dealing ingenuity, inhuman relish for destruction, and witty intimacy with the audience provoke laughter in spite of his evil.[1]

1. See Bernard Spivack's treatment of this tradition, *Shakespeare and the Allegory of Evil* (New York, 1958), especially pp. 337–386.

No matter what shape the comedy may take, however, its bloody context inevitably transforms it into an experience that is somehow grotesque and thus, in theory at least, enables a playwright to link such an experience to the over-all emotional tone of his revenge play. An examination of the ways in which the figure of the comic accomplice is manipulated in some early revenge plays will reveal some of the problems associated with integrating comic effects within revenge tragedy and will also illustrate the tendency of comic functions in this genre to move from parody to satire, from a confrontation with style and method to a confrontation with human weakness, folly, and vice.

Kyd, as usual, provides us with a starting point. His archvillain in *The Spanish Tragedy,* Lorenzo, cunningly contrives to do away with two servants, Pedringano and Serberine, who have helped him to murder Horatio. Though neither servant is conceived as a stock comic figure, Pedringano is maneuvered into a situation that becomes laughably ironic. Commissioned by Lorenzo to kill Serberine, and assured that he will be granted royal pardon, Pedringano confronts both judge and executioner with mocking audacity, not knowing that the box which he thinks contains his pardon is in fact empty. Kyd indulges in literal "gallows humor": Pedringano and the hangman exchange witty insults and conceits for some seventy lines, during which Pedringano's impudence is encouraged by the gestures of the boy who holds the box supposedly containing the pardon. The boy himself is enjoying the grim joke, for he knows already that the box is empty; in fact, the speech that Kyd earlier provides the boy has given the audience a preview of this bizarre scene:

. . . I must goe to *Pedringano,* and tell him his pardon is in this boxe, nay, I would haue sworne it, had I not seene the contrary. I cannot choose but smile to thinke, how the villain wil flout the gallowes, scorne the audience, and descant on the hangman, and al presuming of his pardon from hence. Wilt not be an odde iest, for me to stand and grace euery iest he makes, pointing my finger at this boxe: as who would say, mock on, heers thy warrant. Ist not a scuruie iest, that a man should iest himselfe to death. Alas poore *Pedringano,* I am in a sorte sorie for thee, but if I should be hanged with thee, I cannot weep.

(Spanish Tragedy [1592], III.v.1448–1458) [2]

2. Malone Society Reprint, ed. W. W. Greg and D. Nichol Smith (Oxford, 1948 [1949]).

Nor would Kyd's audience be likely to weep at a scene so deliberately constructed for accentuating comic ironies. But to what end? If Pedringano's removal were merely a further index of Lorenzo's Machiavellian policy, neither the boy's complicity nor the elaborated banter between hangman and murderer would be necessary. Kyd's tactics here show clearly his concern for underlining the grotesque irony, as well as the curious justice, of the whole scheme. Such a concern is clearly related to the later and far grimmer deception of the play within the play, which becomes the vehicle for Hieronimo's final revenge. It is related, too, to the staging of the lovers' rendezvous that ended in the murder of Horatio (who was both hanged—like Pedringano—and stabbed—like Lorenzo and Balthazar). There (II.iv) Horatio and Bel-imperia engage in lovers' banter, exchanging witty conceits about love as war and death, ignorant of the literal death that is about to strike. The shade of irony is blacker, the characters more noble and sympathetic. But the theatrical strategy is of the same sort that Kyd uses for his critical scenes throughout the play: he poses his victims within a situation that appears to them pleasurable, even triumphant, but which the audience sees as hideously contradicted in reality. The comic delusion of Pedringano is a parodic reflection of the delusions that beset the others: Horatio, who thinks he is approaching sexual "death" rather than his own execution; his mother, whose insane attack on the arbor marks her supposed revenge upon her son's murderers; Lorenzo and Balthazar, who believe they are but actors in the final tragedy. Even when Pedringano's death is considered only in relation to Lorenzo's craft, a further ironic delusion appears: instead of eliminating a potential threat to the secrecy of his crimes, Lorenzo contributes to his own undoing, for Pedringano's letter, written in prison and on his person at the gallows, becomes Hieronimo's final proof that Lorenzo is his son's killer. The Machiavellian policy that would effect security by liquidating accomplices leads directly to the undesired disclosure. Lorenzo's grim joke on Pedringano becomes a joke on himself.

Kyd's handling of the Pedringano episode thus fits fairly well into the play's texture of melodramatic intrigue and ironic cross-purposes; the character is much less important than the ironic situation; and indeed the same can be said of the treatment of Horatio and Bel-imperia. The play is punctuated by its three highly theatrical trap scenes: Horatio's death in the arbor, Pedringano's hanging, and Hieronimo's play. For each, Kyd has provided a careful prelude, so that the audience will be well prepared to appreciate the grotesque ironies of the verbal ambiguities and "playing" that take place in each case before the trap closes. The first and the last trap are the more horrible; the central one is offered as a kind of parodic interlude, muted in its emotional intensity to set off the more lurid tones of the others.

Kyd's Pedringano is an example of an accomplice who starts out as a servant who can be threatened and bribed into treacherous and murderous ways; he becomes comic only within the context of a contrived event. Marlowe's Ithamore in *The Jew of Malta,* on the other hand, is a grotesque caricature from first to last, but the dramatic world he inhabits and the master he serves also share that quality. As accomplice to Barabas he serves several functions, the foremost of which is to act as a dark and comically distorted mirror of his villainous master. This relationship begins even before he has a line to speak, when he stands on the slave-block in the market place, visibly leaner and more bedraggled than the more expensive slaves. Barabas buys him because he is cheaper and will be easier to keep up, and also because he needs one to "doe much villanie" (II, l. 898).[3] Barabas elaborates on the kind of service he has in mind in his famous autobiographical résumé of sadistic crimes ("As for my selfe, I walke abroad a nights / And kill sicke people groaning under walls . . ."). The young Turk takes his cue readily and replies in the Jew's own vein, so that Barabas can gloat:

> Why this is something: make account of me
> As of thy fellow; we are villaines both.
>
> (II, ll. 978–979)

What marks this new fellowship most of all is its farcically exaggerated character. The catalogue of crimes is ludicrous in itself, but the offhand way in which it is recited, the macabre delight behind the whole conception, draw the two together in what is less a sinister and threatening partnership than a diabolical comedy team; one almost looks forward to their antic evils. This effect is partly due to the dramaturgical image of the Vice that lies behind this sort of happy malignity,[4] and it is enhanced in

3. *The Works of Christopher Marlowe,* ed. C. F. Tucker Brooke (Oxford, 1910).

4. See Spivack, pp. 346–352. J. B. Steane, *Marlowe: A Critical Study* (Cambridge, Eng., 1964), pp. 166–203, explores several comic strands in the play.

the ensuing action of the play by both the ingenious vitality of the new team and the generally unsympathetic nature of the victims. Mathias and Lodowick are little more than stock rivals, and it is more fascinating to watch the way Barabas manipulates them into hostility than it is compelling to pity their destruction: Marlowe's pacing of the action and handling of asides lend that familiar hectic quality of farce that adds to the comic distancing. Ithamore's gusty laughter at the whole episode must necessarily hurt Abigail's feelings more than the audience's. In the case of the hypocritical friars, there is hardly reason for anyone's feelings to be stirred; their greed and envy provide the villains with the key to their destruction, in much the same way that the vices of Jonson's scavengers in *Volpone* make them ripe for gulling. Pathos intrudes only in the case of Abigail, that figure of virtue and ordinary human feelings so strangely out of place in Marlowe's Malta. The quality of Barabas' deceptions becomes increasingly bizarre in the company of Ithamore. The Jew finds in the Turk not only a handy accomplice but also an appreciative audience for his secret crimes; their mutual gloating reinforces the pleasures of villainy. By this time, of course, revenge is only a convenient rationalization for the Jew's stratagems, which are actually ends in themselves. Ithamore's giddy admiration of Barabas' tactics serves to accentuate this shift in focus.

It has often been pointed out how the abstract and absolute quality of Barabas' evil is heightened when he disowns Abigail and "adopts" Ithamore as his new heir. But Marlowe does not permit even the Jew's alter ego to find a genuine place in Barabas' affections. Almost at the very moment that he makes this gesture, Barabas recoils in his characteristically deceitful way: "Here take my keyes," he offers in one breath, and in the next half-line retracts: "I'le giue 'em thee anon." "Goe buy thee garments," runs the echo, followed swiftly by "But first goe fetch me in the pot of Rice." When Ithamore dashes out, it becomes clear that Barabas' offer is only a ruse:

> Thus euery villaine ambles after wealth
> Although he ne're be richer then in hope:
> But, hush't.
>
> (III, ll. 1354–1356)

Marlowe is underlining not only the Jew's double-dealing but, more importantly, the radical theme of the play: the cynical accent on greed as the basic motivation of all men, or, as the Bashaw puts it in the next scene, "The wind that bloweth all the world besides, / Desire of gold." In terms of plot, this confidence of the Jew's also looks forward to the removal of his comic accomplice. Even before Ithamore provides Barabas with a reason for enmity by his blackmail project, the Jew has made his inner decision. As Ithamore dashes off with the poisoned porridge to the convent, he says, "Pay me my wages for my worke is done." Alone, Barabas comments, "Ile pay thee with a vengeance *Ithamore*."

The vengeance strikes in the latter half of the fourth act, which is devoted to the farcical seduction of Ithamore by the Courtesan and her associate thief, Pilia Borza, "a fellow . . . with a muschatoes like a Rauens wing, and a Dagger with a hilt like a warming-pan." Marlowe's grotesque exaggeration reaches its consciously ludicrous heights in these scenes, which include Ithamore's mock-lyric speech that parodies Marlowe's own "Passionate Shepherd" at the same time that it comically accents Ithamore's absurd delusions:

> Content, but we will leaue this paltry land,
> And saile from hence to *Greece*, to louely *Greece*,
> I'le be thy *Iason*, thou my golden Fleece;
> Where painted Carpets o're the meads are hurl'd,
> And *Bacchus* vineyards ore-spread the world:
> Where Woods and Forrests goe in goodly greene,
> I'le be *Adonis*, thou shalt be Loues Queene.
> The Meads, the Orchards, and the Primrose lanes,
> Instead of Sedge and Reed, beare Sugar Canes:
> Thou in those Grouves, by *Dis* aboue,
> Shalt liue with me and be my loue.
>
>   (IV, ll. 1806–1816)

The entire blackmail affair, as has been frequently remarked, operates as a parody of the political extortion that establishes the outer limits of the plot, and it reasserts the "desire-of-gold" motif. The comic accomplice thus becomes the center of a brief subplot in which he is both victim and would-be victimizer. Barabas is only momentarily embarrassed. He gets to use a disguise, a new kind of poison, and even feigns his own death before the incident is over, and the accomplice is no more. Afterwards, Marlowe swiftly expands the scope of the Jew's practice: Barabas moves from the small-time extortioners to the great ones, manipulating whole armies and governments in the ingenious way he had once exploited lovers, friars, pimps, and slaves. He graduates from the bowl of steaming porridge to the boiling cauldron but makes his inevitable mistake when he takes into his confidence a man less foolish and mechanical than was Ithamore.

The dramatic experience Marlowe gives us is totally different in kind from the one Kyd provides in *The Spanish Tragedy*. It depends basically on grotesque caricature and develops situations in order to allow the caricature to display itself most freely. The situation itself is not the central concern; unlike Kyd, who was interested more in accenting graphic horror and in turning ironic play into shocking deaths, Marlowe pitches his melodramatic extravagances at a zany angle in order to prompt an intellectual response. Marlowe's ironies have an edge to them which cuts in one direction: the revelation of greed masked in various modes of hypocrisy and exploitation. Jew, Turk, and Christian are all representatives of the same gross vice. In Ithamore it is naked and perhaps most "innocent"; in Barabas it is far less important and vital than the masquerade itself; in the Christians it is the most insidious because the least acknowledged. Though Ithamore may be an absurd parody of evil, the play in which he lives moves generally in the direction of satire.

It remains a curious fact, however, that we are less conscious of the satire, less aware of the biting edge of Marlowe's cynical humor, when the parodic element is allowed its greatest liberties. Ithamore's scenes with Barabas in the market place and with Bellamira and Pilia Borza are those with the least moral abrasion. The exaggeration here provides a maximum of comic distance, and despite all the vice on display there are no uncomfortable familiar recognitions. The caricature seems to take on a life of its own and for the time being severs its connections with the realities of deceit and hypocrisy upon which it was originally modeled. Not until the more normal characters come back into view is the satiric tension reestablished.

Closely related to Marlowe's Ithamore is the comic accomplice in Henry Chettle's *Tragedy of Hoffman,* Lorrique. That Chettle must have had Marlowe's play in mind is obvious not only from the near duplication of the Mathias and Lodowick episode, which even uses the identical names for the rivals, but also from the initial scene, which presents Lorrique's swift conversion from the service of Otho to that of the maniacal revenger Hoffman:

> HOFFMAN
> Were I perswaded that thou couldst shed teares,
> As doth the Egyptian serpents neere the Nile;
> If thou wouldst kisse and kill, imbrace and stabbe,
> Then thou shouldst liue, for my inuictiue braine
> Hath cast a glorious proiect of reuenge
> Euen as thou kneel'st, wilt thou turne villaine speake.
>
> LORRIQUE
> Oh sir when was I otherwise, from my creation nothing else, I was made of no other stuffe, villany is my onely patrimony: though I bee an irreligious slaue, yet I beare a religious name, though I want courage, yet in talke, I'le put them all downe. . . .
>
> (I.i.82–92) [5]

Lorrique is of course frantically arguing for his life, but after this speech he never betrays any remorse about his conversion, nor does he hesitate to assist with alacrity in the immediate execution of his true master. His confession near the end of the play is a patent exhibition to keep himself out of danger when he realizes that Hoffman's secrets are no longer safe. He is consistently a cleverer servant than Ithamore, but he ends up none the less as Hoffman's final victim.

Hoffman himself, though like Barabas a master of deception and a gloater over his destructive victories, does not have the cool-headed wit of Marlowe's villain. He is given to impassioned speeches of great emotional force, and it is clear that his mania for excessive revenge is more deep-seated a feeling than Barabas possesses. For him the true delight lies in the completion of revenge, not in the ingenious means contrived to effect it. Chettle conceives him as one driven by insane passion; not only his revenge but also his sudden lust for the mother of the murdered Otho illustrates the pattern. His speech is consistently elevated, metaphorical, self-dramatizing; he does not indulge in the swift alterations of kind assurances and villainous asides so characteristic of Barabas in his "working" moments. Hence, the relationship between his comic accomplice and

5. Malone Society Reprint, ed. Harold Jenkins (Oxford, 1950 [1951]).

himself is tuned differently. Lorrique becomes a fellow villain but not quite a mirror of Hoffman; he does not share his hates and savage feelings. He acts with equal energy and ingenuity, can counterfeit just as well, but has enough common sense about him to recognize the enormity of Hoffman's horrible plans and deeds. Though he lacks normal feelings about such things, he does not lack the insight that renders explicit the outlandish aspect behind them. As he confides sarcastically to the audience in the second act:

> . . . yet this *Clois* [Hoffman] is an honest villaine, ha's conscience in his killing of men: he kils none but his fathers enemies, and there issue, 'tis admirable, 'tis excellent, 'tis well 'tis meritorious, where? in heauen? no, hell.
>
> (II.iii.661–664)

Chettle, writing early in the seventeenth century, is apparently aware of the risks of putting such a ranting villain as Hoffman on stage at this point in the history of the revenge play, when Kyd's Hieronimo had already become the butt of mocking allusions and parody. That he is interested in the graphic scene of horror is clear from the opening of the play, where Hoffman's solitary vows of revenge are chanted to the accompaniment of thunder and lightning and where, hung before Hoffman's cave, is the dangling skeleton of his dead father. The gruesome execution of Otho by means of the burning crown is clearly in the same vein. The histrionics of such scenes are acknowledged in a way by a series of Hoffman's comments using the metaphor of the tragic performance:

> This but the prologue to the'nsuing play.
> The first step to reuenge, this seane is donne
> Father I offer thee thy murtherers sonne.
>
> (I.i.237–239)

> He was the prologue to a Tragedy,
> That if my destinies deny me not,
> Shall passe those of Thyestes, Tereus,
> Iocasta, or Duke Iasons iealous wife;
> So shut our stage vp, there is one act done
> Ended in *Othos* death; 'twas somewhat single;
> Ile fill the other fuller. . . .
>
> (I.iii.407–413)

Lorrique, now or neuer play thy part:
This Act is euen our Tragedies best hart.

(III.ii.1341–1342)

Such comments appear to be a way of putting the melodramatic excesses
into a plausible perspective; somehow the exaggeration is less likely to be
criticized if something in the play can point explicitly to the quality of
exaggeration itself, to rationalize its presence there. Lorrique's reaction to
Hoffman is in the same line: it points to the absurdity in the revenge, but
acts less as a moral judgment than as an aesthetic safety release. The
monstrosity, once acknowledged as such, can be tolerated more easily.
Ultimately, then, such a perspective on Hoffman allows Chettle to keep
him in the unrestrained vein without subjecting him to ridicule. The use
the dramatist makes of Hoffman's rival for power, Prince Jerome, indicates the same purpose. Jerome is a combination braggart warrior and
foolish simpleton, the shame of his father, a thorn to Hoffman, and
ultimately the victim of Lorrique's poison. He is the other major comic
figure in the play and serves, like Lorrique, to set Hoffman in superior
relief. When the Duke his father disinherits him in favor of the sounder
Hoffman (disguised as Otho), Jerome launches into a revenge vow that
parodies the earlier ones by Hoffman:

> Well, sword come forth, and courage enter in,
> Brest breake with griefe; yet hold to be reueng'd:
> Follow me *Stilt;* widdowes vnborne shall weepe,
> And beardlesse boyes with armour on their backes
> Shall beare vs out, *Stilt* we will tread on stilts,
> Through the purple pauement of the court,
> Which shall bee, let me see, what shall it be?
> No court, but euen a caue of misery.
> Ther's an excellent speech *Stilt.* . . .

(II.i.514–522)

The parody, of course, works to the disadvantage of Jerome. He becomes
a foolish braggart-revenger who unconsciously mimics the grim words
and deeds of Hoffman himself. He is a comic figure who cannot quite
carry the burden of a Senecan passion.

I do not think that Chettle's efforts to accommodate his own indulgence
in exaggeration are ultimately very successful, but it is interesting to see

the experiment in operation. There is perhaps a similar program behind the eccentricities of John Marston's *Antonio's Revenge,* which is either a poor revenge tragedy or, as R. A. Foakes has suggested, a good parody exploiting the use of child actors to mock the old ranting styles of Kyd and Marlowe.[6] That the spirit of burlesque invades the play is undeniable; that it underlies the whole structure as a basic conception is less evident.

The weird tonalities of *Antonio's Revenge* stem in part from its position as a sequel to *Antonio and Mellida,* a free-wheeling romantic comedy stuffed with the stock comic figures so favored by the boy companies: witty maiden, parasite and flatterer, bombastic tyrant, foppish would-be man of fashion and of wit, braggart warrior. They are jumbled together in a world of folly and excess, which the critic Feliche can chide at nearly every turn. Burlesque is the predominant tactic employed in the presentation of the fools; but the spectacle is framed in Feliche's satiric perspective. The Induction to the play ends with a very tentative forecast of a second part, "which, if this obtaine gratious acceptance, meanes to try his fortune."[7] It seems dubious, however, that Marston had clearly in mind the kind of play he would eventually append, for the Induction also promises to Feliche greater scope and "more exact accomplishment in a second Part"—and Feliche is only a corpse in *Antonio's Revenge.* Several of the inflated comic characters of the first play are reduced to roles of minimal importance in the second, but the foppish fool, Balurdo, remains as a comic accomplice figure. A second comic accomplice is provided in the person of Gaspar Strotzo. The satiric commentator is replaced by a role more pertinent to the revenge theme: a Senecan Stoic. The serious dimension of the play resides in the interaction of the philosophical Stoic and the passionate revenger, Antonio. It begins as a fairly conventional Senecan debate between the man of reason and the man of passion but ends in a total rejection by the Stoic himself of the rational alternative. At the same time, Marston seems to be fascinated with the motif of madness that Kyd had used to such effect, and it is not altogether clear that this motif or the Stoic one is envisioned as burlesque. There are so many other Elizabethan plays, including several acted by boys, that exploit such

6. "John Marston's Fantastical Plays: *Antonio and Mellida* and *Antonio's Revenge,*" *PQ,* XLI (1962), 229–239.

7. *Antonio and Mellida and Antonio's Revenge,* ed. W. W. Greg, Malone Society Reprint (Oxford, 1921 [1922]).

conventions and mingle bombast with farce that one hesitates to justify such maneuvering as parody.

Gaspar Strotzo, however, is certainly a figure conjured up to reflect comically the bizarre execution of Kyd's Pedringano. Marston's archvillain, Piero, elaborates Lorenzo's trick on Pedringano with characteristic gusto. He persuades Strotzo to make a public confession of the murder of Andrugio (Piero's own crime), promising him that he will grant mercy after the revelation. But Piero goes right ahead with the execution, strangling the surprised Strotzo on the spot. Unlike Kyd, however, Marston is not interested in letting his gulled accomplice dramatize his confidence that everything will turn out all right. Marston does not exploit the ironies of the situation; he shows it only as another successful chapter in Piero's book of black deeds.

Piero himself has been colored black and Vice-like in this play. He opens it exulting in his hypocrisy and vengeance toward Andrugio and punctuates it regularly with choruses of gloating self-praise at each new villainy. "O rare!" is his favorite expletive in this context, foreshadowing Volpone's idiom of delight in artful exploitation. He takes the foolish Balurdo into his service because he can use unthinking tools but later sends him to prison for showing sympathy with a wronged courtier. Balurdo, whose inanities are sprinkled heavily throughout the play, finally becomes one of the revenging masquers who slay the wicked Piero.

Balurdo's presence at the assassination is no more disturbing an element than elsewhere. It accentuates the sadistic dimension of the scene, but then the sadism seems only another aspect of making the punishment fit Piero's crimes. Balurdo's earlier interactions with Antonio, where he presents a parody dream in response to Antonio's description of his foreboding nightmare, and where he enviously mocks Antonio disguised as a natural fool, seem less understandable. In each case he brings ridicule upon himself rather than Antonio, and this effect does not seem to fall in line with Foakes's suggestion that the melodramatic bombast is being consciously criticized. Balurdo distracts from the rant and passionate bombast in the play; he does not deflate it or underline it. He seems so extended an exaggeration himself that he cannot recognize exaggeration elsewhere. Like most other fops and wittols, he continually exposes himself rather than others. His role as an accomplice is perfunctory; and one is hard pressed to find a valid means to integrate him into the play, whether it be parody or not. The unfortunate truth may well be that his success as a character in *Antonio and Mellida* is the only justification for his appearance here. (This is certainly true of the songs which carry over from one play to the next.)

Marston's comic accomplices, then, represent in little the disjointed quality that most critics have detected in this play. Perhaps the best that can be said for them is that they serve a function analogous to Prince Jerome's in *Hoffman*. Their self-deflating absurdities may help to keep the audience from feeling that the highly wrought expressions of pathos by Antonio, Maria, and Pandulpho are less grave than they are meant to be. Some confirmation of this is offered by Marston's use of theatrical imagery, which is somewhat similar to Chettle's. Like Chettle, Marston wants to build exaggerated passions but make them plausible at the same time. Thus, Pandulpho's early rejection of hysterical grief is couched in these terms:

> Would'st haue me cry, run rauing vp & down,
> For my sons losse? would'st haue me turn rank mad,
> Or wring my face with mimick action;
> Stampe, curse, weepe, rage, & then my bosome strike?
> Away tis apish action, player-like.
>
> (I.ii.485–489)

Antonio later echoes the theme: "Madam, I will not swell like a Tragedian, in forced passion of affected straines" (II.ii.824–825). That the tactic can work successfully may not be evident in these plays, but in Hamlet's soliloquy on the Player's passion we have the finest witness that it can.

When he turned the revenge play into a tragicomic pattern in *The Malcontent,* Marston was able to do much better things with his own comic gifts. Written originally for a boys' company, it turns back to the basic strategy of *Antonio and Mellida* but pursues its themes with more energy and sophistication. The overinflated burlesque figures are on grand display once more, and in place of Feliche stands the railing Malevole. The foolish, flattering, lecherous world around him offers ample scope for his biting comments, and the tendency of satire to take over where parody leaves off is once more in view. In later revenge tragedy it appears in several forms. The dark cynicism of Webster's Flamineo in *The White Devil* is one familiar and important development; it is reflected weakly and awkwardly in the role of the pander Roxano in *The Bloody Banquet.* The satirist's perspective on corruption pervades that intricate dance of death, *The Revenger's Tragedy,* where Vindice, both revenger and accomplice, continually links the fantastic and grotesque world of the play with the world of the audience. The humor in these Jacobean plays tends always to grow more grim; the bizarre horrors projected by the need to outdo past variations on the revenge conventions are kept from becoming totally detached from an imitation of life by the satiric impulse to see the images, however unrestrained, as emblems for the passionate and destructive urges in mankind.

The parodistic impulse in the earlier plays is part of a dramatic tradition at least as old as the English mystery plays (one thinks immediately of the Wakefield Cain and his mocking boy Garcio, for instance). It is prompted largely by an awareness of exaggeration and extremes, but, unless used with a careful thematic control, it tends to distance the world of the play still further from the real world. In the revenge play, a genre so committed to displaying the experience of horror, the Elizabethan dramatist seems to have sensed a particular need for some kind of balancing perspective or mood. The parodic postures of comic accomplices dramatized by Kyd, Marlowe, Chettle, and Marston can be viewed as one kind of attempt to provide such a balance. But staged parody, like the revenge play itself, all too easily becomes the victim of its own indulgences in style and in spectacle. The audience is invited to appreciate the implausible for its own sake, to laugh at the momentary incongruity or to shudder at the extravagant cruelty without asking what connection there may be between them or between the play and reality. The twists and turns, surprises and shocks, become part of a game wholly distinct from life. The play becomes a thing wherein no consciences are caught because the action is no longer emblematic of the human condition. In such a context the comic accomplice is no more than a funny, stupid, unpitied victim, a supposedly pragmatic but invariably frustrated dupe of the major villain or revenger. Kyd and Marlowe make some attempts to link the careers of their accomplice figures with the ironic fate of their archvillains: the self-aggrandizing spirit who will play all tricks to prosper is caught short in the end. Both master and servant are made to die victims of their own craft. Chettle and Marston, less concerned with structural analogies, use parodic accomplices mainly to accentuate the superiority of their evil protagonists and to accommodate by explicit recognition the extravagant emotional outbursts of their revengers.

The satirical accomplice of the Jacobean revenge play, wiser and often more bitter than his Elizabethan counterpart, serves a broader purpose. He characteristically plays upon moral ironies besides illustrating theatrical ones, and thereby insists on the relevance of the play's action to the life of its audience. Yet even he seems circumscribed by his own focus on corruption. Open to the absurd follies of human pretensions and hypocrisies, aware always of the rottenness of things, he is somehow shut off from any sensitivity to the sadness of things. There is no counterpart in revenge tragedy for the kind of relation between the comic and the tragic that Shakespeare so magnificently orchestrated in *King Lear* by using the Fool. In the revenge plays the grandeur and the littleness in man, the passion and the insight, the pathos and the humor seem to stay in separate compartments, never to merge in the telling way that gives life to *Lear* and attests its validity as an image of life itself.

Critical Myths
and Chapman's Original
Bussy D'Ambois

ROBERT P. ADAMS

Is it possible, at this late date, that a Jacobean tragic masterpiece, close in time to *Hamlet* and *Othello,* one notable for its individualized treatment of justice versus tyranny and of sexual power as a tragic force, may be brought to light if we can clear away a mass of critical myth [1] or persistent fallacy that has densely obscured it? I suggest that the answer is yes and that the tragedy is George Chapman's original *Bussy D'Ambois.* Written between 1600 and 1604, first printed in 1607, this remarkable drama received its first modern scholarly edition only in 1964. [2]

1. Rather unoriginally, I here use "myth" to indicate "a usually traditional story of ostensibly historical events that serves . . . to explain a practice, belief, or natural phenomenon"; also as "a thing having only an imaginary or unverifiable existence," or "an ill-founded belief" (*Webster's Collegiate Dictionary*).

2. George Chapman, *Bussy D'Ambois* [1607], ed. Nicholas Brooke, Revels Plays (London, 1964); hereafter cited as "Brooke." *Bussy's* composition is dated 1604, with 1600–1604 limits, by S. Schoenbaum in his revised edition of Alfred Harbage, *Annals of English Drama 975–1700* (London, 1964), p. 86. Apart from Brooke, all other modern editions are of the 1641 *Bussy,* or are conflations of 1641 with 1607 (see Brooke, pp. lxxiv–lxxv). The 1641 text was most recently edited by R. J. Lordi (Lincoln, Neb.,

I do not propose to rehearse the marked differences between the 1607 play
(here called *Bussy I*) and the often edited posthumous 1641 version (here
called *Bussy II*), or who may be responsible for the second work.[3] The
customary view, to be sure, has been that the 1641 text is merely an
ordinary revision of the 1607. Of course there is dispute as to whether
Chapman alone devised *Bussy II* or whether other hands also worked on
it. My position here is quite independent of this perhaps insoluble problem. Concerning texts, at least three fairly solid facts stand out. First, that
of *Bussy I* is the nearest and best thing we have for revealing Chapman's
original intentions in what is by general consensus his one tragic masterpiece. Second, no one seems to doubt that the 1607 text came from
Chapman himself. Third—and of greatest significance—*Bussy I* and
Bussy II are so different from each other that, if we seriously respect the
integrity of texts, it is only good sense to treat these plays as two different
works of art. Close comparison indicates that the differences between
them have been inadequately weighed. Moreover, Chapman's artistic
achievement in the original *Bussy D'Ambois* has been obscured by a
number of persistent views which, however valid they may be for *Bussy II*
or especially for other and later of Chapman's tragedies, are substantially
invalid when applied to *Bussy I*. This essay seeks to identify some of these
critical myths (now usually accepted as truth) and to suggest that they be
discarded. When this is done, it may be feasible to perceive what Chapman actually accomplished in the original *Bussy*. To begin with, we may
notice at least five broad-spectrum myths of textual identity and integrity,
of critical focus, and of critical method.

1964); cited as "Lordi." The 1641 edition cited is in *The Tragedies of George
Chapman*, ed. T. M. Parrott (London, 1910); cited as "Parrott." *Bussy D'Ambois*,
ed. F. S. Boas (Boston, 1905)—hereafter cited as "Boas"—gives the 1641 text with
conflations from 1607.

3. Summaries and comparisons of selected 1641 *vs.* 1607 differences have been
made, e.g., by Berta Sturman, "The 1641 Edition of Chapman's *Bussy D'Ambois*,"
HLQ, XIV (1950–1951), 171–201. Cf. Peter Ure, "Chapman's 'Tragedy of Bussy
D'Ambois': Problems of the Revised Quarto," *MLR*, XLVIII (1953), 257–269; cf.
Lordi, p. xxx; Brooke, pp. lx–lxxiv. Brooke (pp. lxv–lxxi) remarks ways in which
the author or authors of the changes often tend to be " 'theatrical' in a bad sense,"
especially in the amazing mishmash made of the crucial Act V in 1641. He surmises
it not unlikely that "this conversion was [made] by sheer inadvertence" (p. lxix).

I

The first and most crucial myth is the notion that the text of *Bussy II* (1641) is substantially equivalent to that of *Bussy I* (1607). At least two fairly radical differences indicate that these two dramas should be considered not as variants but as separate creations. In the original *Bussy* the second scene of Act II begins with a 49-line section that is absent from the posthumous play. When closely studied, this passage emerges as of decisive importance for the understanding of the singular heroine, Tamyra, and for the major theme of "affections' storm" of sexual love for D'Ambois which overwhelms her reason and social inhibitions. Most crucially, the entire fifth act, which develops the catastrophe and suggests to the audience many subtle modes of response to it, is so altered in the 1641 text as to be completely changed in dramatic effect and in tragic meaning. The total cumulative force of these radical changes and of a host of lesser ones has been precisely stated by Brooke: the difference established between *Bussy I* and *Bussy II* is ". . . enormous. . . . I do not think it is too much to say that [in 1641] the last Act has been turned from tragedy into melodrama (rigged out with tragic trappings) . . ." (Brooke, p. lxix).

It is not possible to undertake here a closely detailed comparison of the two versions, but some of the major achievements of *Bussy I* may be enumerated by glancing at the fifth act. First, the role of the Friar in V.i and of the Friar-Ghost in the climactic V.iii seems designed throughout to point great tragic issues such as those of honor, justice, mercy, and of a singular "Christian reconcilement." Second, Bussy's chamber scene (V.ii), in which he resolves at whatever risk to aid Tamyra should she summon him, sets his concept of love and honor in bold, ironic contrast to the parallel concepts of Montsurry, stressed in V.i as he tortures his defenseless wife in the name of honor and Christian manhood. Third, the doubly cynical dialogue in V.iii.1–56 between the play's great villains, Monsieur and Guise, is "placed" to furnish an ironic frame through which the audience may retrospectively view Bussy's readiness for self-sacrifice and prospectively may prepare to view the hero's imminent destruction by a gangster murder planned by the two would-be tyrants, who play a psychologically active role as they remain to supervise it silently, in V.iii.57–193, after which they probably exit. Fourth, throughout V.iii Bussy D'Ambois plays a dominant part in the tragic design, a part both psychologically and morally active even from his death at line 193 to the Friar-Ghost's final elegy over the hero's body, with which *Bussy I* ends. Fifth, the subtle drama of "Christian reconcilement" is developed powerfully in one unbroken flow (ll. 199–264); *Bussy II* breaks it (ll. 119–146, 154–221). Sixth, the Friar-Ghost's remarkable elegy to D'Ambois' antityrannical spirit is finely integrated to form an artistically meaningful closing (in *Bussy II* the speech, "placed" at ll. 147–153, effects a rather melodramatic anticlimax).

Like Nicholas Brooke, its editor, I am persuaded that the original *Bussy D'Ambois* is very much superior to the more familiar second play: superior poetically, theatrically, in terms of character development, in its psychological realism, and in the clarity with which it transmits a tragic vision which may still be meaningful today. But in any event the best available assurances are that Chapman's original tragic intention and achievement are best represented in the 1607 text. Even if it could be proved, instead of dubiously assumed,[4] that Chapman alone was responsible for the 1641 play-text, the fact is that the plays are radically different.

II

Failure to recognize that these two plays are not textually interchangeable or equivalent has in part resulted in the fallacious idea that criticism of *Bussy II* really amounts to full, adequate, and relevant evaluation of *Bussy I*. Actually, at present there exists almost no discussion strictly of the original tragedy and based on respect for its textual integrity. As far as I know, only Brooke, in his 1964 "Revels Plays" edition, keeps his eye exactly on the 1607 text (e.g., in his pp. xxvi–liv). Virtually all other commentators tacitly ignore the major differences between the two *Bussy* texts or seem to assume that no harm results either from conflating the two or from treating them as simple variants. For these two tragedies, only continued critical confusion can result from such a practice. Interest-

4. T. M. Parrott, "The Date of Chapman's 'Bussy D'Ambois,' " *MLR*, III (1908), 134; cf. Sturman, as cited in *HLQ*, XIV (1950–1951), 172.

ing as the extensive critiques of *Bussy II* may be, they are just that, no more and no less. Discussions of the 1641 play cannot clarify Chapman's achievement in his first masterpiece. Brooke's brief comparative analysis suggests indeed that the deviser or devisers of the posthumous play saw many things in ways so unlike the Chapman of *Bussy I* as to turn tragedy into melodrama. Nevertheless, underlying the idea that criticism of the 1641 *is* essentially valid for the 1600–1607 play seems to be the fallacious notion that Chapman was fantastically consistent in his ideas, emotions, and values over a long period of his life.[5] This almost amounts to saying that, even if the two texts were, as they are, often sharply unlike, Chapman remained unchanged and hence the differences should not matter. Such an idea appears nonsensical. Elias Schwartz rightly pointed out that such assumptions of "consistency in Chapman's thought" amount to a "begging of the critical question."[6] Soundly, it seems to me, he observed that "there is no warrant for assuming that what a man believes to be true at thirty, he still holds to at forty or fifty. And the proper way to discover what a writer believed at a particular time is to understand what he wrote *at that time*" (Schwartz, p. 164 n.). The best way to discover what Chapman accomplished in his tragic masterpiece nearest to *Hamlet* and to *Othello* is surely to study the original play as closely as possible, keeping in mind its values realizable in the theater. The truth seems to be that the most remarkable things in the original *Bussy D'Ambois* are there because, for at least once in his life, Chapman escaped enslavement to his own theories of morality and of tragedy. Peter Ure seems most to the point when he observes that (even in the 1641 play) "The evidence suggests that in *Bussy D'Ambois* something not perfectly within the moralist's control came up from below the threshold of his mind, and

5. See, e.g., Ennis Rees, *The Tragedies of George Chapman* (Cambridge, Mass., 1954), p. 1. This criticism of the 1641 play is hereafter cited as "Rees."

6. Elias Schwartz, "Seneca, Homer, and Chapman's [1641] *Bussy D'Ambois*," *JEGP*, LVI (1957), 164 n.; cited hereafter as "Schwartz." His comment was applied especially to Rees and also to J. W. Wieler, *George Chapman: The Effect of Stoicism upon His Tragedies* (New York, 1949). Miss Sturman, cited in n. 3, above, derived general ideas on tragedy and poetic diction from Chapman's pre-*Bussy I* writings; she then found that "the fidelity with which the early version of *Bussy* conforms to these precepts is remarkable" (p. 178). Her method extracts passages from dramatic context and thereby tends, I think, to miss what is most important, namely, the ways in which *Bussy I* shows a tragic vision exceeding even Chapman's own theories.

that it was this that transformed a moral spectacle into a piece of tragic theatre."[7]

Even critics of *Bussy II,* with but few exceptions,[8] take that play to be Chapman's only unmistakable tragic masterpiece. I have suggested that the original *Bussy D'Ambois* is by far the superior work of art.

III

A third broad-spectrum critical myth that obscures Chapman's achievement, even in the later play, is the idea that the best way to assess it is through a survey of all his tragedies, or of several lumped together. For the original *Bussy* is not only Chapman's first great tragedy; it is also his only play worthy of that accolade. After its creation, as a writer of dramas which can potentially come alive in the modern theater because they have meaning for our time and a structure adequate to the tragic vision, his progress was essentially downhill. The reader's perception of what happens in *Bussy I* (or even the later play) is, at the very least, sadly blurred when it is not disengaged from the lesser work. This effect can be seen, for instance, in Edwin Muir's essay on "Royal Man," in which he treats the character of Bussy (of 1641) together with that of Byron (in *Byron's Tragedy* of 1607–1608). Muir generalizes interestingly about heroes, yet to do so he invents a composite figure never seen on any actual stage.[9] The result is to draw D'Ambois down toward Byron's more static and more didactic level.

How a much more enlarged and more typical kind of critical overview ends by inflicting a theatrical, if not poetical, kiss of death on Chapman's sole masterpiece can be seen clearly in the conclusions reached by Peter

7. "Chapman's Tragedies," *Jacobean Theatre,* ed. J. R. Brown and B. Harris (London, 1960), p. 236; cited as "Ure."

8. One is Robert Ornstein, *The Moral Vision of Jacobean Tragedy* (Madison, 1960), pp. 50–60; cited as "Ornstein." On his view, cf. Brooke, p. lvii. Another is Cyrus Hoy, in *Research Opportunities in Renaissance Drama VIII,* ed. S. Schoenbaum (Evanston, Ill., 1965), p. 12.

9. " 'Royal Man': Notes on the Tragedies of George Chapman," *Essays on Literature and Society* (London, 1949), pp. 20–30; cited as "Muir." This essay has been identified (Ure, p. 230) as most exactly summing up the "general direction of [Chapman] criticism."

Ure: "The relative merits of Chapman's different tragedies have . . . the effect . . . of a long *decrescendo* [which] cannot be overcome. . . . The story of his work is in part the story of how [his response to 'greatness'] generated an antithetical rigour, binding some of his work with frost, but permitting some of it to rise to the level of elegy" (Ure, p. 244). As though such a dismal conclusion to a survey were not enough to sink *Bussy I* (still in most minds equivalent to *Bussy II*) from consideration for the modern stage, Ure proceeds to consider the "body of [Chapman's] work," perforce including the one masterpiece, along with "the Roman tragedies of Jonson and Samuel Daniel" (*ibid.*). Chapman might as well have a huge dead weight tied to his artistic neck and be thrown into the Thames.

IV

No less fallacious than the survey approach, at least as far as *Bussy I* is concerned, is the idea that the meaning of a drama's subordinate elements can be well perceived when they are abstracted from the onmoving design of action, the play being regarded primarily as a printed text to be examined in the study. The resulting distortions are likely to be especially far-reaching for a subtle psychological work wherein much that is most significant is suggested, even by close textual study apart from the theater, as developing beneath the surfaces of the progressive poetic flow. Dover Wilson cogently deplored in much *Hamlet* criticism "the vicious habit of taking stock of the whole play at once, instead of treating it as a serial work of art in which incidents and events are arranged in a certain order and intended to be apprehended in that order. . . ." [10] For most *Bussy* criticism the confusions similarly generated are proportionately far worse because virtually all commentators have taken stock of *Bussy I* and *Bussy II* simultaneously, without recognition of their major differences.

A common variation of myth IV bears on the admittedly complex problems of Chapman's style. Its investigators have usually examined passages lifted from their dramatic context and have treated them virtually as discrete poems. What in consequence has tended to appear is the

10. *What Happens in Hamlet* (Cambridge, 1935), p. 202; cited as "Wilson."

idea that in *Bussy II*, the poetically superior *Bussy I* being usually ignored, Chapman has a single characteristic style with occasional deviations that result when allegedly he loses judgment or control. He is not often credited with disciplined mastery of a variety of dramatic idioms. Thus, at a tense point in the fourth act of the original *Bussy D'Ambois*, Brooke observes the "strikingly terse" language given to the hero but thinks that Bussy soon "recovers his normal rhythm" (pp. xlviii–xlix). I would suggest rather that for his hero, and for the major figures generally in *Bussy I*, Chapman invented a wide range of rhythms, tones, and imagery, all reflective of "character" as shown in response to the pressures of the action. His stylistic control cannot be perceived simply by attempting to notice deviations from an assumed norm. I cite here but two examples such as are often lifted from their dramatic setting, usually in order to denounce what are said to be characteristic qualities of "turgidity and obscurity," [11] or to prove that Chapman's language in *Bussy* is, as Dryden put it when removed from the theater in the privacy of his study, ". . . to sum up all, uncorrect English, and a hideous mingle of false poetry, and true nonsense. . . ." [12] Dryden's contempt might have been excited by two rhetorically violent satiric speeches of D'Ambois', one in his role of the

11. Cf. Moody Prior, *The Language of Tragedy* (New York, 1947), p. 106 (criticizing *Bussy II*); cited as "Prior." He does note that these are first impressions, "defects of his style and not its characteristics."

12. "Dedication of *The Spanish Friar* [1681]," in *Essays of John Dryden*, ed. W. P. Ker (Oxford, 1900), I, 246. Brooke (p. lv) notes the passage and says that *"Bussy* was quickly revived after the Restoration . . . and . . . Dryden . . . saw Charles Hart in the rôle." Was *Bussy I* revived? I rather surmise it was some stage adaptation of the sensationalized, melodramatic 1641 play. Brooke remarks that Dryden "does at least indicate how successful Chapman's verse could be on the stage." This last is a major point. Dryden found that *Bussy* "amazed me . . . upon the theatre." Earlier in this same dedication, however, Dryden shows contempt for "the play-house . . . cunning of a juggler" (*Essays,* ed. Ker, I, 245). I suggest that Chapman originally wrote for a theater which thrived on strong poetry and strong effects. Dryden's colder, more bookish Restoration tastes appear in his increasingly rigid ideas of "uncorrect English," i.e., he preferred verse more like reasoned prose in syntax and imagery. Brooke's remarks (pp. liii–liv) are far more relevant now than Dryden's, at least for today's audiences, which have learned to respond to Brecht or Beckett and are perhaps far better prepared to appreciate Chapman's range in *Bussy I* than Dryden was, at least in his study.

"King's Eagle" (III.ii.7–59), the other in his verbally spectacular "flyting" with the villain, Monsieur (III.ii.336–411). I suggest that in their context, and as imagined when projected on stage, these are fairly in character for the blunt-spoken D'Ambois. They express the intense vigor, concreteness, and clear vision with which he perceives and despises common courtly corruption, bogus greatness, and would-be tyrants such as Monsieur and Guise. All these qualities are indeed marked from the play's beginning (e.g., I.i.1–139). First, as "King's Eagle," D'Ambois sets and then closes a trap to catch, further expose, and politically weaken the Guise. When, in the second passage cited, Bussy is alone with Monsieur, we are shown a deadly kind of joking; and even in this one sequence the controlled stylistic expression shows a wide range which should make very strong good sense to an audience which has realized the fateful subsurface duel taking place. For, underneath a mask of outrageous humor, Monsieur, who sets the tone and idiom, conducts his last subtle trial: can he "use" Bussy to kill the King? (Cf. Brooke, p. xlv.) It is as fallacious for the original *Bussy D'Ambois* as it is for *Hamlet* to disregard the nature of the play as a strictly serial work of art.

V

Thus far, discussion has dealt with a cluster of broad-spectrum myths of textual identity and integrity, of critical focus, and of method. At present also regarded as fairly well-established truth are what I suggest to be fallacies concerning Chapman's relation to Marlowe.

A fifth myth, namely, that Chapman is more or less slavishly trying to imitate Marlowe, usually appears in one of two forms. Either Tamburlaine is alleged to be the pattern for Bussy D'Ambois as a tragic hero, or Chapman is said to be (unsuccessfully) imitating *Dr. Faustus* in his use of the supernatural. Tucker Brooke's neat summation is fairly typical:

While Tamburlaine scourges kingdoms with his conquering sword, Bussy [1641] domineers over a peculiarly ignoble group of courtiers and is assassinated by the husband of the lady he has seduced. The earth-shaking vaunts of

Tamburlaine and the occult agencies of *Dr. Faustus* often seem absurd in *Bussy*. . . .[13]

The issues are best divided: first, the tragic-hero idea; second, the use of the occult or supernatural. *Bussy II* criticism repeats over and over the notion that Chapman intended his hero to be a "Marlovian superman" or "titan."[14] Even while claiming that Chapman's heroes closely resemble Marlowe's, one critic is puzzled that they "have no ambition to achieve an earthly crown. . . . Bussy does not try to gain power over others, but merely to live after the pattern of 'royal man.'" At the same time it is said that the poetry of both Marlowe and Chapman "is inspired by a philosophical idea of man, not by human life as the observer sees it" (Muir, p. 29).

I suggest that, for the original *Bussy D'Ambois,* in major respects Chapman was not intent upon realizing either a form of the Marlovian superman or the so-called "perfect" man. Marlowe's epic figure of Tamburlaine is an exotic evocation of events long past and, to him, apparently romantic. By contrast, in *Bussy I,* Chapman, as I understand him, seeks to represent—and most refreshingly too—a credible modern court society, with mixtures of well-observed good and evil embodied in its men and women, who are as visibly engaged in a pursuit of happiness as most men seem to be today. Actually Bussy does not affect Tamburlainian "earth-shaking" vaunts at all. His highly energetic powers of language, which in Chapman as in Marlowe become a form of symbolic action, are used to pinpoint, satirize, and expose localized corruption and potential tyranny. A serial critique of *Bussy I* shows a large part of Acts I–III to be publicly dominated by a subtle struggle on the part of the just and strong King Henry, choosing Bussy as his aide or "Eagle" (by III.ii), against the would-be tyrant, Monsieur. No superman or "perfect man," Bussy's very

13. *The Renaissance (1500–1660)* (New York, 1948), pp. 556–557.

14. E.g., R. H. Perkinson, "Nature and the Tragic Hero in Chapman's Bussy Plays," *MLQ,* III (1942), 266; by p. 270 he has "the super-man, or perfect man." In his view, Chapman soon got into confusions because "the Marlovian super-man" lacked "true humanity and the equivalent of a tragic flaw" (p. 263). Shifting ground slightly, he then thought Chapman characterized Bussy as "the Stoic 'complete man' . . . [as] part of his attempted rationalization of the theoretical Marlovian super-man" (p. 266). Prior (p. 108) sees Bussy as a "superman" brought low by "Fortune." Ornstein (p. 48) thought Chapman "turned away from the Marlovian titan" which he found presented in *Bussy II.*

human frailties are strongly marked, nowhere more powerfully than by himself in his own death speech.[15] Although Tucker Brooke found only "peculiarly ignoble" men and women in the court "world" staged in *Bussy II* and alleged that the hero domineered over them indiscriminately, closer analysis of *Bussy I* suggests that Chapman drew clear distinctions where nobility is concerned. One of these, often overlooked, is that between comic and tragic hypocrisy, especially as embodied in the heroine, Tamyra (tragic), vis-à-vis such creatures of both common and peculiar corruption as the Duchess of Guise (comic). In the original *Bussy* the hero subtly or strongly satirizes the commonly degraded courtiers, while he respects and comes to love Tamyra, who is not sexually vicious. (Like Brooke [p. xliii], I see no value in rehearsing "the crudities of moral indignation that have been urged against Tamyra [hardly tolerable anyhow when Freud is every man's familiar].") Furthermore, the persistent superman myth takes little or no account of the refreshingly down-to-earth human scale and proportion of the Tamyra-Bussy love affair. For therein, with a sensitive psychological realism, Chapman shows how two strong people, seeking happiness in a world whose commonplace corruption they never made, may at least temporarily be subject to an overwhelming passions' storm of sexual love.

As for the use of the supernatural—the "occult agencies" of *Dr. Faustus* said to be "often absurd" in *Bussy II*—even the first modern editor of the original tragedy seems to censure Chapman as failing to provide for his summoned spirits the spectacular language which Marlowe devised for Mephistophilis. In *Bussy I* (IV.ii.18–138) Friar Comolet calls up a spirit, Behemoth, in an effort to secure information on the plots of the villains and their dupe, Montsurry, while a bit later (V.ii.45–67) D'Ambois recalls the spirit to get clearer information, if possible. Brooke remarks: ". . . my

15. See Brooke, pp. li–lii, where he observes how wrong T. S. Eliot was in his notion that the Bussy of 1641 perished "in the odour of Seneca." Sensibly, Brooke observes (p. lvii, n. 7) that the "assertion [Ornstein, p. 59] that Bussy 'dies triumphant, certain that he has achieved immortal fame in his fight against evil' is a very strange interpretation of V.iii.178–193 [= V.iv.131–146 in Parrott's edition of 1641, which Ornstein (p. 281) used]." Brooke surmises that "Ornstein's general contempt for Act V is in part the result of the maladroit revision in the later [1641] text" (see Brooke, p. xlix). In Schwartz (p. 175) persists the idea of Bussy as a superman who, although "a murderer and an adulterer," is said to be, "within the play's ethical context, . . . consistently . . . a hero of impeccable virtue" (i.e., like Tamburlaine).

reference to *Faustus* points the weakness: Behemoth has nothing like the words Marlowe gives to Mephistophilis; Chapman has valid uses for his spectacle, but he barely succeeds in making them explicit" (p. xlvii). I suggest, however, that Chapman endeavors to invent for his Behemoth no such language as Marlowe did for Mephistophilis because these dramatic figures and their purposes in the actions are radically unlike. In contrast to Marlowe's mighty devil-figure, Behemoth has very limited knowledge and even less power. Indeed in *Bussy I* (unlike the 1641 text) he and his aides are not actually identified as "devils" at all but, at most, as "spirits." [16] Dramatically, Behemoth functions as a sort of spirit-intelligencer. As such, the effect of his limited powers is to enforce a humanist tragic concept that the fate of men depends decisively upon men and, with this, the idea that modern man is his own worst enemy. Chapman simply has no dramatic need for Mephistophilis' poetic mode. I think Brooke is on the right track when he observes that the really meaningful question is "the value, to the play, of this spirit spectacle" (p. xlvii). In the resourceful theater of today, the spirit spectacle—given an intelligent nonnaturalistic production—could work very adequately.

Nevertheless, the Chapman of the *Bussy I* does, I think, owe something of vital importance to Marlowe. It has been most precisely defined by Peter Ure, even though essentially he evaluated only the 1641 play and its hero: "What distinguishes Chapman and what made it possible for him to write his masterpiece in tragedy is a fiery and imaginative response to 'greatness' and its role among men" (p. 244). Through his tragic design in *Bussy I,* Chapman does seem to suggest that in modern society there may be other work for authentic great men than laboring to gain power over others or to achieve earthly crowns. Coming into view in the original *Bussy D'Ambois* is a form of tragedy in which the hero strives with all his powers to aid justice, to defeat would-be tyranny, and to achieve happiness through shared love. To say the least, Chapman's alleged more-or-less slavish imitation of Marlowe is very much exaggerated as a creative force in the original *Bussy.*

16. In Brooke's edition the printed identification in stage directions marking Behemoth and company as "Devils" seems to be Brooke's editorial addition (at IV.ii.40.1–2; IV.ii.138.1; V.ii.51.1; and V.ii.67.1). In the 1607 text itself (and even in Parrott's edition of 1641), these figures are at most "spirits."

VI

A third cluster of interrelated critical myths (VI–X) has grown up concerning Chapman's power to express his tragic vision in the theater, both broadly regarded and, more narrowly, involving characterization.

My sixth myth holds that generally Chapman lacked creative force to invent and to control plot structures adequate to his purposes. By those content to take over-all views of his tragic output, this idea is fairly well accepted as part of the conventional wisdom. Thus Ornstein thinks that Chapman "consistently lacked the ability to construct plots which would translate his vision of life into vital dramatic terms" (p. 54). Muir concluded that Chapman cared only about

the crisis as a thing in itself, for in the crisis the real drama of his heroes is born and they rise into their own world; he therefore tries to reach it without the wearisome labour of working towards it through a methodical arrangement of situations (Muir, pp. 21–22).

My concern here is only with the degree to which this idea actually fits the original *Bussy D'Ambois,* not with such validity as it may have for other of Chapman's tragedies. Perhaps once again discussion can be clarified by separation of the issues. The questions then are: What vision of life does *Bussy I* express? What sort of plot structure conveys it? How vital are its dramatic terms?

I suggest that close serial analysis of this particular tragedy shows that, for it, this myth embodies major error. Virtually no element in the plot is left to chance or Fortune; rather Chapman roots the entire tragic design in character skillfully revealed by actions which spring from the conflicts of strong personalities. For the first three acts, two major themes are developed in parallel. In the sector of public life at court there emerges the idea of political power as a force making for tragic strife. This struggle is subtle, but it is unmistakably between the just King Henry and the great man who seeks tyrannic power ruthlessly, Monsieur, who brought D'Ambois to court as a likely instrument for achieving the crown, if necessary by killing the King. But Henry brings to bear a counterpolitic of justice, draws D'Ambois to his own side, and sets in motion a long-overdue campaign for exposing corruption in high places. In reaction Monsieur swiftly forms a coalition with Guise to destroy the hero. But Acts I–III, in the sector of private, personal, and emotional life, sensitively develop also the theme of sexual power as a force for joy or suffering. Thus rises the issue of personal happiness. As Act IV begins, these two major structural themes fuse in the action and work together dynamically to the end. During Acts IV–V the burden of representing active tyranny is transferred by the villains to their dupe and tool of murder, Montsurry, who in the last act emerges as a great "character" during and after the torture scene (V.i).

A critically important element in this plot design is the time scheme. All the events fall in firmly linked sequences on two consecutive days and nights. Through this time structure Chapman seems to suggest that the forces which generate suffering in modern society appear when passion and reason meet, with their intense conflicts compressed to the utmost in time. Symbolically, time and passion become great powers, almost characters, in the tragedy. The structurally central Bussy-Tamyra love relationship (in the original play she takes more obvious initiative than he does), which is far clearer in *Bussy I* than in the melodramatic second play, suggests that, in strong men and women, passion may rise from below "consciousness" to rule or overwhelm reason. Chapman long anticipated such analysts as Freud in his perception of the pervasive power of sexuality in society. His tragic vision incorporates the passions'-storm theme into the dramatic structure, which does indeed yield "the sense that their [the lovers'] coming together is a dark but deep compulsion far removed from the ordinary life of the shallow or beastly courtiers who surround them" (Ure, p. 236). Closely held and sustained within a carefully built dramatic structure, Chapman's tragic vision transcends the tidy formulations of systematic moralists.

VII

An allied fallacy is that Chapman leaves the tragic hero unaffected and untested by the action and therefore leaves him essentially unknown to the audience. Counter to this fairly common view (see, e.g., Muir, pp. 30, 22), which of course tends to be applied even more sweepingly to the lesser characters, I suggest that the original *Bussy D'Ambois* presents every major figure with a varied succession of tests or challenges. Chapman's characters best reveal themselves by their choices of responses made from the spectrum of possibilities available at a given dramatic moment. This pattern may be illustrated, ironically enough, from a figure whom Muir (pp. 20–21) mocked as a dramatic nobody, mere "cardboard," one of the "minuses whose very names seem unreal." This is the heroine's husband, Montsurry. During the first three acts he appears as a mere sycophant and toady for the "great" would-be tyrants, Guise and Monsieur. But during Act IV and above all in Act V he emerges as a figure of great and even frightening proportions, when he joyously tortures Tamyra and seeks to carve her into an image of all adultery. Before the tragedy's final phase, I find no less than nine major tests which the action is designed to present to him. Here I cite only the final challenge, which comes during the anguished drama of love against hate after D'Ambois' death. The ghost of Friar Comolet urges Montsurry to achieve forgiveness and "Christian reconcilement" with Tamyra. The audience can sense that such heroic achievement may be possible if Montsurry can summon up sufficiently daring and imaginative powers of creative love. Instead, self-persuaded that he is virtually without human frailty, and self-enslaved by curiously rigid and contradictory ideas of honor, he shows in his great final speech how he chooses symbolic suicide (V.iii.159–264).

This challenge-and-response pattern and dramatic method for revealing the depths of human nature is distinctive of the treatment accorded the major tragic figures in *Bussy I*. (This excludes Monsieur and Guise, whose coldly cynical viciousness is controlled by prudent *amour-propre*.) As an observer of human nature under stress, Chapman is most subtle and original, as well as nearest in sympathy to our own age, when he invents dramatic means to show how passions may arise from below consciousness to affect the course of the action decisively. Indeed, this poignant understanding of the complexities of the passion-reason conflicts in men distinguishes the Chapman of *Bussy I*. Even in the inferior 1641 play it accounts, I think, for what Ure (p. 235) called the "double vision of its hero." What this kind of vision signifies is the perhaps permanent tragic dualism generated between man and society. Not only the hero but Tamyra and Montsurry as well are shown to the audience by means of this "double vision," for they are no less tragically ambiguous.

VIII

Side by side with the idea that the tragic hero remains unknown to the audience coexists the myth that *Bussy* is a one-character play and that Chapman lacked virtually all powers of characterization. This myth has divers variations: e.g., that, with one or two exceptions, all the figures (even in *Bussy II*) are stock types [17] or that Chapman is interested only in "the man of excessive virtue or spirit or pride." [18] By 1910, in his edition of *Bussy II,* Parrott singled out King Henry in particular to illustrate how Chapman allegedly failed in characterization because Henry does not exhibit the qualities modern historians discern in him, namely, a "strange compound of sensualism, superstition, cowardice, and ferocity." The comment, too long to quote here, includes *inter alia* the stock comparison with Shakespeare as a "yardstick," and with it the lumping-together of all Chapman's tragedies. Of course *Bussy* is depreciated in the process. Included is the assertion that not only the King but Monsieur and Guise are mere stock types, the King a mouthpiece for conventionally uplifting royal platitudes (Parrott, p. 544).

I propose that these generalizations break down when *Bussy I* receives close, consecutive scrutiny as a work whose meaning must be fully imagined in the playhouse. Such a critique indicates rather that the King, Monsieur, and Guise (who has brutal strength but is the least of them; cf. Brooke, p. xliii, on economy in his representation) emerge as figures of considerable interest. Contrary to Parrott's assumption, I suggest that Chapman evidently never intended his King Henry to copy the last of the Valois. His King is his own invention, one designed to fit the purposes of his plot structure, no mere King qua King who mouths royal sentiments and never acts on them; he is shown rather as dry, sharp, shrewd, witty, resourceful politically, and tough-mindedly just.

As for Monsieur's portrait in *Bussy I,* it far surpasses in wit and depth any mere type of the "ambitious and villainous intriguer" (Parrott, p. 544) or the stock "satanic Machiavel" (Ornstein, p. 54). For him Chapman invented a singularly cruel, obscene wit and humor. Close scrutiny of

17. Parrott, p. 544; Muir, pp. 20–21; Ornstein, p. 54; Ure, p. 230.
18. Muir, p. 20; Ure, p. 230.

the dialogue's undermeanings reveals the powerful "stench of corruption" and "perverse appetite" (Brooke, p. xl) characteristic of him. But when these subtleties go unobserved, much of the characterization is lost to sight. The brilliant fifth-act exchange of wit between Monsieur and Guise, on the imminent murder of the hero (V.iii.1–55), illustrates the point. It has, of course (for 1641), been taken as "choral," [19] that is, as relatively static material. Or the passage is said to show Chapman belatedly, if not clumsily and arbitrarily, imparting "the 'correct' moral interpretation," so that, at the end, D'Ambois' death may gain "heroic significance" (Ornstein, p. 59). I reason, rather, that this Monsieur-Guise interchange in the original *Bussy D'Ambois* should be read "in character." Then it seems that when the villains—who have skillfully engineered the plan for D'Ambois' murder from ambush by gangsters—appear to discuss the coming atrocity, they come as supervisors who wish to check up on and enjoy their handiwork. From the audience's viewpoint, therefore, they play not a passively choric but a psychologically active role until the hero's death, when, in 1600–1607, they probably left the stage "above." Their witty talk (V.iii.1–55) of "Nature" as being to blame for the outrage is, I think, a fantastic piece of their obscene humor (cf. Ure, pp. 232–233).

IX

Hard upon the heels of the notion that Chapman lacked virtually all powers of characterization comes a quite ingeniously reasoned critical myth, that his talents in *Bussy* do not include a psychological realism which is meaningful in twentieth-century terms. His great heroine, Tamyra, is usually a center of such commentary. Of course even critics of *Bussy II* have long been at odds over Tamyra and indeed over the whole question as to why her love affair with the hero was made so important in the tragic design.[20] Perhaps the key idea is that the heroine's struggle against sexual passion is too brief to be credible. Actually in *Bussy I* this problem is paralleled by that of the suddenness of Bussy's response and,

19. E.g., Irving Ribner, *Jacobean Tragedy: The Quest for Moral Order* (London, 1962), p. 33; cited as "Ribner."
20. See Parrott, p. 545; Ornstein, p. 54; Ure, p. 235; Brooke, p. 40 n.

even more strikingly, by that of the speed with which the heroine's
husband, Montsurry, gives way to an outbreak of pathological jealousy,
which results in his torturing his wife in V.i. While no one seems to have
examined with care this phenomenal passions' storm in Montsurry, the
Tamyra-Bussy relationship has attracted much attention. Hardin Craig
studied Tamyra's sudden passion for Bussy (II) and, with it, certain
similar events in Heywood's *A Woman Killed with Kindness* (1603).
Rightly he saw that Chapman gave to drama a new turn, one toward a
psychological "tragedy of passion," of which he found Chapman to be
"our first great writer." Yet to him Tamyra "makes no struggle" against
"irresistible passion." Craig found an adequate explanation for what he
saw in the view that Chapman was rigidly and even pedantically devoted
to an Elizabethan system of psychology, one which he applied almost
mechanically to Tamyra's characterization.[21] In Craig's view, the suddenness of the passion and of the sequent action by which Tamyra and Bussy
become lovers must seem incredible today, while even historically it
makes sense to him only on the assumption that Chapman had swallowed
whole certain then-conventional notions about women's "nature," i.e., that
for a woman to be sexually tempted is for her to fall.[22]

Whatever validity such reasoning may have for Heywood's simpler
tragic vision, Craig's criticism does not, I think, fit very well the complexities or even the text of the original *Bussy D'Ambois*. In *Bussy I* appears
one of the most significant passages which concentratedly represents
Tamyra's inward struggle against a rising passions' storm, the speech
which includes her remarkable soliloquy beginning "I cannot cloak it"
(II.ii.1–49). As it happens, the melodramatic *Bussy* of 1641, which Craig
examined, lacks this key passage entirely (Parrott, pp. 22, 563–564).
Secondly, what is of crucial importance for Tamyra is that the thrust of
passion which overwhelms reason and the conventional protective wis-

21. Hardin Craig, *The Enchanted Glass* (New York, 1950), pp. 131–136, *passim*.
Discussing all of Chapman's plays, he finds "that one could almost reconstruct the
subject of Elizabethan psychology from . . . [them] alone" (p. 126). In context, the
view that "Chapman was pedantic" (p. 126) seems virtually to suggest that he was
too enslaved by current psychological theory to observe human nature for himself.

22. Hardin Craig, "Ethics in the Jacobean Drama: The Case of Chapman," *Essays
in Dramatic Literature,* ed. Craig (Princeton, 1935), pp. 28–39, *passim*.

dom (social restraints, official morality, piety, custom, etc.) comes from within the depths of personality, or from that mysterious region which today we should term subconsciousness. (For some odd reason Bussy is usually labeled a seducer. Since in *Bussy I,* however, the heroine actually takes a degree of initiative after an eruption of desire she cannot restrain at that time, it would perhaps be more accurate to describe the lovers' meeting as—in an un-Platonic sense—one of "true minds.") It seems to me that Craig's view of the so-called "reasonable modern view of probabilities in both character and act" fits far better some of the work of Ibsen than it does either the facts or the vision of life shown dramatically in the original *Bussy* or widely observed in investigations by Freud and others. By now, I think, it has been sufficiently well established that everyone, no matter how seemingly secure and reasonable (like the Tamyra of *Bussy I,* whose marriage seems happy until we watch Montsurry complacently counsel her to "bear with" Monsieur's sexual assaults), has breaking points where his social defenses and self-controls may give way. In *Bussy I* the instant when reason crumbles before the drive of passion is the moment of the highest poetic, theatrical, and human interest. There is nothing necessarily incredible (*pace* Craig) in "one recorded struggle." For there is no way to know surely how many went unnoticed because their signs were ambiguous or obscure (e.g., as Montsurry, in II.ii.1–33, is so obtuse that he does not perceive indications of growing passionate turmoil in his wife, although the more acutely observant Beaupré does see them and enables the audience to do so as well). I do not find Chapman enslaved, any more than Shakespeare, by the theories of Renaissance psychology, although both artists use them when it helps. In short, I suggest that in the original *Bussy D'Ambois* Chapman is master of a very powerful form of psychological realism, one well able to move us today to look thoughtfully into the mysteries of our own humanity.

X

Finally we come to the semimyth that Chapman is a philosopher and that consequently the main interest of his plays lies in his philosophy. This notion, if accepted, would transfer the value of the original *Bussy*

D'Ambois from the realm of playhouse drama to that of abstracted ideologies. Of course I have no reason to differ with the view that the tragic vision expressed in *Bussy I* conveys ideas about human suffering that are still important. Critics preoccupied with Chapman's philosophy seem to be concerned with ethics or at least with morality, with ideas on "Nature," and with concepts of Bussy as a tragic hero but one so detached from the dramatic structure as to become a sort of free-floating image of man. Thus Muir has it that "Chapman is not interested in human nature, or in practical morality, or in evil, but in the man of excessive virtue or spirit or pride" (p. 20). Or, apparently in all seriousness, Bussy is proposed as almost the literal embodiment of Golden Age man or "natural man" (e.g., Ribner, pp. 24–27). When several of Chapman's heroes are fused into "royal man" by Muir, the resulting composite figure is said to flourish although the "dramatic machinery" of the tragedy goes to havoc (pp. 24–25).

This tenth myth implies that Chapman's tragedies in general should be relegated to the study and presumably be forever abandoned by the living theater. I suggest one exception—the original *Bussy D'Ambois*. To consider at least one moot point of so-called philosophy, proponents of the hero-as-Golden-Age-man at once point to King Henry's strong praise of D'Ambois after the King has forcefully arrested the second Bussy-Guise quarrel (III.ii.90–110). Yet within the dynamic structure of the action this praise is both subtly "in character" for Henry and works as part of his adroit struggle to expose and neutralize the play's bogus "great" men and would-be tyrants, Guise and Monsieur. Moreover, I propose that a 1600–1604 audience in London did not expect or crave the literal return of the Golden Age any more than we do today. But Muir did make an excellent point concerning the effect of Henry's praise of the hero: "Bussy d'Ambois and Byron are unfallen men among the fallen, but their virtues are not Adam's; they are not equipped with innocence, but with native noblesse, spirit and state, genius and an ingenuous soul, the virtues of the Renaissance" (Muir, p. 25). This last qualification is of notable force. At least partly, it embodies an idea of a humanist tragic hero which may still have validity. I would myself suggest that, in his original *Bussy,* Chapman represents his own individualized idea of an active courtier, soldier, and scholar, perhaps to be contrasted with Hamlet's introspective inactivism.

In the original *Bussy D'Ambois,* moreover, this ideal of a modern heroic man is firmly anchored into a strongly coherent dramatic structure.[23]

23. This essay is drawn from the introduction to a forthcoming study, "Passions' Storm: What Happens in Chapman's Original *Bussy D'Ambois,* and Shakespeare's Tragedies."

The Faithful Shepherdess:
A Fletcherian Experiment

MARCO MINCOFF

EW PLAYS of the Beaumont and Fletcher canon are quite as puzzling as *The Faithful Shepherdess*. Not that there is anything engimatic in the play itself—the authorship is unusually well attested, the date comparatively so, and, though the pastoral play is not otherwise very fully developed in England, it follows the pastoral pattern sufficiently closely to present few difficulties on that score. What is tantalizingly puzzling, however, is that a play which, just because of its assured position in Fletcher's works, might be expected to form the cornerstone of any understanding of his development is in style, meter, and structure so utterly unlike anything else he produced that it hardly seems possible to relate it to the rest of his work as a whole; it remains floating in a void. It is therefore of some interest to see at least what it was that Fletcher was attempting in this work, how it differs from his other plays, and why. But also, since it seems to be Fletcher's first singlehanded attempt at tragicomedy (although of a rather special kind), the play is of some importance in suggesting, first, the origin of his use of the tragicomic impasse and, second, the reason for the attraction it exercised on a period and a class that was reshaping the drama to its own aesthetic and moral needs.

Wallis believes that *The Faithful Shepherdess* was the first attempt at serious drama, not only by Fletcher alone, but by the Beaumont and

163

Fletcher combine, and that a realization of their mistakes here and in *The Knight of the Burning Pestle* led the friends to concoct together in *Philaster* a coolly calculated theatrical success which was to determine the whole trend of their further development.[1] But, in the first place, the probabilities of dating seem to me to speak for *Philaster* as the earlier play;[2] and second, it seems doubtful whether any lesson could be learned from the failure of either the burlesque or the pastoral, except the overwhelmingly obvious one that the audience would not swallow anything too different from their ordinary fare.

Fletcher and his friends were indeed quite clear in their minds as to the main causes of the play's failure on the stage. The audience had expected

a play of coñtry hired Shepheards, in gray cloakes, with curtaild dogs in strings, sometimes laughing together, and sometimes killing one another: And misling whitsun ales, creame, wasiel & morris-dances, began to be angry.[3]

They were disappointed, Jonson declared,

> since it had not to doe
> With vices, which they look'd for, and came to.[4]

Or because, as Chapman put it, it

> Renews the golden world; and holds through all
> The holy lawes of homely pastorall;
> . . . .
> Where forrests flourish but in endlesse verse;
> And meddowes, nothing fit for purchasers.[5]

1. *Fletcher, Beaumont and Company* (New York, 1947), p. 184; cf. Frank Humphrey Ristine, *English Tragicomedy* (New York, 1910), p. 110. The idea seems also to be accepted by Clifford Leech, *The John Fletcher Plays* (London, 1962), p. 33.

2. The date of *Philaster* is, of course, quite uncertain. My chief reason for putting it *c.* 1607 is the line of development of one of the central motifs, mentioned below, running *Othello–Philaster–The Faithful Shepherdess*. But also the fact that *Philaster* seems to have been produced before the taking-over of Blackfriars by the King's men, and that productions during a large part of 1608–1609 were cut down on account of the plague, lends a certain support to an early date.

3. *The Works of Francis Beaumont and John Fletcher*, ed. A. R. Waller (Cambridge, Eng., 1905–1912), II, 522.

4. *Ibid.*, II, 447.

5. *Ibid.*, II, 520.

It was, in short, too namby-pamby and divorced from reality for the robust tastes of an audience nurtured on Jonson, Marston, Middleton, and the other early Jacobean playwrights. The subject was at fault, not the author's theater-craft, and there was nothing for Fletcher to learn from his failure except to avoid such themes in future, which he certainly did. It is improbable, therefore, that the pastoral elements of *Philaster* and the wounding of the heroine by the hero were borrowed from this play.[6] On the contrary, the wounding of Arethusa was, like so much else in *Philaster,* certainly modeled on, and probably inspired by, *Othello;* and it was more probably the success of *Philaster,* and perhaps the impact of the *Astrée,* which Fletcher had probably read in manuscript at this time,[7] that induced him to go a step further and attempt an innovation that came at least ten years too early. The aristocratic part of the audience, which was in tune with the pastoral tradition, approved the play. But its tastes had not yet succeeded in imposing themselves on the mass of playgoers— whom Beaumont characteristically accused of illiteracy [8]—and, to achieve success on the boards, *The Faithful Shepherdess* had to await the revival of 1634.

Of course a pastoral play was not in itself an innovation;[9] Fletcher's only experiment consisted in presenting a diversion admired and appreciated by the select and artificial audiences of the European courts on the public stage of London. And in doing so, he took no pains to adapt it to the requirements of the average playgoer by means of comic relief and realistic interludes. He was fully aware, apparently, that he was attempting a new species with rules of its own, and it is his adherence to those rules, his exclusion of his ordinary style and stagecraft, that makes *The Faithful Shepherdess* so difficult a work to place. He had approached the drama as a whole with new conceptions and was evolving a new form of

6. Wallis, p. 110; Ristine, p. 112.

7. Cf. Charles Mills Gayley, *Beaumont the Dramatist* (London, 1914), p. 90.

8. *Works,* II, 446.

9. Besides the semipastoral entertainments of Lyly and the more lyrical *Arraignment of Paris*—all courtly plays—there had been Daniel's *The Queen's Arcadia* (1605), which actually did combine the artificial pastoral with the heavily satirical tendencies of the time, and translations of Tasso's *Aminta* (1587) and Guarini's *Il Pastor Fido.* See W. W. Greg, *Pastoral Poetry and Pastoral Drama* (London, 1906). p. 242.

comedy that anticipated the main lines of development for generations to come.[10] Here he was attempting something almost more revolutionary: trying to restore—for a generation that had wallowed in the starkest realism, that had introduced into its poetry the rhythms and melodies of everyday speech and the imagery of everyday life—the romantic beauty and poetry of a past age and of a class with which most of the audience were not in sympathy. That he would have persisted in the experiment, even if the play had been successful, is hardly likely. He would have known that, at best, a lyrical drama could only exist as a contrast to something else and not as a model for future drama; but for the nonce he was ready to devote his powers to lyrical expression and the evocation of the pastoral atmosphere. Chapman saw very truly that the play's peculiarity lay in its being "both a poem and a play"; and it is in fact chiefly as poetry that the play must be regarded—the drama takes only a secondary place. It is for this reason that Fletcher abandoned even for the blank-verse passages his usual light, tripping meter, his end-stopped lines and feminine endings, his accretive, appositional sentence structure, by which he was used to achieve a verse demanding to be spoken rapidly and easily, and introduced instead a full, sonorous line that would have to be declaimed weightily to gain the full effect of every word. To place the accent on the dramatic form is to misunderstand Fletcher's intentions. For the form, no less than the style and meter, is essentially different from that of his true dramas. It is, indeed, much less original, more regular, balanced, and symmetrical, looking back to the past rather than forward to the future.

There is, to begin with, none of that spreading-out of the tension to secure a series of peaks—so characteristic of both the comedies and the serious plays—and none of the chain structure of separate attacks directed toward a single goal. The action sets in slowly, not in the least *in medias res,* rises gradually to the complex misunderstandings of the wood that fill out the third and fourth acts, and dies away slowly again in the last act. The evening and morning songs of the old priest at the opening of the second and fifth acts form two equally balanced points of rest that mark

10. I believe, though it is by no means certain, that he had already produced *The Woman's Prize,* if nothing else. At least Beaumont could hardly have spoken of him as "the man, whose wit ne'r had a stain, / Upon the publick Stage" (*Works,* II, 446) if this was his first play.

off the introduction and the resolution from the rest. Nor have we the two clear, bold lines of action so characteristic of the comedies, but instead a network of intersecting actions as in the earlier structural type of Jonson and Chapman. As in *Il Pastor Fido* or, less obviously, the *Astrée*—the technique was common with Jonson and others, too—pastoral love is presented in a number of contrasting types, ranging from the pure, passionless memory of it in Clorin to the wanton flirtations of Cloe and the animal passion of the Sullen Shepherd,[11] treated with an eye to contrast and parallelism in the situations. The action in the night scenes flows rapidly and easily—more easily than in earlier drama—with theatrical effects of surprise, sudden reversals, changes of mood and determination leading to swift death and marvelous resuscitations; such effects could equally well be borrowed from the Italian pastorals or the Alexandrian romances by which they had themselves been influenced.

The deficiency of motivation in the modern sense, i.e., motivation depending on personality, and the presentation of fluctuating emotions, as in Fletcher's later tragicomedies, are obvious enough; but to claim with Wallis [12] that the play is constructed on the variety of emotional impact and emotional patterning—whatever that may mean—is surely, in spite of the admission that the patterning is somewhat obscured by lyrical and descriptive interludes, to push a principle, correct enough in the main for Fletcher's other works, too far. For the emotion here is always subordinated to the poetry and the pastoral mood; the same charming woodland haze engulfs all the situations, deadening the emotions and imposing the same atmosphere on them all. As in Italian pastoral, the soliloquy predominates, and long set speeches tend to replace the give-and-take of conversation—even more than in the originals, for Fletcher does not take over the Italian and classical technique of confidants.

This is how the half-bestial Sullen Shepherd expresses the heat of his lust as he chases Amaryllis:

> Stay thy pace,
> Most loved *Amaryllis,* let the Chase
> Grow calm and milder, flye me not so fast,
> I fear the pointed Brambles have unlac'd

11. Wallis, p. 188.
12. *Ibid.,* p. 190.

Thy golden Buskins; turn again and see
Thy Shepherd follow, that is strong and free,
Able to give thee all content and ease.
I am not bashful, Virgin, I can please
At first encounter, hug thee in mine arm,
And give thee many Kisses, soft and warm
As those the Sun prints on the smiling Cheek
Of Plums, or mellow Peaches; I am sleek
And smooth as *Neptune,* when stern *Eolus*
Locks up his surly Winds, and nimbly thus
Can shew my active Youth; why dost thou flye?

                                                              (V.i)

The lust is only to be perceived intellectually, by the contrast with the
praises of chastity that have set their artificial moral standard and by the
strictures of the priest that immediately follow. Poetically the speech is as
calm, decorative, and languid as Amoret's lament:

This place is Ominous, for here I lost
My Love and almost life, and since have crost
All these Woods over, never a Nook or Dell,
But I have sought him, never a bending brow
Of any Hill or Glade, the wind sings through,
Nor a green bank, nor shade where Shepherds use
To sit and Riddle, sweetly pipe, or chuse
Their Valentines, that I have mist, to find
My love in. *Perigot,* Oh too unkind,
Why hast thou fled me? whither art thou gone?
How have I wrong'd thee? was my love alone
To thee worthy this scorn'd recompence? 'tis well,
I am content to feel it: but I tell
Thee Shepherd, and these lusty woods shall hear,
Forsaken *Amoret* is yet as clear
Of any stranger fire, as Heaven is
From foul corruption, or the deep Abysse
From light and happiness. . . .

                                                              (IV.i)

Running through both speeches is the same decorative woodland imagery,
the same richly beautiful vision. It is around that that the drama is
integrated, that and the theme of chastity, while the play of the emotions
merely forms little waves and eddies on the surface.

     It is this use of poetry as an integrating element that sets *The Faithful*

Shepherdess so markedly apart from Fletcher's other work, making it indeed "a poem and a play." And in his use of the pastoral background and woodland scenery, the constant flow of nature imagery, Fletcher also differs very markedly from his Italian models, where the background is only introduced in occasional songs and set praises of nature, but the emotion is defined rather than presented. He was in fact following the English tradition of Spenser and Shakespeare, with their rich visual backgrounds, *A Midsummer-Night's Dream* being probably of some importance in this respect.[13] To Spenser's Garden of Adonis Fletcher probably owes the strong undercurrent of images expressive of fecundity and growth, of nature as an active, life-giving principle; and to the English Petrarchists in general, a second strain of images of fire and flames to represent the passion of love; while yet a third leitmotiv, the moon, seems to derive from *A Midsummer-Night's Dream*. But it is worth noting that for Fletcher the moon is merely a decorative embellishment by which to suggest the beauty of the night; of Shakespeare's further symbolical play with the moon as suggestive of the changeability and illogicalness of the sublunary sphere, which so piquantly underlines the comedy of errors in the woodland scenes, there is nothing. Even here, the only one of his plays in which Fletcher applies the poetry of suggestion and symbol at all, his world remains in the main, as elsewhere, one of strictly human causations in which suggestions of metaphysical powers and influences have small part.

To Spenser, too, Fletcher probably owes his conception of the satyr as a friendly and beneficent being, representing a kindly and motherly Nature; in his Italian models, in which the satyr was a standing pastoral requisite, he represents ferocious sensuality, the role that Fletcher reserved for his Sullen Shepherd.[14] Whether Wallis is correct in attributing to Spenser Fletcher's use of the theme of chastity around which to organize the plot, as in *The Faerie Queene,* Book III,[15] is rather more doubtful. For

---

13. D. M. McKeithan, *The Debt to Shakespeare in the Beaumont-and-Fletcher Plays* (Austin, 1938), pp. 91–98. The parallels of incident discussed on pp. 84 ff. are more ingenious than convincing, however, though there is a certain similarity of structure.

14. Wallis, p. 288. Possible Italian sources for the concept are cited by McKeithan, pp. 84 ff.

15. Wallis, p. 188.

in his comedies, also, Fletcher made use of intellectual concepts to unify his plots in a way very different from Spenser's, and the theme of chastity itself was probably suggested in the first place by Guarini, who, although he did not make his play such a laudatory ode on the beauty of chastity, had at least placed the concept in the center through the strict laws of Arcadia punishing its infringement by death; for on that his whole plot hinges. And the Alexandrians too were very fond of stressing the value of virginity.

More important however, but quite independent of any question of influence, is the way in which Fletcher's concept of chastity differs from Spenser's. For him, as for Guarini, in fact, chastity is mainly a technical point; he admits the idea of chaste love, it is true, but his highest embodiment of chastity is nevertheless the sterile virginity of Clorin, in which he seems to point forward to *Comus* rather than to recall Britomart and Amoret, whose ideal is certainly not virginity. He anticipates, in short, an age in which a social code governed by clearly formulated general rules was to be of more importance than the ethical attitude of the individual. Fletcher has indeed been accused of cynicism in his superficial and conventional attitude toward chastity,[16] even of maintaining an undercurrent of satire.[17] The latter charge is certainly a perversion of the facts, which are that, in order to stress the purity of his heroines, Fletcher keeps up a running comment of surprise at the possibility of such superhuman virtue; and even the charge of cynicism is somewhat exaggerated, though there is more than a little truth in the suggestion that Fletcher was paying lip service to a virtue that actually left him rather cold. His concept of love, even at its most elevated and declamatory, was always tinged by a voluptuous eroticism, very shocking to Victorian critics, who felt compelled to protest their innocence of condoning the idea of the body or the senses playing any part in love—a tradition which perhaps still haunts some men who would consider it priggish to speak of Huxley or D. H. Lawrence in the same vein.

What is really wrong with Fletcher's presentation of love is usually not the voluptuous strain but the frigidity, the lack of any warming touch of intimacy or friendliness. He belonged to an age that was beginning to

16. Greg, p. 274.

17. Gayley, p. 285; Leech (pp. 42 ff.) also, I think, goes too far in seeing a deliberate system of paradoxical contradictions.

recognize the rights of the body more fully, perhaps to overemphasize them on that account; even the Puritan conduct books, as Schücking has pointed out, at times exhibit a glowing eroticism which Milton was not ashamed to reflect [18]—and he belonged to a class which had long delighted in elaborate games of flirtation. That this class should, in the artificial form of pastoral, in which it gave vent to its sense of oversophistication, have chosen chastity as the typical virtue of the simple life is as little surprising as that its picture of chastity should in its artificiality be on a level with its picture of shepherd life. There is no cynicism involved, unless we regard the whole pastoral idea, the artificial praise of simplicity by a sophisticated society, as cynical in itself.

From the historical point of view, however, the chief interest of *The Faithful Shepherdess* lies perhaps not so much in its well-worn pastoral themes as in what was originally a side issue, namely, Fletcher's often quoted Preface, which represents the first attempt in English at a theoretical definition of tragicomedy, even though it was only a reassertion of Guarini's positions. But actually, though even Fletcher did not really turn to it in his independent works until later, tragicomedy was not in any way a new form; what was new was its recognition as an independent genre, neither tragedy, nor comedy, nor a mixture of the two, but to be defined rather by its differences from either:

A tragie-comedie is not so called in respect of mirth and killing, but in respect it wants deaths, which is inough to make it no tragedie, yet brings some neere it, which is inough to make it no comedie: which must be a representation of familiar people, with such kinde of trouble as no life be questiond, so that a God is as lawfull in this as in a tragedie, and meane people as in a comedie.[19]

Though that form had been achieved long before Fletcher's days, its significance had not been realized nor yet, indeed, its independent position; and for that reason its possibilities had not been very fully exploited either. That was to remain one of the most obvious achievements of Beaumont and Fletcher.

Tragicomedy might easily be regarded as an offshoot of romantic

18. Cf. L. L. Schücking, *Die Familie im Puritanismus* (Leipzig and Berlin, 1929), p. 71.
19. *Works,* II, 522.

comedy, for the earlier Renaissance comedy based on interwoven and contrasting plots had usually given one of the strands a more pathetic coloring that might even approach tragedy, although the outcome was bound to be happy. *The Merchant of Venice* and *Much Ado about Nothing* are comedies of this type, that remain comedies only by virtue of the relative importance given to the purely comic strands; and it would be easy to derive tragicomedy from such plays by a simple accentuation of the pathos. But actually *Damon and Pythias* (1564) and *Promos and Cassandra* (1578) are tragicomedies earlier in date than any known comedy of the Lylian or Shakespearean type, and the once popular romances of which Sidney complained, now only represented by chance survivals like *Clyomon and Clamydes,* should also be reckoned to the genre. So that it would actually be truer to say that romantic comedy developed out of tragicomedy by an accentuation of the comic underplots, though the point is mainly of academic interest; for the earlier practice scarcely recognized a difference, and the romances mostly went under the name of histories, less often of comedies.[20] Various other early plays could also be reckoned as tragicomedies, and the type persisted into the early Jacobean period, though the romanticism of Elizabethan days was considerably docked, and the comic strain tended toward heavy satire, heavier than in comedy proper, or toward themes now regarded as unpleasant, as, for example, in *The Malcontent, Measure for Measure,* and *The Honest Whore*. To find a common denominator for these very varied productions might indeed prove hard; even Fletcher's fairly elastic formula does not cover them entirely. What they show is the straining after a new kind of drama whose actual birth was still in the future.

The term "tragicomedy" seems in some guise or other to be as old as the form itself, although seldom applied, and to have been current among specialists, though regarded at first as unsuitable for the general public.

20. E.g., *The Historie of the two valiant Knights, Syr Clyomon . . . : And Clamydes; The Historie of Orlando Furioso; The Comicall Historie of Alphonsus King of Aragon; The most Excellent History of the Merchant of Venice; The History of Antonio and Mellida,* and *Troilus and Cressida* passed as a history in the quartos. On the other hand we have *The excellent Comedie of . . . Damon and Pithias; A most pleasant Comedie of Mucedorus; The Old Wives Tale. A pleasant conceited Comedie; The pleasant Comodie of Patient Grissell,* and even *The Mayor of Queenborough, a comedy,* printed as late as 1661.

Thus the entry in the Stationers' Register for 1567–1568 runs, "ye tragecall comodye of Damonde & pethyas," but the play itself was published as an "excellent Comedie." (Gascoigne's *The Glass of Government* [1575] did, however, actually appear as "A tragicall Comedie so entituled, bycause therein are handled aswell the rewardes for Vertues, as also the punishment for Vices.") The compound apparently appears first in Samuel Brandon's classical drama of *The Virtuous Octavia* (1598) and in Daniel's *The Queen's Arcadia* (1606), both of them plays appealing to a superior class of readers. More popular plays escaped the specification, however—not only *The Malcontent* (in spite of its entry in the Register as a *Tragiecomedia*) and *The Woman-Hater* (although it drew attention to itself as neither comedy nor tragedy in the Prologue), but even *The Faithful Shepherdess* itself, and all the Beaumont and Fletcher plays. It was not, in fact, until the 1630's that the term became popular, and its acceptance was certainly due to the popularity given to the species by the practice and theory of the pair. And it was, in its turn, the theory and practice of the Italian pastoral drama that helped them to clarify their concepts and to establish a form of tragicomedy that did differ in many ways from its Elizabethan predecessors. It is scarcely of importance in this connection whether *Philaster* succeeded *The Faithful Shepherdess* in time or not, but if, as seems probable, *Philaster* was the earlier play, the pastoral elements in it are all the more important if, instead of reflecting memories of the unsuccessful play, they are to be derived directly from the Italian models.

Tasso's *Aminta* had presented a very simple plot in which, in classical fashion, events were related instead of represented and the accent lay entirely on the emotional impact on the participants. Long monologues, complaints, and laments fill out the body of the play, and the chief emotion aroused is a sentimental pity for the plight of the hapless lover, who seeks refuge from his pains in suicide—a suicide that all suppose, until the final act, to have taken place. Then it is suddenly announced that he is alive and none the worse for his plunge from the rocks, and sorrow is unexpectedly turned to joy. That is an effect of resuscitation obviously borrowed from Achilles Tatius, on whom Tasso also based the greater part of his second scene.[21] And by its very simplicity Tasso's play

21. *Aminta,* ed. Carmelo Previtera (Milan, 1936), p. 9.

admirably exemplifies the essential effect of seventeenth-century tragicomedy, which is pity, a sentimental pity that turns to rejoicing through
some unexpected and fortuitous circumstance. The further tragic element
of terror is lacking, or reduced at least to insignificance; and other even
more important effects that Aristotle perhaps undervalued—awe, or admiration, and acquiescence in the inevitable—are still more conspicuously
absent. Pity such as we are invited to feel for Tasso's hero would be an
impertinence if felt for Prometheus, Oedipus, Macbeth, or even Hamlet;
our pity for them is swallowed up in admiration for the sense of greatness
they inspire.

The elevation that tragedy achieves by such means is achieved here by
the adherence to a superhuman code of virtue, love, duty, honor, by
admiration not for the hero himself but for his code, through which he is
caught in a net of suffering. Since the implication is that any infringement
of this code would be despicable, he hardly wins even the admiration that
his steadfastness might entitle him to. The stress lies instead on his
unhappiness, and there is nothing left but to pity him for the impasse into
which he is forced, an impasse that is nevertheless scarcely felt to be
inevitable, since it depends neither on his own personality, as in Shakespearean tragedy, nor on an inexorable fate, as with the Greeks, but on a
merely human convention. Aminta goes to his death in accordance with a
pattern of Platonic adoration. If we accept the pattern, we cannot admit
that he has any choice in the matter; to represent an internal struggle
would be to convict him of treachery to his code, which we have
by definition accepted as the supreme good. If we do not accept it, the
whole is likely to appear to us as a piece of frigid and artificial casuistry.
And the author himself hardly helps to convince us, for his acceptance
remains only half-hearted; he dare not put his code to the supreme test by
letting it work itself out to its logical conclusion, for that would awake
questions as to its validity or would at least suggest accusations of cruelty
against the code he wishes to glorify. It must justify itself, therefore, by
leading to a happy end. Hence the essential weakness of tragicomedy and
the sense of artificiality that it inevitably inspires once the code is no
longer in force. As long as it remains valid, however, even if only as a
fashionable convention, the impasses to which it leads and the emotions
they arouse are effective enough. And they offered a speciously attractive

basis for drama to an age that was seeking to evolve a dramatic form of its own to embody a moral code that was to work without the support of religious sanctions. The pitting of a hero against a glorified code of behavior became the basis of most serious drama in Europe during the seventeenth century.

Tasso's *Aminta* was, however, too classical in form for a stage that owed its vitality to its resolute opposition to the classical structure, and it was *Il Pastor Fido,* with its more complex plot—again largely influenced by Alexandrian romance—that provided an example much closer in spirit to the type of play popular in England. Though it still differed considerably from the kind of tragicomedy that Fletcher was to achieve, it helped toward its evolution; it did so less, perhaps, than the romances it had itself been influenced by, but still it contributed something. Technically, Guarini's plot falls into two distinct strains. One is a complex network of intrigue in the manner of comedy, centering in the love of Mirtillo and Amarilli, with Corisca's jealous attempts to ruin them, which practically swamps the second strain, the love of Dorinda for the Adonis-like figure of Silvio, an action so simple and so little developed that it actually provides only a few episodic interruptions to the main plot. The interlinking of these two themes is of the weakest, being provided only at the beginning of the play by the fact that Silvio has been forced into the position of Amarilli's betrothed, so that his figure remains always in the background of the main plot, though he plays no real part in it. The main plot rises skillfully to the climax of complications before the mouth of the cave, when all the strands merge together (much as with the complications beside the well in *The Faithful Shepherdess*); it then moves on to a brilliant denouement, the effect of which is heightened by the introduction of fresh impediments as soon as the last has been cleared away, until the knot, which has steadily been growing more and more hopelessly entangled, is finally loosed by a surprise discovery. In spite, however, of their love for brilliant and surprising denouements, this technique of a deferred solution was never applied in its full force by Beaumont and Fletcher. Nor can it be said that Guarini had any marked effect on their structure as a whole—especially on Fletcher's. There it was the romances themselves, with their series of reversals and turns of fortune, that were of much greater importance. Nor does Fletcher, outside *The Faithful*

Shepherdess, make use of a type of chain-grouping of the lovers that was a constant motif of pastoral drama [22] and continued into heroic romance—Coridone and the satyr pursue Corisca, who pursues Mirtillo, who loves Amarilli, who is betrothed to Silvio, who falls in love with Dorinda. Such complicated grouping leads inevitably to the network pattern that Fletcher was avoiding even in comedy.

There was, however, one feature of the Italian pastoral tragicomedies that was of real importance: their artificial, sentimental, romantic atmosphere. This, it is true, is the atmosphere of Alexandrian and Renaissance romance, and it was free to any dramatist to transfer the high-flown sentimentality thence to the stage. But Tasso and Guarini were the chief pioneers in this transference, and by their concentration on scenes of emotional pathos, on the presentation of emotions rather than action, they were offering a new technique. This technique was again perhaps not new in itself, for much of it was borrowed from classical tragedy, but they applied it in a new manner and to themes sufficiently novel to catch the ears of their contemporaries—even of contemporaries brought up in an essentially different tradition. In this respect Guarini is of much greater importance than Tasso, for he elaborated a technique not only for the static display of emotions, as in the *Aminta,* too, but also for the evocation of swiftly changing moods, especially with Corisca and her sudden transitions from blandishments to outbursts of anger and abuse, and in the sudden stirring of Silvio's love after he has shot the enamored Dorinda by mistake—brilliantly brought out by his imprecations, immediately preceding, against the goddess of love. Typical, too, is the seesaw effect of his deferred denouement, where the emotion sways tremulously between despair and fresh hope through the greater part of his longest act. Such effects we do find in the Beaumont and Fletcher plays; and though Fletcher does not make much use of fluctuating emotions in *The Faithful Shepherdess*—where his changes of mood and intention are apt to fall between the scenes, so that each scene is devoted to a separate emotion—in his later plays emotional transitions and the development of changes of mood begin to play an extremely important part. But even in *The Faithful Shepherdess* the play of emotions, the elaboration of scenes of contrasting emotions, even sudden changes of emotion, are already of

22. As in Racan's *Les Bergeries;* cf. further examples in Greg, pp. 174, 176.

importance, though hardly occupying the central position that Wallis would assign to them; and the line of the emotions that any single character undergoes is of considerable variety.

That is a rather important point, which Waith, in his otherwise sensitive and important paper on Fletcher's characterization, overlooks in attempting to minimize Guarini's influence in this respect. Guarini's characters do not, it is true, represent such a rigid scheme of ethically determined attitudes as Fletcher's,[23] though a more cautious formulation might put it that in this point Fletcher was following the didactic allegorical tradition in general rather than Comicall Satyre, with its simplified and extreme types, in particular; possibly even he had already come on the *Astrée,* that compendium of erotic attitudes. Nor must it be forgotten that Guarini himself, and the pastoral tradition as already exemplified in *As You Like It,* gave a very strong hint in this direction. Of Guarini's six main characters, hero and heroine represent ideal love, as do Fletcher's Perigot and Amoret. Corisca is sophisticated lust (Fletcher's Cloe), and the satyr as the embodiment of brutish lust is repeated in the Sullen Shepherd. The remaining pair—Dorinda, the hapless pursuer, and Silvio, the cold Adonis—are not directly repeated by Fletcher, but, with their sexes reversed, their relations are roughly paralleled by Clorin and Thenot, while Dorinda's role is also repeated by Amaryllis, who at the same time schemes against the ideal pair like Corisca. Thus, Fletcher's grouping actually does show a rather close connection with Guarini's, though he has enriched it by the addition of the bashful lover Daphnis and the passionate lover Alexis, a sharply contrasted pair of rivals for Cloe's love, balancing the other contrasted pair: Amoret and Amaryllis. The great difference between the dramatists is that with Guarini the complications depend upon outward circumstance—the wishes of the parents and the laws of the country—while with Fletcher events arise solely out of the impulses of the varied characters and their interactions. And with the final purgation of those impulses, through the havoc they have caused, we do in fact get one of the basic effects of Comicall Satyre—an effect that Fletcher did not resort to in his comedies.

---

23. Eugene M. Waith, "Characterization in John Fletcher's Tragicomedies," *RES,* XIX (1943), 150 ff.; cf. Waith, *The Pattern of Tragicomedy in Beaumont and Fletcher* (New Haven, 1952), pp. 7 ff., where Jonson is not invoked as a model.

The White Devil, or Vittoria Corombona?

R. W. DENT

APPRECIATION OF WEBSTER'S *The White Devil* has recently benefited from valuable editions in the Revels and New Mermaid series, from books on the tragedy's relationship to its historical and nonhistorical sources, and from a score of less restricted critical studies. For these we can all be grateful, both for illumination and for the challenge of conflicting interpretations. Our understanding of the play can at present most profit, I believe, from a reexamination of certain aspects of structure, characterization, and theme, especially as these involve our proper assessment of Vittoria's and Flamineo's roles.

I

According to the title page of the first two quartos, *The White Devil* is "The Tragedy of *Paulo Giordano Ursini,* Duke of *Brachiano,* With the Life and Death of Vittoria Corombona the famous Venetian Curtizan." The head title, however, calls the play the tragedy of both Brachiano and

Vittoria, while the running title is merely "Vittoria Corombona."[1] Our lone early praise of the play, Samuel Sheppard's epigram of 1651,[2] names Vittoria but third in its catalogue of Webster's "lively" creations: murderous Brachiano, Flamineo "the Devils darling" (perhaps implying he thought Flamineo, or conceivably Brachiano, the devil of the title), Vittoria, "that fam'd Whore," "Desp'rate Lodovico," and "Subtile Francisco." Ten years later, however, at the opening of an age of actresses, an unenthusiastic Pepys went to see "Victoria Corombona," and in the quartos a few years later only Vittoria remains on the title page. That of 1665 reads "The White Devil, Or, Vittoria Corombona, A Lady [*sic*] of Venice. A Tragedy"; that of 1672, "Vittoria Corombona, Or, The White Devil. A Tragedy." Brachiano has disappeared, and Flamineo, of course, has never been there. In the abundant criticism since Lamb, she has maintained that priority. That she is the white devil of the title has remained an almost unquestioned assumption. And only in recent years—thanks especially to Clifford Leech, Travis Bogard, and B. J. Layman—has Flamineo, or even Brachiano, been considered a possible rival to her centrality. Flamineo's importance, I believe, is still underestimated and in part misinterpreted.

Small wonder that A. W. Ward, like many another with a conventional conception of the play as principally Vittoria's, complained that "the catastrophe seems to lag too far after the climax,"[3] or that W. W. Greg, despite being responsible for the act division, found Act V "inordinately long."[4] The objection persists, most recently in M. R. Ridley's observation on Webster's "childishly incompetent" plot construction: "The fifth act composes a full third of the whole play. It is therefore, not unnaturally, overweighted."[5]

---

1. How much of this varied focus in titles was determined by Webster is open to conjecture; no other quarto of the period approaches it.

2. *The Works of John Webster*, ed. F. L. Lucas (London, 1927), I, 101. All Webster citations are from this edition. Sheppard's admiration of Flamineo is expressed far more fully than is that for any other character.

3. *A History of English Dramatic Literature*, rev. ed. (London, 1899), III, 57.

4. "Webster's 'White Devil': An Essay in Formal Criticism," *MLQ*, III (Dec., 1900), 125.

5. *Second Thoughts* (London, 1965), p. 80. Harold Jenkins, assuming *The White Devil's* structure is explicable strictly in revenge-play terms, implies a comparable

Traditional emphasis upon Vittoria combines with modern editorial practice to provoke such judgments. Unlike the slightly later *Duchess of Malfi,* which was originally published in five acts and was clearly so constructed, *The White Devil* first appeared without acts or scenes, and there is no good reason to suppose Webster planned it with a five-act structure in mind.[6] Restoration quartos made a muddled effort to divide the play into acts, and these divisions were in turn followed, varied, or ignored in subsequent editions. Then Greg proposed the act and scene divisions now generally followed. Yet, as he almost conceded despite his five-act recommendation, the play falls more naturally into three parts than five: our present I–II (859 lines), III–IV (1109 lines), and V (1046 lines). These correspond roughly to the old protasis, epitasis, and catastrophe, although the protasis is unusually long because two families are involved, and the catastrophe is unusually long because of Flamineo's role in the plot.

Part one, while presented with a maintenance of dramatic tension that conceals its expository character, is fundamentally an exposition of the initial situation prior to the commission of the murders. A trio of villains, individually motivated, imbed themselves deeper and deeper in evil, first over the foolish obstruction of a ridiculous husband, then over the protests of virtuous kindred of both low and high estate. The movement ends with a pair of murders, resolved upon before even hearing the futile protests of the high, then ruthlessly pursued.[7] The counteraction is ready to begin. The second movement includes its initial stages. It is first dominated by Monticelso, uncle of Vittoria's murdered husband, and is directed primarily at Vittoria. Then, with the news of the second murder, the loving

---

judgment ("The Tragedy of Revenge in Shakespeare and Webster," *Shakespeare Survey 14* [1961], pp. 50–52).

6. Clifford Leech has recently implied the contrary, but without any supporting argument. See his *Webster: "The Duchess of Malfi"* (London, 1963), p. 29. Presumably he would concur with Greg's arguments.

7. Dumb shows economically present the murders themselves while emphasizing Isabella's devotion, Brachiano's brutal indifference, and Flamineo's merriment in murder. I disagree with those who think the dumb shows a means of distancing, thereby allowing subsequent sympathy for the guilty. Vittoria, who as false wife to Monticelso's nephew will be the target of the initial counteraction, is "distanced" by her absence despite the dumb shows being presented in her home.

brother of Brachiano's duchess takes over, and the counteraction shifts from legal procedure to blood revenge, now directed primarily at Brachiano. But Francisco takes an unbloody step first; poisoning Brachiano's "fame" before his body, he tricks the infatuated duke into marrying "a whore; what can be worse?" (IV.iii.57–59). The blood revenge, all executed on the day of marriage, comprises a major part of the third movement. Francisco remains on the scene long enough to see his principal foe destroyed, then leaves the remnant "foul vermin" to his tool-villain "Franciscans."

Thus far, this summation has centered upon the great of the play: two powerful dukes and a cardinal about to be elected pope. In a sense, following the *Mirror for Magistrates* tradition, Brachiano's fall is the "tragedy" of the play, as the 1612 title page asserts, and he may well have been intended as its white devil. Vittoria has been the prime target of Monticelso, understandably, but the famous trial scene, however effective, is merely an early step in the development of the counteraction. Thereafter she attracts little attention from the great, and her brother Flamineo still less. But Webster was concerned with more than the great. Hence he provided a kind of subplot, mainly to trace the fortunes of Flamineo.

Something other than the natural focus produced by the counteraction was requisite if Webster wished Flamineo to be a center of interest and suspense. The dramatist could have made him the influential confidant and counselor of Vittoria, or of Brachiano, or of both. This he clearly is not; though he tries to be such a figure, he is ignored almost as completely by them—insofar as this is possible—as by their powerful enemies. Such means of emphasis would have required a kind of change in the characterization of Brachiano and Vittoria, and in the portrayal of the latter, contrary to Webster's apparent aims. Unwilling to give Flamineo the sort of role he later created for Bosola, he provided him instead with an episodic sequence of his own.

Although he is on stage almost perpetually throughout the first two-thirds of the play, Flamineo's active role is necessarily subordinate. With the completion of the first movement his actual services as tool villain are completed. He has twice eliminated Camillo, once by "gullery," once by murder, the former in an episode which serves principally to reveal his own character and situation, together with that of his sister, Vittoria. More important, his individual purposes have been emphasized by a bitter quarrel with his mother, from which we learn through Flamineo's eyes his past, present, and future. He is the only one of the trio to attempt a sincere defense of his villainy, and he does so with both Cornelia and Marcello before the counteraction gets under way. While Vittoria's purposes remain half-hidden by a screen of the dramatist's own making, Flamineo's self-centered ambition is given a special stress from the start. This resolute "poor secretary" of Brachiano is no mere hireling, no Dr. Julio whom Brachiano "must employ." He is playing for bigger and less immediate reward, for "preferment," and not (in his own opinion) as a petty pander and murderer. He is an apprentice "politician," modeling himself on the Machiavellian practices he sees in his betters. What more could Webster do at this stage of the play to make clear the importance of Flamineo's career in the action to come?

In the second movement, nevertheless, Flamineo remains subordinate. As the enemies of Vittoria and Brachiano begin to strike, he does nothing which even promises to speed or retard their progress. His own interests are dependent upon Vittoria's, and most of his speeches naturally reflect that concern. His antic dispositions before and after her trial may seem of principal value in heightening suspense, in foreshadowing, in sharpening effects by contrast, or simply in providing a necessary relief lest the dramatic tension become overstrained. Such functions are often served by his garrulity. But in neither episode is he merely a talker. In the first occurs a highly serious argument with Marcello, in the second a fight with Lodovico, his eventual murderer. Webster wasted no time in getting Flamineo doubly involved in the final blood revenge. But he did more than that. Prior to the Brachiano-Vittoria quarrel of IV.ii, Brachiano first calls him "Pandar." Startled, Flamineo is indiscreet enough to forget his station and defy his lord, even threatening to break *his* neck as he had Camillo's, the very thing his "politic wisdom" should have warned him against. A few lines later, in almost the first words his sister has spoken to him, even including I.ii, Vittoria's contempt for the "Pandar" is first made explicit, and again he is startled by the word. Soon after, pleased by the reconciliation of Brachiano with Vittoria yet blindly unaware how little he is a part of it, despite his "Court wisedome" he holds the stage to stress once again the progress of his hopes. In the middle portion of the play, in other words, not only are his individual purposes reemphasized, but he has an anticipatory quarrel with Marcello, acquires the personal enmity of the tool revenger whose station is most like his own, and estranges the already contemptuous duke on whom his "preferment" depends. Vittoria, who at the end will be his last hope of "reward," shows her contempt for him. Even more than for Vittoria or Brachiano, the supposed triumph which begins the last section is for Flamineo an illusion.

As the final movement opens, the happy wedding party crosses the stage. Only Flamineo remains, to address a minor figure of the court:

> FLAMINEO
> In all the weary minutes of my life,
> Day nere broke up till now. This mariage
> Confirmes me happy.
>   HORTENSIO
>   'Tis a good assurance.
> Saw you not yet the Moore that's come to Court?
>
>   (V.i.1–4)

In these opening lines Webster has indicated the foci of the extended catastrophe: the disintegration of Flamineo's happiness and the completion of the blood revenge. Brachiano appears but three times, once to welcome the disguised revengers, once to "pardon murther," then to be murdered himself. He is dead before this last portion of the play is half over. His new duchess, Vittoria, appears only at his death scene (where she says and does very little) and in the cutthroat chaos of the finale. On the other hand, the revengers, especially Francisco, are frequently on stage; Webster thereby stresses the imminence and ingenuity of the revenge, the villainy of its principal victim, and the dubious character of the revengers themselves. But the most central figure of all is Flamineo, on stage almost continually, speaking 403 of the 1046 lines, and, above all, "falling to peeces" before the revengers can strike. As in the preceding parts, much that he says and does concerns the actions of others, especially Brachiano and Vittoria, and affects our estimation of them as well as of him. But the career of Flamineo, necessarily subordinated to that of his sister and the duke earlier in the play, is subordinated no longer.

The entire fabric of villainy presented in I.ii now falls apart internally, each of its members betraying, or at least denouncing, the others.[8] When

---

8. Brachiano denounces Vittoria only in his death ravings, in which he condemns himself as well. See my *John Webster's Borrowing* (Berkeley, 1960), pp. 146–150.

the virtuous members of Flamineo's family, having accepted the fruits of evil,[9] refuse to accept its morality, the creature who has by policy been partially responsible for their rise is by temper responsible for their fall—and for the disintegration of his own prospects in the process. The same turbulence of spirit which enforced his original evil now causes his collapse. High-spirited at the opening of V.i, for the first time Flamineo speaks in honest, even enthusiastic, admiration of a supposedly virtuous, but wise, man (ironically, the disguised Francisco). Just as he had claimed in III.i to have "made a kind of path" to his own and his sister's "preferment," he now obviously thinks himself responsible for the preferment of his entire family. At first he jokingly refuses to take his brother's reproaches seriously and intentionally taunts him about the "fan of feathers" which has replaced Marcello's former "shamoyes." The gradual progress to mutual anger is skillfully handled. Thus "I have brought your weapon backe" (V.ii.14) is Flamineo's indignant, impulsive response to the fact that the brother he has advanced should actually have sent him a sword in challenge. It is an act like his later bursting-in on the mother he has maddened, an act almost immediately regretted, or like his earlier threat to Brachiano; it is wholly unlike his merrily premeditated murder of Camillo. After this unintentional slaughter of Marcello,[10] his disintegration into the desperate violence of the final scene is rapid and sustained. Brachiano first punishes him for his earlier indiscretion, then in his death ravings repeatedly stresses Flamineo's imminent death for past evils, then,

---

While in his right mind, or wrong mind perhaps, he remains a pleased and devoted newlywed—at least until his final ambiguous outcry. Throughout the present essay I have tried wherever possible to avoid repeating arguments earlier presented in my book. See pp. 27–31 on Monticelso and Flamineo, and several notes in the commentary, especially on the title and on Vittoria's dream.

9. In IV.ii.221 f. Brachiano had told Flamineo to bring Marcello to the wedding "If you can worke him to it," promising to "advance you all." That he has been won is apparent from the passage over the stage opening V.i and by his words to his unrecognized former master: "I have bin a souldier too," one who "thriv'd . . . poorely" (V.i.113 f.). When, in dying, Marcello says "this it is to rise / By all dishonest means," he includes himself.

10. His "I'le to sanctuary, / And send a surgeon to you" (V.ii.18 f.) implies he did not intend murder, and his "It was my misfortune" (l. 46) is an evasion but no lie. Strictly, Cornelia is telling the truth in ll. 61–63; perhaps only her concluding lines should be taken as provoking the page's "This is not trew."

as a ghost, further confirms that ominous prediction. In intervening episodes Flamineo is made "a Court ejectment" by the new and virtuous Duke Giovanni, then impulsively "discovers" the "superstitious howling" of the mother he has driven mad. Still resisting the repeated suggestion to "study [his] praiers," he sums up this sequence of "horrours":

> . . . the disgrace
> The Prince threw on mee; next the pitious sight
> Of my dead brother; and my Mothers dotage;
> And last this terrible vision.
>
> (V.iv.138–141)

He is ready for his dying "My life was a blacke charnell," although still attempting to avoid the consequences. In a last frantic attempt to salvage his prospects, he will go to Vittoria.

In most tragedies of the period there is an unexpected resolving element late in the action. The swift execution of the blood revenge is unexpected only to its victims. The audience knows well enough that the supposed security of the trio is an illusion, and only the form and timing of the revenge bring surprise and suspense. But the sudden focus upon Flamineo and the consequences of his violence, carefully prepared for in the first two parts of the play, provides an unexpected yet probable movement to a kind of double destruction: for himself especially, for his murderous sister as well. Both are doomed, whether the revengers arrive or not. Some action of this sort was essential if the machinations of the blood revengers were not to overshadow completely the evil of Flamineo and his sister, as they tend to do in the case of Brachiano.

If the tension excited by imminent revenge seems unduly protracted, then, this is largely because it has been supplemented in the last third of the play by the tension of a complementary action. There is, in fact, a kind of circularity in the movement of the play. *The White Devil* opens and closes with Lodovico, the violent enemy, and yet the instrument, of crafty greatness. Within that frame the initial focus is upon the house of Camillo, corrupted by the influence of Brachiano's greatness. Closing the scene is Cornelia's condemnation of her children, her prediction that the house will fall to ruin if they persist, and Flamineo's extended reply in defense of ambitious villainy. The world then shifts to one of greatness, into which Vittoria enters by her alliance with Brachiano and her relationship to Monticelso. Cornelia is unseen, Zanche silent, Marcello, Lodovico, even Flamineo kept subordinate. But greatness begins to vanish from the play even as Vittoria and Flamineo appear to approach it. Monticelso disappears in IV.iii; Francisco assumes a debasing disguise and then withdraws entirely after the murder of Brachiano. Meanwhile the relatively lowly, whose fortunes have depended on Vittoria's, take more and more of the stage. Even Zanche becomes an actively traitorous and lustful villain as the expanding evil descends to her level, and in the final scene she proves a useful counselor to Vittoria herself. By that scene the great have all vanished, the virtuous of Camillo's house have perished, and the vicious are busily betraying and murdering one another. The pursuit of greatness has ended in chaos and, at the last, death by hired villains.

II

It is difficult to know just how Webster expected us to regard the tragedy of his protagonist trio. Certainly our attitudes are complicated not only by his oft noted overdevelopment of individual scenes (which especially obscures the Flaminean "subplot" in the play's middle) but by his affection in this play for delayed revelations and for what I interpret as underdevelopment. Delayed revelations may provide an effective dramatic irony or shock, as when the master revenger is welcomed at the wedding before being identified for the audience, or when his supposed Capuchins are not identified as "Franciscans" until just after they have poisoned Brachiano.[11] But the effect is not always so clear. The purpose of "Send Doctor *Julio* to me" (I.ii.297) is concealed until II.i.288, where we abruptly realize—or should, I believe—how totally futile the preceding dialogue has been and how deceptive Brachiano has been. Here the treatment somewhat resembles that for Vittoria, a matter to be discussed later. Sometimes the delayed revelation combines with underdevelopment seriously to obscure an aspect Webster probably intended as significant. Unaware of Francisco's purpose in sending his "love letter" to Vittoria, we witness the magnificent quarrel scene intent on Brachiano and Vittoria rather than on how they are fitting into their enemy's plan. Francisco's

11. As I have elsewhere argued, Francisco, not Flamineo, should make this identification (see *MP*, LVIII [1961], 276).

briefly expressed exaltation in IV.iii.57–59 does not materially alter our impression, especially when the remaining third of the play contains not the slightest hint that Brachiano has indeed "poison'd" his reputation by marrying Vittoria. So too with the new pope's pronouncement of excommunication and banishment—followed by the presence of the papal ambassadors at the wedding. I do not interpret this as Websterian cynicism but as underdevelopment spiced with a touch of muddle and a love for spectacle. Even here, however, we should remember the irony of the poisonous "extreame unction" and last rites administered by the "Franciscans." In turn, our attitudes are further complicated by Webster's partially discrediting Monticelso and the blood revengers, although he does so far less than many critics assert.[12] Most complicating of all, however, is the portrayal of the protagonists themselves.

Had all the major characters of *The White Devil* been presented as fully and consistently as Flamineo, the problem of effect would be relatively simple, although still complex. They are not. One's impressions are frequently confused, often by obstacles to interpretation which Webster can scarcely have intended. *The White Devil* is a play, of course, not a body of material for a court of law. One's attitude toward the characters depends upon a sequence of related impressions in a sequence of dramatic situations, not upon a sifting of evidence or a weighing of justice in the scales. Some difficulties, for example, result from the implications of seemingly

---

12. This matter demands too much consideration of details to be examined here. In *John Webster's Borrowing* (p. 28) I argued that the consistent portrayal of Monticelso as a virtuous churchman (although one not above taking advantage of his authority for partly personal reasons, and of concealing those reasons) is muddled by his apparently recommending a treacherous blood revenge in IV.i. Conceivably the latter could be explained as a deception by which Monticelso tries to discover Francisco's intentions. It could be so acted. But IV.i appears generally so muddled, undigested, and implausible that I remain skeptical (although generally agreeing with Leech's view of Monticelso as a figure on the side of virtue). In IV.i, for instance, Francisco tells us he has pretended "innocence" in order to conceal his plans from Monticelso, but he then immediately asks to borrow the Cardinal's "blacke book" and even asks him to "foulde downe the leafe" where murderers are listed—murderers with which, we later learn, he is already provided. Even disregarding much in IV.i, however, one must concede that Webster considerably debases the loving brother of Isabella who was so sympathetically portrayed in the first half of the play. Especially debasing are his deception of Lodovico in IV.iii and his repeated emphasis upon the art and "glory" rather than the justice of his revenge.

minor details in the text. These should be given no greater significance than one has reason to think they might be given by Webster's audience. They cannot, however, be disregarded simply because they interfere with otherwise tidy impressions, although some of them may in the last resort be discounted as mere bits of carelessness, of inconsistency.

Of the protagonists the "adulterous duke" requires least discussion. He is shown at his worst in Act II, brutally offensive to his devoted wife, contemptibly ready to accept and assist her concealment of his conduct, casual in then proceeding to provide for her murder, callous on witnessing the manner of her death and that of Camillo, as if watching the removal of mere trivial obstacles unworthy of his consideration. His murderous intentions are formed before that act begins, although we are at most only dimly aware of this as we watch his angry quarrel with Monticelso and Francisco, his pretense of reconciliation, his abuse of Isabella. Opposition apparently only increases his evil conviction that "Small mischiefes [adultery] are by greater [murder] made secure." [13] He is a "politic" villain, undoubtedly—one who commits adultery and murder without a qualm, who deceives skillfully, who acts treacherously. It is this aspect of him which makes Flamineo regard him as a great "devil," a model "politician" (see III.ii.313 f., IV.ii.58–63, V.iii.59–67), and which is stressed by the revengers in Act V [14] and even confessed by Brachiano himself in parts of his death scene.

Yet in Brachiano's own activity, from his opening "Quite lost" to his final cry, the romantic aspects are stressed throughout most of the play. He appears in a sense both better and worse than the other members of the villainous trio, at once their ally, their support, and their victim. Even in Act II we see as much of the spoiled, arrogant, infatuated nobleman as of the politic villain, and both Monticelso and Francisco seem at first to regard his relationship with Vittoria as an aberration from a previously

13. II.i.315. This is the only traditional villain's tag Webster gives to Brachiano. Its emphasis has little in common with those later given Francisco in IV.i, however.

14. In V.iii.150 ff. especially. Comparable taunts by the triumphant revengers in *The Revenger's Tragedy* begin with Vindice's cry: "Royall villaine, white diuill!" (III.v.153). Gustav Cross thought this the source for Webster's title; yet the habitual identification of Vittoria as the white devil kept him from even considering its possible application to Brachiano. See "A Note on 'The White Devil,'" *N&Q*, N.S., XXI (March, 1956), 99 f.

commendable life, a "lascivious dreame" from which he must if possible
be awakened. Call his passion lust if you will, as do many of the characters
in the play, including Flamineo and Vittoria; it is never represented on
the level of bestial animality common to so many lustful villains of
Jacobean drama. Nor is he made to glory in his politic art, a self-conscious,
self-praising Machiavellian such as Francisco becomes. More of the lion
than of the fox is made apparent in him, and more of infatuated willful-
ness than of either. When he is murdered during the celebration of his
wedding to Vittoria and dies with a last desperate—but ambiguous—
appeal to her upon his lips, the reaction of an audience, however moral,
could be no simple satisfaction in seeing a villain destroyed.

Our rather complex emotional response depends in a considerable degree upon our estimation of the "love" which caused his fall. Are the
implications of his death ravings the best commentary on his relationship
with Vittoria? [15] Or is his dying cry? Did Vittoria make him not only a
villain but a fool as well? At the moment of his death we cannot be sure;
by the end of the play we have every reason to suspect it. Our suspense is
akin to that at the death of Antony in Shakespeare's slightly earlier
tragedy, but our final impression is in sharp contrast.

Undeniably, Vittoria is a fascinating dramatic creation, with her mur-
der-provoking dream, her "brave spirit" at the trial, her passionate quarrel
with Brachiano. She so dominates the stage in these scenes that it is
somewhat distracting to realize how seldom she appears or how little she
speaks.[16] Scenes vary in importance, it is true, and a dramatic silence—or
absence, even—may excite an interest and suspense which the omnipresent
garrulity of Flamineo does not. Flamineo resists silence even after catch-
ing his "everlasting could"; his sister rarely speaks as much as the dramatic situation might easily warrant.

Throughout the nineteenth century, critics always stressed her unmiti-
gated but fascinating evil. "Fair as the leprosy, dazzling as the lightning,"

15. See *John Webster's Borrowing,* pp. 146–150.

16. With her less than one-tenth of the play's lines contrast the Duchess of Malfi,
who, despite her early death, speaks almost as much as Bosola and far more than any
other character. For comparative statistics, including the tragedies of Shakespeare,
Jonson, and Beaumont and Fletcher, see T. W. Baldwin, *The Organization and
Personnel of the Shakespearean Company* (Princeton, 1927), plates opposite pp. 198,
228, 435.

"a masterstudy in womanhood in its deadliest perversion," "unquenchable wickedness," "a proud, conscious, dazzling, and defiant woman of sin, in life as in death"—these are typical summations. Such a view is supported in detail by John Addington Symonds [17] but is shared by few except Leech (and in part Gunnar Boklund) among recent critics. W. W. Greg first suggested, with admirable moderation, that Symonds was less charitable than the evidence warranted; Vittoria, he felt, was motivated as much by passion as by ambition. Sampson, in his edition of 1906, agreed. Lucas then moved a step further, to insist that "few virtues are as moving as the courage and devotion of these lovers, who have been so ruthless and guilty in all else" (I, 96). Subsequently, critic after critic, whether discussing Webster in detail or merely alluding to his play, accepted without question the validity of Vittoria's love. In this more sympathetic tradition few deny her evil any more than did Lucas; like him they stress an extenuating element which their predecessors did not even consider: her "devotion." This romantic aspect now in turn appears on the wane— fortunately. It rarely occurs with the stress retained in Bogard's Chandler edition (San Francisco, 1961), and only a partial shadow remains in Elizabeth Brennan's able New Mermaid (London, 1966), where Vittoria, "one woman hounded to death by men," is conjecturally characterized as "responsive to love and to goodness, but unable to resist the power of evil in the world around her" (pp. xix, xxviii).

For me, difficulty in interpreting Vittoria centers around three problems, each of which affects my estimation of the extent and character of her evil: (1) the degree to which Monticelso's condemnation of her in the trial accurately reflects her past; (2) the degree of her complicity in the murder of her husband and Brachiano's wife; and (3) the nature of her attitude toward Brachiano and the motivation for her initial association with him (lust, love, ambition, adventure, or a complex of these). That Vittoria is an adulteress is made perfectly clear, although Monticelso's charge of her general promiscuity is not; that she is a murderess from the start is somewhat obscured but is almost certainly a part of our final impression; that her attitude toward Brachiano was expected to resemble even remotely what so many now call "love" seems to me incredible.

The first of these problems, while less significant than the others,

17. "Vittoria Accoramboni," *Italian Byways* (New York, 1883), pp. 157–161.

certainly affects the direction of our sympathies, especially during the progress of the trial scene. A willingly adulterous Vittoria is part of the "given" of the play. We are nevertheless encouraged to form an impression of her past—which in turn affects our opinion of her present—yet are denied the kinds of signs by which it might be made clear. The first reference to her (I.i.38–44) is by Lodovico, already a resentful enemy; it suggests, notwithstanding, a Vittoria whose "honour" is yet unstained, though threatened with corruption by the persistence of Flamineo and Brachiano. Flamineo's speeches in I.ii encourage a contrary impression, one of her lust and incontinence, but we soon learn with what qualification his comments about others must be taken.[18] Cornelia and Marcello, in turn, strengthen the opinion of her past originally suggested by Lodovico, and Vittoria herself encourages this view on several occasions.[19] At the trial, however, Monticelso asserts she has long been "a most notorious strumpet" and sentences her accordingly, although the fundamental basis of that sentence is her adultery, for which "the proofes are evident." [20] Dazzled by her spirited self-defense, as is Monticelso himself, we may perhaps share the English Ambassador's opinion (made before the murder charge) that her enemy is "too bitter," but we know too little about Vittoria to assume he is ever lying or, on the other hand, to assume that Cornelia and Marcello have been deceived by her guile. One might continue to present such sources of impression and counterimpression at length, but with little profit. We are given directly opposed views of her past, not merely views conflicting in emphasis, and we have no means of

18. In the middle of the play we see him twice excited to anger when Vittoria is called a "whore" (III.iii.105, IV.ii.45), but his anger is probable whether or not he thinks the charge true.

19. See Cornelia's speeches in I.ii, Marcello's in III.i. Vittoria's self-defense (especially in I.ii.283–285, IV.ii.110–121) consists of dramatic speeches, perhaps no more worthy of credit than her bold lies at the trial.

20. As the French Ambassador asserts (III.iii.18) and as Monticelso clearly believes (III.i.6–7). Vittoria's judges are propagandists, who make the charge of murder only for rhetorical purposes. In taking advantage of their specially delegated power, their action is less admirable than understandable; there is little ground, however, for the critical tradition which calls them hypocritical, malicious, and wicked. Leech is again an admirable exception, but the play provides no evidence to prove or disprove his assertion that Monticelso "speaks nothing that is not true" (*John Webster* [London, 1951], p. 55).

judging between them. True, such a judgment, either way, would only slightly qualify our final estimation of Vittoria, only slightly alter our response to her rise and fall.[21] Whatever her implied conduct in the past, it is her conduct in the present which mainly concerns us. Thus the ambiguity here considered occasions but a minor complication to our sympathies, though a definite one.

Whether we regard Vittoria as a murderess or not is obviously of far greater importance. When she recites her "dreame" to Brachiano, her brother provides what appears to be a satisfactory commentary:

> Excellent Divell.
> Shee hath taught him in a dreame
> To make away his Dutchesse and her husband.
>
> (I.ii.246–248)

Harold Jenkins is virtually alone in rejecting Flamineo's interpretation: her dream "we must surely take . . . as a dream and not as a fabrication on her part" (p. 51). Yet this view is as defensible as the conventional one. At least one of Vittoria's statements in the dream would encourage a Jacobean audience to suspend judgment,[22] to wait for further confirmation of her murderous intention, especially since neither Brachiano nor Cornelia interprets the dream as a suggestion to commit murder. They would wait in vain. Almost all signs prior to the last scene of the play, in fact, would point toward her innocence in this particular respect, although these signs are so indirect, so faint, that they can scarcely be called signs at all. This much is clear: there is no confirmation.

With so sketchy a summation of this second problem, let us turn to the third, the "love" of Vittoria for Brachiano. In the first three acts of the play we have little reason to believe Vittoria motivated by anything nobler than lust or ambition. By the time of her quarrel with Brachiano in IV.ii such a critic as Symonds is already assured she is a consummate villain. Undistracted by the apparent sincerity of her passion (which is probable enough, after all, without endowing Vittoria with "devotion"), he

---

21. It is essential, however, to those who think Vittoria changes for the worse as the play progresses. Most recent is Edwin B. Benjamin, who says of V.vi: "The real tragedy is what has happened to Vittoria" ("Patterns of Morality in *The White Devil*," *ES*, XLVI [1965], 6).

22. See *John Webster's Borrowing*, pp. 87 f., in support of this entire paragraph.

admires the extraordinary artistry with which she turns her lover's rage into a proposal for marriage. More sympathetic critics, aware that the proposal does not come until after the reconciliation of the "lovers," attempt some psychologically plausible compromise between passion and design or deny design altogether. Actually, we have not the evidence to know. If we suspect at all, we must reserve our judgment until we learn more of Vittoria, in the last third of the play. We shall see little more of her, however, until the final scene.

For reasons in part indicated above, the degree of Vittoria's evil, the possibly extenuating quality of her relationship with Brachiano, must be inferred almost wholly from the evidence of her own speeches and actions. Others may complicate our impression; they do not clarify it. On her first appearance we see, or at least are encouraged to suspect we see, how skillfully she can disguise a murderous intention within "a foolish idle dreame." At her arraignment we know enough of her past action to recognize the boldness with which she gives falsehood the ring of truth,[23]

---

23. In *Endeavors of Art* (Madison, 1954), p. 139, Madeleine Doran cites the following lines from the trial scene as especially evoking an audience's admiration and pity: "Summe up my faults I pray, and you shall finde, / That beauty and gay clothes, a merry heart, / And a good stomacke to [a] feast, are all, / All the poore crimes that you can charge me with" (III.ii.215–218). I have always thought the effect of this particular speech quite different and its audacious proclamation of innocence one of the few instances in the trial where we can be absolutely certain that Vittoria is lying rather than merely evading or equivocating or countercharging. But Webster may have intended a further effect that few in an audience, Jacobean or modern, could catch. Vittoria's "poore crimes" strikingly resemble those in *Revelationes sancte Birgitte*, VI.xv (I cite a Nuremberg edition of 1500, sig. r3ᵛ): "Quid enim facere solet meretrix? Utique solet esse procax in verbis: levis in moribus: pulcra facie: ornata vestibus." Thus John White, probably echoing some earlier controversialist: "Nun-Bridget sayes, the markes of a whore are foure, *Shamelessnesse in words, Levitie in manners, A faire face, And gay clothes*" (*A Defence of the Way to the True Church* [1614], p. 12). White thereby helps prove the Church of Rome to be the Whore of Babylon. The possible relevance of such anti-Rome materials to the play has yet to be assessed; "white devil" itself was mainly popular in such contexts prior to Webster. Certainly there may have been an intended irony in Vittoria's outraged and outrageous promise on being sentenced to the house of convertites: "My minde shall make it honester to mee / Then the Popes Pallace" (III.ii.301 f.). Just after doubting the efficacy of Rome's "Monasteries of the Convertites," Bishop Jewel voiced a popular Protestant charge: "The Popes Palace *at Laterane*, sometime the harbour of Holy Saints, is now become a Stew of whoores"

and we are impressed by her capacities as an actress. The scenes which principally suggest her romantic passion for Brachiano are yet to come, and prior to them we have good warrant for thinking her an extraordinary villain and for distrusting any appearance of sincerity or passion. Symonds' suspicions have abundant grounds.

Vittoria does not seem the result of confused characterization, and yet the presence of conflicting signs compels us to hold in suspense any completed opinion of her. The principal reason for this, ignored by almost all critics except Layman and Brennan, is the limitation of means and of dramatic situations by which she is presented. Webster has employed none of the conventional Elizabethan devices by which her intention and motivation might be made clear. Prior to the last scene she does not once qualify a speech with an aside,[24] does not once speak in soliloquy, although the use of both aside and soliloquy is common in the play. Meanwhile, she stands alone. Her servant Zanche is never represented as her confidante nor Flamineo as a partner in whom she confides. For her intention we are continually left to inference without being sure of our inference. Then—and this is important—in the last scene of the play we finally see her clearly.[25] We have the opportunity to measure her grief for the death of Brachiano, debated a few minutes before by Flamineo and Francisco, and we find it wanting. V.vi.84–87 includes some fine words of her love for Brachiano, but there is no reason to think any part of them sincerely spoken; our knowledge that the last half is a lie, and in a context

---

(1565; *Works* [1609], p. 346). I see no clear Protestant bias in Webster's handling of the trial scene, however, and certainly none whatever in the papal election and the new pope's subsequent behavior (except in Monticelso's misunderstanding the doctrine of confession [IV.iii.109–113]). Lodovico's having "tane the sacrament to prosecute / Th'intended murder" (IV.iii.75 f.), while emphasizing his belief in the rightness of his cause, implies no awareness or sanction of his intentions by the church.

24. In V.vi.55 ff. asides to Zanche make clear a hypocrisy which would soon be thoroughly apparent without them. In this sense of "aside" she is given one early whisper to Flamineo (I.ii.154), which simply indicates her desire that Camillo be gulled out of the way. Three very short speeches at her death are in effect soliloquies, her only ones in the play.

25. She enters with a prayer book, but this does not long affect our impression of her behavior. We may recall that even the "devil" Brachiano is credited with using a prayer book; cf. V.i.67.

of obvious deceptions, helps to discredit the first half as well. Thereafter Vittoria scarcely refers to Brachiano at all, except to regret, in an impersonal dying couplet, that she ever met him. We hear her first words of exultation, not at the wedding, but minutes after the death of her husband on their marriage day—and while she is triumphantly stamping on the brother she thinks she has just murdered:

> This thy death
> Shall make me like a blazing ominous starre,
> Looke up and tremble.
>
> (V.vi.132–134)

Earlier in the scene we watch her obvious wiles with Flamineo; moments later we see her frustrated attempts with the revengers. We still cannot wholly know what complexity of motivation Webster would have allowed her. Ambition appears predominant, most so in her final couplet. Although her share in the initial murders remains unclarified, we have at last seen her capacities for murder undisguised—even if in self-defense more undeniable than that claimed in her original "dreame." One thing seems clearest of all: we have seen no "tragic love."

The very ambiguity of Vittoria's portrayal, I believe, is in large part responsible for her fascination as well as for our mixed response even at the end of the play. Her role could be so acted, with winks and sly looks aside to the audience, that the mystery would be removed—and all semblance of tragedy with it. Indeed, much of her role in V.vi is not far from this level. On the other hand, it could scarcely be acted so that a Symonds might credit the sincerity of her passion for Brachiano. Until V.vi we have only her speeches before others by which to judge, only her appearance in a series of challenging situations, and we know her capacities for disguise.

That Webster intended to employ ambiguity or encourage suspended judgment in this degree cannot be proved. It does seem an extraordinary artistic procedure for a Jacobean dramatist, although in some ways akin, for example, to Shakespeare's handling of Cleopatra or even, much earlier, of Bolingbroke in *Richard II*. Yet the consistency of treatment seems too great to be accidental: the singular absence of asides, soliloquies, confidences, or quarrels over ends and means (all of which we have for Flamineo). It may be pointed out that Webster is often ambiguous, that his treatment of action, character, and theme is frequently confusing.

There is no other instance, however, in which lack of evidence consistently obstructs our interpretation of a major character's action. Only with Vittoria are we kept in doubt from stage to stage—until the debasing revelation of the close. It is for this reason, principally, that I am inclined to believe her, if anyone, "the white devil" of the title.

In Flamineo Webster created a figure whose apparent inconsistency is a sign of complexity, as a good actor could show. Vittoria, at least by comparison, is a theatrical rather than a tragic creation. She is the product of an ingenious intention, rigorously followed, a dazzling façade Webster might well have endowed with the "flesh and blood" he gave to the heroine of his second tragedy. He did not choose to do so.

Of Flamineo's characterization little more need be said. Like many recent critics I thoroughly agree with Leech that he is "in many ways the most interesting figure in *The White Devil*" and that, more than Vittoria, he "seems to have come white-hot" from Webster's imagination.[26] A passage from Joseph Hall's *Heaven upon Earth* (1606) well illustrates the type of character Webster apparently conceived, or at least one essential aspect of that type:

. . . there are some firme & obdurate forheads, whose resolution can laugh their sinnes out of countenance. There are so large and able gorges as that they can swallow & digest bloody murders, without complaint, who with the same handes which they have since their last meal embrued in blood can freely carve to themselves large morsels at the next sitting. Beleevest thou that such a mans heart laughs with his face? will not hee dare to be an Hypocrite that durst be a villaine? These glow-wormes when a night of sorow compasses them, make a lightsome and fierie shew of ioy, when if thou presse them thou findest nothing but a cold & crude moisture. Knowest thou not that ther are those, which count it no shame to sin, yet count it a shame to bee checked with remorse especially so as others eies may descry? to whom repentance seems base-mindednesse, unworthy of him that professes wisdome and valour. Such a man can grieve when none sees it, but himselfe can laugh when others see it, himselfe feeles not. Assure thy self that mans heart bleedeth when his face counterfeits a smile. . . .

(Sec. IV, pp. 28–31)

Other elements complicate him further. He is a scorner of pride obsessed by pride, a pursuer of greatness with a professed contempt for greatness, a lover of craft with too little self-control to be successfully crafty, and so on. But Hall's passage stresses the primary key to his creation, the key that makes intelligible his vehemence, his vulgarity, his laughter, his unpredictability—above all, his behavior in the final movement of the play. When he dies, we cannot but be aware of the misdirected energy, the wasted vitality, that dies with him. Unlike Vittoria and Brachiano, he has not one good word said for him by anyone in the play (except one line by stupid Camillo). None of the other characters qualifies the general contempt by admiring his "brave spirit" (though he has one) or by suggesting that his evil is in part the fault of others (which it is). Less glamorous but more genuine than his shadowy sister, he is at the end of the play the more impressive figure. We cannot regret his death, but our feelings are far from simple when he dies. More than Vittoria's, his has been "an expense of spirit in a waste of shame."

III

In my earlier discussion of the play's structure I largely ignored I.i. As Travis Bogard has to a considerable degree demonstrated, *The White Devil* has a highly functional beginning:

The opening scene . . . states the theme of the play: the evils of courtly reward and punishment. . . . During Lodovico's lament and his friends' remonstrances, the larger theme . . . is divided into three parts for later development: first, the rotten prodigality of court life; second, the evils of a social system in which sycophants flatter a lord for an uncertain living; third, the treachery of a prince's capricious "justice." These are the chief aspects of the theme which appear in action and comment throughout the play, and Webster never loses sight of them.[27]

Bogard then effectively develops this thesis,[28] except that to strengthen his case he goes beyond the evidence of the play to blacken wholly both Monticelso and Francisco, to suggest that, in such a world, Webster offers Flamineo and Vittoria no honest alternative to their course of evil, and to

27. *The Tragic Satire of John Webster* (Berkeley, 1955), pp. 119 f.
28. Accordingly, we rarely now find the scene disapproved, as in Ridley's recent study, where it is condemned as "a misleading bit of bad workmanship" (p. 78).

imply that Flamineo falls despite being a master in the courtly art of pursuing preferment. I have in part already argued against these views, but, since all are common in current criticism, it may be useful to take a further look at I.i's prologue relationship to the play.

As Bogard has partly shown, I.i introduces us to the world of the play and to its dominating attitudes. Where he principally errs, I believe, is in implying that Lodovico's viewpoint—like that of the far more important but parallel Flamineo later—approximates that of Webster. On the contrary, it seems to me essential that one recognize both characters as strictly dramatic creations, whose cynical judgments can be trusted only to the degree that the play actually supports their bias. An "understanding Auditory," such as Webster lacked at the Red Bull, would need to recognize Lodovico's perverted evasions of responsibility despite the vehemence with which he shifts the blame and despite the fact that he may prove partly justified in doing so. We are entering a world where the protagonists will forever thus evade, sometimes sincerely (like Lodovico here), sometimes by design (as in their charging Monticelso with a cozening greed in III.ii, iii). In the first of the play's ironic uses of "charity" (I.ii.298–300) Brachiano will blame "uncharitable" Cornelia for his ensuing evil and will then proceed to further evasions, sincere or hypocritical, in succeeding scenes. Vittoria, master of evasion throughout, will die with an evasive couplet on her lips. Flamineo will blame his prodigal father, or princely example, or Fortune,[29] or even Giovanni as a "villainous" young wolf. Too often modern criticism takes these evasions as Websterian truths, discrediting even Isabella or Giovanni, not to mention the more vulnerable Monticelso or Francisco. Some have even taken Lodovico's speech at the close of Act IV as a Websterian essay on the universal hypocrisy of the great, both religious and secular, although we know that Lodovico has there just been tricked into a revived cynicism. One must be as wary with "point of view" in Webster as in many a modern novel.

Admittedly, the responsibility of the great for the play's pervasive evil is

---

29. Indeed, Lodovico's complaint that "Fortun's a right whore. / If she give ought, she deales it in smal percels, / That she may take away all at one swope," far better describes the eventual careers of Flamineo and his sister than it does Lodovico's past.

a key thematic element, even if exaggerated by Lodovico and Flamineo. Cornelia's protest to Brachiano is as true as it is fruitless:

> The lives of Princes should like dyals move,
> Whose regular example is so strong,
> They make the times by them go right or wrong.
>
> (I.ii.279–281)

In *The White Devil* the times mainly go wrong, and they are scarcely remediable by punishments at a subprincely level. Lodovico's own banishment, we hear, was intended by "the law" as a "gentle pennance [to] both end [his] crimes, / And in the example better these bad times"; later, the law through Monticelso will base Vittoria's mild sentence on her "publicke fault, / Joyn'd to'th condition of the present time" (III.ii.266 f.). Such moderate action proves futile, for both Lodovico and Vittoria have great dukes to lead them in a contrary direction. Lodovico's greatest offense, we learn, was in having "acted certaine Murders" (as he will again at the play's end, this time to pay with his life). These he regards as mere "flea-bytinges"—just as the great duke Brachiano and his "ape" Flamineo will regard the murders of Camillo and Isabella. Like Lodovico, the protagonists will thereby discover what it is "to have great enemies," whether lawful or unlawful, but like Lodovico they will be "justly dom'd." Lodovico may complain, citing Brachiano for his example, that "great men scape / This banishment"; IV.iii will prove him wrong.[30] Thereafter, like Vittoria and Flamineo, Brachiano will perish by lawless violence largely of his own begetting. The "great enemies" are given great cause, not depicted as habitually evil. But Francisco, whom Giovanni was once successfully taught to "imitate . . . / In vertue" (III.ii.321 f.), proves subsequently as corrupting a "dial" as Brachiano.

---

30. Many find scant reassurance at the play's end in Giovanni's "All that have hands in this, shall tast our justice," and they regard Francisco's survival as a significant fact. This seems unfair. Like the much darker and more complex *Duchess of Malfi* (with its initial marriage rather than murder, and its Ferdinand-Cardinal rather than Francisco-Monticelso), *The White Devil* ends with at least the hope of a new generation. Whether Giovanni will prove a "dial" of the right kind, and whether Francisco will go unpunished, is another story, not essential to the moral view of the tragedy. Even with respect to "justice," moreover, the violence of the revengers is less simply evil than Giovanni yet realizes.

One further aspect of I.i as prologue deserves attention: the moral counsel which Lodovico, along with many a modern, regards as mere "painted comforts": [31]

> Perfumes the more they are chaf'd the more they render
> Their pleasing sents, and so affliction
> Expresseth vertue, fully, whether trew,
> Or ells adulterate.
>
> (ll. 47–50)

Admittedly, the idea is a Renaissance commonplace, platitudinously expressed, but it should not therefore be disregarded as a mere irrelevant cliché. Perhaps Webster relied too heavily upon tradition for support; perhaps he should have bulwarked his idea both by poetry and by more fully developed examples. But the concept of affliction as the test of virtue, the discriminator between true and false jewels, is essential to the play. Typically, Vittoria will offer a version of it in her false boast when sentenced to the nunnery: "Through darkenesse Diamonds spred their ritchest light." The world of the play is one dominated by "darkenesse," by punishments rather than rewards, both earthly and heavenly, although the illusory prospect of earthly reward may obsess its Flamineos and Vittorias. Just as earthly evil is emphasized over good, so too the prospect of heavenly punishment takes priority over that of salvation, although neither receives much consideration. Unlike *The Duchess of Malfi* with its mortified heroine, *The White Devil* scarcely hints at the possibility of salvation. Vittoria may claim an intention of going "weeping to heaven on crutches" (IV.ii.124), but this will soon prove one more false diamond. Damnation, on the other hand, is made a recurrent threat; witness especially the triumphant revengers over dying Brachiano or triumphant Vittoria over supposedly dying Flamineo. Yet only Lodovico seriously considers it a deterrent, and he is soon tricked out of his momentary lapse into Christian morality. For Flamineo it is never more than an immediately passing concern, quickly replaced by one for how long he has to live. "That's the most necessarie question" (V.iv.125). Like his model Brachiano (V.iii.14–16), his strong heart's "covenant" is with this world. Even

---

31. The speakers become tool revengers in Act V, but this should not discredit the validity of their moral commonplaces at the opening.

Marcello, after all, pleads only in terms of this world: "For love of vertue beare an honest heart" (III.i.60), and such counsel is of course rejected by a Flamineo who dislikes even more than the early Bosola the thought of an age where "onely the reward of doing well, is the doing of it." [32] He cannot conceive as a valid alternative to his own pursuit of preferment that *"Integrity of life"* [33] which Webster surely meant in a traditional sense rather than in some peculiarly Websterian one such as Bogard's [34] or even Irving Ribner's.[35] The prime "affliction" Webster gives to Flamineo and Vittoria is in their initial situation, one that thwarts their every impulse and gives them abundant reason to dislike a passive resignation to their fortunes. By their standards the "vertue" or "integrity" of Cornelia and Marcello spreads no rich light in the darkness, understandably. As Marcello implied, it has no prospect of reward beyond itself, not even enough to satisfy Marcello himself when a modest compromise with himself appears possible later. In these "bad times," nevertheless, it is the only alternative Webster suggests. And it is a real one, although characteristically rejected in the opening prologue.[36]

IV

Probably, as with comparable abstract titles in other Jacobean tragedies, *The White Devil* was intended to refer to some single character, most plausibly one of the protagonists. Two have virtually equal claim, with Vittoria's perhaps the better. Flamineo alone is ineligible. He deceives almost no one but himself; only Camillo can be so foolish as to mistake him for "a vertuous brother" (I.ii.145). But the title, somewhat like that of *The Changeling,* may well have a thematic relevance far more significant

---

32. *The Duchess of Malfi,* I.i.33 f.

33. *The Duchess of Malfi,* V.v.145.

34. Pp. 38–44; see also his recent edition, and Ian Scott-Kilvert, *John Webster* (London, 1964), p. 15.

35. *Jacobean Tragedy* (London, 1962), pp. 98 ff.

36. In less significant ways several details in I.i suggest that Webster wrote this scene after completing the play and with its final scene especially in mind. Most interesting, perhaps, is Lodovico's scornful remark about those "ready to be executed . . . growne familiar / With the knave hangman"; cf. V.vi.193 ff. (Flamineo) *vs.* 210 ff. (Vittoria), where Lodovico has become the "hangman."

than any reference to a single character. If Vittoria's façade hides the devil which brings Brachiano to his "eternal ruin," Brachiano—or rather the spurious greatness which he represents—brings Vittoria and Flamineo to theirs. Similarly, a spurious concept of "glory," of "fame," of what is "noble" (wholly unlike that in *A Monumental Columne* or in those later *Characters* which are indubitably Webster's) dominates much of the blood revenge. Late in the play, especially, the vocabulary of those "in a mist" is repeatedly undercut (e.g., "glorious act" *vs.* "blacke deed" [V.v.9, 12], "glorious villaines" *vs.* "bloudy villaines" [V.vi.272, 284], "noble deede" *vs.* "murderer" [V.vi.280, 292]). Indeed, Flamineo thus undercuts himself, juxtaposing "glorious" with "vicious," in that praise of Vittoria's "noble" death which so many have taken as Webster's (V.vi.241–247). Obviously, Webster admired a "brave spirit," and never more than in facing death. Yet the bravery shared at the close by Lodovico, Flamineo, Zanche, and Vittoria (least so by Vittoria, incidentally) is at most but a semiprecious jewel. *The White Devil* has no terrified Cardinal, no frantic Cariola. In this one respect the contemptible Zanche proves more "noble," if you will, than is the foil to the Duchess of Malfi in the latter's truly noble death. Bosola's response to "I am Dutchesse of *Malfy* still" was first spoken by a briefly "happy" Flamineo; its irony is essential both to him and to his play:

> Glories, like glow-wormes, afarre off shine bright
> But lookt to neare, have neither heat nor light.
>
> (V.i.38 f.)

The Idea of a Theater
in Jonson's The New Inn

HARRIETT HAWKINS

S INCE ITS FAILURE ON THE STAGE in 1629 *The New Inn* has received very
little sympathetic attention. Negative critical attitudes have prevailed
to such a degree that hardly anyone bothers to read the play, much
less discuss what Jonson may have been trying to do.[1] There is, however,
an exceptionally good witness for the defense. E. B. Partridge's sympathetic discussion of the play is at once fruitful and suggestive. *The New
Inn,* Partridge says, involves "the true relation of the understanding and
the things of sense, or of reality and appearance," and the plot may be seen
to provide "hilarious comments on the absurd situations of romance."[2]

1. John Enck, who usually is favorably disposed toward Jonson, says we had best
ignore this play, since "Jonson seems to have nodded during the labor of composition" (*Jonson and the Comic Truth* [Madison, 1957], p. 220). Jonas Barish mentions
"the unabashed romance plots of *The New Inn* and *The Magnetic Lady,*" and finds
that "this resumption of old-fashioned themes . . . testifies either to a decline in his
[Jonson's] experimental energy or to a more aggressive wooing of his dwindling
audience" (*Ben Jonson and the Language of Prose Comedy* [Cambridge, Mass.,
1960], p. 241). Herford and Simpson discuss the improbable plot and conclude that
Jonson "plies the traditional machinery of transformation and disguise with a vigour
which comes near to effacing every vestige of the characters it is applied to" (*The
Works of Ben Jonson* [Oxford, 1925–1952], II, 194; all Jonson quotations are from
this edition, hereafter cited as *Works*).

2. *The Broken Compass* (New York, 1958), pp. 198–199, 190. See also Robert E.
Knoll, *Ben Jonson's Plays: An Introduction* (Lincoln, 1964), pp. 183–184.

Indeed it seems possible to show that, throughout the play, Jonson uses plot and characterization in order to examine the nature of illusion in general, and theatrical illusion in particular. Within the play Jonson teaches his audience that certain illusions are required in the world of the theater, where a boy actor may appear to be a lady, where costume establishes the rank of a character, where an hour can be presented in ten minutes. He explores various problems concerning reality and illusion that arise from these theatrical conventions through his bold manipulation of the conventions themselves, and he extends his examination of dramatic illusion to include "illusions" common in ordinary life—dreams and love. Jonson's use of an improbable romance plot and of the "traditional machinery of transformation and disguise" may be explained in terms of the thematic content of the play. But I do not believe they represent any "wooing" of his audience, for in fact Jonson fills *The New Inn* with experiments in comic organization that make far too many demands on his audience. Still, the highly experimental features in the play that may well contribute to its failure also make it a work of continuing interest because of the idea of a theater which these features imply and which the play itself embodies.

Throughout *The New Inn* Jonson coaches the audience to consider plot and character in terms of theatrical practices, in relation to conventions which produce dramatic illusion. From the beginning to the end, Jonson stresses the fact that his play, through almost outrageous "feigning," can teach the audience significant truths about various kinds of illusion within both the world of the theater and the "theater of the world." He establishes a metaphorical relationship between the world and the stage at the outset, when Lord Frampul, who is introduced to the audience in his disguise as the Host of the New Inn,[3] discusses the well-known idea of the *theatrum mundi*:[4]

3. It is well to note here that Jonson's spokesman is an actor playing the role of a character who, within the play, "feigns" to be what he is not—and in this feigning the Host is typical of the other major characters in the play. The original audience would not have read the summary of plot and characters which Jonson attached to the printed edition of the play and would have accepted characters as they are introduced in the beginning. It thus seems more fruitful to consider plot and character as they appear within the play itself.

4. See Anne Righter, *Shakespeare and the Idea of the Play* (London, 1962), pp.

> I imagine all the world's a Play;
> The state, and mens affaires, all passages
> Of life, to spring new *scenes,* come in, goe out,
> And shift, and vanish; and if I haue got
> A seat, to sit at ease here, i'mine Inne,
> To see the *Comedy;* and laugh, and chuck
> At the variety, and throng of humors,
> And dispositions, that come iustling in,
> And out still, as they one droue hence another:
> Why, will you enuy me my happinesse?
>
> (I.iii.128–137)

The Host suggests a relationship between his inn and the comic stage [5] and also identifies himself with the audience watching this particular play. Like the Host, the audience sits at ease to see the comedy and laugh at the variety and throng of humours that come in and out. And if "all the world's a Play," the individuals in the audience are by extension and analogy participants in the comedy. They share the point of view of the Host and perhaps, like him, play roles. A shifting, extended relationship between the audience in the theater and the actors on the stage is implied here and stressed elsewhere in the play. Indeed, *The New Inn* is governed by the idea of the world as a stage; and, by the time Jonson uses the *theatrum mundi* metaphor in this comedy, a number of themes especially significant to a playwright had become attached to the concept. Since Jonson explores several of these themes, it is well to give a few examples of significant meanings which the concept had acquired.

In the *Discoveries* Jonson uses the metaphor to make the point that men—like several of the characters he presents in *The New Inn*—lose sight of their own identities by adopting false "roles" within the theater of the world:

64–86; Ernst Robert Curtius, *European Literature and the Latin Middle Ages,* trans. Willard R. Trask (New York, 1953), pp. 138–144; Samuel C. Chew, *The Pilgrimage of Life* (New Haven, 1962), pp. 160–161; Richard Bernheimer, "Theatrum Mundi," *Art Bulletin,* XXXVIII (1956), 225–247; Thomas B. Stroup, *Microcosmos: The Shape of the Elizabethan Play* (Lexington, 1965), pp. 7–36; and Frances Yates, "New Light on the Globe Theater," *New York Review of Books,* VI (May 26, 1966), 16–22.

5. C. G. Thayer, in *Ben Jonson: Studies in the Plays* (Norman, 1963), pp. 202–232, considers this aspect of *The New Inn.* See also T. B. Stroup's discussion of the Inn as a microcosm of the world in *Microcosmos,* pp. 29, 164.

I *have* considered, our whole life is like a *Play:* wherein every man, forgetfull of himselfe, is in travaile with expression of another. Nay, wee so insist in imitating others, as wee cannot (when it is necessary) returne to our selves. . . .

(Works, VIII, 1093–1096)

In Erasmus' *Praise of Folly,* which is certainly one of the most important books for an understanding of Jonson, theatrical illusion is explicitly compared to illusion in everyday life, and Folly's discussion of the *theatrum mundi* concept provides an excellent introduction to *The New Inn:*

So lykewise, al this life of mortal men, what is it els, but a certayne kynde of stage playe? where as men come foorth disguised one in one araye, and another in another, eche playing hys parte, till at last, the maker of the playe, or Bookebearer causeth them to auoyde the skaffold, and yet sometime maketh one man come in, two or three times, with sundrye partes and apparell, as who before represented a king, being clothed al in purple, hauing no more but shifted himself a litle, shuld shew hymself againe like a woe begon myser. And al this is done vnder a certaine veile or shadow, which taken away once, the play can no more be played.[6]

According to Folly, all the world is a play, and like a play the world requires the acceptance of certain illusions, of the veil or shadow without which the play cannot be played. The implications of this statement to a playwright are evident. If the world is a stage, the stage is a kind of world wherein the "maker of the playe" may allow one of his characters to appear in various guises, may have an actor come in, two or three times, with "sundrye partes and apparell," as Jonson so frequently does throughout *The New Inn.*

The theater was not only the realm of illusion, it was also a place where men could go to be instructed. The connection between a "theater" and teaching is stressed in a work by Pierre Boaistuau, who uses *Theatrum Mundi* as the title of his explicitly didactic book. The Introduction indicates that this "Theater of the World" is set forth so that man, in his pride, may learn of his true nature. Since man is "of himselfe so masked and disguised that he knoweth not himselfe," Boaistuau says, "I haue

---

6. *The Praise of Follie,* trans. Sir Thomas Chaloner (London, 1577), D8ᵛ-E1ʳ. All citations to *Praise of Folly* are to this translation.

addressed to him this Theatre, in the which he may contemplate & be aduised of his infirmitie and miserie, & not withdrawne from himselfe . . . and if we will be equall Iudges in humane actiōs: what else is this world but a Theatre?"[7] Here the theater is described as a place of instruction, a microcosm and mirror of the great world it reflects, where men may learn about themselves.

Boaistuau's emphasis on the didactic function and Folly's emphasis on the illusory nature of the theater come together in an Italian *impresa* which shows a stage and has as its motto *Fingit at docet.* The commentary beneath the picture provides a summary of conventional interpretations of the *theatrum mundi* commonplace. It describes the stage as a "scene of the world, made according to nature." "The appearance is of a comedy" because people on the stage appear to be what they are not. An ignorant man may play a learned man: "You will find one pretending to be the other, and the others playing the parts of others." From another point of view, however, the scene of the world may be considered tragic. In both instances the stage teaches by feigning: *"Et io Fingit, at Docet"* (see Figure 3).

In *The New Inn* Jonson constantly stresses, for comic purposes, the feigning and teaching themes which the *theatrum mundi* commonplace had acquired. Throughout the play we find Jonson toying with his own art, frequently alluding to dramatic conventions and theatrical illusion at the very time he is exploiting them on the stage, constantly suggesting that the "feigning" on the stage, the illusions of the various characters, are analogous to the feigning and illusions inherent in everyday life. In a play based on errors and "supposes," in which almost every character at one point or another appears, or endeavors to appear, to be something which he is not, Jonson continually reminds us of the willing suspension of disbelief by which the events that an audience sees on the stage are both obviously feigned and accepted as real.

Within the play there are characters like those described in the *Discoveries,* who have lost sight of their own identities by adopting poses. By participating in, or viewing the play within the play, these characters learn the truth about themselves and others, just as men were to learn of their

7. Pierre Boaistuau, *Theatrum Mundi* (London, 1581), ¶2ᵛ–¶3ʳ.

618   Teatro d'Imprese,

SCENA, APPARATO.

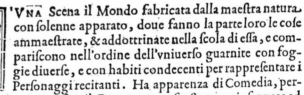

'Vna Scena il Mondo fabricata dalla maeſtra natura con ſolenne apparato, doue fanno la parte loro le coſe ammaeſtrate, & addottrinate nella ſcola di eſſa, e compariſcono nell'ordine dell'vniuerſo guarnite con foggie diuerſe, e con habiti condecenti per rappreſentare i Perſonaggi recitanti. Ha apparenza di Comedia, perche ſi vede vno ignorante fare il Dottore; vno ſcoſtumato inſegnare ad altri i coſtumi, & i ſauij eſſere giudicati da ſciocchi; & l'inette perſone vſurpare l'honoreuolezza, & i gradi douuti à meriteuoli: Et all'incontro vn buono, vn virtuoſo ſeruire, & eſſere nel ſeruire ingiuriato, che pare appunto eſſere fatto ſcherzo, e giuoco della fortuna, e riuſcire ridicoloſa la rappreſentatione, e coſi fingere traueſtiti e gli vni, e gli altri l'attioni altrui, come proprie. Ma s'hà ſembianza di Comedia la vita noſtra per queſti ſcherzi, e modi apparenti, ſi conoſce il fine eſſere tragico, poiche ſi veggono i Re, i Principi, & il tutto in morte terminare malamente, di cui ſi può con verità dire LVDIS FVNERALIBVS ACTA EST, come ſcriſſe ad vno apparato di Comedia, per cui inteſe la vita ſua, il Rota, fatta per lo dolore conceputo nella morte di ſua Moglie. Et io FINGIT, AT DOCET.

FIGURE 3. Illustration photographed from Giovanni Ferro, *Teatro d' Imprese* (Venice, 1623), II, 618, with the kind permission of the Folger Shakespeare Library.

own nature through Boaistuau's *Theatre*. Further, individual characters learn that a certain kind of feigning may in fact teach, for, through feigning, truth may be revealed, and, as Folly implied, certain illusions are as necessary to the theater of the world as they are to the world of the theater. The actors who play such characters, and the playmaker who brings them on and off the stage, pass this information on to members of the audience at *The New Inn,* who are themselves participants in the comedy of the world.

Along with the Host's speech emphasizing the relationship between the world and the theater, there are further key references to the stage in the opening scenes. We learn that in the world of the New Inn—again linked rhetorically to "all the world" (I.iii.107)—characters may choose the parts they will play:

> It being i'your free-will . . . to choose
> What parts you would sustaine. . . .
>
> (I.iii.108–109)

All the major characters introduced in the first act have chosen certain parts within the play itself. From the Host, who is really Lord Frampul, to the guests and servants, the various characters either play, or attempt to play, certain roles which conceal their true rank, sex, or nature from other characters and from the audience, either by their costumes or by their acting. Whether they assume physical disguises, or attitudes contrary to their natures, the characters "feign." In the beginning of the play Jonson presents these characters in disguise, deliberately withholding information concerning their true identities from the audience. Thus he exploits the conventions of acting and costume which require other characters on the stage, as well as the audience, to accept an actor, or a character within a play, for what he is not. For example, in the first scene we meet "Frank," who appears to both audience and characters to be a boy. It is only in the fifth act that Jonson reveals to the audience (and to all but one of the figures on the stage) that "Frank" is a girl of noble birth who has been disguised as a servant boy. At the outset, however, Jonson stresses, through the vocabulary of the play, the fact that the theater gives "Frank" at least two identities, that "Frank" is both a character within the comic world of *The New Inn* and also, in terms of the world of the theater itself, really and always a boy actor:

> O Lord, Sir, he prates Latine
> And 'twere a parrat, or a *play-boy*.
>
> (I.iii.4–5; emphasis mine)

Just as "Frank" is really a "play-boy" at the same time that conventions
of theatrical illusion allow him to exist in turn as the Host's boy and as
the nobly born Laetitia, so other characters simultaneously play different
roles. When Lady Frampul dresses her servant Prue for her role as queen
for a day, the discussion of costuming functions on several levels at once:

> LADY FRAMPUL
> 'Tis rich enough! But 'tis not what I meant thee!
> I would ha' had thee brauer then my selfe,
> And brighter farre. 'Twill fit the *Players* yet,
> When thou hast done with it, and yeeld thee somwhat.
> PRUDENCE
> That were illiberall, madam, and mere sordid
> In me, to let a sute of yours come there.
> LADY FRAMPUL
> Tut, all are *Players,* and but serue the *Scene*.
>
> (II.i.33–39) [8]

Here again Jonson uses the *theatrum mundi* commonplace simultaneously to create and to fracture illusion. Lady Frampul's speech reminds
us of dramatic conventions, and we are coached to view the action from
several perspectives. Of course the boys playing Prue and Lady Frampul
are serving Jonson's scene, and the beautiful costume is already in the
hands of the players. The theatrical practices described are also exhibited,
as the audience watches the "play-boy" acting the part of Prue adopt the
rich costume appropriate to still another role. For both Prue and Lady
Frampul, like "Frank" and the Host, play "roles" within the play itself.
"Prue," played by a boy actor who exists at one and the same time as a
player and as Lady Frampul's servant, appears within the play both as a
mere servant and as the reigning queen of the play within the play. As we

---

8. Lady Frampul's translation of the traditional motto of the Globe, *Totus
mundus agit histrionem,* repeats the commonplace which is so influential within the
play and which was also used by contemporaries to defend the stage. See Thomas
Heywood's *Apology for Actors* (London, 1612), a4ᵛ: "All men haue parts, and each
man acts his owne."

shall see, Prue's role within the play, whereby she adopts a costume
appropriate to her wit and virtue, is a means by which she becomes a
noblewoman in the end of the play. Costume, in this instance, functions to
reveal the truth about a character, though we shall see that in other
instances it is the source of many of the mistakes people make concerning
appearances throughout the play.

The New Inn is also concerned with disguises and mistaken identities
at a deeper level than those involving external costume. Lady Frances
Frampul, who poses as "love's heretic," masks herself by attitude and
behavior rather than by dress, and only later in the play does she admit
this to herself and to others:

> frowardnesse sometime
> Becomes a beauty, being but a visor
> Put on. You'l let a Lady weare her masque, *Pru.*
> PRUDENCE
> But how do I know, when her Ladiship is pleas'd
> To leaue it off, except she tell me so?
>
> (IV.iv.293–297)

The discarding of a mask of behavior is less apparent to others than the
change of a garment. Lady Frampul's disguise, mask, costume of attitude
is also harder to penetrate than, say, the externally inappropriate costume
of Pinnacia Stuffe, the ridiculous tailor's wife who wears a garment
beyond her merit or station. In fact, discussions of Lady Frampul's fine
acting ability raise the complex question: where does acting leave off, and
where does the truth begin? What is the relationship between the way one
acts and what one really is? When Lady Frampul, who has held to the
attitude of Love's heretic, speaks as if she were in love, various characters
debate whether she is acting or not:

> PRUDENCE
> Well *fain'd,* my Lady: now her *parts* begin!
> LATIMER
> And she will *act* 'hem subtilly.
> . . . .
> PRUDENCE
> Excellent *actor!* how she hits this passion!
> . . . .

LATIMER
But doe you thinke she *playes?*

(III.ii.178–179, 210, 214) [9]

LOVEL
Tut, she dissembles! All is personated,
And counterfeit comes from her!

(III.ii.259–260)

PRUDENCE
Or you can faine!
My subtill and dissembling Lady mistresse.

(IV.iv.144–145)

PRUDENCE
I sweare, I thought you had dissembled, Madam,
And doubt, you do so yet.

(IV.iv.310–311)

Of course the boy playing Frances Frampul is "feigning" all the time. But in an interesting Renaissance example of the James-Lange theory, when the character he plays, Lady Frampul, begins to act as if she were in love, she actually falls in love. Her "acting" serves as a revelation, and she ultimately becomes what she acts. Just as Prue, who acts the part of a queen in the Court of Love, becomes a noblewoman in the end, Lady Frampul, who acts the part of a lover, finally becomes one. "Roles," or disguises, in several instances ultimately reveal identity. "Frank," who is really a noble girl, is costumed as such, and the "disguise" even involves the adoption of her true name.[10] Prue and Lady Frampul also take on new

9. The emphasis in these quotations is mine. For further discussion of Lady Frampul's acting, see the following passages:

10. Throughout the play, Jonson uses names in a significant way. Lord Frampul (disguised as the Host) assumes the name Good-Stock, which hints at his noble birth. "Frank," who is really his daughter, is described as "descended of a right *good stock,* Sir" (II.vi.23; emphasis mine), and this suggests the true relationship between them. "Frank" is ostensibly named "Francis," while Lady Frampul's first name is Frances (II.ii.19–23), and the Lady tells "Frank" her name "is the same with yours" (II.ii.23). Indeed it proves to be, since they are sisters, only the similar name is not the first but the last. Jonson apparently uses these discussions of names, and puns on names, as clues to the real identities of the various characters, but I doubt that an audience would have time to catch these clues in performance. I did not notice them until after several readings of the play, though the innumerable puns on the names

identities and become what they act—noblewoman and lover; but "Frank" simply acts what she really is. What appears to be real in the first scene is in fact a costume, and what appears to be a false role (that of Laetitia) proves to be real. The function of costume and roles within the play is complex, affording numerous parallels and contrasts. Yet if the nature of the three female characters all in one way or another is revealed through what they play or wear, the audience is reminded that they are in fact play-boys, who, on the stage, remain what they are but take on the appearance of what they are not. Quite late in the play Prue reminds us again that her rich costume is in truth a "play-boyes brauery":

> I will not buy this play-boyes brauery,
> At such a price, to be vpbraided for it,
> Thus, euery minute.
>
> (IV.iv.321–323)

These references to play-boys, acting, masks, parts, function within the play on the stage and extend beyond it to remind the audience that what they are watching is always "feigning," always a dramatic illusion. And there are implied references to theatrical illusion which serve to underscore the explicit ones. For example, after the Court of Love scene, Lady Frampul feels that the hour has gone by too quickly:

> I should haue thought it scarce had run ten minutes,
> When the whole houre is fled.
>
> (III.ii.243–244)

The scene she describes would take approximately ten minutes' acting time. This statement of the lover's theory of the relativity of time operates within the context of the play, describing Lady Frampul's feelings, and it also provides a kind of comment on dramatic illusion, whereby an hour may be presented in ten minutes.

At the end of the play within the play, we find references to the sensations which an audience and actors feel when a performance is over, when "The Court's dissolu'd, remou'd, and the play ended" (IV.iv.247). The play within the play is seen by various characters as mere illusion,

---

of characters in the low-life scenes—Fly, Jordan, Ferrett—obviously are stressed for comic purposes. The most important pun, on Lovel's name, is discussed below.

unrelated to any kind of truth, and the players appear to be reduced to what they were before the Court of Love began. The dramatic illusion over, "reason" returns:

LOVEL
. . . I ha' not lost my reason,
Though I haue lent my selfe out, for two howres,[11]
Thus to be baffuld by a Chambermaid,
And the good Actor, her Lady. . . .

(IV.iv.275–278)

Lady Frampul's revelation of love is reduced to good acting, and Prue is reduced to her former role of chambermaid. Lovel's speech is part of Jonson's customary fourth-act reversal, where everything in a play appears to run backwards. Subsequent events, the ultimate resolution of the tangles, indicate that Lovel's "reason" is wrong, that his comic "bafflement" was right, that acting and illusion may reveal truth as well as conceal it. But at this point in the play various characters reject illusions. Prue says she will put off her "play-boyes brauery" (which is precisely what the boy playing Prue will do when the performance of *The New Inn* is over). The Host compares himself to a playwright and metaphorically likens the actions he has manipulated, and their apparently unsuccessful outcome, to the manipulations of the comic poet, Jonson himself:

I had thought to ha' sacrific'd,
To merriment to night, i' my light Heart, *Fly,*
And like a noble Poet, to haue had
My last act best: but all failes i' the plot.

(V.i.24–26)

The Host's expression of doubt concerning the outcome must lead the audience to wonder how Jonson will resolve the difficulties he has set for himself. Other characters contribute to the suspense, agreeing that previous events had no relation to truth. Beaufort calls the strange "errors" of the play the *"Supposititious* fruits of an Host's braine" (V.v.41). All appears to be confusion. Lovel and Lady Frampul seem estranged. Prue is angry. "Frank" is supposed to be the Host's son. Then a new set of

11. The Court of Love scene is supposed to have lasted two hours—the acting time of a contemporary play.

recognitions and reversals takes place. The lovers are reconciled; Prue decides to marry Lord Latimer; and "Frank," the Host, and the Nurse prove to be the family of Lady Frampul. Lovel describes these revelations by comparing them to a dream and wonders whether the happy ending is a significant dream or a mere phantasm: [12]

> Is this a dreame now, after my first sleepe?
> Or are these phant'sies made i' the light Heart?
> And sold i' the new Inne?
>
> (V.v.120–122)

In *The New Inn* Jonson makes artistic use of widely held contemporary theories that poetry and dreams may be, in one sense, illusions but that they may also be a means by which reason is transcended and truth revealed. Throughout the play he distinguishes between "phantasms," which have no relation to reality, and "visions," which can be of high import. As the play ends, Lovel speaks of his "vision" and recognizes that the happy ending is in fact a dream come true, an "illusion" which is meaningful, not "supposititious" or baffling (V.v.149–150), and thus Jonson coaches us to see the play as an extreme example of dramatic illusion and also as a poetic consideration of the kind of reality illusions may have. The subplot contributes key lines which function in terms of this theme:

> PEIRCE
> O you haue had some phant'sie, fellow *Peck;*
> Some reuelation—
>
> . . . .
>
> FERRET
> We shall ha' some truth explain'd.
>
> PEIRCE
> We are all mortall,
> And haue our visions.
>
> (III.i.112–113, 129–130)

12. In his earlier masque, *The Vision of Delight,* and again in *The New Inn,* Jonson adopts Macrobius' widely known classification of dreams and distinguishes between dreams known as "phantasms," which are meaningless or deceptive and which have no relation to truth, and "visions"—dreams through which profound truth may be revealed. I discuss Jonson's exploration of traditional dream theory in *The Vision of Delight* in my doctoral dissertation, *Ben Jonson: Five Poetic Worlds* (Washington University, 1964).

In some instances visions may be closer to the truth than "reason." But certain false illusions, deceptive "phantasms" with no relation to nature and truth, must be discarded:

> These are fits, and fancies,
> Which you must leaue, good *Peck*.
>
> (III.i.138–139)

From the outset Jonson uses the term "phant'sie" or "fancy" to describe misleading roles or attitudes which various characters adopt. Lovel's absurd Love Melancholy is described as such a "phant'sie" (I.iv.17), and so is Lady Frampul's exaggerated and false pose as Love's heretic (I.v.51). These are "fits and fancies" which the characters must "leaue" before the play can come to a happy ending. And like the deceptive roles and dreams, certain costumes are misleading and unrelated to any reality, and these are ultimately discarded, while others, which serve to reveal the truth, are retained. If the costume or "role" adopted suits the true nature of the character, it may be a means by which this nature is fulfilled and perfected. On the other hand, if it is unrelated to any reality, it represents a false and ridiculous "fancy" which results in unhappiness. Jonson explicitly contrasts Prue and Pinnacia, two women who wear gowns above their station. With Prue, the rich costume proves appropriate and reveals her true nature:

> Sweet *Pru*, I, now thou art a Queene indeed!
> These robes doe royally! and thou becom'st 'hem!
> So they doe thee! rich garments only fit
> The partyes they are made for!
>
> (V.ii.1–4)

Pinnacia Stuffe, as opposed to Prue, is ridiculous in her assumed finery. The rich garments

> [did] shew on good'y *Taylors* back!
> Like a Caparison for a Sow, God saue vs!
>
> (V.ii.5–6)

Jonson's deliberate juxtaposition of the two characters stresses the idea that costumes or "roles" adopted in the world must reflect some kind of truth or they are worthless, ridiculous, and ultimately will be exposed.[13]

False attitudes can be as unfortunate or comic as inappropriate costumes. Lovel is melancholy because he conceals his feelings from Lady Frampul. The moment he begins to reveal them, she responds. His disguise of his feelings is analogous to her adoption of the misleading role of Love's heretic. It is only when the two characters play new parts in the Court of Love—Lovel appearing as Love's advocate and Lady Frampul as Love's convert—that the couple may be united. And still another role which reveals the truth, "Frank's" disguise as Laetitia, brings about the removal of the various false disguises which had kept the family separated and makes reunion and a happy ending possible.

Throughout the play the various roles the characters adopt are compared, contrasted, and held up to question. And so are the conventional guises in which love appears—courtly, Platonic, sensual. The character Lovel enables Jonson to present the standard attitudes and compare them to one another. Lovel is introduced to the audience in the role of the conventional "melancholy" lover, rather like Orsino in *Twelfth Night,* but his melancholy is qualified and questioned by its contrast with the mirth of the Host. In the Court of Love scenes Lovel adopts the role of the Platonic lover, but Jonson contrasts Lovel's Platonic theory with the "practice" of the Ovidian philosophy recommended by Beaufort:

LOVEL

Loue is a spirituall coupling of two soules,
So much more excellent, as it least relates
Vnto the body; circular, eternall;
Not fain'd, or made, but borne: And then, so pretious,
As nought can value it, but it selfe. So free,

13. For a discussion of significant costume in *The New Inn* see E. B. Partridge, *The Broken Compass,* pp. 199–205, where he gives particular attention to the Pinnacia Stuffe episode in terms of the imagery of the play as a whole. In connection with the Stuffe episode, it is interesting to observe how Jonson's presentation of Pinnacia provides, in little, a parallel to the presentation of the more important characters in the play. She first appears to be a great lady, but later we learn that she is not at all what she seemed to be. Through the Stuffe episode Jonson may have tried to hint at the series of recognitions at the end of the play, when we discover that the Host, "Frank," and the Nurse are not what their garments and acting led us to believe they were in the beginning; but, again, I think he expects far too much from an audience.

As nothing can command it, but it selfe.
And in it selfe, so round, and liberall,
As where it fauours, it bestowes it selfe.
                    BEAUFORT (*kissing Frank*)
And, that doe I; here my whole selfe, I tender,
According to the practise o'the Court.
                    NURSE
I, 'tish a naughty practish, a lewd practish. . . .
                                        (III.ii.105–115)

In this scene idealistic theory and the more common practice of love are presented in a kind of debate. As Frank Kermode suggests, Lovel woos Frances

by giving her a full exposition of the true Florentine Art of Love. But Lord Beaufort, a less scholarly gentleman, is seized with an un-Platonic desire for Laetitia, and in this the contrast resides. . . . Lovel speaks for Ourania, Beaufort for Pandemos, illustrating his case with kisses stolen from Laetitia, which are qualitatively very different from that formal, licensed, Platonic kiss, mixture of souls, which is to be Lovel's reward from Lady Frampul.[14]

And, Kermode goes on to say, "Jonson does not allow the high-minded view all its own way, and there may be ironic references to the cult-Platonism of the contemporary court."[15] Jonson does appear to be having gentle fun implying that the two kinds of love ultimately result in the same sort of action. The two kisses may be very different conceptually, but they are both kisses. Though Lovel discounts the senses, his speech appeals to Lady Frampul's "taste," and she calls our attention to several senses in her response to what she earlier termed "loue, or language" (III.ii.172):

O speake, and speake for euer! let min⟨e⟩ *eare*
Be *feasted* still, and filled with this *banquet!*
No *sense* can euer surfet on such truth!
                            (III.ii.201–203; emphasis mine)

This reaction to Platonic truth involves a vocabulary striking in its similarity to that used by Beaufort in describing an Ovidian banquet of sense:

14. "The Banquet of Sense," *JRLB*, XLIV (1961), 74–77.
15. *Ibid.*

BEAUFORT
I relish not these *philosophicall feasts;*
Giue me *a banquet o'sense,* like that of *Ovid:*
A forme, to take the eye; a voyce, mine *eare.* . . .
                                    (III.ii.125–127; emphasis mine)

The descriptions at first glance appear to be in opposition, but the common vocabulary may suggest that they are not so far apart after all. In the following year Jonson examined various kinds of love in a masque, *Love's Triumph through Callipolis,* where he contrasts Platonic love with the crudest sensual love:

> *Loue is the right affection of the minde,*
> *The noble appetite of what is best*
>   (*Works,* VII, ll. 54–55)

as opposed to those loves

> *that in the sensuall schoole*
> *Of lust, for their degree of brute may passe.*
> *All which are vapor'd hence.*
> *No loues, but slaues to sense:*
> *Meere cattell, and not men.*
>   (ll. 92–96)

But in the end of the masque, perfect fulfillment proves to be the incorporation of physical love within the context of the higher, ideal love:

> *Here, stay a while: This! this*
> *The Temple of all* Beauty *is!*
> *Heere, perfect* Louers, *you must pay*
> *First-fruits; and on these altars lay*
> (*The Ladyes breasts*) *your ample vowes,*
> *Such, as* Loue *brings, and* Beauty *best allowes!*
> CHORUS
> *For* Loue, *without his obiect, soone is gone:*
> Loue *must haue answering loue, to looke vpon.*
>   (ll. 115–122)

Again in 1634 Jonson raised the question of reconciliation between Platonic and sensual love:

CHORUS
If Love *be call'd a lifting of the* Sense
To knowledge of that pure intelligence,
Wherein the Soule *hath rest, and residence:*

1. TENOR
When were the Senses *in such order plac'd?*

2. TENOR
The Sight, *the* Hearing, Smelling, Touching, Taste,
All at one Banquet?

BASS
　　　　　　　　　　　　　　　'Would it ever last!

1. TENOR
Wee wish the same: who set it forth thus?

BASS
　　　　　　　　　　　　　　　　　　Love!
(*Loves' Welcome at Bolsover, Works,* VII, ll. 3–9)

The same problem is posed in *The New Inn,* and its solution is not the denial of the sensual but rather sensual love properly contained within a higher context which gives it significance. As Barbara Everett notes, the song Lovel sings at the end of the play, describing his Vision of Beauty, involves, at this point, a real as well as an ideal situation.[16]

Also, Lovel's theory of Platonic love, like his theory of Stoic valor, is held up to question by his own behavior. As C. G. Thayer points out, Lovel

delivers a highly Platonic discourse on disinterested and perfect love while he himself is consumed with passion. . . . He delivers a highly articulate Senecan discourse on valor (which here means Stoic fortitude), convincing everyone in the room of the truth of what he is saying, and then, in an agony of unrequited love, takes to his bed like Troilus or Aurelius.[17]

For example, Lovel describes the man of valor:

He can assure himselfe against all rumour!
Despaires of nothing! laughs at contumelies!

16. "Analysis: Ben Jonson's 'A Vision of Beauty,'" *Critical Quarterly,* I (1959), 244.

17. *Ben Jonson: Studies in the Plays,* p. 206.

> As knowing himselfe aduanced in a height
> Where iniury cannot reach him. . . .

(IV.iv.134–137)

But injury does reach him, and he is plunged into despair not by "all rumour" but by "one word":

> From what a happinesse hath that one word
> Throwne me, into the gulfe of misery?
> To what a bottomlesse despaire? how like
> A Court remoouing, or an ended Play
> Shewes my abrupt precipitate estate. . . .

(IV.iv.249–253)

If nothing can trouble "him that's valiant" (IV.iv.149), Lovel shows something other than valor here. The statement, however, affords a humanizing contrast to Lovel's earlier description of love:

> True loue hath no vnworthy thought, no light,
> Loose, vn-becoming appetite, or straine,
> But fixed, constant, pure, immutable.

(III.ii.122–124)

The Senecan and Platonic ideals, as expressed by Lovel, are all very well and good, but Jonson's comic exaggeration functions to show that they are almost inhumanly abstract and severe. As Erasmus' Folly puts it:

. . . the *Archestoike Seneca* strongly gainsayeth mee, who in no wyse will a wyseman should haue any manner affection in hym. But when hee taketh that away, hee leaueth man, no man, but rather a newefounde GOD without bodily sense, suche as neuer was, nor neuer shall be. Yea, to speake playnlier, hee dooth naught else than fourme a stone Image of a man, without feeling, or any manner inclination perteyning to a man in deede.[18]

Through the action Jonson implies that Lovel's speeches advocating Platonic love and Stoic valor at their most extreme tend to contradict Lovel's own nature. To read Lovel's speeches as dogmatic statements of Jonson's philosophy is to ignore the context in which they occur.[19] Lovel's

---

18. *The Praise of Follie,* E2ʳ.
19. Herford and Simpson consider Lovel a character who "appears, and is meant to appear, an ideal" (*Works,* II, 196). John Enck feels that "Lovel's rapturous

comparison of his "precipitate estate" to "a Court remoouing, or an ended Play" indicates the way we are to view his anguish—in a properly theatrical, properly comic, context. To take his speeches too seriously is to distort Lovel, who is attractive enough as a character but, from the beginning, does not know whether he loves ill or loves well:

> HOST
> But is your name *Loue-ill,* Sir, or *Loue-well?*
> I would know that.
> 　　　　　　LOVEL
> 　　　　　　I doe not know't my selfe,
> Whether it is. But it is Loue hath beene
> The hereditary passion of our house. . . .
> 　　　　　　　　　　　　　　　　　　(I.vi.95–97)

Lovel is like his family "passion" not only in his ambiguous name, for he himself appears in the various guises of love at different points in *The New Inn*. Seen in relation to the courtly, Platonic, and sensual attitudes, he is not inappropriate in a play where a character like Frank is referred to in terms of three separate identities (play-boy, "Frank," Laetitia) or a low character like Fly has a number of titles (II.iv.32–35). And at the end the various kinds of love come together in the proper combination. Dreams, ideal visions, and "roles" appear in relation to reality when the courtly Lovel speaks to his lady mistress of his vision of ideal beauty before they go to bed:

> 　　　　　　　　　　　Stay, let my M^{rs}
> But heare my vision sung, my dreame of beauty,
> Which I haue brought, prepar'd, to bid vs ioy,
> And light vs all to bed. . . .
> 　　　　　　　　　　　　　　　　　(V.v.148–151)

Thus love, like a play or a vision, properly involves truth encompassed by an "illusion" or poetic context which gives it enriched significance. This play, like *A Midsummer-Night's Dream,* is a comic exploration of the power of feigning—of illusion, acting, and poetry—rather than a denial of it. The very facts that play-boys can appear to be ladies, that a costume can evoke an attitude toward a character, that an hour can be

---

improvisation . . . must be written off as philosophizing, in the worst sense of the word, for its own sake" (*Jonson and the Comic Truth,* p. 220).

presented in ten minutes, are indications of the power of dramatic illusion. Further, members of the audience are, in the theater of the world, "all mortal" and have their "visions," and this play explores and exhibits some of the common "visions" of ordinary life in a form which underscores the material it conveys—for these illusions are presented in a context which Jonson insists is always an illusory one.

Within the play Jonson so daringly manipulates theatrical conventions that his very manipulation of them becomes unconventional. He makes extreme demands on his audience, for he deliberately withholds a very large supply of information concerning his characters until the final scenes of the play. In the beginning the audience is expected to accept "Frank" as a boy, the Host and the Nurse as nothing more than Host and Nurse. In the fifth act the audience, coached by theatrical convention to judge by appearance and behavior, would be as surprised as the characters on the stage to learn that the Host, the Nurse, and "Frank" are not at all what they first seemed to be. Just as the servants at first judge Pinnacia's rank according to her fine clothes, the audience would be taken in by Jonson's initial presentation of his major characters. In the end, though, nothing is as it seemed in the first act. Every major character has undergone some kind of transformation. Jonson previously had withheld full information concerning the sex of Epicoene and the power of Tiberius until the final acts of *The Silent Woman* and *Sejanus,* but here he withholds information concerning three major characters; and when he published the play, he found it necessary to supply relevant information. Jonson probably intended the final set of recognitions to come as a comic revelation to the audience, a surprise dependent upon the powers of acting and costume which make it possible for an audience to accept an actor, or a character in a play, for what he is not. For, as Erasmus' Folly indicates:

If one at a solemne stage play, would take vpon him to pluck of the plaiers garments, whiles they were saying theyr partes & so discipher vnto the lokers on, the true & natiue faces of the players, shoulde hee not (trow yee) marre all the matter? . . . yee shoulde see yet straightwayes a new transmutation in thinges: that who before played the woman, should than appeare to be a man: who seemed youth, should shew his hore heares: . . . Yet take away this errour, and as soone take away all together, in as much as the feigninge and counterfetinge is it, that so delighteth the beholders.[20]

20. *The Praise of Follie,* D8^{r-v}.

The world of the theater is based upon the acceptance of certain illusions, and in *The New Inn* Jonson uses theatrical terms and conventions to call our attention to this acceptance, to emphasize the illusory nature of the world of the theater; and he may be said to very nearly "discipher vnto the lokers on, the true and natiue faces" of the players. For he reminds us that the female characters are boy actors in order to stress that on the stage, as in the world, "all are *Players,* and but serue the *Scene,*" and in the end he pulls the rug out from under his audience in order to prove that members of the audience are completely taken in by external appearance in the theater, just as they are in the world at large. The play by no means represents a decline in Jonson's "experimental energy." According to Jonson, "rules are ever of lesse force, and valew, then experiments" (*Discoveries* [*Works,* VIII], ll. 1757–1758), and this play may be said to err on the side of experiment. Nevertheless, the experiment is there for a specific and significant purpose, for the sake of Jonson's comic exploration of an idea of a theater which, through feigning and illusion, can inform men in the "theater of the world" of their own nature.

Deception and Social Dislocation: An Aspect of James Shirley's Drama

RICHARD MORTON

THE TEMPTATION TO CLASSIFY minor literary figures as transitional can hardly be resisted in the case of James Shirley, who was born in 1596, the year of the second volume of *The Faerie Queene,* and died exactly 300 years ago, in 1666, Dryden's *Annus Mirabilis.* As a comic dramatist, he has frequently been identified as a link between Jonson and the Restoration playwrights, between the comedy of humours and the comedy of manners. There is much to support such a view. Forsythe's thorough documentation [1] has revealed Shirley's indebtedness to the Elizabethan and Jacobean stage. The regular appearance in his plays of courtly fashion and the Truewit-Witwoud-Witless ritual of outwitting,[2] so popular in the reign of Charles II, counters Dryden's celebrated rejection of his works as meaningless to the new age:

> Heywood and Shirley were but types of thee,
> Thou last great prophet of tautology.[3]

1. R. S. Forsythe, *The Relations of Shirley's Plays to the Elizabethan Drama* (New York, 1914).
2. Described in T. H. Fujimura, *The Restoration Comedy of Wit* (Princeton, 1952), pp. 65–66.
3. "MacFlecknoe," ll. 29–30.

Pepys, for example, seems to have had some warm responses to his plays, which were among the more popular of the old dramas at the Restoration court.[4]

To concentrate on the transitional aspects of a playwright's works has some disadvantages; it tends to shatter the integrity of the individual pieces, to label one scene or character an echo of the past, another a prefiguration of the future. Shirley's plays have perhaps suffered too much from such scholastic mayhem. Ashley H. Thorndike typifies this approach in his generally admirable and perceptive pages:

> No earlier dramatist presents so many reminiscences of Shakespeare . . . and he often imitates Jonson. . . . But his plays in their main characteristics naturally adapt themselves to the models of Fletcher and Massinger. . . . He is almost as close to the heroic play, the tragicomedy and the comedy of manners of the Restoration as to the romances and comedies of Fletcher.[5]

Shirley's plays are doubtless conventional, but they are independent works of art, achieving their effects by their intrinsic qualities rather than by their position in literary history. My purpose here is to notice one of those aspects of Shirley's plays which give them coherence and effectiveness.

I

The direction of comedy in general is toward reconciliation of discordant elements, and its method in Renaissance drama is most commonly the intrigue, in which, typically, the young outwit the old. The Jonsonian comedy of humours may show the reformation of the eccentric individual; the Restoration comedy of manners frequently shows the resolution of conflicting ways of life—a whole element of society is eccentric. Shirley's comic method has elements of both: he has many "humours" characters, and in his best plays he draws on the fluid and rapidly changing world of Caroline London to produce a comedy of conflicting social elements which seems, perhaps because of its source in a world of

4. See Eleanore Boswell, *The Restoration Court Stage* (Cambridge, 1932), pp. 105–106.

5. Ashley H. Thorndike, *English Comedy* (New York, 1929), p. 236.

genuine social conflict, to have unique urgency and validity. Characteristically, the plot of a play by Shirley depends on a trick or a misunderstanding. As with Renaissance drama in general, the deception of husband by wife, father by daughter, suitor by witty mistress, and foolish citizen by elegant courtier is commonplace and easily anticipated. When, for example, in the delightful comedy *The Lady of Pleasure* we see Aretina fashionably kicking her heels in courtly London, flaunting her noble connections and wasting the estates of her husband, Bornwell, we may well expect him to expostulate fruitlessly in Act I and then, in Act II, to attempt subterfuge. Aretina's appropriate reformation, in Act V, is both timely and inevitable:

> Already
> I feel a cure upon my soul, and promise
> My after life to virtue.[6]

As Father Curry has neatly observed: "On the Elizabethan stage the race of dupes, both native and exotic, flourished in a prolific variety of breeds, and the hunting was both merry and determined."[7]

With Shirley's best plays the irony implicit in the deception situation, where one character misunderstands another or is deliberately duped, serves as more than a source of laughter at the foolishness of the gull. It illuminates the contrast between the viewpoints of the trickster and the tricked, reveals their difficulties of communication, and, when the differences are at a social level, demonstrates the conflicts within the society portrayed.

Shirley's plays show him to have been particularly aware of these conflicts. The well-known tensions between the servant and the master, the countryman and the townsman, the tradesman and the fop, are as staple to his plays as to those of his contemporaries, but he is unusually sophisticated in his perception of conflicts among the various groups of

6. Act V, scene i; James Shirley, *The Dramatic Works and Poems*, ed. William Gifford and Alexander Dyce (London, 1833), IV, 99. With the exception of passages from *The Traitor* and *The Cardinal*, which have recently been well edited, quotations are from the Gifford-Dyce edition, now available in a photographic reprint (New York: Russell & Russell, 1966).

7. John V. Curry, *Deception in Elizabethan Comedy* (Chicago, 1955), p. 6.

leisured city-dwellers.[8] The famous comedy, *The Ball,* devotes so much
attention to documentation of distinctions between the higher levels of
London life that the plot, for want of weeding, is confused and neglected.
The Constant Maid puts on stage a neat abstract of the dramatist's
London. Hartwell is a young descendant of the minor gentry, unwilling
to hold the office by which his father had eked out an archaic, hospitable
squire's existence. Playfair is a courtly gallant of elegant phrase and
considerable means, which he devotes to the pursuit of intrigue. He is the
nephew of Sir Clement, the somewhat old-fashioned justice in whose
house the action takes place. Startup is a foolish rustic who inevitably
becomes the rival suitor. A farcical plot, involving swapping of clothes
and misidentification, puts into opposition these three typical figures of a
fluctuating society. Decayed gentry, prosperous courtier, and *nouveau
riche* farmer meet on approximately equal social terms but differ markedly in interests, attitudes, and behavior. Naturally, then, they live side by
side but do not really understand or trust one another. Confusions, the
basis for comedy, arise. Shirley's world of fashion is exclusive, intricate,
formal, and slightly debauched; his gentry and mercantile classes are
commonsensical, but they are frequently bewildered by the elaborate
courtiers. So Julietta, in *Hyde Park,* a perfectly respectable gentlewoman
of leisure, is explicit when she must entertain the courtly Lord Bonvile:

TRIER
—Sweet lady, pray
Assure his lordship he is welcome.

JULIETTA
I want words.

LORD BONVILE
Oh, sweet lady, your lip in silence
Speaks the best language.

JULIETTA
Your lordship's welcome to this humble roof.
(II.iii; Gifford and Dyce, II, 481)

It is this failure to communicate easily across the bounds of social class
which forms the basis for the tricks or misunderstandings so frequently
found in the plays.

8. The best treatment of this aspect—indeed one of the best discussions of Shirley's
art in general—is in Kathleen M. Lynch, *The Social Mode of Restoration Comedy*
(New York, 1926), pp. 34-42.

Conventionally, of course, the honest woman tempted by her superior reveals or feigns a modest failure to communicate or understand. So, in *The Traitor,* Sciarrha tests the honor of his sister, Amidea, by telling her of the Duke's lusts:

SCIARRHA
You must to court. Oh happiness!
AMIDEA
                              For what?
SCIARRHA
What do great ladies do at court, I pray?
Enjoy the pleasures of the world, dance, kiss
The amorous lords, and change court breath, sing loose
Belief of other heaven, tell wanton dreams,
Rehearse your sprightly bed scenes, and boast which
Hath most idolators, accuse all faces
That trust to the simplicity of nature,
Talk witty blasphemy,
Discourse their gaudy wardrobes, plot new pride,
Jest upon courtiers' legs, laugh at the wagging
Of their own feathers, and a thousand more
Delights which private ladies never think of.
. . . .
AMIDEA
                    You make me wonder.
Pray speak that I may understand.
SCIARRHA
                              Why will you
Appear so ignorant? I speak the dialect
Of Florence to you.[9]

In this passage, as elsewhere in Shirley's plays, we have a richly documented description of the life of a certain social group. The influence of formal satire and the character books is clearly at work; the society Shirley draws requires a fine discrimination which would no doubt be appreciated by the leisured classes in his audience. In *Hyde Park* and *The Traitor* the contest is not between rich and poor, powerful and impotent; rather it is between the apparently closer levels of courtier and gentry. Shirley is not dealing with the extravagant and unlikely union of Fair 'Em and King

9. James Shirley, *The Traitor,* ed. John Stewart Carter (Lincoln, 1965), II.i. 182–194, 204–207.

William but with possible and plausible affairs such as that between Kenelm Digby and Venetia Stanley, which Professor Harbage feels may be dealt with explicitly in *The Wedding*.[10] The dramatic situation is rooted in the life of London and made particularly relevant to a court audience, for whom these matters of class relationships in the upper levels of society would inevitably be of major import.

The failure of comprehension between different groups is sometimes deliberately exploited in a trick, sometimes it grows spontaneously from the dramatic interplay of character. But in Shirley's plays it normally produces uncertainty, discomfiture, and, at last, when the misunderstanding is clarified, discovery and increased self-awareness. Aretina realizes that she cannot really understand or live in the extravagant fashionable world and so, at the end, returns to a proper and decent position of subservience to her husband and the ideals of the minor gentry.

Shirley's devotion to the trick as a dramatic device is demonstrated by his best-known play, *The Cardinal,* which, while a revenge tragedy, opens with a deception more nearly allied to the comic. Although the action begins with a scene of ominous political discussion, stressing for the audience the solemnity of the play, the trick played on the stern soldier Columbo comes from the comedy of manners. In the lively chatter between Rosaura and her maids, he is castigated as uncourtly and uncouth. On stage he confirms this impression, using, as Professor Forker has aptly noted, "military metaphor for court etiquette"[11] in a way calculated to display his personality. The ladies in waiting, Valeria and Celinda, discourse of Columbo's valorous and noble figure in the language of Fletcher's court maidens; their witty dialogue, toying conceitedly with the concept of a soldier as a lover, neatly stimulates the audience's awareness of the distinction between the stiff general and the brilliant court.

When Columbo receives the Duchess' letter, his impatience with the messenger's romantic dialect stresses again the gulf between his manners and those of the Duchess. He interrupts the flood of eloquence with a curt "No Poetry" (II.i.124). His failure to understand the purpose of the letter

10. Alfred Harbage, "James Shirley's *The Wedding* and the Marriage of Sir Kenelm Digby," *PQ,* XVI (January, 1937), 35–40.

11. James Shirley, *The Cardinal,* ed. Charles R. Forker (Bloomington, 1964), p. 18 n.

arises from his incompetent attempt to think in the unaccustomed vein of
a lover:

> [*Aside*] I have found it out, the Dutchess loves me dearly,
> She exprest a trouble in her when I took
> My leave, and chid me with a sullen ey;
> 'Tis a device to hasten my return;
> Love has a thousand arts; I'l answer it,
> Beyond her expectation.
>
> (II.i.128–133)

His instinctive response—to reject the letter with fury—was the right one.
He falls into Rosaura's trap because he tries to affect a habit of mind he
does not possess. Thus this episode, the first step in a dark and bloody
tragedy, is a variation of the gulling of the Witwoud, whose affectations
lead him into pitfalls which his native good sense would have avoided.

Columbo's revenge for his injury is quite deliberately based on his
awareness of the difference between his manners and those of the modish
court. The murder of D'Alvarez in the midst of festivities and before
royalty is, for the court as for the audience, above all else a shocking
breach of decorum. It is his insulting and arrogant disregard of etiquette
which the King finds most distressing:

> This contempt
> Of Majesty transcends my power to pardon,
> And you shall feel my anger Sir.
>
> (III.ii.229–231)

Professor Forker comments: "Note here the shabbiness of the King's
motive, the selfishness implied by his capacity to look upon sudden
murder (in the presence of the bereaved) as primarily a breach of court
etiquette" (p. 63 n.). It may rather be thought that the focus on manners
is inevitable in a play which marries tragedy and comedy of intrigue.
Inevitably, the deception and the misunderstanding have comic overtones,
but their principal purpose within the drama is surely to focus attention
on the incompatibility of the characters and to stress the tension between
the modes of life which they represent.

If the ritual of deception can be central to an effective tragedy, it is not
surprising that Shirley can use it to a significant degree in his comedies, to

lend clarity and coherence to their structure. Examples from some of
Shirley's less well-known plays may show how he develops and refines the
use of misunderstanding. In the early *Love Tricks* the conflicts and
deceptions are farcical and entertaining but lack any coherence. In *The
Gamester* the deceptions are more meaningfully related to character, and
the plot has a genuine direction. In *The Example* and *The Opportunity*
we can see the deceptions related significantly to character and to the
patterns of society; these plays are consistent and valid analyses of social
life, cast in the mode of comic drama.

II

Love Tricks, or The School of Compliment has a plot constructed
around a complex series of deceits, which take various forms of gulling,
disguise, masquerade, and self-deception. Much of the interest of the play
comes from Shirley's skillful maintenance of a wide and dizzy range of
confusions. The grotesque tricks played by Gorgon and Gasparo on the
aged Rufaldo are conventionally farcical. The temporary irrationality of
the beautiful Selina, who believes that she wishes to marry the old man, is
a stranger love trick. Both Rufaldo and Selina realize that they have been
deceived. Rufaldo rages at his tricksters, while Selina wonders at her folly
and exiles herself to life in a pastoral landscape. But at the play's end they
both come to self-awareness and accept their proper places. Rufaldo
abandons his lusts and welcomes his daughter's wedding, and Selina
marries her beloved Infortunio.

A series of similar episodes shows this basic pattern in the adventures of
other characters: a movement from deception and blindness to anger or
distress and then to eventual self-awareness. But Shirley seems to have
no single theme in the play; it wanders amiably and loosely from episode
to episode. The scenes at the School of Compliment, a witty series of
parodies on books of polite instruction, do, however, show some social
awareness. In this School, where the clownish come to learn sophistication, the fluid society of the 1620's reveals its many problems of behavior
and communication for the new rich. The desire of Aretina in *The Lady
of Pleasure* to make a great figure in the fashionable world is foreshad-
owed in the Oaf, who is brought to the School to receive polish and

progresses so well that he can soon make a convincing imitation of the speech of a cynical fop:

A younger brother, sir; born at the latter end of the week, and wane of the moon; put into the world to seek my own fortune; got a great estate of wealth by gaming and wenching, and so purchas'd unhappily this state of damnation you see me in.

(III.v; Gifford and Dyce, I, 54)

The School scenes demonstrate Shirley's interest in social affectation—an affectation which is the up-to-date form of the humour and consists of the improper and mistaken decision to behave in a way at odds with one's genuine personality. Rufaldo and Selina are basically sensible; temporarily they affect the lover and the martyr. Aretina and the Oaf affect a social class not properly theirs; the dramatic function of their eccentricities is not different from that of Rufaldo and Selina. Carol, the socially affected and flighty heroine of *Hyde Park,* is similar to the egregious Sir Gervase Simple in *Love in a Maze,* a Jonsonian rustic who is either dumb or incoherent in company. Carol flirts vivaciously and nervously; Sir Gervase loosens his tongue with alcohol. They both affect a competence they do not naturally have. The affected person inevitably falls into confusion and is ripe for deception.

The plot of intrigue and the rather static School scenes are not integrated in *Love Tricks,* but they show, side by side, Shirley's skill in manipulating affectations and portraying fashionable London. In his best comedies these elements come together.

The Gamester rapidly sets on stage the irreconcilable views of life which clash throughout the play, giving it a focus sharper than that of *Love Tricks.* Men of overnice honor devoted to the dangers and romance of swordplay are introduced; a wounded duelist, Delamore, is carried on, and his high-minded opponent and sometime friend, Beaumont, is arrested. Meanwhile, Wilding, who is so lacking in honor as to ask his wife's help in debauching his ward, cynically discusses dueling with Hazard, the gamester:

Is't not a great deal safer, now, to skirmish
With a petticoat, and touze a handsome wench
In private, than be valiant in the streets,
And kiss the gallows for't? Hang, hang this foolery!

(I.i; Gifford and Dyce, III, 194)

The audience is assured of a sharp contrast between the two groups shown on stage.

Throughout the play Shirley maintains consistently the tension between the romance of Delamore and Beaumont—in a subplot of supposed death and tearful reconciliation—and the cynicism of Wilding or, to a lesser degree, Hazard. As usual, the plot develops through a trick, but the deception practiced on Wilding is not a conventional device. It is exactly and shrewdly chosen to suit his personality—first to batten on his libertinism, then to force him to discover his own unworthiness and actively struggle to regain a way of life that is honorable in the Delamore sense. Believing himself to be cuckolded, he analyzes, in two involved soliloquies, his supposed position, attempts to work a way out, perceives his own villainy, and realizes the full implications of his predicament:

> I am justly punish'd now for all my tricks,
> And pride o' the flesh. I had ambition
> To make men cuckolds; now the devil has paid me.
> . . . .
> And spight of [all] these tricks, am a Cornelius.
>   (V.i,ii; Gifford and Dyce, III, 260, 272)

The libertine is reformed by jealousy, the vice of the man of honor, but logically irrelevant and meaningless to a Wilding. He is led into the trap, not because he is ambitious, lustful, or foolish; indeed, he is shown from the beginning of the play as sympathetic in some ways. Rather, his view of life is the result of an affectation. Unable to sustain consistently the part he has chosen to play, he falls into self-contradiction and confusion. Wilding is not stupid; his mind, under the influence of the affectation, just does not work in the same way as that of Mrs. Wilding, and consequently he cannot understand or communicate with her. The trick is designed to force an adjustment back to his proper view of life; the romantic subplot provides a symbol of the appropriate direction in which to move.

The Gamester is a neat and actable play, with some good scenes of London life, particularly those connected with the gambling tables; but the passages of realistic social comment are not meaningfully integrated into the main plot, and the play, while less diffuse than *Love Tricks,* is by no means completely unified.

The Gamester is built around conflicts between views of life. *The Example,* an excellent, fast-moving comedy, unfairly neglected, is built around the conflict between two different ways of life—that of the noble courtier and that of the old-fashioned gentry. Shirley is here able to incorporate his social awareness into the comic structure. The court is represented by Lord Fitzavarice, who mixes shrewd business dealing with arrogant libertinism and provides himself with a scrivener and a poetaster, Confident Rapture, to manage the two sides of his destructive activities. The honest and upright gentry are represented by the Lady Peregrine, whose husband, Sir Walter, has been forced into exile as a debtor, and her uncle, Sir Solitary Plot, so paranoiac that he watches nervously through the night, convinced of the dangers of the modern world and dreaming of plots in everything. The servants, what with waiting on Lady Peregrine through the day and Sir Solitary through the night, are chronically incompetent from lack of sleep. The expected trick played on Sir Solitary has the effect of shaking him from his humour; Lord Fitzavarice is persuaded by Lady Peregrine's honesty and purity to reject his vicious way of life.

Significant is the way in which these two key characters, in their tensions and their eventual return to decent behavior, consistently speak of themselves and their manners in terms of their social status. The action occurs because of the problems created by the interaction of the different classes. Sir Solitary's fears arise from his terror of bravoes in the streets, with their lascivious intent, and from his distrust of the high, fashionable life of gambling and the ball. Fitzavarice's assaults on Lady Peregrine seem to him perfectly proper, in view of his nobility and her genteel penury. His page, we may notice, defines her scruples as uncourtly:

> You are the first
> Lady within my observation,
> That has took time to ask her conscience
> The meaning of a jewel, sent by a lord,
> A young and handsome lord too; 'tis a thing
> At court is not in fashion, and 'twere pity
> One with so good a face should be the precedent
> Of such superfluous modesty.
>
> (I.i; Gifford and Dyce, III, 291)

The actual courtship, whether by the proxy wit of Confident Rapture or by Fitzavarice himself, stresses the nobility of the wooer and assumes that his status deserves her submission.

Moreover, he is convinced that he can purchase her love by his promise
to repair her husband's fortunes. This is the typical misunderstanding of a
Wilding—an assumption that one's own desires (in this case, cupidity)
are generally shared, in other words, an affectation of consensus. But the
courtship of Fitzavarice is more than the conventional nobleman's lust.
He is governed by a sense of his own position, which forces him into
continuing even after he regrets his precipitation:

> I must have
> Some way to enjoy her body for my credit;
> The world takes notice I have courted her,
> And if I mount her not, I lose my honour.
> (I.i; Gifford and Dyce, III, 296–297)

> Most invincible; no temptation
> Can fasten on her: would I had ne'er laid siege to her!
> The taking of her province will not be
> So much advantage to me, as the bare
> Removing of my siege will lose me credit.
> (II.i; Gifford and Dyce, III, 302)

Later he is forced into dueling with Sir Walter, against his wishes but
impelled by a sense of his honor, which, he claims, is precarious in a world
of malice. Lord Fitzavarice is indeed the courtier, dependent on the
maintenance of a fragile reputation—as much a prisoner of his honor as
Sir Solitary is of his timidity. Sir Walter's valid question, "Can lords /
Be cowards?" (IV.iii; Gifford and Dyce, III, 344) is apt. It is the Lord's way
of life, even his social status, that forces him into an intolerable position.
Neither he nor Sir Solitary can comprehend the environment into which
they fall; their actions are repugnant to common sense yet seem essential
to them. Both are restored to society by a general rejection of their follies,
and, as has been made clear throughout, both are in essence decent and
sensible. The relief with which Lord Fitzavarice' wicked ways are abandoned is neatly suggested in a scene which shows his page returning to
Lady Peregrine, this time on a proper errand:

> I meet
> Honest employments with more cheerfulness.
> . . . .

When I go upon
Lascivious errands, madam, I take money
There is no other benefit belongs to 'em;
But good ones pay themselves.

(III.i; Gifford and Dyce, III, 320)

By stressing a failure of understanding rather than of morality, by relating the failure to understand to the social environment, and by showing the eccentric behavior as a temporary affectation, Shirley has made convincing and even moving the reformation and reconciliation scenes at the end of the play. We do not suddenly see a rake turning angel in Act V; rather we have the discovery, by a basically sympathetic character, that his way of life has been misdirected. This is perhaps more clearly seen in an admirable passage in *The Witty Fair One*. Fowler has been attempting to trick Penelope by feigning sickness. She organizes an elaborate series of deceptions to confront him with his supposed death and funeral. At first the jest is lighthearted and witty; then Fowler gradually realizes the solemnity implicit in the device and laments his loose ways.

The problems inherent when one social group comes into contact with another are skillfully and imaginatively revealed in the romantic comedy *The Opportunity*. The theme of mistaken identification is ancient and conventional, though we might expect the love affairs which arise from the comedy of errors to be permanent. That the transient soldiers, Aurelio and Pisauro, leave Urbino unattached, that their influence in the city is a temporary aberration, is made to seem inevitable as a result of the social contrast between their characters, as straightforward military men, and the intricate courtly environment into which they fall. Always in the background of the Duchess' affairs is the significance of her lofty political status. Lucio, a courtier, observes:

Although I honour Borgia [Aurelio],
And wish him heartily advanced, I would
Not kneel to him; my voice is for Ferrara,
He is a prince; I would not for my state
This should break off his treaty.

(II.ii; Gifford and Dyce, III, 393)

Pisauro becomes delighted with the prospect of power, and Aurelio himself is shown unromantically balancing political and amorous success:

Betwixt the duchess and Cornelia
My soul divides: I must not be a fool,
And for the fable of [mere] amorous love
Leave state that courts me with a glorious title.
（II.iii; Gifford and Dyce, III, 400）

The audience is not allowed to forget the implications of the action, nor does Shirley ignore the distinctions between the heroes and the courtiers around them. He uses the device of a trick to demonstrate this distinction. The Duchess has encouraged the diffident Aurelio by dictating a love letter which includes a broadly hinted assignation. Aurelio, uncertain if this is the opportunity he must grasp, happens on the Duke of Ferrara, who quotes what he had overheard on a previous occasion and persuades the unhappy soldier that the letter belongs in nobler hands. The Duke's trick works because Aurelio is out of his depth, confused in the courtly atmosphere around him. The nature of the deception and the Duke's easy and fluent dissimulation convince the audience that the traveling soldiers, while they may make a brief impression in Urbino, have really no proper place there. Aurelio's high hopes are an affectation, which the Duke's trick exposes.

A somewhat similar situation is found in *The Humorous Courtier,* where the ambitious courtier Contarini imagines that the Duchess is in love with him. He attributes his confusion, not entirely without reason, to the allusive nature of royal conversation:

'Tis great pity custom should make princes
So reserv'd in wooing.
（V.iii; Gifford and Dyce, IV, 606）

Typically, the Jacobean or Caroline romantic drama tends to be distant from reality; artifice and a fairy-tale atmosphere seem to deny any opportunity for social comment. Conversely, the realistic dramas of the day tend to submerge any general purpose beneath the details of everyday behavior and life in the London streets. Shirley's continuing interest in social status marks both romantic plays such as *The Opportunity* and realistic pieces such as *Hyde Park,* giving to the one a relevance and to the other a consistent theme. Romantic comedy with valid social comment, and realistic comedy with a firm dramatic focus, are Shirley's particular gifts to the theater of his time.

III

The failure of understanding, revealing the different modes of thought in differing social groups and forcing the rejection of affectation, is seen at its clearest and most sophisticated in the celebrated comedy *The Lady of Pleasure*. The central deception has an ironic inversion: Aretina is never found out by the fop she tricks. The comic movement toward understanding and reformation works here through a trick, but it is the successful trickster who undergoes the change. Aretina, who has ambitions to step into fashionable life, is unable to cope with the ways of that life. But her change of heart comes from the spontaneous collapse of her affectation following her moment of insight. Doubtless, Shirley's recognition of the essentially introspective nature of the self-discovery makes him have her withdraw from the stage to recover her composure behind the scenes.

The usual dramatic purpose of the comic trick is to reveal the character of the gull; in the case of Wilding and the others, the revelation is to themselves. In *The Lady of Pleasure* the trick reveals the true character of the fops to Aretina. The gull's character, as well as her own, is made plain; it is the trickster who, shocked at what she sees, reforms her behavior. The gull, Kickshaw, never learns the truth.

Critics have tended to be severe on Aretina. As Professor Knowland comments: "Aretina . . . having enjoyed her sin is 'converted' and left unpunished; but the awakened sense of guilt is just another theatrical trick." [12] But it is possible that a dramatist can show a convincing reformation without the external urges of public scorn or poetic justice. Aretina does indeed fall victim to the deception played by her husband, who pretends to be as devoted as she to a life of fashionable luxury and feigns riot to the point of apparent ruin. His miming of her affectations and extravagance acts as a comic mirror to show her the flaws in her own life, which she first sees vaguely and then, as his deception continues and bankruptcy threatens, perceives in full degree (V.i; Gifford and Dyce, IV, 82, 85).

Aretina's realization that the fashionable life is dangerous and

12. *Six Caroline Plays,* ed. A. S. Knowland (London, 1962), p. x.

inappropriate is illustrated by a number of excellent comic devices. The effect of her ambitions on her nephew, Frederick, is well shown. He first appears as a mild-mannered if rather oafish student, fresh from college in his *sub-fusc*. Determining to civilize him, she gives him over to her steward for tuition. Frederick proves a most apt pupil, becoming a fashion-obsessed buffoon and drunkard. When he attempts to court his aunt, she finally realizes the disastrous results of her educational experiment and packs him off again to the university. She is less able to undo the effects of her infatuation on her steward. He has first appeared as a typical old-fashioned retainer, and his greeting of Frederick shows him as a genuine friend of the family: "Welcome home, sweet master Frederick!" (II.i; Gifford and Dyce, IV, 24). But he rapidly sinks into the dissolute urban life, and the last we hear of him is Frederick's comment:

> Your steward has some pretty notions too,
> In moral mischief.
>
> (IV.ii; Gifford and Dyce, IV, 71)

Through *The Lady of Pleasure* the audience is shown the true significance of the life of fashion. Throughout they are aware that Kickshaw and Littleworth are, as their names tell us, of no account. The portrait of the elegant Celestina, a more polished and witty figure, though scorned by Aretina and the fops, shows some of the true value of the high life.

Several passages explicitly contrast the life of fashion and the ideal life of the past, which Aretina has rejected. The play opens with her vivacious description of the country life she hates; while intentionally a rejection, the speech develops into an elaborate and splendid image of the old world, which conflicts with the similarly ornate invective against city luxury delivered by her husband. As their dialogue progresses, the imagery stresses the essentially destructive impact of luxury:

> BORNWELL
> I could accuse the gaiety of your wardrobe,
> And prodigal embroideries, under which
> Rich satins, plushes, cloth of silver, dare
> Not shew their own complexions; your jewels,
> Able to burn out the spectators' eyes,
> And shew like bonfires on you by the tapers.
>
> (I.i; Gifford and Dyce, IV, 8)

Such passages underline the falsity of Aretina's position in general moral terms. Elsewhere the dramatist skillfully shows the incompatibility of the lives of the gentry and the fops. In Act I, scene i, Kickshaw and Little-worth visit Aretina and are briefly entertained by Bornwell. All three try to be pleasant. Kickshaw and Littleworth are not arrogant Restoration beaux, Bornwell is no clownish squire. But they do not succeed in communicating with each other; their small talk dissolves into misunder-stood compliment and unanswered question:

> KICKSHAW and LITTLEWORTH
> Save you, sir Thomas!
> BORNWELL
> Save you, gentlemen!
> KICKSHAW
> I kiss your hand.
> BORNWELL
> What day is it abroad?
> LITTLEWORTH
> The morning rises from your lady's eye:
> If she look clear, we take the happy omen
> Of a fair day.
> BORNWELL
> She'll instantly appear,
> To the discredit of your complement;
> But you express your wit thus.
> KICKSHAW
> And you modesty,
> Not to affect the praises of your own.
> BORNWELL
> Leaving this subject, what game's now on foot?
> What exercise carries the general vote
> O' the town, now? nothing moves without your knowledge.
> KICKSHAW
> The cocking now has all the noise; I'll have
> A hundred pieces on one battle.—Oh,
> These birds of Mars!
> LITTLEWORTH
> Venus is Mars' bird too.
> KICKSHAW
> Why, and the pretty doves are Venus's,
> To shew that kisses draw the chariot.

LITTLEWORTH

I am for that skirmish.

BORNWELL

When shall we have
More booths and bagpipes upon Bansted downs?
No mighty race is expected?—But my lady
Returns!

(I.i; Gifford and Dyce, IV, 12–13)

The passage is worth quoting at length to illustrate Shirley's skill in documenting embarrassment. Bornwell's simple questions, about the weather or about local news, attract witty extravagance and private jokes instead of replies. His final question about Banstead Downs elicits only stunned silence. Happily, Aretina appears, to set effective conversation again in motion. In this scene Shirley gives an abstract of his comic subject: the two levels of society exist, but they cannot meaningfully dwell together. The wealth and attractions of an Aretina may link the two groups for a time in courtship or intrigue, but, as discovered in *The Opportunity,* the liaison is temporary. A trick may recoil, a character may reconsider, and the persons in the play must return to their original, unaffected ways of life.

The comedy of intrigue generally suffers from the excessive virtuosity of its practitioners. Manipulation of a complex plot is more important than a single-minded dramatic purpose. Shirley's effective linking of the deception episode with a consistent view of English life permits him uniquely to turn the scampering plots of Renaissance theater into meaningful social commentaries.

Professor Knights quotes from a source in 1622:

For nowadays most men live above their callings, and promiscuously step forth vice-versa into one another's ranks. The countryman's eye is upon the citizen: the citizen's upon the gentleman: the gentleman's upon the nobleman.[13]

In a period of rapid social change, inevitably a sense of dislocation will be felt by many individuals. The uncertainty of their position will be reflected in confused behavior, affectation, or an exaggerated awareness of

---

13. L. C. Knights, *Drama and Society in the Age of Jonson* (London, 1937), p. 108.

status. The satirist and the comic writer will work effectively with the materials of snobbery and the stupidity of social ambition. James Shirley's contacts with the polite world of London and with the gentry of the provinces provided for him a rich experience of the uncertainties and foolishness of much contemporary society. His range is perhaps more limited than that of his predecessors, his wit less incisive than that of his successors; he may, to speak of him again as transitional, lack the variety of Jonson and the modish glitter of Etherege. But he is admirable in his grasp of the conflicts in the middle range of society and fruitful in his development and manipulation of the conventional intrigues. His use of the trick and the deception to illustrate the social situation of his comedy gives to his best pieces a consistency of purpose and a unity of plot not often met with in English comedy of the Jacobean and Caroline periods.

Renaissance and Restoration Dramatic Plotting

CYRUS HOY

I

THE AUTHOR OF THE ANONYMOUS *Some Remarks on the Tragedy of Hamlet* (1736) [1] found a distinction in the play which its modern admirers are unlikely to consider very striking. He observes that *Hamlet*

strikes us with a certain Awe and Seriousness of Mind, far beyond those Plays whose Whole Plot turns upon vehement and uncontroulable Love, such as are most of our modern Tragedies. These certainly have not the great Effect that others have, which turn either upon Ambition, the Love of one's Country, or Paternal or Filial Tenderness. Accordingly we find, that few among the Ancients, and hardly any of our Author's [i.e., Shakespeare's] Plays, are built upon the Passion of Love in a direct Manner; by which I mean, that they have not the mutual Attachment of a Lover and his Mistress for their chief Basis. Love will always make a great Figure in Tragedy, if only its chief Branches be made use of; as for instance, Jealousy (as in *Othello*) or the beautiful Distress of Man and Wife (as in *Romeo* and *Juliet*) but never when the whole Play is founded upon two Lovers desiring to possess each other: And one of the

---

1. The author has often been said to be Sir Thomas Hanmer, but the attribution has been challenged (e.g., by Clarence D. Thorpe, "Thomas Hanmer and the Anonymous Essay on *Hamlet*," *MLN*, XLIX [1934], 493–498).

Reasons for this seems to be, that this last Species of that Passion is more commonly met with than the former, and so consequently strikes us less. Add to this, that there may a Suspicion arise, that the Passion of Love in a direct Manner may be more sensual than in those Branches which I have mention'd; which Suspicion is sufficient to take from its Dignity, and lessen our Veneration for it.

(pp. 4–5)

A fundamental difference in the subject matter appropriate to tragedy and comedy is here being invoked, one that is classic in its origin and of which the eighteenth-century critic would have been well aware. The point that the author of *Some Remarks* is making is succinctly echoed a few years later by the anonymous contributor to *Miscellaneous Observations on the Tragedy of Hamlet* (1752):

Love, the usual Subject of modern Tragedies, our Poet has very wisely refused Admittance into his best Compositions, it is a Passion truly comic, and when introduced in Tragedy deserves our Contempt and Derision, rather than Pity or Compassion.

(p. vii)

The wave of the future is already discernible here ("Love, the usual Subject of modern Tragedies"), and so inured to romantic tragedy were later generations to become that the treatment of passionate love would seem quite the normal subject for tragic representation. Shaw was never more the literary iconoclast than when he announced, in the Preface to *Three Plays for Puritans:*

Besides, I have a technical objection to making sexual infatuation a tragic theme. Experience proves that it is only effective in the comic spirit. We can bear to see Mrs Quickly pawning her plate for love of Falstaff, but not Antony running away from the Battle of Actium for love of Cleopatra. Let realism have its demonstration, comedy its criticism, or even bawdry its horselaugh at the expense of sexual infatuation, if it must; but to ask us to subject our souls to its ruinous glamor, to worship it, deify it, and imply that it alone makes our life worth living, is nothing but folly gone mad erotically—a thing compared to which Falstaff's unbeglamored drinking and drabbing is respectable and rightminded.[2]

2. Bernard Shaw, *Three Plays for Puritans* (Penguin Books, 1962), pp. 30–31.

Although English tragedy's early affinity for romantic story made certain that the treatment of love would never be entirely absent from it (more of Shakespeare's plays are built directly upon the passion of love than the critics of 1736 and 1752 seem to have imagined), the formal distinction between both the matter and the manner appropriate respectively to tragedy and comedy is preserved, however loosely, through the end of the sixteenth century. As for "matter," it may be enough to say that, for the Renaissance, tragedy has it, whereas comedy deals with common things (among which the 1736 critic would include the subject of "two Lovers desiring to possess each other"); this is the distinction which Hieronimo makes in *The Spanish Tragedy* (IV.ii.156 ff.) between

> *Tragedia cothurnata,* fitting Kings,
> Containing matter, and not common things

and comedy, merely "fit for common wits." As for "manner," the distinction between the tragic and the comic is described by Elyot, who found it prefigured in the movements of contrasting dances:

. . . the maiestie of princes was shewed in that daunse, whiche was named *Eumelia,* and belōged to tragedies: dissolute motiōs, and wanton countenaunces, in that whiche was called *Cordax,* and pertained to comedies: wherein mē of base hauiour only daunsed.

(The Governor, 1531 ed., 81ᵛ)

By the end of the first decade of the seventeenth century, the nature of tragedy has changed, both in matter and manner, and the change permanently affects the shape of English tragic drama thereafter. The subject matter of tragedy becomes frankly romantic; the manner becomes informed with the dramatic, situational equivalents of what Elyot termed "dissolute motions and wanton countenaunces." The change is accompanied by a breakdown of conventional distinctions between comic and tragic modes that is most immediately apparent in the area of dramatic plotting. Comedy flourishes throughout the Jacobean and Caroline periods, and dramatists go on writing titular tragedies, though of a distinctly melodramatic kind. But after about 1612 the output of all the principal dramatists who are active between that date and the closing of the theaters—Fletcher, Middleton, Massinger, Shirley, Ford—consists mainly of plays that fall into that intermediate region of tragicomedy, the most remarkable feature of which genre is its capacity for decorating the slender, intricate, but often highly resilient and often distinctly elegant structure of comic intrigue and romantic purpose with great garlands of tragic, or quasi-tragic, or pseudo-tragic passion, with festoons of rhetorical ornament, with histrionic tableaux of stunning intensity and variety. One must not be blind to the essentially comic design of Jacobean tragicomedy, with its intrigue-ridden plots and with romantic love—the time-honored subject of comedy—the ground of all its arguments. Onto the design is imposed a burden of more or less tragic implication; emotional intensities mount beyond normal comic temperatures, and mental agitations possess a more than comic shrillness. If the essence of the baroque style consists in a profound tension between form and content, manner and subject material, then Jacobean tragicomedy is the most truly baroque creation in English literature. To understand it aright, one must understand the two qualities which it incorporates in uneasy fusion: the comic logic of its formal design and the irrational pathos let loose within this symmetrical structure when love—the natural subject of comedy—is raised unnaturally to a tragic power.

II

The kind of dramatic plotting that I wish to examine has reference to the tragicomedies and the tragedies (which regularly bear the imprint of the tragicomic manner) of the late Jacobean and Caroline periods and to the Restoration heroic play (where the tragicomic manner is pervasive). Thematically, and as regards the formal arrangement and movement of the action, the plays of both periods exhibit a number of similarities, which is not surprising since, fundamentally, they are all concerned with the same thing, namely, erotic passion. Here the treatment of passion regularly serves a double purpose. The plays of both periods, from Beaumont and Fletcher to Dryden, are explicit in their depiction of the destruction worked when passion goes unchecked and of the salvation that is achieved when passion is mastered by reason. The emotional content of these plays is very high. Temptations are painfully resisted or desperately yielded to; and the atmosphere is charged with frustrated passions that must patiently be borne, if virtue is to be saved, until either death or a patently contrived theatrical coup provides a release from pain. The frustrations of passion, so prominent in the plotting of these plays, serve in themselves as so many temptations to vice—which explains the apparent anomaly that the highest virtue in this drama very often consists in doing nothing. To act, as often as not, is to open the way to sinning; and the typical hero or heroine of Jacobean, Caroline, and Restoration tragedy and tragicomedy shows his mettle by steadfastly enduring the afflictions of an unkind fate. This accounts for the curiously suspended states in which the principal personages of the drama of these periods regularly find themselves. They are emotionally agitated to a well-nigh convulsive degree, but at the same time they are poised on an ethical dilemma which, their sense of honor being what it is, fixes them in a paralyzing relationship one to another. This outer rigidity of movement and gesture, contrasting so strongly with the emotional turbulence of the characters' inner lives, is reflected in the contrivance of the plots of these plays, where figures are grouped in intricate and highly formalized arrangements around which swirls a seemingly endless stream of violence. The special quality of such plots derives from the extent to which they are generated by contrary forces: one static, the other agitated and ceaselessly active; and the bustle and stir of which they have more than enough must not deafen us to the stillness that reigns at the psychological center of the storm. There stands the hero, internally wracked by contending passions but suspended meanwhile through the power of a tormenting indecision until events settle the issue of his destiny. For all the battles that he wins, for all the kings that he makes and unmakes, Almanzor's love for Almahide in *The Conquest of Granada* remains in abeyance throughout the ten acts of Dryden's gigantic play, until her husband is conveniently dispatched at the end of the drama.

We can see this sort of plot taking shape in the later Elizabethan drama, where the conflict in tragedy comes to center on man in opposition with himself. As a tragic issue this is sufficiently redoubtable; witness, in Greek tragedy, the *Bacchae* or the *Hippolytus* of Euripides, or any of the major tragedies of Shakespeare. But in lesser hands the conflict of man in opposition with himself is likely to result in a mere tug of war between his inclination to virtue and his inclination to vice. The manner in which plots in the Beaumont and Fletcher plays turn on ethical dilemmas is typical of the drama of the Jacobean, Caroline, and Restoration periods. The principal issues that hold the stage in the Jacobean and Caroline theater are more or less frankly sensational in nature, and the dilemmas which they pose take the form of so many tantalizing questions. Will Amintor, in Beaumont and Fletcher's *Maid's Tragedy*, kill the king who has made him a cuckold, or will he persist in his loyalty to a ruler who, whatever he is as a man, is still his anointed monarch? Will Arbaces, in Beaumont and Fletcher's *A King and No King*, surrender to his incestuous passion for the woman he believes to be his sister, or will he not? Will Giovanni, in Ford's *'Tis Pity She's a Whore*, engage in incestuous relations with the girl he knows to be his sister, or will he not? Will the elder Malefort, in Massinger's *Unnatural Combat*, engage in incestuous relations with his daughter, or will he not? Will Bianca and Ferando, in Ford's *Love's Sacrifice*, commit adultery, or will they manage to restrain their unruly affections?

The action in all of these plays of the Jacobean and Caroline periods turns on frustrated passion, and frustrated passion is the mainspring of the action in the typical Restoration heroic play. Thus, in Dryden and Howard's *Indian Queen* Montezuma loves Orazia, daughter of the Inca of Peru, but her father forbids their union. Later, when all three have fallen into the hands of Zempoalla, the usurping Queen of Mexico, the relationship of the lovers is further complicated, for Zempoalla conceives a passion for Montezuma, while her general and erstwhile favorite, Traxalla, is enflamed by the beauteous Orazia. *The Indian Emperor,* Dryden's sequel to *The Indian Queen,* is a tissue of frustrated love relationships. Almeria, daughter of the now deceased Zempoalla (twenty years have elapsed since the end of the preceding play), is the beloved now of Montezuma, whose Orazia is also dead. But Almeria receives his love with scorn, determined as she is to avenge the memory of her mother. Almeria loves Cortez, but he in turn loves Cydaria, Montezuma's daughter.

Such a sequence of one-sided and, as it were, interlocking love relationships can be elaborated to the point where it comes to serve as a kind of structural principle in seventeenth-century baroque tragedy. Before *The Indian Emperor* Dryden had already employed it in his second play, the tragicomedy of *The Rival Ladies,* where Don Manuel loves Angellina, who, together with Honoria, loves Don Gonsalvo, who loves Julia, who loves Don Rhodorigo. In the realm of pure tragedy Racine's *Andromaque* provides an outstanding instance of this sort of thing, where Oreste loves Hermione, who loves Pyrrhus, who loves Andromaque, who is dedicated to the memory of Hector. In Dryden's *Tyrannic Love* Placidius loves Valeria, who loves Porphyrius, who loves Berenice, who is bound in marriage to Maximin, Emperor of Rome. Maximin himself loves St. Catharine of Alexandria, but her heart is set on martyrdom, and so his passion must remain unsatisfied, like that of nearly everyone else in the play. The convoluted relationships exhibited in *Tyrannic Love* are merely more numerous than in the average Restoration tragedy; the principle which they demonstrate remains the same throughout the period, and it can be applied on almost any scale.

The fact that it can be almost endlessly varied does not disguise the fact that it quickly comes to be reduced to a formula. Thus the structural principle on which Dryden's *Aureng-Zebe* is built is the same as that which had already served Dryden and Howard in *The Indian Queen*. Aureng-Zebe and Indamora, like Montezuma and Orazia, love each other. And as Montezuma and Orazia are, respectively, the unwilling objects of the passion which Zempoalla and Traxalla, that disaffected couple, conceive for each, so Indamora and Aureng-Zebe are confronted with the unwelcome attention paid to each by, respectively, the Emperor of India and his licentious wife, Nourmahal. Here a certain fillip is given to the situation by the fact that the Emperor of India is Aureng-Zebe's father—who thus, in pursuing Indamora, becomes a rival to his own son—and by the further fact that Nourmahal is Aureng-Zebe's stepmother, so that her overtures of love to him are not merely adulterous but incestuous as well. The architectonics—and the word is used advisedly—in two such plays as *The Indian Queen* and *Aureng-Zebe* are identical; in each, the same pressures are exerted from the same quarters. Repeatedly, in baroque tragedy, one has the impression of architectural principles at work: of masses artfully arranged, of forces duly balanced, of thrust opposed to counterthrust, as the virtuous arm themselves against the onslaughts of the wicked. Tensions and strains are calculated with a fine precision, all in the interest of determining at what point the passion-driven creature might be expected to break and just how much the rational hero or heroine can reasonably be expected to bear. A hero like

Aureng-Zebe is sorely tried: by his father, by his stepmother, by his rebellious younger brother, even by his Indamora; but the praise to which he has aspired as son and lover is his by the end of the play, as indeed it has been throughout. Indamora, that cynosure where all loves meet, is exposed to the force of sundry passions (Aureng-Zebe loves her purely, the Emperor loves her impurely, Morat begins by loving her impurely but is redeemed under her influence, Arimant loves her hopelessly), but her virtue is proof against all that is unchaste.

Often in Restoration tragedy it is virtue itself which, for a time at least, stands between the hero and heroine's consummation of their passion, for the heroine is bound to another (through no fault of her own), and honor forbids her to violate her marriage vows. The mutual love of Almanzor and Almahide in *The Conquest of Granada* may be acknowledged, but it cannot be fulfilled because Almahide is bound in marriage to the weak and jealous King Boabdelin. So it is, too, with Porphyrius and Berenice in *Tyrannic Love,* for Berenice has been forced into a loveless marriage of state with the tyrannical Emperor Maximin. Otway's Don Carlos is forever deprived of the love of Elizabeth of Valois, to whom he was once promised in marriage, because his father, Philip II of Spain, has married her himself. So heavy is the air of Restoration tragedy with frustrated longings and thwarted desires that not even marriage can always assure the lovers that their afflictions are at an end. In Congreve's *Mourning Bride* Almeria and Alphonso, though married, have been separated by shipwreck on their wedding day; and even after they are restored to each other, their union remains unconsummated because Almeria's father, the King of Granada, keeps Alphonso imprisoned in a subterranean vault. The structural principle at work in *The Mourning Bride* is the same as that present in *The Indian Queen* and *Aureng-Zebe*. To add to the woes of the lovers, Almeria is sought after by Garcia, the candidate for her hand selected by the King her father; and Alphonso is pursued by the passionate Queen Zara. Plots of this sort may end either tragically or not. In *Don Carlos* the lovers die. In *The Indian Queen, The Indian Emperor, Tyrannic Love,* and *The Mourning Bride* the lovers are at last united by the timely death of the person or persons who have kept them apart. In *Aureng-Zebe* Nourmahal dies, the Emperor gives over his intemperate passion for Indamora, and the way is cleared for her union with the hero.

III

Plots which turn on the relationships of a group of frustrated lovers had been a staple of the seventeenth-century English stage at least since the days of Beaumont and Fletcher. Prior to Beaumont and Fletcher such plots, when treated at all, had been dealt with in terms of the sheerest comedy, as in *As You Like It,* where Silvius loves Phebe, who loves the disguised Rosalind, who loves Orlando; or in the Orsino-Olivia-Viola triangle in *Twelfth Night,* where affections are passed around until they come full circle (Orsino loves Olivia, who loves the disguised Viola, who herself loves Orsino). Elizabethan comic plots of the more romantic variety regularly turn on triangular love relationships, as in such a play as Greene's *Friar Bacon and Friar Bungay.* Where this is the case, cross-wooing furnishes a natural source of comic complication. Jonson, in *Every Man out of His Humour,* jeers at such arguments of comedy as would have "a duke to be in loue with a countesse, and that countesse to bee in loue with the dukes sonne, and the sonne to loue the ladies waiting maid" (III.vi.195 ff.). The manner in which such plots come to be treated seriously and problematically in the plays of Beaumont and Fletcher marks a turning point in English drama.

The complications arising from misplaced love, traditionally a subject for comic invention, come increasingly to provide materials for the depiction of tragic—or near-tragic—suffering in the plays of Beaumont and Fletcher and in the later Jacobean and Caroline dramatists. Thus, in Fletcher and Massinger's *The Custom of the Country* the tyrannical Count Clodio pursues the pure Zenocia, beloved of Arnoldo, who is pursued by the wanton Hippolyta, who herself has a faithful lover in the sea captain Leopold. There is a point in Beaumont and Fletcher's *A King and No King* where Spaconia loves Tigranes who—for the moment— loves Panthea, who finds herself returning the seemingly incestuous love of Arbaces. In Beaumont and Fletcher's *Philaster,* in what amounts to a variant of the *Twelfth Night* triangle, Euphrasia loves Philaster, who loves Arethusa, who returns his love but is falsely accused for a time of loving Euphrasia when the latter is disguised as the page Bellario. In *The*

Maid's Tragedy Aspatia loves Amintor, but he marries Evadne, only to discover on his wedding night that she is the mistress to the King, to whom she intends to be entirely faithful. The tragedy of misplaced love is fully realized in this play, as it is not in the case of Euphrasia's love for Philaster or in Arbaces' love for Panthea, where the lovers conceive a mutual passion despite the belief that they are brother and sister, suffer exquisite pangs of conscience as they find themselves drifting inevitably to the sin of incest, but are delivered from the threat of this guilt by the timely revelation that they are not brother and sister after all. This is typical of Fletcherian tragicomedy, which depends for some of its most spectacular dramatic effects upon a fairly shameless exploitation of situations wherein passion is aroused only to be denied its fulfillment, for a time at least. In Fletcher's *A Wife for a Month* Frederick, the libidinous and usurping King of Naples, loves the chaste Evanthe, who loves the noble Valerio. Evanthe and Valerio are permitted to marry, but with the stipulation that Valerio must die at the end of a month, which he is willing to do for the sake of even so short a period of bliss shared with his beloved. But then the fiendish Frederick makes Valerio's situation even more intolerable by forbidding the husband to consummate his marriage upon pain of death to his wife. All of which paves the way for one of those scenes of enforced continence on the wedding night, so dear to the hearts of both Beaumont and Fletcher (cf. as well *The Maid's Tragedy* and *Thierry and Theodoret*).

What the future held for the dramatic treatment of this sort of aphrodisiac occasion is suggested by a scene (V.i) in Fletcher, Massinger, and Field's *Knight of Malta*. The amorous proposals that the noble hero, Miranda, makes to the virtuous heroine, Oriana, must be rejected because she is another man's wife and he is a probationer in the order of St. John. In the course of the scene Miranda lets it be known that he was only testing Oriana when he asked her to "regard / The torturing fires of [his] affections." Be this as it may, she rises splendidly to the occasion; and when Miranda congratulates her on the virtue she has displayed in the face of temptation, she rejoins with a speech that is worth quoting for the evidence it displays of the new love ethic that has entered English drama:

>   my spirits
> Doe embrace thine, my minde doth thy mind kisse,
> And in this pure conjunction we enjoy

A heavenlyer pleasure then if bodies met:
This, this is perfect love, the other short,
Yet languishing fruition, every Swaine
And sweating Groome may clasp, but our's refinde
Two in ten ages cannot reach unto;
Nor is our spirituall love, a barren joy,
For mark what blessed issue we'll beget,
Deerer then children to posterity,
A great example to mens continence,
And womens chastity, that is a childe
More faire, and comfortable, then any heire.

(1647 ed., p. 93)

What is remarkable about this speech is that the continence it celebrates is self-enforced. Physical love is rejected in favor of a high Platonic ethic which cultivates spiritual love, which is to say, love which remains unconsummated in the flesh. This same love ethic persists into the Restoration, where it produces such grandiose utterances as Berenice's statment of her love for Porphyrius as she is being led to execution at the command of her husband the Emperor, in *Tyrannic Love* (V.i):

In death I'll own a love to him so pure,
As will the test of heaven itself endure;
A love so chaste, as conscience could not chide;
But cherish it, and keep it by its side.
A love, which never knew a hot desire,
But flamed as harmless as a lambent fire;
A love, which pure from soul to soul might pass,
As light transmitted through a crystal glass;
Which gave Porphyrius all without a sin,
Yet kept entire the right of Maximin.[3]

The dramatist of frustrated passion par excellence in the late Jacobean and Caroline periods is Ford; and given his acknowledged interest in love melancholy as diagnosed by Burton, it is not surprising to find him addressing himself to the dramatic treatment of heroical passion. In *The Broken Heart* Penthea has been forced by her brother into a loveless marriage with the insanely jealous Bassanes, and honor keeps her faithful to him, even though her love has long been pledged to Orgilus, and his to

3. *The Works of John Dryden,* ed. Walter Scott (London, 1808), III, 426–427.

her. In *Love's Sacrifice* Bianca, Duchess of Pavia, conceives a passion for her husband's favorite, Fernando, and he for her, but she is tormented at the thought of violating her marriage vows. She comes to Fernando's chamber (II.iv) and offers herself to him, but with the stipulation that, if he take her, she will kill herself on the morrow. *Love's Sacrifice* anticipates, in a number of ways, the shape of things to come in the tragedy of the Restoration. In the second part of *The Conquest of Granada* there is a scene (IV.iii) in which Almanzor appeals to Almahide to "give a loose to love":

> Love eagerly; let us be gods to-night;
> And do not, with half yielding, dash delight.[4]

She rebukes him sharply, affirming in part as follows:

> If I could yield, —but think not that I will, —
> You and myself I in revenge should kill;
> For I should hate us both, when it were done,
> And would not to the shame of life be won.

"Deny your own desires," is the sum of her counsel to Almanzor, but he persists, stoutly maintaining that "love's the best return for flesh and blood." Whereupon she declares:

> You've moved my heart so much, I can deny
> No more; but know, Almanzor, I can die.
> Thus far my virtue yields; if I have shown
> More love than what I ought, let this atone.

And, according to the stage direction, she makes a motion to stab herself. At this desperate move, Almanzor cries out, "Hold, hold!" and promises never to ask such a favor again. The Platonism dramatized in this scene (Almahide has some words of praise for "that secret joy of mind, / Which great souls only in great actions find," and which ought not to be lost "for one tumultuous minute"—a point which Oriana has made to Miranda in *The Knight of Malta*) is at one with the Platonic love ethic on exhibit in such a play as *Love's Sacrifice;* and as Ford's tragedies have thematic connections with the tragedy of the Restoration, they have their

---

4. *Ibid.,* IV, 181. All subsequent quotations from this play are found on pp. 181–182.

structural affinities with that tragedy as well. *Love's Sacrifice* is built on the same structural principle that I have defined in *The Indian Queen, Aureng-Zebe,* and *The Mourning Bride.* Fiormonda, the lascivious sister of the Duke of Pavia in Ford's play, loves Fernando, who comes to love the Duchess Bianca after she has given him the signal, but the Duchess is bound in marriage to the Duke. Passion drives Fiormonda to confess her love to Fernando; he tells her that he has "vowed to live a single life,"[5] but she is not long in guessing that the Duchess has his heart. Whereupon she betrays the lovers to the Duke, driven by an ambivalent mixture of love and hate to destroy what she cannot possess. Restoration tragedy is full of ladies like her: Almeria in *The Indian Emperor,* Nourmahal in *Aureng-Zebe,* the Duchess of Eboli in *Don Carlos,* Zara in *The Mourning Bride,* who epitomizes herself and all her kind in a famous couplet:

> Heaven has no rage, like love to hatred turned,
> Nor hell a fury, like a woman scorned.[6]

The difference between the Fiormondas, the Nourmahals, and the Zaras, on the one hand, and the Biancas, the Almahides, and the Indamoras, on the other, is that the former seek to fulfill their passion at any cost and must therefore be branded wicked, while the latter, who seek to suppress their passion at any cost when fulfillment implies a violation of honor, are therefore to be accounted virtuous. And suppression counts for much in drama such as this, where everything turns on the success with which erotic passion is kept under the control of reason. In plays such as *Love's Sacrifice* and the typical tragedies of the Restoration, to surrender to natural instinct is to court death: to die to honor, if not to suffer the physical death of the body. That is why love and death are so often associated, both in Ford and in Restoration tragedy; for the original meaning of passion is suffering, and the ultimate in suffering is death.[7] Characters like Ford's Bianca and Fernando in *Love's Sacrifice* and Penthea and Orgilus in *The Broken Heart,* like Dryden's Almanzor

5. Act I, Scene ii. *John Ford (Five Plays),* ed. Havelock Ellis (New York, 1957), p. 274.

6. Act III, Scene ii. *William Congreve (Complete Plays),* ed. Alexander Charles Ewald (New York, 1956), p. 415.

7. See Denis de Rougemont, *Love in the Western World,* trans. Montgomery Belgion (New York, 1957), *passim,* especially pp. 32–36, 41–45.

and Almahide in *The Conquest of Granada* and Porphyrius and Berenice in *Tyrannic Love,* are kept apart by an internal necessity which
binds them to a rigid code of honor, the violation of which is death. Like
the equilibrists in Mr. Ransom's poem, they may yearn for each other,
they may even offer themselves to each other, but what they say is
straightway unsaid with the words "Honor, Honor" that come so inevitably to their lips and deliver them from what, in the Platonic code,
must stand as the final shame. For those who give way to their passion,
the end is death and madness, generally both.

IV

The first two acts of the anonymous Elizabethan chronicle play *Edward
III* (printed in 1596) present a romantic plot which contains the germs of
a number of emotional details that would be developed, refined, and
embellished by dramatists in the years ahead. There King Edward finds
himself desperately enamored of the virtuous Countess of Salisbury. He
declares his passion to her, and she is moved to hear of it; but she sensibly
reminds him that the love he would offer her is due his Queen and that
the love he solicits of her is due her husband, who is away, fighting the
King's wars. And announcing her belief that the King but tempts her in
her husband's absence, she closes the interview. But the King's passion is
undiminished. He meets the Countess' father, the Earl of Warwick, and,
in a scene that Beaumont and Fletcher must have remembered when they
composed the scene in *A King and No King* (III.iii) wherein Arbaces
tells the honorable Mardonius of his incestuous love and solicits his aid in
satisfying it, all is revealed. Warwick, who—like Mardonius—has noticed
that all is not well with his royal master, opens the interview by asking
what is wrong and whether he can help. The King extracts an oath that
Warwick will do his bidding and then demands that the nobleman go to
his daughter and win her to become the King's mistress. Warwick is left
to ponder his dilemma: either to play the pander to his daughter or break
his oath to his King. It is the sort of emotional impasse in which the
Jacobean drama of a decade hence will delight. Ten years later Warwick,
in a Jacobean tragicomedy or tragedy, would disguise himself as the
King's pandering agent and go to his daughter for the purpose of testing

her honor, as Marston's Malevole tests his wife's, and Tourneur's Vindice tests his sister's. But what is remarkable about the treatment of this potentially sensational and highly suggestive episode in *Edward III* is the utter simplicity with which it is handled. Warwick, announcing himself "an atturnie from the Court of hell" (II.i.381),[8] reports to his daughter what his oath demands, she responds with disgust, and he confirms her in her virtue. The episode concludes with a final meeting between the Countess and the King. She comes to him, and he assumes that she is ready to consent to his desire. She implies that she will if first he will kill her husband and his Queen. To this he consents, whereupon she produces two daggers and delivers herself as follows:

> Here by my side doth hang my wedding knifes:
> Take thou the one, and with it kill thy Queene,
> And learne by me to finde her where she lies;
> And with this other Ile dispatch my loue,
> Which now lies fast a sleepe within my hart:
> When they are gone, then Ile consent to loue.
> Stir not, lasciuious king, to hinder me;
> My resolution is more nimbler far,
> Then thy preuention can be in my rescue,
> And if thou stir, I strike; therefore, stand still,
> And heare the choyce that I will put thee to:
> Either sweare to leaue thy most vnholie sute
> And neuer hence forth to solicit me;
> Or else, by heauen, this sharpe poynted knyfe
> Shall staine thy earth with that which thou would staine,
> My poore chast blood. Sweare, Edward, sweare,
> Or I will strike and die before thee heere.

> (II.ii.173–189)

This drastic speech has the desired effect: the King swears as she requires, his sense of shame is reawakened, and he goes off to conduct the French wars.

I have dwelt thus in detail on this subsidiary plot of *Edward III* because it presents with the utmost clarity a dramatic situation the general lineaments of which will be familiar to all students of Jacobean and Caroline tragedy and tragicomedy—one which is fully stocked with a store of romantic, not to say erotic, potential which the Jacobean dramatists and

8. *The Shakespeare Apocrypha,* ed. C. F. Tucker Brooke (Oxford, 1908).

their successors would prove themselves adepts in the art of exploiting but which is entirely unexploited here in its Elizabethan instance. King Edward, though his passion for the Countess is by no means unmixed with revulsion for himself, is a model of uncomplicated determination beside the tormented indecision of such a character as Beaumont and Fletcher's Arbaces; and the Countess' threat of suicide, whereby her honor will be confirmed, unlike that of Ford's Bianca, is to be carried out before, not after, an adulterous coupling. The Elizabethan treatment of the situation is straightforward and direct, largely consisting in the plain depiction of a clash of purposes and a setting-forth in bold, clear strokes of the responses of the individual wills that are in opposition. The Jacobean treatment of comparable situations is far more oblique, concerned as it is with depicting, not merely a character's response to the dilemma on which he is impaled or the conflict in which he is trapped, but his response to his response, and his response to other characters' responses to his response. Things can become very inward in Jacobean dramatic situations, and the requisite technique for representing this inwardness will perforce be one capable of projecting a complex variety of knowingly assumed moral and emotional attitudes, each of which is the stylistically decreed response to a specific dramatic occasion and absolute in itself, however equivocal the sum total of such attitudes may seem when viewed in the aggregate. The example of the subplot of *Edward III,* when viewed against the handling of similar plots in later plays, is instructive for what it tells us of the manner in which the details, the implications, the total meaning of a given dramatic subject are transformed according to the rhetorical colors, the histrionic decoration, and the psychological contours of the garment of style in which it is set forth. In its small way, comparison of the subplot of *Edward III* with corresponding plots in plays of the Jacobean, Caroline, and Restoration stage points to some of the larger transformations, of form and spirit, which dramatic style was to undergo in the transition from Renaissance to Baroque.

V

In judging the plots on which the foregoing discussion has been focused, it is well to understand what the dramatists who made them had in mind. This is perhaps most readily viewed in the light of Addison's often quoted statement to Bishop Hough in 1700 concerning Boileau and the passions aroused by tragedy: "Aristotle, says he, proposes two passions that are proper to be raised by tragedy, terror and pity, but Corneille endeavours at a new one, which is admiration." [9] Of this, Bonamy Dobrée says that Addison "might have added that to endeavour at admiration had been the hallmark of all English tragedy for the last forty odd years." [10] One might add that Dobrée might have said that to endeavor at admiration had been the purpose of English tragedy and tragicomedy for the past eighty-odd years—since, that is, the days of Beaumont, Fletcher, and their followers and imitators. For what, if not admiration, is one to feel for such characters as Amintor in *The Maid's Tragedy?* What passion, if not admiration, could Massinger conceivably have hoped to raise in his audience with his succession of virtuous heroines: Cleora in *The Bondman,* Camiola in *The Maid of Honour,* Sophia in *The Picture?* And what is one to make of Calantha's dance at the end of Ford's *Broken Heart,* as she steadfastly treads its measures while death after death is announced to her, if one does not accord to this display of Spartan endurance the wonder which it is so obviously intended to arouse? For to evoke admiration is to evoke wonder, and to arouse a sense of wonder is the whole endeavor of the drama of the late Jacobean, Caroline, and Restoration periods. In the presence of it we are invited to wonder at life's complexities—complexities of relationship as well as emotional response—in the same moment that we are invited to wonder at the shaping power of imagination which reduces them to order. [11] We are invited to wonder as well at the opposing

9. Quoted by Bonamy Dobrée, *Restoration Tragedy, 1660–1720* (Oxford, 1929), p. 14.

10. Dobrée, p. 14.

11. Regarding the power of the creative faculty in these matters, see Dryden's Dedication to *The Rival Ladies,* where he speaks of the time when his play "was only a confus'd Mass of Thoughts, tumbling over one another in the Dark: When the Fancy was yet in its first Work, moving the Sleeping Images of things towards the Light, there to be Distinguish'd, and then either chosen or rejected by the Judgment. . . ." And later, where he defines the dramatist's task in the composition of such works as the present tragicomedy: "To conduct his imaginary Persons, through so many various Intrigues and Chances, as the Labouring Audience shall think them lost under every Billow; and then at length to work them so naturally out of their Distresses, that when the whole Plot is laid open, the Spectators may rest

extremes of human experience here artfully juxtaposed: extremes that embrace passionate indulgence and rational restraint, sensual abandon and godlike forbearance, and which, in the plots of the plays examined here, mark the ways that end, respectively, in vice and virtue.[12]

---

satisfied, that every cause was powerfull enough to produce the effect it had; and that the whole Chain of them was with such due order Linck'd together, that the first Accident would naturally beget the second, till they all render'd the Conclusion necessary." (*The Works of John Dryden* [Berkeley and Los Angeles, 1962], VIII, 95.)

12. The baroque dramatist's rationale for the play with a double ending (fortunate for the virtuous, miserable for the vicious) is stated by Corneille in his *Discours du Poëme Dramatique*: "C'est cet intérêt qu'on aime à prendre pour les vertueux qui a obligé d'en venir à cette autre manière de finir le poëme dramatique par la punition des mauvaises actions et la récompense des bonnes, qui n'est pas un précepte de l'art, mais un usage que nous avons embrassé, dont chacun peut se départir à ses périls. ... Le succès heureux de la vertu, en dépit des traverses et des périls, nous excite à l'embrasser; et le succès funeste du crime ou de l'injustice est capable de nous en augmenter l'horreur naturelle, par l'appréhension d'un pareil malheur." (Corneille, *Théâtre Complete* [Bibliothèque de la Pléiade, 1950], I, 11.)

Pictures for the Reader:
A Series of Illustrations
to Comedy *1591–1592*

LOUISE GEORGE CLUBB

I N SIXTEENTH-CENTURY ITALY regular comedies and illustrated books
abounded, but illustrated editions of regular comedies were rarer than
Indian pearls. Helen M. C. Purkis' description and discussion of the
woodcuts adorning Gonzaga's *Gli inganni* (Venetia, Giovan Antonio
Rampazetto, 1592) [1] are therefore singularly interesting. Now her conclusions are offered extension by the discovery that a year before the publication of Gonzaga's comedy a number of the same woodcuts had been used
in the second editions of two other comedies: Cristoforo Castelletti's *I torti
amorosi* and Sforza Oddi's *Prigione d'amore,* also published in Venice but
by different printers (gli Heredi di Marchiò Sessa, and Girolamo Polo, Ad
Istantia di Filippo Gionti [*sic*], respectively).[2]

1. "The Illustrations to Curzio Gonzaga's *Gli inganni:* Variations On the Comic
Scene of Serlio," *Letterature moderne,* VII (1957), 342–348.

2. The copies I use of the 1591 *Torti* and of the sole edition of *Inganni* belong to
the Folger Shakespeare Library. The University of Toronto Library has provided a
microfilm of its copy of the 1591 *Prigione.* Giunti's Florentine press had published
Oddi's comedy first, as the colophon indicates: "Stampata in Fiorenza, & ristampata
in Venetia."

Examining the twenty illustrations of stage action [3] used thirty times in the course of *Inganni,* Dr. Purkis observes that for the first fourteen scenes (except II.v, which is not illustrated), each picture is used only once and accurately represents the text. But after III.iii repetitions occur, and the number of actors depicted does not always correspond to the number called for by the playwright. Repetitions in the 1591 editions of *Torti* and *Prigione* begin with the first act, in the last scene of one and the fourth of the other. Further comparison reveals minor differences and major resemblances which indicate the similar use of the woodcuts by Rampazetto, Sessa's heirs, and Girolamo Polo, and—more important—the purpose for which the woodcuts were originally intended.

Although *Inganni* is in octavo and the 1591 *Torti* and *Prigione* are both in duodecimo, the pictures are the same size in all three.[4] They seem larger in *Inganni* because Rampazetto added ornamental scrolls to the sides of each cut and also because he achieved a clearer impression. The two sets of detached figures in *Inganni* noted by Pandolfi [3] do not appear in *Torti* or *Prigione.* On the other hand, the Prologue and all forty-three scenes of *Torti* are illustrated, three of them twice, adding up to forty-seven illustrations, while in *Prigione* two Prologues and thirty-nine scenes are illustrated, eleven of them twice, coming to fifty-two all together.

The total, however, represents only twenty-nine individual woodcuts. In *Inganni* there are twenty depictions of stage action, eight of which are

3. In addition there are in *Inganni* two sets of four detached figures (each used twice: $15 = 52$; $26v = 71$) of costumed actors without backgrounds, not described by Dr. Purkis but mentioned by Vito Pandolfi in *La commedia dell'arte,* II (Florence, 1957), 336, as an example of iconography connected with the *commedia dell'arte.* To my best knowledge, these have nowhere been reproduced, but two of the illustrations of stage action are included without discussion in Pierre Duchartre's *La commedia dell'arte et ses enfants* (Paris, 1955), p. 61. One of these two also illustrates Dr. Purkis' article, together with nine others. In short, eleven of the woodcuts in *Inganni* are available in modern reproduction, but neither the detached figures nor any of the illustrations used only in *Torti* or in *Prigione* exist except in the original editions. An enlarged portion of one of the *Inganni* cuts is used on the cover of the edition of Bruno's *Candelaio* (Turin, 1964) in the Einaudi series of drama texts, but the reproduction is too incomplete to constitute a representative sample of the woodcuts.

4. The woodcuts from *Torti* and *Prigione* are reproduced here in their natural size, those from *Inganni* slightly smaller.

repeated once (10v = 69; 15v = 39; 27 = 66; 27v = 52v; 34v = 71v; 47v = 64; 50 = 61v; 59 = 73) and one twice (37v = 44 = 49). Of the twenty-one woodcuts in *Torti*, four are repeated once ([5] = 169; [11] = 145; 46 = 87; 68 = 77); two twice (107 = 158 = 178; 18 = 41 = 94); two three times (57 = 111 = 130 = 196; 124 = 134 = 175 = 198); one five times (28 = 56 = 116 = 150 = 165 = 172); and one seven times (23 = 33 = 51 = 65 = 128 = 152 = 192 = 201). Twenty-six of the twenty-nine pictures so far discovered in the series are used in *Prigione*, four repeated once (17 = 103v; 20 = 89; 36v = 81; 59 = 84v); two twice (4 = 85v = 101v; 57v = 60v = 66); three three times (25 = 32 = 70v = 99v; 28v = 48v = 74 = 90; 33 = 55v = 87 = 96); one four times (39 = 82 = 92 = 98 = 107); and one five times (10v = 22v = 31 = 54v = 65 = 95). Only fourteen of the woodcuts appear in all three plays, and ten in two of them:

Inganni		Torti		Prigione		Inganni		Torti		Prigione
9	=	124	=	10v		77v	=	211		
15v	=	46	=	57v						
22	=	28	=	4		10v	=			36v
23	=	18	=	73v		17v	=			76
27	=	57	=	102v		21	=			97
27v	=	[11]	=	27v		34v	=			77v
32v	=	83	=	51v		50	=			56v
37	=	107	=	33						
37v	=	23	=	39				[5]	=	20
41	=	97	=	25				17	=	35v
45	=	62	=	17				141	=	59
47v	=	68	=	28v				203	=	112
56	=	30	=	34						
59	=	185	=	69v						

This leaves *Torti* with two (76, 118) and *Prigione* with three (6, 38, 45) woodcuts not shared, and *Inganni* with none (except for the detached figures mentioned in note 3). The five may be called unique only because there has been no report of their being used to illustrate editions of other comedies, although it is obvious that the entire series was designed expressly to provide illustrations for any regular example of the genre. Knowledge of the full size of the series and of the range of effects it offered must wait on future discoveries.

Inganni 9

Inganni 15v

Inganni 22

Inganni 23

Inganni 27

Inganni 27v

FIGURE 4. Woodcuts photographed from Curzio Gonzaga, *Gli inganni* (1592), and Cristoforo Castelletti, *I torti amorosi* (1591), with the kind permission of the Folger Shakespeare Library. Woodcuts photographed from Sforza Oddi, *Prigione d'Amore* (1591), with the kind permission of the University of Toronto Library. [This figure is continued through p. 274.]

Inganni 32v

Inganni 37

Inganni 37v

Inganni 41

Inganni 45

Inganni 47v

Inganni 56

Inganni 59

Inganni 77v

Inganni 10v

Inganni 17v

Inganni 21

Inganni 34v

Inganni 50

Torti 5

Torti 17

Torti 141

Torti 203

Torti 76

Torti 118

Prigione 6

Prigione 38

Prigione 45

Inganni 15

Inganni 26v

Yet even with only three examples of the use of these pictures it is possible to see how the results could differ. In *Inganni* the woodcuts are distributed sparingly, not for economy, but in order to achieve a high rate of correspondence between picture and text. In *Prigione,* with half again as many illustrations, and in *Torti,* with nearly as many as *Prigione,* a disregard of such niceties is apparent in the blurred reproduction and in the discrepancies caused by the more generous use of woodcuts.

Dr. Purkis concludes from the variety and arrangement of backgrounds in perspective used in *Inganni* that the artist was not thinking of the stage designer's problems or of any particular performance but that the illustrations suggest the range of possibilities in stage sets for comedy of the period. The hypothesis that might have been sensed waiting around the corner—that the entire group of cuts was an all-purpose series, designed for the *reader* of comedy—is confronted and confirmed by the appearance of the 1591 *Torti* and *Prigione.* While *Inganni* and *Torti* are set in Rome and *Prigione* in Ferrara, the illustrator employed generalized architectural motifs appropriate to almost any Italian city. There are Florentine towers, Bolognese arcades, Roman domes, but without identifiable particulars; moreover, none of them is set in relation to surrounding buildings so as to suggest a real and specific city. In one picture (*Inganni* 27v = *Torti* [11] = *Prigione* 27v) the pair of dark figures hammering a bell atop an arch are recognizably the famous *Mori* of Venice. But the view of them is one impossible to obtain in reality, for the long, narrow street flanked by houses leading toward the arch did not exist in the real sixteenth-century Venice any more than it does today. Then, as if to emphasize the unreality (and perhaps as a signature of the Venetian artist?), the motif is repeated: the *Mori* reappear (*Inganni* 37 = *Torti* 107 = *Prigione* 33) on a quite different arch at the end of a different street. In one of the woodcuts unique to *Prigione* (45) the background at first glance suggests Piazza San Marco as seen from the Piazzetta, but closer examination reveals a tower where there should be an arch, a stairway where none should be, and so on. In their humble way some of these woodcuts are akin to the games of fantastic juxtaposition later played on canvas by Canaletto.

Each of the twenty-nine separate cuts has a different background, with diminishing perspective and a considerable variety of buildings. The basic principle common to all is the idea of comic scene authorized by Serlio, but no two vistas are the same. Not only would it have been impossible, as

Dr. Purkis has observed, to effectuate so many changes within the physical limits of the comic stage at that time, but it would also have broken the fairly strict custom of employing a single set for comedy while indulging the contrasting taste for elaborate machinery in the *intermedii*. Therefore, there could have been no thought of staging in the mind of the artist, who was deliberately jumbling and departicularizing familiar architectural types to make his illustrations a suitable accompaniment to the reading of any comedy.[5]

The disposition of human figures in the woodcuts is determined likewise, not by the exigencies of a specific performance or even of a specific play, but by those of the genre. As a result, the cuts represent the most common grouping of characters in comedy of the period. The general similarity in *favola* and relationship of characters from play to play made possible a degree of accuracy which, if not exact, was sufficient to permit the same set of illustrations to serve many comedies. On the other hand, variations in the manipulation of characters by the individual dramatist would have prohibited any single series from meeting every contingency, without being swollen to an unmanageable size. These variations account for the discrepancies between illustration and text in *Inganni, Torti,* and *Prigione,* especially after the epitasis is well under way, when the intrigue proper to the genre customarily becomes more complex and involves as many encounters as the playwright could arrange without confusing his audience.

The series includes at least one woodcut of each of the basic groupings, beginning with a solo depiction of each stock figure reduced to its lowest common denominator: old gentleman, young gentleman, young lady, male servant, female servant. Of each of these, however, regular comedies generally contain a minimum of two, with variations creating more precisely designated characters. Young gentlemen may be lovers, soldiers, Neapolitan poetasters, or girls in disguise; young ladies may be boys, real ladies, or well-dressed courtesans, costume being the determining element. Next come depictions of two of each type, and variously composed pairs, then trios, and so on. By cross-addition the artist could make twenty-nine

5. An earlier analogous use of woodcuts to illustrate comedy is described in another article of Dr. Purkis. See T. E. Lawrenson and Helen Purkis, "Les éditions illustrées de Térence dans l'histoire du théâtre: Spectacles dans un fauteuil?", *Le lieu théâtral à la Renaissance,* ed. Jean Jacquot (Paris, 1964), pp. 1–23.

combinations in no time. Moreover, the possibilities increase with the growth of the group which occurs in the last scenes of many comedies. In twenty-seven of the woodcuts in this series, four is the largest number of characters represented, but the last scenes of *Inganni* and *Torti* are illustrated by a picture of three women and six men (77v = 211), and the penultimate scene of *Torti* and the last of *Prigione,* involving respectively five and eight characters, are allotted a woodcut of nine men (203 = 112). Apparently the series did not include pictures of groups of five, six, seven, or eight. To some comedies the omissions would not matter, but *Inganni, Torti,* and *Prigione* occasionally call for groups of intermediate sizes. A stranger gap in a series providing such variety, however, results from the artist's failure to place human figures in any of several windows and balconies shown, although, like most regular comedies, these three include scenes played from above.

A count of the repetitions of woodcuts dictated by the texts reveals the following predominance, in descending order of frequency: male servant with young gentleman (*Inganni* 37v = *Torti* 23 = *Prigione* 39), male servant solo (*Inganni* 22 = *Torti* 28 = *Prigione* 4), young lady with female servant (*Inganni* 27 = *Torti* 57 = *Prigione* 102v), male servant with old gentleman (*Inganni* 9 = *Torti* 124 = *Prigione* 10v). The student of Italian Renaissance comedy will recognize these as exactly the most common combinations. Not despite its generality but because of it, this series of woodcuts offers a pocket-sized panorama of the conventions of the character groupings as well as of the scenery proper to Italian regular comedy and a hint as to the interest which had developed by the 1590's in the *reading* of plays.

An Approach
to French Renaissance Drama

DONALD STONE, JR.

IT IS HARD TO CONCEIVE of an aspect of the French Renaissance that has
been more systematically neglected than the drama. Yet total neglect
might have been preferable to the prejudicial treatment the genre has
received in the past and continues to receive today. I hope that the years to
come will show an increase in studies in French Renaissance theater, but
not before serious thought is given to the work now before us on this
subject. The following pages offer a brief survey of significant studies on
sixteenth-century drama in France and attempt to show that present views
on Renaissance tragedy may well hinder rather than help our appreciation
of its place in French literature.

I

At the present time a student interested in French Renaissance drama
will have little success in finding a satisfactory survey of the genre or an
unbiased evaluation of its accomplishments. Raymond Lebègue's *La Tragédie française de la Renaissance* contains a bare 109 pages. Rigal's *Le
Théâtre française avant la période classique* does not even discuss the
sixteenth century, and later, when he seems to have regretted this

omission, he was content to devote a chapter of *De Jodelle à Molière* to "La Mise en scène dans les tragédies du XVIᵉ siècle." The title of a recent Sorbonne thesis, *La Tragédie française de Jodelle à Corneille*[1] suggested that the long-awaited study had been made. Unfortunately, the subtitle of the thesis, "Le Thème de la vengeance," reveals the book's true content: a long enumeration of Renaissance plays where the theme of vengeance appears.

When the familiar manuals refer to the genre, they all tell the same story. Castex and Surer:

En 1552, Jodelle, âgé de vingt ans à peine, fait représenter devant la Cour la première tragédie en français, *Cléopâtre captive*. Sa pièce était dépourvue, sinon de beauté poétique, du moins d'intérêt dramatique. ... Mais Ronsard et ses amis saluèrent cette pièce comme un événement littéraire, et c'en était bien un, puisqu'elle inaugurait en France la tragédie.[2]

Lagarde and Michard:

Jodelle ... avait vingt ans lorsqu'il fit jouer devant la cour sa *Cléopâtre captive,* notre première tragédie. L'événement fut célébré avec enthousiasme par Ronsard et les autres poètes de la Pléiade. Aujourd'hui la pièce nous paraît longue et lente, et nous y trouvons fort peu d'action dramatique. ... Il en sera de même de toutes les tragédies du XVIᵉ siècle. Cependant, cette oeuvre annonce le théâtre classique par sa composition en cinq actes ... et par l'apparition des trois unités. La rupture est complète avec la tradition médiévale.[3]

This story in no way betrays the analysis of longer studies but, as we shall see, reproduces them with depressing exactness. French Renaissance drama is the victim of both the negligence of critics and their prejudices.

Enea Balmas in his excellent volume on Jodelle protests against the traditional interpretation of the poet in these terms:

È gratuito supporre che Jodelle abbia voluto scrivere una tragedia "regolare," e non vi sia riuscito; ed è sterile accusarlo di essersi mostrato maldestro in

1. E. Forsyth, *La Tragédie française de Jodelle à Corneille* (Paris, 1962).

2. P. Castex and P. Surer, *Manuel des Études littéraires françaises* (Paris, 1946), II, 50.

3. A. Lagarde and L. Michard, *Les Grands Auteurs français du programme* (Paris, 1949), II, 167.

un'impresa alla quale egli si è certo accinto con criteri diversi da quelli che gli si vorrebbero attribuire.[4]

It is significant that the first recent voice of protest should come from a critic who is not French,[5] as the prejudicial treatment of French Renaissance drama is in many ways related to a general tendency among French critics to glorify their classical period. The brilliant success of the seventeenth-century theater has tended to close their eyes to all other efforts with tragedy. They can accept or approve only what conforms to Aristotle and resembles Corneille and Racine. Moreover, implicitly or explicitly, Renaissance tragedy is "le théâtre avant Corneille," or "les origines du théâtre classique" (the two manuals could not make this more clear). The consequence of such an unbounded appreciation of the classical theater—Balmas is only too well aware of this—is a confusion of traditions and intentions which has been fatal to the study of Renaissance drama and yet is so easily explained if one gives the plays in question a superficial glance.

Jodelle designated both *Cléopâtre captive* and *Didon se sacrifiant* as tragedies; for the most part he wrote in alexandrines, and he divided the plays, which relate tales of tragic love, into five acts. In form and content, then, the plays have nothing in common with the medieval theater; rather both aspects so strongly suggest Racinian drama that Lebègue assures us, "... Jodelle rompt complètement avec le théâtre médiéval; il ne lui emprunte rien. ..."[6] And naturally, since Renaissance drama looks like classical tragedy, it can be judged as such. "Pas d'incertitude, pas un conflit intérieur. Rien n'est plus vide," says Lebègue of *Cléopâtre captive;*[7] "comme la *Cléopâtre,* la *Didon* reste une pièce élégiaque, sans action ...,"

---

4. Enea Balmas, *Étienne Jodelle* (Firenze, 1962), p. 309.

5. I am not forgetting G. Lanson's excellent remark in his *Esquisse d'une histoire de la tragédie française* (New York, 1920), p. 13: "Erreur de considérer la tragédie de la Renaissance comme une tragédie classique mal faite, procédant de la même conception que celle de Racine et de Corneille et n'ayant besoin que d'être améliorée." Unfortunately, his words were not heeded.

6. Raymond Lebègue, *La Tragédie française de la Renaissance* (Brussels, 1944), p. 30.

7. *Ibid.,* p. 31.

notes Forsyth.[8] In both cases the judgment is clearly based on a comparison with the classical tragedy of Corneille and Racine.

Even more injurious to the genre is the fact that for most critics this elegiac quality derives from an erroneous interpretation by Renaissance humanists of the meaning of tragedy. In the words of Maurice Valency, "The Italian dramatists had thought tragedy should make one shudder. The French thought it should make one cry."[9] H. W. Lawton notes that Seneca is a contributing factor: "The choice of Seneca as the model in tragedy led to an important and lamentable development in the character of the genre: it became lyrical or rhetorical rather than dramatic."[10] Nevertheless, his ultimate judgment leaves us with the same impression: French humanists were not of the same stature as their classical successors. They betrayed the nature of tragedy. They betrayed that antiquity whose aesthetics Aristotle had so conveniently codified and, by inference, the seventeenth century had so carefully followed. There is no escaping the dominance of the classical moment here; it even represents the very historical point ("le théâtre avant Corneille") from which we set out to judge Renaissance drama. But what a different picture emerges when we begin at the beginning of tragedy in France in the sixteenth century, that is, with the medieval theater and early humanists like George Buchanan.

II

Prior to the Renaissance medieval drama had undergone a significant evolution as it left the church, even the cathedral square, to become an interminable divertissement, costly, formless, as crude as it was edifying. Its content became at the same time more and more didactic, with its message communicated through allegory and lament—the same kind of lament (and the same didacticism) that we find in such early humanist dramas as Buchanan's *Jephthes, sive Votum*.

Written between 1539 and 1544, when Buchanan was a professor at Bordeaux, *Jephthes* has no acts, just a series of episodes (more than five),

8. Forsyth, p. 149.
9. Maurice Valency, *The Flower and the Castle* (New York, 1963), p. 28.
10. H. W. Lawton, *Handbook of French Renaissance Dramatic Theory* (Manchester, 1949), p. xxi.

separated by the Chorus. The Scot also had the misfortune to write in Latin, not French, so that, for reasons of language as well as form, the manuals could not properly cite his work as the beginning of French classical tragedy. Buchanan may not be dismissed so rapidly, however. If his plays have not every trait of the seventeenth-century tragedy, they are still far from reproducing the interminable mixture of comedy and didacticism characteristic of medieval *mystères*. The humanist has brought the drama back to a classical simplicity. At the same time, he chooses a biblical subject, yet shows the firm influence of Euripides' *Iphigenia in Aulis*.

The play is taken from a short episode in the Old Testament (Judges XI.29-40). Jephthah vows that if God will give him victory, he will sacrifice whoever comes from his house to greet him after the battle. God delivers the Ammonites to Jephthah, but the first person to meet him is his only child, a daughter. He weeps and reveals his vow to her. She accepts her fate, asking only that she may go to the mountains to bewail her virginity. When she returns, the sacrifice is accomplished. Buchanan could not have transformed this story into a full-length play without embellishing it somewhat. Interestingly enough, his development begins even with the *données* of the Bible tale. Unlike the biblical source, Buchanan's Jephthah does not tell his daughter immediately of the vow. She must learn of her fate from another. With her mother she begs Jephthah not to fulfill his vow and then serenely consents to die—all traits which Buchanan borrowed from Euripides.[11]

Given that the humanist's intentions were not exclusively literary, he did not stop at incorporating a few touches from Greek tragedy. Like Erasmus, Buchanan used literature to expound on religious issues. *Jephthes'* preoccupation with the problem of vows lays bare the true *raison d'être* of Buchanan's tragedy. To the original framework, Buchanan added the figure of the high priest and a long episode in which Jephthah and the priest debate whether the fatal vow should be kept. The discussion is not very different in kind from the confrontation between Satan and the shepherds in Marguerite's *Comédie de la Nativité* or the situation which concludes the *Moralité nouvelle d'un empereur qui tua son neveu*. Lebègue is doubtless right in suggesting that the humanists

11. For further discussion see *Four Renaissance Tragedies,* ed. Donald Stone, Jr. (Cambridge, Mass., 1966), pp. xiii-xiv.

wished to bring the theater back to a form more compatible with the works of antiquity. But changes in form did not necessarily bring about changes in content and, in particular, in the conception of tragedy. On the contrary, the persistence of a biblical subject and the continued interest in didacticism suggest that the difference in tragic vision between medieval and ancient drama—so great for us—was in point of fact rather minimal for Buchanan, a suggestion rather well borne out by the play itself.

From the outset the meaning to be ascribed to the misfortune which will befall Jephthah is unclear. According to the angel of the Prologue, God will cause tragedy to fall on Jephthah's house in order that "l'insolente audace / N'aura plus dans son coeur aucunement de place." [12] To what is the angel referring? Is the tragedy an arbitrary act of God (in keeping with the classical dramas of Euripides and Seneca), or is He punishing an act (Jephthah's vow) which is repugnant to Him (in keeping with the medieval drama of sin and retribution)? Jephthah's conversations with his daughter, his wife, and the high priest in no way serve to clarify the issue. [13] But then, given contemporary views on tragedy, there was no reason for Buchanan to do otherwise.

Lanson showed long ago that the early Renaissance inherited from the Middle Ages a simple but adequate definition of tragedy: that of Donatus. [14] This commentator on comedy sought also to distinguish comedy from tragedy, where one found "the characters exalted, the terror great, the outcome calamitous." [15] No mention of catharsis, of when and where the action should begin; no mention of how the play should show action rather than narrate it. No mention of Aristotle at all. Consequently, when Buchanan wrote a play about a general's family and a terrible sacrifice, he had fulfilled all the aspects of Donatus' requirements.

As a result, the obscurity which surrounds the meaning of Jephthah's sacrifice as well as the scene of religious discussion says less about Buchanan's talent than about a general concept of tragedy at this time, a concept

12. *Jephté ou le Voeu*, trans. Florent Chrestien, vv. 71–72. The entire text is reproduced in Stone, *Four Renaissance Tragedies.*

13. See Stone, *Four Renaissance Tragedies*, pp. xvi–xviii.

14. See G. Lanson, "L'Idée de la tragédie en France avant Jodelle," *RHLF*, XI (1904), 541–585.

15. Quoted in H. W. Lawton, *Handbook*, p. 11.

no more complex than that of Donatus and hardly destined to exclude the lament or didacticism of medieval drama.[16] Quite the contrary. When Buchanan fills his play with monologues of lament, his decision may well reflect Seneca's influence, but it also underlines that continuing association of tragedy and elegiac lament already so entrenched in medieval drama.

In view of these remarks, can we be as confident as Lebègue that Jodelle "rompt complètement avec le moyen âge"? In a recent issue of *Neophilologus* I published an article on certain adaptations of the Dido and Aeneas story by members of the Pléiade and especially on the third book of the *Franciade* and *Didon se sacrifiant*.[17] In each case the poets prove to be quite indifferent to the internal drama of Vergil's couple. The proud queen of eastern blood who abandons herself to a passion she knows to be contrary to her vows to Sychaeus becomes a woman struck down by Fortune, unjustly abandoned by "pariure Enee."[18] I suggest at the close of the article that the absence of internal drama in the portrait of Dido (or Ronsard's heroine modeled on her), as well as the moral judgment of Aeneas (or Francus' poignant awareness of the moral problems inherent in his situation), derives from a continuing medieval influence upon the Pléiade. My own recent work with the tragedy makes me even more inclined to adopt such a position, despite the formal changes wrought by Jodelle in his plays.

Jodelle's reworking of the Dido and Aeneas story reverses completely the characterizations of the *Aeneid*. Vergil's Trojan remains, even within the fourth book, the hero of the epic. He has momentarily succumbed to pleasure in the form of Carthage and Dido's attentions, but throughout he is the "pius Aeneas." Confronted by Mercury, he is frightened and confused as to what plan of action to adopt, but there is no doubt in his mind that he should obey. Dido appears as the victim of divine machinations in

16. Note Lazare de Baïf's revealing definition of tragedy in his Preface to a translation of Sophocles' *Electra* (1551): "... une moralité composée des grandes calamitez, meurtres et adversitez survenues aux nobles et excellentz personnaiges." Not only is Donatus' influence quite clear, but tragedy is also seen as a kind of *moralité!*

17. "Dido and Aeneas, Theme and Vision in the Third Book of the *Franciade,*" *Neophilologus,* XLIX (1965), 289–296.

18. E. Jodelle, *Didon se sacrifiant,* v. 448, in Stone, *Four Renaissance Tragedies.*

the scene between Juno and Venus. Elsewhere Vergil lavishes his poetic
powers upon a portrait of the passionate queen who gradually forgets
rank, vows, and country for the sake of her love.

Didon se sacrifiant begins with a speech by the Trojan Achates. He
fears that their departure from Carthage may bring down the wrath of the
gods upon them for their "unjust flight," which may cause the death of
Dido. He is countered in this view by Ascanius, now a young man, and
Palinurus, who persuade their companion that the gods must be obeyed
and that the death of Dido would be a lesser misfortune than the Trojans'
failure to fulfill the promise of their race. This exchange raises the
essential themes of the play: Aeneas' base treatment of Dido, who has
been led on by a faithless adventurer, and the gods' omnipotent control
over human destiny. It matters little that Aeneas, too, has misgivings
about leaving; the gods have chosen him, not Dido, as their favorite. Her
love for Aeneas has brought her to new heights of joy, but the gods have a
penchant for turning upon mortals in just such a situation.

Thus, Dido's tragedy, like Jephthah's, revolves around her relationship
to those forces outside man which regulate his life. Whether they are
called God or Fortune is of little importance. The humanist drama
attempts, as did its medieval counterpart, a moral lesson on man's destiny
and could not be less interested in a study of human psychology as a
complex phenomenon. To compare the love theme of *Didon se sacrifiant*
and *Phèdre* with the intention of proving that Racine was the better
psychologist contorts entirely the function of love in the Renaissance play.
Whereas love is the source of tragedy for Racine, for Jodelle love is but the
framework for his tragedy. Dido's love for Aeneas has made her happy;
now the wheel of Fortune will turn.

> Que l'homme ... contemple
> En ce departement fatal,
> Comment la Fortune se iouë
> D'vne grand' Roine sur sa rouë,[19]

chants the Chorus at the end of Act I to provide a fitting definition of
Jodelle's intentions. Of course, Seneca's choruses make the same point. But
essential to Dido's fall is a firm recognition, even by Aeneas' own men,

19. *Ibid.,* vv. 421–424.

that his departure is an unjust act. Jodelle could not have found this element in Vergil, nor the association made by the Carthaginian women that Aeneas has been chosen by the gods to effect the destruction of Dido's life.[20] (Dido's feelings after hearing of Mercury's commands are directed against Aeneas, "Nec tibi diva parens generis" [v. 365], and her allusion to the gods reeks of scorn for what she believes Aeneas' fabrication, "Scilicet is superis labor est, ea cura quietos / Sollicitat" [vv. 379–80].) Balmas has gone so far as to see in *Didon se sacrifiant* a profound antireligious bent;[21] but however we interpret these departures from Vergil and Seneca, it is clear that the more medieval subjects of innocence, guilt, and punishment heavily influenced Jodelle's rendering of Dido's tragedy.

III

A study of how Renaissance tragedy differs from classical drama does not, however, also explain why it differs so fundamentally from that of the seventeenth century. Racine's portrait of love has vastly more in common with Vergil's analysis of Dido than does *Didon se sacrifiant*. Yet Jodelle was easily as proficient a Latinist as Racine, and the ugly charge of a betrayal of antiquity inevitably returns.

However tempting this charge appears as a simple explanation of all our difficulties, the texts do not corroborate a view that Renaissance humanists betrayed their models (Euripides and Seneca) by writing an elegiac drama full of lamentation. There is not space enough here for a long analysis of Euripides and Seneca, but when so distinguished a student of Greek drama as H. D. F. Kitto writes of Euripides, "This is . . . a tragedy lyrical in conception. . . . Pathos and lamentation replace energy and tragic action, static scenes illuminated by intellectual analysis take the place of the ever changing drama of Sophocles,"[22] then

20. C'est que pecheurs nous sommes,
   Et le Ciel se faschant,
   Fait pour punir les hommes
   Son bourreau d'vn mechant.
21. Balmas, *Jodelle,* p. 346.
22. H. D. F. Kitto, *Greek Tragedy: A Literary Study* (New York, 1954), pp. 280, 287.

the parallel with French Renaissance drama is patent. Thus, if the humanists are guilty of not capturing all the intensity of Vergil's story, the crime was committed in the name of a splendid fidelity to the Greco-Latin tradition they knew best. If seventeenth-century tragedy somehow escapes Jodelle's adaptation, we must presuppose a change of attitude toward tragedy, independent of source; in fact, contrary to the example offered by the source. And as French society and literature evolved, such a change took place.

Although the form of humanist tragedy is nearly that of seventeenth-century drama, the development of theater from the Pléiade to Corneille is not a simple linear progression. In the early 1600's tragedy was almost eclipsed by the pastoral and the tragicomedy. When the theoreticians, Mairet, and the Academy brought tragedy back into prominence, the literary context which produced the humanist drama had long since died. Medieval theater was no longer an influence. The salons of the *précieuses* demanded a literature that pleased, not preached; and the subject which pleased most easily was love, conceived now as the psychological drama that Ariosto and Tasso in particular had recently revealed to the French public.

Few documents of the time point so markedly to an evolution in attitude toward the theater than Corneille's Preface to *Clitandre*. In this tragicomedy of 1631, the moralizing choruses have disappeared; the love story exudes the influence of the pastoral and the *précieuses*. But Corneille also insists on writing several scenes of violence whose presence in the play he explains in the Preface:

... quiconque voudra bien peser l'avantage que l'action a sur ces longs et ennuyeux récits, ne trouvera pas étrange que j'aye mieux aimé divertir les yeux, qu'importuner les oreilles, et que me tenant dans la contrainte de cette méthode j'en aye pris la beauté sans tomber dans les incommodités que les Grecs et les Latins qui l'ont suivie, n'ont su d'ordinaire, ou du moins n'ont osé éviter.[23]

At last a playwright shows concern for that element of action so sorely missed by the critics in Renaissance drama, but, interestingly enough, Corneille's concern does not stem from a deeper understanding of Aristot-

23. Pierre Corneille, *Clitandre*, ed. R.-L. Wagner (Lille and Geneva, 1949), p. 9.

le or antiquity. Corneille sees quite correctly that the "longs et ennuyeux récits"—those speeches that modern critics deplore in Jodelle and his successors—are products not of a betrayal of antiquity but, on the contrary, of an excessive faithfulness to its ways. Corneille wants to "divertir les yeux": a tribute to his own dramatic sense, but also an early sign, I think, of the canon of "plaire" to which La Fontaine, Molière, and even Racine will have recourse in justifying innovations not entirely approved by the academicians. There is no little irony in these remarks, especially if we compare them to the traditional views. For, just as the humanists have proven to be most faithful to the dramatists of antiquity they knew well, so Corneille shows that certain essential qualities of the most immediate ancestor of classical theater derive from a distinct reaction in technique against the theater of antiquity.

From two different social and literary contexts come two very different tragedies. Their common form, their common sources, are misleading parallels to say the least, and both theaters deserve to be analyzed and appreciated as separate entities far more than has been the case in the past. Buchanan and Jodelle knew the late medieval theater, hardly an influence on Corneille. More important, if Jodelle and Racine both read Vergil, Jodelle had only Donatus, Euripides, and Seneca to direct his thinking on love and tragedy. None of these authors suggests that love and passion are the essence of human tragedy. Racine knew the same authors but also belonged to a period which had passed through long exploitation of Tasso's *Aminta,* Racan's *Les Bergeries,* Ariosto's *Orlando Furioso.* This literature of love and tragedy cared little about Fortune's Wheel. Passion, jealousy, longing, and devotion—here was material enough for drama; and it reflected an attitude that could not help opening Racine's eyes to new dimensions of Vergil's story of Dido. In short, by insisting that the differences between a Jodelle and a Racine are distinctions of talent and intelligence rather than chronology and tradition, critics merely accuse Renaissance dramatists of not doing what in fact they never intended to do, and at the same time pursue comparisons that rarely lead to the essential differences which divide the two centuries as well as their literatures. Unless we recognize at the outset that Renaissance tragedy is not a poor attempt to do what classical tragedy alone achieved but that each is a separate genre, we must inevitably fail to see how rich both can be in observations upon the periods that conceived and developed them.

Review Article

Irwin Smith. *Shakespeare's Blackfriars Playhouse: Its History and Its Design.* New York: New York University Press, 1964. Pp. xx, 577. $15.00.

I
RWIN SMITH IS WELL KNOWN to Elizabethan scholars as the author of
Shakespeare's Globe Playhouse: A Modern Reconstruction (New
York, 1956), which provides a hypothetical delineation of this famous
theater and its stage. His recent book on Blackfriars is also noteworthy
and is obviously the product of much enthusiasm by the author for his
subject. In this review article I offer an appraisal of Smith's reconstruction
of the stage at Blackfriars by making a close analysis of the staging
requirements of fourteen King's men plays for which we have records of
performances and whose texts carry markings related to prompt-copy. In
so doing, it is not my intention to discredit Smith's work; instead, I hope
to suggest refinements in methodology that may lead to a more discriminate selection of textual evidence in future studies of pre-Restoration stage
conditions.

Smith's handsomely illustrated volume is important and useful in several respects. It first traces the history of Blackfriars from the settlement of
the Dominican Friars at Ludgate in 1275 until the dissolution of this
religious establishment in 1538; it then offers a concise history of theatrical
activity there from 1576, when Richard Farrant established the First

Blackfriars Playhouse, until 1642, when the theaters were closed by order of parliament. By a thorough examination of architectural remains, old maps, and legal records, the author assembles a meticulously documented plan for the complex of buildings that comprised Blackfriars precinct. An appendix of 121 pages reprints forty-six contemporary documents relating to the history of Blackfriars.

A major contribution to our knowledge of Blackfriars is provided by the author's convincing argument that plays were performed in the Parliament Chamber or Great Hall, the top floor of the so-called "Upper Frater," rather than in the lower section of this building, as suggested earlier by Wallace and Adams.[1] Smith bases his contention on three important factors: (1) The Great Hall at Blackfriars had a large audience capacity and had served for several major assemblies of historical importance; it was here that Henry VIII held the trial preceding his divorce from Katherine of Aragon, and it was also the scene of Cardinal Wolsey's trial. (2) James Burbage's Deed of Purchase (1596) seems primarily concerned with the upper floor and access thereto; the Deed describes this level of the building as "all those seven great upper rooms as they are now divided, being all upon one floor and sometime being one great and entire room. . . ." Presumably Burbage eliminated the partitions for the seven rooms and restored the space to a shape suitable for theatrical performances. (3) The lower story would have been unsuitable for use as a theater. The weight of the upper floor would require that the space underneath it have a heavily vaulted low ceiling supported by pillars that would block audience sight lines.

Smith also makes some knowledgeable conjectures concerning the dimensions of the playhouse. Whereas the Survey of 1548 gives the dimensions of the Upper Frater as 107 by 52 feet, or 101 by 46 feet within 3-foot walls, the Hawkins deposition of 1609 gives the dimensions of the Great Hall as 66 by 46 feet. Smith notes that the width of the Hall agrees with the presumed interior width of the Parliament Chamber but that the length is 35 feet shorter. He therefore suggests that when Burbage made his renovations he set up a partition that screened off 35 feet of the Hall

---

1. Smith, pp. 167–168, cites Charles W. Wallace, *The Children of the Chapel at Blackfriars, 1597–1603* (Lincoln, 1908), p. 40, and Joseph Quincy Adams, *Shakespearean Playhouses* (Boston, 1917), pp. 192, 197.

from view of the audience, thereby providing a backstage area for a
tiring house.

Concerning the stage at Blackfriars, Smith states:

> No contemporary drawing or description of the Blackfriars stage is known to
> exist. In the absence of any direct information as to its design and equipment,
> we can reconstruct it only by analyzing the demands made upon the stage by
> the plays performed upon it, and so recognizing the physical resources that
> enabled the stage to meet those demands (p. 210).

On the basis of a wide variety of external and internal evidence, Smith
compiles a list of 133 titles that he describes as the repertories of the
Chapel-Revels Children and the King's men at Blackfriars. Stage directions and allusions in the dialogue of these plays serve as the basis for his
theories about the stage equipment discussed in his final three chapters:
"The Platform," "The Rear Stage," and "The Upper Stages."

The stage facilities that the author deems necessary for performances at
Blackfriars are treated under the subheadings: "The Platform Trap,"
"The Stage Curtains," "The Rear-Stage Walls," "The Rear-Stage Trap,"
"Dimensions of the Rear Stage," "The Tiring-House," "The Window
Stages," "The Tarras," "The Side-Wall Galleries," "The Inner Stage on
the Upper Level," "The Stage Stairs," and "The Music Room." All of
these structural features are given precise positions and dimensions in five
detailed and artfully executed floor plans and elevations.

This hypothetical reconstruction of the stage at Blackfriars is an imaginative piece of work that should certainly be taken into account in any
study of early English playhouses. It is necessary, however, to raise serious
objections to some of the evidence that Smith uses to support his theories.
Although he relies heavily on the texts of plays that were presumably
performed at Blackfriars, he does not fully answer two important questions concerning each of these plays: (1) What reliable external evidence
is there to indicate that it was, in fact, performed by the King's men before 1642? (2) What bibliographical evidence is there to suggest that the
earliest extant text of the play may reflect the manner in which it was
produced? Although Smith gives a presumed date of first production
for each work on his play list, he does not there specify the place and
date of actual performance, if any, nor does he give the date of the edition that he cites. This lack of information can be misleading. For

example, two of Smith's most important pieces of evidence concerning a
"curtained rear stage" are taken from *The Parson's Wedding,* listed in his
repertory as by "Thomas Killigrew: 1639–40," and *News from Plymouth,*
listed as by "William Davenant: 1635." At first glance this evidence seems
convincing:

From *The Parson's Wedding* (V.ii):

*The fiddlers play in the tiring-room; and the stage curtains are drawn, and
discover a chamber, as it were, with two beds, and the ladies asleep in them;
Mr. Wild being at Mrs. Pleasant's bed-side, and Mr. Careless at the Widow's.*
(As cited by Smith, p. 345)

From *News from Plymouth* (IV.ii):

*A Curtain drawn by Dash (his Clerk) Trifle discover'd in his Study, Papers,
Taper, Seale and Wax before him, Bell.*
(As cited by Smith, p. 346)

But closer study reveals that Smith has apparently not made use of some
important historical and bibliographical scholarship.

Bentley notes that the dialogue of *The Parson's Wedding* makes reference to Blackfriars, but he states that scholars disagree as to whether this
work was ever performed at this playhouse (Bentley, IV, 703).[2] The text
was not printed until 1663; the title page of this edition states that the
work was "Written At Basil in Switzerland." The earliest extant record of
performance is a notation by the Master of the Revels for 1663–1664
indicating that the play may have been licensed in these years. In his

2. The following secondary sources are cited parenthetically hereafter in this text:
R. C. Bald, *Bibliographical Studies in the Beaumont & Fletcher Folio of 1647,*
Supplement to the Bibliographical Society's Transactions, No. 3 (1938); Gerald
Eades Bentley, *The Jacobean and Caroline Stage* (Oxford, 1941–1956); E. K.
Chambers, *The Elizabethan Stage* (Oxford, 1923); W. W. Greg, *Dramatic Docu-
ments from the Elizabethan Playhouses* (Oxford, 1931). All citations to the Beau-
mont and Fletcher Folio of 1647 are to the Dartmouth College copy. Act and scene
numbers cited are those in *The Works of Francis Beaumont and John Fletcher,* ed.
A. R. Waller (Cambridge, Eng., 1905–1912). Dramatic manuscripts are cited by page
numbers in modern printed transcriptions. Stage directions in seventeenth-century
playbooks are normally italicized, but with the names of characters set in roman.
Here stage directions in the folio of 1647 are cited entirely in italics; all citations to
dialogue and to manuscript stage directions are set in roman within quotation
marks.

Diary, Pepys (11 October 1664) refers to this work's being acted by the King's company. Since Killigrew, the author of the play, was the manager of this company at the time the work was printed, it seems more than likely that the first edition reflects stage conditions of the Restoration playhouse rather than those at Blackfriars over twenty years earlier.

News from Plymouth was first printed in the Davenant folio of 1673; besides late printing, this text offers further difficulties. The play was licensed for performance on 1 August 1635, at which time the King's men would have been playing at the Globe instead of Blackfriars; this is confirmed by allusions in the Prologue. Furthermore, the Epilogue of the play, as Bentley observes, contains a dozen or more alterations that suggest the work was revised for revival during the Commonwealth or Restoration periods (Bentley, III, 209–210). In the latter period the play would most likely have been acted by the Duke of York's men, of which Davenant was the manager from 1660 to 1668. Thus there is conflicting evidence concerning the playhouse at which the 1673 text of *News from Plymouth* may have been performed, but none of this evidence points to production at Blackfriars.

One of the texts that Smith uses to support his theory about an "upper stage" at Blackfriars is Brome's *The Novella.* This title is included on the list of plays protected for the King's men by the Lord Chamberlain in 1641, but there is no specific record of performance. Furthermore, the work was not printed until 1653, over twenty years after the presumed date of composition (Bentley, III, 84–85).

From these examples we see that Smith has included in his play lists at least three late printed texts that are of only secondary value as evidence concerning pre-Restoration stage conditions. Still another, less obvious, problem must be considered. Although Smith states that his lists "include only those extant plays that presumably were written specifically for performance on the Blackfriars stage" (p. 210), he does not acknowledge that the King's men performed many of these plays, e.g., *News from Plymouth,* at the Globe, or at court, or on tour of the provinces. There is no direct evidence that any of these plays were written specifically for Blackfriars. Given the production history of this company, a more suitable approach for the study of staging would be to describe a *mode of production* for the King's men rather than attempt a hypothetical reconstruction of the stage at Blackfriars.

The index to Smith's book shows that *The Parson's Wedding, News from Plymouth,* and *The Novella* are cited a total of forty-three times to support his theories about the stage at Blackfriars. In contrast to his reliance on these late printed texts, Smith gives only passing notice to the extant manuscript prompt-books from the repertory of the King's men: *Believe as You List, The Honest Man's Fortune, The Second Maiden's Tragedy,* and *Sir John van Olden Barnavelt;* these four texts are cited a total of twenty-two times. Smith lists these plays in the repertory of the King's men, but he does not identify them as manuscripts, nor does he discuss their textual characteristics. It should be obvious that these contemporary documents provide a higher order of evidence than plays surviving only in late printed editions.

These prompt-books not only offer significant evidence concerning staging methods; they also provide touchstones that may help to determine the nature of the copy supplied to the printer of a given playbook. Although Smith cites thirty of the thirty-four plays first printed in the Beaumont and Fletcher folio of 1647, he makes no reference to an important study by R. C. Bald, who has given careful consideration to the nature of the copy that may lie behind the printed texts in this volume. Bald finds that many of the folio texts carry markings that are probably related to prompt-copy, while others do not. His bibliographical research is clearly relevant to a discussion of staging methods by the King's men.

Although it is beyond my present scope to discuss all 133 texts that Smith cites in his study, it may be instructive to examine in some detail a representative sample of plays from the repertory of the King's men. There is clear evidence that all of the plays listed below were produced by this company between 1611 and 1642; all fourteen of the texts—five contemporary manuscripts and nine plays first printed in the Beaumont and Fletcher folio of 1647—carry notations that appear to be derived from the prompter. While it cannot be established with certainty that all of the folio plays on the list were printed directly from prompt-copy, all show characteristics that Greg and others have associated with manuscripts marked for production.[3]

3. W. W. Greg, *The Shakespeare First Folio* (Oxford, 1955), pp. 105–161. The following plays in the folio of 1647 are not included as evidence concerning staging methods by the King's men because their production histories are ambiguous or nonexistent: *The Little French Lawyer* (Bentley, III, 357), *Nice Valor* (Bentley, III,

The Manuscripts

Beggars' Bush (Fletcher, with Massinger?). At Whitehall, 27 December 1622; at the Cockpit in Court, 30 November 1630; at Hampton Court, 19 November 1636 (Bentley, III, 313). This work was printed in the 1647 folio, but more useful for my purpose here is the manuscript included in the Lambarde volume in the Folger Shakespeare Library. Bald states that this manuscript was "clearly transcribed from the theatrical prompt-copy of the play, since it incorporates a number of obvious prompter's directions not to be found in the printed text" (p. 62).

Believe as You List (Massinger). Refused Revels license by Herbert, 11 January 1630/1; prompt-book carries Revels license dated 6 May 1631; acted by the King's men 7 May 1631 (Bentley, IV, 762–765). British Museum MS. Egerton 2828 has been edited by Charles J. Sisson (Malone Society Reprints, 1927). Also see Greg, *Dramatic Documents,* I, 293–300.

The Honest Man's Fortune (Fletcher, Massinger, *et al.*). Revels license for revival by King's men, 8 February 1624; prompt-book carries license by Herbert with same date (Chambers, III, 227). Bald offers a comparison of the manuscript with the text printed in the folio of 1647 and finds that the manuscript is more closely related to performance than the printed text (pp. 53–57). MS. Dyce 9 at Victoria and Albert Museum has been

---

382), *The Double Marriage* (Bentley, III, 329), *Love's Cure* (Bentley, III, 363), *The Queen of Corinth* (Bentley, III, 398), *The Woman's Prize* (Chambers, III, 222), *Bonduca* (Chambers, III, 228), *The Humorous Lieutenant* (Bentley, III, 343), *Wit at Several Weapons* (Chambers, III, 232), *Valentinian* (Chambers, III, 229), *Women Pleased* (Bentley, III, 431). The following plays in the 1647 folio are not included as evidence because, as Bald observes, "it has not been possible to find any directions which suggest, even remotely, the specific influence of the prompter" (pp. 109–110): *The Noble Gentleman, The Captain, The False One, The Laws of Candy, The Island Princess, The Pilgrim, Four Plays in One.* Three other plays have been excluded because evidence is scanty or inconclusive: *A Wife for a Month, The Prophetess, The Sea Voyage.* Two otherwise acceptable texts, *The Coxcomb* and *The Mad Lover,* are not included because of serious dislocations probably caused by the restoration by the printer of scenes cut in performance. See Humphrey Moseley's "Stationer to the Reader" in the 1647 folio.

edited by J. Gerritsen (Djakarta, 1952). Also see Greg, *Dramatic Documents,* I, 288–293.

The Second Maiden's Tragedy (Anonymous). Revels license, 31 October 1611 (Chambers, IV, 45). British Museum MS. Lansdowne 807, f. 29, has been edited by W. W. Greg (Malone Society Reprints, 1909). Actors' names in the text identify it as a King's men play. Also see Greg, *Dramatic Documents,* I, 264–268.

Sir John van Olden Barnavelt (Fletcher, with Massinger?). Mentioned in letters by Thomas Locke dated 14 and 27 August 1619 (Bentley, III, 415). British Museum MS. Add. 18653 has been edited by W. P. Frijlinck (Amsterdam, 1922), who notes censorship markings initialed by George Buc, Master of the Revels; actors' names in the text are those of King's men. Most of the text is in handwriting identified as that of Ralph Crane, a scribe who worked for the King's men. Also see Greg, *Dramatic Documents,* I, 268–274.

Plays in the Beaumont and Fletcher Folio of 1647

The Chances. At the Cockpit in Court, 30 December 1630; at the Cockpit in Court, 22 November 1638 (Bentley, III, 319). Actor's name in stage directions (Bald, p. 103).

The Custom of the Country. At Blackfriars, 22 November 1628; at Hampton Court, 24 October 1630; at the Cockpit in Court, 27 November 1638 (Bentley, III, 324).

The Fair Maid of the Inn. Revels license for Blackfriars, 22 January 1625 / 6 (Bentley, III, 337). Prompter's stage directions (Bald, p. 106).

The Knight of Malta. Revels Office records, 1619–1620 (Bentley, III, 337). Prompter's stage directions (Bald, p. 105).

The Lovers' Progress. Revels license, 6 December 1623; at Whitehall, 1 January 1623/4; Revels license for revival, 7 May 1634 (Bentley, III, 360). Frequent traces of prompter's additions (Bald, p. 107).

Love's Pilgrimage. Revels license for revival, 16 September 1635; at Hampton Court, 16 December 1636 (Bentley, III, 367). Actors' names in the text (Bald, p. 103).

The Loyal Subject. Revels license, 16 November 1618; Revels license for revival, 23 November 1633; at Whitehall, 10 December 1633; at Hampton Court, 6 December 1636 (Bentley, III, 370–371). Anticipatory stage directions (Bald, p. 105).

The Maid in the Mill. Revels license, 29 August 1623; at Hampton Court, 29 September 1623; at Court, 1 November 1623; at Whitehall, 26 December 1623 (Bentley, III, 377). Preparatory stage directions (Bald, p. 105).

The Spanish Curate. At Blackfriars, 24 October 1622; at Court, 26 December 1622; at the Cockpit in Court, 6 December 1638; at Court, 7 January 1638/9 (Bentley, III, 418). Prompter's directions (Bald, p. 104).

It should be pointed out that eight of these fourteen plays were performed at one or more of the entertainment halls at Court. Since other acting companies also performed at these halls, the analysis that follows may be applicable, not only to Blackfriars, but also to the pre-Restoration stage in general. I have tried to avoid following the preconceptions that appear to have guided several earlier studies of stage conditions. Instead of setting up a hypothetical stage and then seeking evidence to support this conjectural reconstruction, I first offer a chart (p. 300) showing what was *required* to produce these plays and then go on to suggest how these requirements may have been met with a minimum of difficulty. If the stage directions specify the manner in which a large property is introduced, this is noted parenthetically on the chart; also noted are the number of scenes in which the acting area above is used in a given play.

It is important to emphasize that the production requirements of all fourteen plays can be met by the stage facilities shown in the extant pictorial evidence concerning the pre-Restoration stage. The first eight plays on the chart can be acted in any hall or playhouse with a stage and a façade such as that shown in the De Witt drawing of the Swan, or with the addition of a trestle stage to the façades shown in Richard Hosley's recently published photographs of the hall screens at Hampton Court Palace (1531–1536) and the Middle Temple (1574). Hosley's observations are relevant to my analysis of the stage directions in these eight plays:

The Tudor hall screen is remarkably similar to the tiring-house façade of the Swan Playhouse as recorded in the De Witt drawing (c. 1596), and the similarity is especially pronounced if comparision of the tiring-house façade is made with a screen having an enclosed gallery. The two doors and windowed gallery of the tiring-house correspond closely to the two doorways and win-

Title	Doors	Large Properties	Above	Hang- ings	Dis- covery
Barnavelt (MS.)	2	Table Bed Bar (brought in) Chairs Scaffold (put out) Coffin	Walls (1) Above (1)	—	—
Beggars' Bush (MS.)	—	Table (out) Table & Stools (set out)	—	—	—
The Chances	—	—	Above (2)	—	—
The Custom of the Country	2	—	Above (1)	—	—
The Fair Maid of the Inn	2	—	—	—	—
Love's Pilgrimage	—	Table (servants) 2 Beds Chair (carried)	Above (1)	—	—
The Loyal Subject	2	Banquet	Above (2)	—	—
The Spanish Curate	—	Bar (set out) Table (set out) Bed (thrust out) Table (out) Table (set out) Chair & Stools (out)	—	—	—
Believe as You List (MS.)	Trap	Table & 6 Chairs (set out) 2 Chairs (set out)	Above (1)	Arras	—
The Honest Man's Fortune (MS.)	—	Banquet (servants)	—	Arras	—
The Second Maiden's Tragedy (MS.)	—	—	Gallery (1)	—	Tomb
The Knight of Malta	2	Scaffold (set out) Stairs (set out) Table (out) 2 Stools (out)	Tarras (1) Above (1)	—	Altar Tomb
The Lovers' Progress	—	Bar (set forth) Table (servants)	—	Curtain	—
The Maid in the Mill	2	6 Chairs	Above (1) Window (1)	Arras	—

dowed gallery of the hall screen; and each of the two façades stands at the rear of an area used for acting; the playhouse stage in the one case, the floor of the hall or a stage set up against the hall screen in the other.[4]

Hosley's measurements indicate that the doorways of the hall screen at Hampton Court are 8'0" wide and 13'3" high, measured from the floor; the doorways of the hall screen at the Middle Temple are 6'0" wide and 10'6" high. These dimensions would allow for the erection of a trestle stage 4' high and still leave room for actors to enter through the doorways and for large properties to be thrust out. It should be noted that Hosley uses the term "windowed" to describe a row of ten unglazed apertures across the top of the hall screen at the Middle Temple. This may be in keeping with the references to "windows" found in a number of pre-Restoration plays. Smith, on the other hand, interprets these references in a narrower sense and includes large casement windows in his hypothetical reconstruction of the stage at Blackfriars.

The remaining six plays on the chart require hangings or a discovery space not shown in the De Witt drawing but clearly evident in the drawings on the title pages of *Roxana* (1632) and *Messalina* (1640).[5] One means of reconciling this apparent discrepancy has been suggested by G. F. Reynolds, and later supported by C. Walter Hodges and Lawrence J. Ross. Surprisingly, Smith does not take the work of these scholars into account in his discussion of the stage at Blackfriars. Writing in 1940, Reynolds suggests:

Instead of a permanently placed rear stage, a structural part of the theater, was there perhaps a curtained framework easily removable, and so not used in all plays and, as it happened, not present on the Swan stage at the time of De Witt's visit? Such a framework is at least a possible way to provide a discoverable space . . . there is nothing essentially unusual about the idea of a removable framework, but the possible uses have scarcely been much considered.[6]

4. Richard Hosley, "The Origins of the Shakespearian Playhouse," *Shakespeare 400,* ed. James G. McManaway (New York, 1964), p. 33.

5. These title pages are reproduced by C. Walter Hodges, *The Globe Restored* (London, 1953), p. 154.

6. G. F. Reynolds, *The Staging of Elizabethan Plays at the Red Bull Theatre* (New York, 1940), pp. 131–132.

Later work by Hodges examines contemporary illustrations of English pre-Restoration playhouses and of theatrical performances on the Continent. From these pictures he reconstructs a large curtained booth, the top of which has been "boarded over and railed in, so that it can be used as an acting place." [7] His hypothesis about a booth would be equally applicable to performances at Court or some other place where a discovery space and an acting area above were not part of the structure of the auditorium. More recently Ross has put forth a plausible theory that *Othello* (performed at Court, 1 November 1604) may have been staged with a curtained booth of "modifiable neutrality" as the center of the play's action.[8]

(1) *Doors*

None of the plays included in this study requires more than two doors. These are mentioned in the stage directions for some scenes in order to designate that the actors arrive on stage from different *directions,* but the doors themselves are not consistently identified with any one place or "house." It should be noted that the word "several" is used in the sense of "distinct or apart" rather than "more than two," e.g., the stage direction in *Barnavelt:* "Enter 2. Captaines: & yeir Soldiers," with the marginal notation by the prompter "severally mr. Rob: mr. Rice" (p. 77). Similar references to "several" doors are found in *The Lovers' Progress* (IV.i), *The Loyal Subject* (III.v), and *The Knight of Malta* (II.v). The wording "one door and . . . the other" is used in the stage directions of *The Fair Maid of the Inn* (III.i), *The Custom of the Country* (IV.i), and *The Lovers' Progress* (II.i).

In some scenes doors are given special dramatic significance. For example, Act V of *The Second Maiden's Tragedy* opens with an unlocalized scene in which Votarius tries to convince Anselmus that his wife is inconstant; Votarius suggests that Anselmus lock himself in a closet in his wife's chamber. Anselmus and Votarius are each given an "exit." In the next scene Anselmus delivers a brief monologue followed by the prompter's notation "Locks him self in" (p. 64). Anselmus' wife and servant

7. Hodges, p. 171.

8. Lawrence J. Ross, "The Use of a 'Fit-Up' Booth in *Othello,*" *Shakespeare Quarterly,* XII (1961), 359–370.

enter, and after their brief conversation Votarius comes "to the door" and asks to be admitted. The servant lets him in, but the wife spurns Votarius' attentions. Anselmus comes from the closet to confront Votarius. Neither door is localized in the scene that follows.

A stage direction in *The Maid in the Mill* calls for a "discovery," but the dialogue makes it clear that one of the entrance doors is used here rather than a more elaborate discovery space. News comes that the King is approaching; Otrante locks Florimel "in a closet" (V.ii). The King enters and asks to see what is in this "little room" and commands that the lock be forced. Two lines later there is the direction *Florimell dicouered,* and she steps forth to play the rest of the scene.

(2) *Trap*

A prompter's warning in *Believe as You List* reads: "Gascoine: & Hubert below: ready to open the Trap doore for Mr Taylor" (p. 60). Twelve speeches later there is another prompter's warning: "Antiochus—ready: vnder the stage" (p. 62). In the next scene a jailer enters and calls to Antiochus, who answers from "belowe." The dialogue suggests that Antiochus rises from his dungeon to play the rest of the scene on stage. A raised platform such as that shown in the De Witt drawing could easily be equipped with a trap door to accommodate this action.

(3) *Large Properties*

The chart indicates that in the manuscript plays most large properties are described as "set out" or "brought in." In the folio plays similar terminology is used to describe the manner in which most large properties are introduced.

(a) *Banquets and Tables.* In *The Honest Man's Fortune* one scene begins with the direction "Enter foure serving in a Banquet" (p. 108). A scene in *The Loyal Subject* starts with the direction *Enter two Servants preparing a Banquet* (IV.v). In *Love's Pilgrimage* (I.i) there is the direction *Enter Hostess and Servants with Table,* and later in this scene *Enter Hostess and Servants with meat.* The prompter's anticipatory directions in *The Spanish Curate* call for the preparation of a banquet used in the scene that follows: *Chaire and stooles out,* and *A Table ready covered with Cloath Napkins Salt Trenchers and Bread* (V.i). The next scene begins with the direction *The Table set out and stooles* (V.ii). Other plays in which stage directions specify that a table, chairs, or stools be set out are *Beggars' Bush* (II.iii and III.i), *Believe as You List* (p. 23), and *The Knight of Malta* (III.iv).

(b) *Bars.* A prompter's stage direction in *Barnavelt* reads "A Bar brought in" (p. 60); a bar is *set forth* in *The Lovers' Progress* (V.i); in *The Spanish Curate* a prompter's warning *The Bar & Book ready on a Table* (III.ii) anticipates the point in the action where these properties are *set out* (III.iii).

(c) *Beds.* Act IV of *The Spanish Curate* opens with Lopez and Bartalus discussing the imminent death of Diego. Here there is the prompter's warning *Diego ready in Bed, wine, cup,* which anticipates the direction twenty-seven lines later *Enter Diego (in a bed) Millanes, Arsenio, and Parishioners.* Soon after this there is the prompter's notation *Bed thrust out.* Although other texts on the list do not specify the manner in which beds are introduced, this notation indicates that thrusting-out of beds was probably normal procedure. The prompter's notation "Son abed" in *Barnavelt* (p. 46) may be a cue to thrust out his bed. A more complex stage direction is found in *Love's Pilgrimage,* in which *Enter Theodosia and Phillipo on several beds* (I.ii). There is a dialogue allusion to a bed in *The Custom of the Country* (I.i), but the stage directions do not mention it.

(d) *Scaffold and Stairs.* Two plays require that a scaffold be set out. In *Barnavelt* there is the marginal stage direction "Enter Prouost Barnauelt: Lords: Guard. (a Scaffold put out) Execution'" (p. 79). A stage direction in the margin of *The Knight of Malta* reads *The Scaffold set out and the staires* (II.v). In the action that follows, Oriana "ascends" to the block and delivers a speech of farewell, but her execution is interrupted and she is set free. Here it is important to note that movable stairs are set in place for the scene in which they are required. This suggests that a stairway was not necessarily part of the permanent structure of every stage on which the King's men performed. So, too, in other King's men plays in which characters ascend or descend, this stairway may have been set in place for the required action.

(4) *Acting Area Above*

Fourteen scenes in nine plays on the list require an acting space above the main stage, but every scene played in this area is limited in scope and duration and is always related to action on the main stage. In *Barnavelt* the Prince of Orange and his followers enter and are greeted by a Captain. A prompter's stage direction reads "Enter Capn. on ye walls" (p. 25). After a brief exchange between the Captain and those below, the scene ends with "exeunt." Later in the play the Burghers engaged in "merry song" are soon joined in their celebration: "Enter wife, aboue" (p. 59). She gives three brief speeches in this unlocalized area before the scene ends with "exeunt" (p. 60). A scene in *The Second Maiden's Tragedy* opens with the direction "Leonella aboue in a Gallery with her loue Bellarius" (p. 63). Her speech here describes the principal function of the acting area above in this and other plays:

> thow knowst this gallerie well tis at thy vse now
> t'as bin at myne full often, thow mayst sitt
> like a most priuat gallant in y'on corner
> see all the plaie and nere be seene thy self.

Leonella leaves Bellarius with the stage direction "Descendet" and nine lines later joins the characters on the main stage. Bellarius observes the action below; later he too appears on the main stage (p. 67).

A prompter's direction in *Believe as You List* reads "Ent: Metellus— fflaminius: & Sempronius (Aboue)" (p. 65). This group overhears a long soliloquy by Antiochus, who has made his entrance from his prison "under the stage." Those above make aside comments among themselves as Antiochus is tempted by a courtesan.

During a scene in *The Custom of the Country* between Arnoldo and Zenocia, *Enter above Hippolyta and Zabulon* (IV.i); the latter pair observe and overhear the conversation of the former pair. Hippolyta and Zabulon later join the action on the main stage. Toward the end of a scene in *The Knight of Malta* Zanthia enters and speaks to two Gentlewomen: "Hist, wenches: my Lady calls, she's entring the Tarrasse, to see the show" (I.ii). The next scene opens with the direction *Enter (above) Oriana, Zanthia, two Gentlewomen, (beneath) Valetta, Mountferrat, Astorius, Castorot, Gomera, Miranda, Attendants of Knights &c* (I.iii). Mountferrat addresses one line to Oriana, who observes the scene below without being seen by other characters. Oriana is the only character who speaks from above. Later in the same play there is a direction in the margin: *Corporall and Watch above singing* (III.i). They observe the action below, and later in the scene *Enter Cor. below and Watch.*

A prompter's warning *Bawd ready above* in *The Chances* (IV.ii) anticipates her entrance in the next scene, *Enter Bawd (above)* (IV.iii). The actors below observe her, but she speaks no lines. Later in the scene she *enters* on the main stage and joins the action there. In the next act of the play, *Enter Duke, Petruchio below, and Vecchio above* (V.i). Vecchio overhears the conversation of the characters below but does not reveal his presence to them. Eight lines after his last aside to the audience he *enters* and admits the callers.

In *Love's Pilgrimage* the action on stage is interrupted by *Enter Roderigo above* (IV.i); he orders a gunner to "make a shot into the Town," and tells the soldiers on stage below to "bring Antonio into my Cabben." *The Loyal Subject* makes an explicit reference to the acting area above being used as an observation post: *Enter Ancient, crying Broomes, and after him severally, four Souldiers, crying other things. Boroskie and Gent. over the stage observing them* (III.v). Later in this play, *Enter Duke above* (IV.vi); he talks with a group of soldiers assembled below and *exit.*

The area above is used in two scenes of *The Maid in the Mill.* In the first, Martine and Antonio enter and come to a "goodly window," after which *Enter Ismena and Aminta above with a Taper* (I.iii). These four characters play a scene that ends with an *exeunt* for the men and an *exeunt* for the women above. In a later scene, *Enter Aminta (above) with a Taper* (IV.iii). She gives a twenty-nine-line soliloquy before she makes her *exit.*

All of the staging requirements discussed thus far could have been met by the two doors and a gallery over the main stage shown in the De Witt drawing or by the addition of a raised platform to the façade shown in Hosley's photographs of the hall screens at Hampton Court and the Middle Temple. Fourteen scenes in nine plays require an acting area above, but in eight of these scenes the action is limited to a brief appearance by a single character. In three other scenes only two characters appear above. In the three remaining scenes more than two characters are described as entering above, but no more than three characters actually speak from above in any one scene. The space above remains unlocalized in most scenes and usually serves as an observation post from which characters comment on, or converse with, characters below. In all of these scenes the action above could have been played in the shallow space provided by a gallery, if the auditorium were so equipped, or by an acting place atop the booth suggested by Hodges. This area should therefore be considered as auxiliary to the main stage rather than as a distinct and separate "upper stage."

(5) *Hangings*

In four plays on the list mention is made of an arras, curtains, or hangings. As with the case of the acting area above, a study of the flow of action in these plays indicates that limited use is made of this facility in any one play. The hangings were not used as a curtain for a "rear stage." Instead, they served as a place of concealment for a maximum of two members of the company while action took place on the main stage. All of these scenes could have been played in the equipment shown on the title page of *Roxana* (1632).

The prompter's anticipatory directions in *Believe as You List* read "Harry: Willson: & Boy ready for the song at ye Arras:" (p. 65). Later in the scene there is the prompter's notation "the Lute. strikes & then the Songe," followed by the direction "Ent: Courtezan" (p. 67). Apparently the song is used as a cue for her entrance, but the singer and the lute-player remain hidden behind the arras. During a scene in *The Honest Man's Fortune* the prompter has the notation "Lamyra showes hir Selfe at the Arras" (p. 73). In an aside Lamyra says, "I will obserue this better." She remains hidden and overhears the conversation of the other characters on stage before the prompter's direction "Ent: Lamyra: from the Aras" (p. 75).

The hangings are also used as a place of concealment in *The Lovers' Progress,* in which *Enter Clarinda with a Taper, and Lisander with a Pistole, two Chaires set out* (III.i). At this point there is the prompter's stage direction *Caliste sitting behind a Curtaine.* Clarinda tells Lisander, "I'll leave ye now, draw but that Curtain, And Have your wish," and she makes her *exit.* There are no stage directions here for Lisander, but the dialogue suggests that he sees Calista asleep in the chair. She awakes, and the two characters play a love scene that is interrupted by *Noise within.* Calista tells him to "retire behind the hangings and there stand close." Her husband Cleander *enters,* and after a brief scene he leaves. Calista then calls forth Lisander, who makes his *exit.* In *The Maid in the Mill* there is the preparatory stage direction *Six Chaires placed at the Arras* (II.i), but the action of this play does not call for the use of hangings. As we have seen, Florimel is "discovered" later in this play, but her entrance is preceded by the business of unlocking a door (V.ii).

(6) *Discovery Space*

The term "discovered" is used to describe the manner in which two major properties, a tomb and an altar, are first introduced to the audience. It may be useful to cite the stage directions that precede these discoveries in order to gain a better picture of the flow of action in these scenes. In *The Second Maiden's Tragedy* the Tyrant asks two soldiers to bring "the keys of the Cathedrall" and "lanthornes and a pickax" (pp. 53–54). One soldier goes out and returns with the keys; the second promises to bring the other items. The Tyrant makes his "exit," and the others follow. The next scene begins with the stage direction "Enter the Tirant agen at a farder dore, which opened, bringes hym to the Toombe wher the Lady lies buried; The Toombe here discouered ritchly set forthe" (p. 55). Later in the scene, "On a sodayne in a kinde of Noyse like a Wynde, the dores clattering, the Toombstone flies open, and a great light appeares in the midst of the Toombe; His Lady as went owt, standing iust before hym all in white, Stuck with Iewells and a great crucifex on her brest" (p. 61). Since the action requires only one other door through which characters enter later in this scene, a plausible interpretation for this discovery may be that the Tyrant opens "the farder dore" to reveal the tomb, which in turn has doors of its own. An alternative explanation may be that the Tyrant enters from "the farder dore" and comes to a curtained booth where the tomb is discovered.

In *The Knight of Malta* the prompter's notation *Discover Tombe* near the end of IV.i anticipates the use of the tomb in the scene that follows. Miranda, Norandine, and Collonna enter a church and hear a groaning "in the wall." They go to the "tomb" and read a "tablet" with a newly inscribed epitaph of Oriana, who soon *rises up* to speak to them. In this scene it seems probable that one of the doorways could be used for this discovery. Later in the play, after thirteen named characters, plus assorted attendants, have assembled on stage, there is the stage direction *An Altar discovered, with Tapers, and a Book on it. The two Bishops stand on each side of it. Mountferrat, as the Song is singing ascends up the Altar* (V.ii).

Since this disclosure is made with great ceremony, and since an altar with steps leading up to it might be too bulky to set forth, it seems likely that this discovery was made by opening the hangings of a curtained booth. The other action of this play gives no indication that the altar would have been placed in a "rear stage." All the action of this play could have been performed in the equipment shown on the title page of *Messalina* (1640) or in the boothlike structure suggested by Hodges.

In summary, Smith offers interesting conjectures about the stage at Blackfriars, but some of his findings rely on evidence of questionable validity. If more rigorous standards are applied in the selection of texts studied, it can be seen that the staging requirements of King's men plays were probably much simpler than Smith suggests and may have been met by the facilities shown in the extant pictures of pre-Restoration stages. Generally speaking, our knowledge of early stage conditions is heavily dependent on textual evidence. It is therefore essential that investigations in this field discriminate between those texts that are related to actual production and those of doubtful provenance. Only by a detailed analysis of the available historical and bibliographical evidence concerning each play can we gain a clear understanding of how this important body of dramatic literature was first staged.

T. J. KING

Notes on Contributors

ROBERT P. ADAMS, Associate Professor of English at the University of Washington, is the author of *The Better Part of Valor: More, Erasmus, Calet, and Vives, on Humanism, War, and Peace, 1496–1535* (1962).

DAVID M. BEVINGTON is Professor of English at the University of Virginia. In 1962 he published *From* Mankind *to Marlowe: Growth of Structure in the Popular Drama of Tudor England,* and he is now finishing a book on topical content in Tudor plays.

M. C. BRADBROOK is Professor of English at Cambridge University. Her numerous publications include *Themes and Conventions of Elizabethan Tragedy* (1935), *The School of Night* (1936), *Shakespeare and Elizabethan Poetry* (1951), *The Growth and Structure of Elizabethan Comedy* (1955), *The Rise of the Common Player* (1962), and *English Dramatic Form* (1965).

JOSEPH S. M. J. CHANG, Assistant Professor of English at the University of Wisconsin—Milwaukee, is engaged in a reassessment of Francis Bacon's role as spokesman of the new science.

LOUISE GEORGE CLUBB is Associate Professor of English at the University of California at Berkeley. Her publications include *Giambattista della Porta, Dramatist* (1965).

311

DOUGLAS COLE is Assistant Professor of English at Yale University. He is the author of *Suffering and Evil in the Plays of Christopher Marlowe* (1962).

R. W. DENT, Professor of English at the University of California at Los Angeles, is the author of *John Webster's Borrowing* (1960).

HARRIETT HAWKINS, Assistant Professor of English at Vassar College, has articles awaiting publication in *Modern Philology* and *Studies in English Literature*.

CYRUS HOY, Professor of English at the University of Rochester, is general editor of the Regents Renaissance Drama Series. Among his publications are *The Hyacinth Room* (1964) and "The Shares of Fletcher and His Collaborators in the Beaumont and Fletcher Canon," which appeared serially in *Studies in Bibliography* (1956–1962).

ALVIN B. KERNAN, Associate Provost of Yale University, is author of *The Cankered Muse* (1959) and *The Plot of Satire* (1965).

T. J. KING is Assistant Professor of English at Dartmouth College. His published work includes an article on pre-Restoration staging in *Theatre Notebook*. He is presently preparing a book on staging methods at Stuart private theaters (1603–1642).

ROBERT C. MELZI is Professor of Romance Languages at Pennsylvania Military College and Visiting Lecturer in Italian at Bryn Mawr College. He is the author of a forthcoming book on Castelvetro.

MARCO MINCOFF, Professor of English and Chairman of the English Department at the University of Sofia, has published papers on Shakespeare and on Beaumont and Fletcher and other dramatists of the period.

RICHARD MORTON, Assistant Professor of English at McMaster University, is studying textual problems in the plays of James Shirley.

L. G. SALINGAR lectures on English literature at Trinity College, Cambridge, and is presently at work on a book on Shakespeare's comedies, of which the essay published in this number of *Renaissance Drama* represents a section.

DONALD STONE, JR., Assistant Professor of Romance Languages at Harvard University, has edited a collection of *Four Renaissance Tragedies* (1966).

Books Received

The listing of a book does not preclude its subsequent review in *Renaissance Drama*.

BASKERVILL, CHARLES READ. *The Elizabethan Jig and Related Song Drama.* New York: Dover Publications, 1965. Pp. x + 642. $2.75 (paper). (Orig. publ. 1929.)

BEAUMONT, FRANCIS, and JOHN FLETCHER. *The Dramatic Works in the Beaumont and Fletcher Canon,* Vol. I, ed. FREDSON BOWERS. Cambridge: Cambridge University Press, 1966. Pp. xxxv + 670. $18.50.

BENNETT, JOSEPHINE WATERS. Measure for Measure *as Royal Entertainment.* New York: Columbia University Press, 1966. Pp. xiii + 208. $6.00.

BERRY, FRANCIS. *The Shakespeare Inset: Word and Picture.* New York: Theatre Arts Books, 1965. Pp. x + 173. $5.75.

BERTRAM, PAUL. *Shakespeare and* The Two Noble Kinsmen. New Brunswick, N. J.: Rutgers University Press, 1965. Pp. x + 306. $10.00.

BRADBROOK, M. C. *English Dramatic Form: A History of Its Development.* New York: Barnes & Noble, 1965. Pp. 205. $5.00.

———. *The Tragic Pageant of* Timon of Athens. An inaugural lecture. Cambridge: Cambridge University Press, 1966. Pp. ii + 38. $1.00 (paper).

BUTLER, FRANCELIA. *The Strange Critical Fortunes of Shakespeare's* Timon of Athens. Ames: Iowa State University Press, 1966. Pp. xiii + 188. $4.50.

CHAPMAN, GEORGE. *Bussy D'Ambois,* ed. MAURICE EVANS. New Mermaid Dramabook. New York: Hill and Wang, 1966. Pp. xxxiv + 126. $1.25 (paper).

Corneille and Racine: Parallels and Contrasts, ed. ROBERT J. NELSON. Englewood Cliffs, N. J.: Prentice-Hall, 1966. Pp. xiii + 176. $3.95 (paper).

Critical Essays on the Theatre of Calderón, ed. BRUCE W. WARDROPPER. New York: New York University Press, 1965. Pp. xvi + 239. $6.00.

CUNLIFFE, JOHN W. *The Influence of Seneca on Elizabethan Tragedy.* Hamden: Archon Books, 1965. Pp. iv + 155. $5.00. (Orig. publ. 1893.)

CUNNINGHAM, J. V. *Woe or Wonder: The Emotional Effect of Shakespearian Tragedy.* Denver: Alan Swallow, 1964. Pp. 134. $1.35 (paper). (Orig. publ. 1951.)

DAWSON, GILES E., and LAETITIA KENNEDY-SKIPTON. *Elizabethan Handwriting 1500–1650.* New York: W. W. Norton & Co., 1966. Pp. ix + 130. $6.95.

Early Shakespeare: A Reading and Playing Guide, ed. JOHN RUSSELL BROWN and BERNARD HARRIS. Shakespeare Institute Studies. New York: Schocken Books, 1966. Pp. 232. $1.95 (paper). (Orig. publ. 1961.)

Five Restoration Adaptations of Shakespeare, ed. CHRISTOPHER SPENCER. Urbana: University of Illinois Press, 1965. Pp. xi + 475. $12.50.

FORD, JOHN. *The Broken Heart,* ed. BRIAN MORRIS. New Mermaid Dramabook. New York: Hill and Wang, 1966. Pp. xxxii + 95. $1.25 (paper).

———. *Perkin Warbeck,* ed. DONALD K. ANDERSON, JR. Regents Renaissance Drama. Lincoln: University of Nebraska Press, 1965. Pp. xx + 114. $1.00 (paper).

———. *'Tis Pity She's a Whore,* ed. N. W. BAWCUTT. Regents Renaissance Drama. Lincoln: University of Nebraska Press, 1966. Pp. xxii + 110. $1.00 (paper).

Four Centuries of Shakespearian Criticism, ed. FRANK KERMODE. New York: Avon Books, 1965. Pp. 571. $1.45 (paper).

Four Renaissance Tragedies, ed. DONALD STONE, JR. Cambridge, Mass.: Harvard University Press, 1966. Pp. xxx + 224. $2.00 (paper).

FRASER, RUSSELL. *Shakespeare's Poetics in Relation to* King Lear. Nashville: Vanderbilt University Press, 1966. Pp. xi + 184. $5.00. (Orig. publ. 1962.)

GREBANIER, BERNARD. *The Great Shakespeare Forgery.* New York: W. W. Norton & Co., 1965. Pp. xii + 308. $5.00.

HALLIDAY, F. E. *A Shakespeare Companion 1564–1964.* Baltimore: Penguin Books, 1964. Pp. 566. $2.25 (paper). (Previous ed. 1952.)

Hamlet: *A Reading and Playing Guide,* ed. JOHN RUSSELL BROWN and

BERNARD HARRIS. Shakespeare Institute Studies. New York: Schocken Books, 1966. Pp. 212. $1.95 (paper). (Orig. publ. 1963.)

HARBAGE, ALFRED. *Conceptions of Shakespeare*. Cambridge, Mass.: Harvard University Press, 1966. Pp. ix + 164. $4.95.

HERRICK, MARVIN T. *Italian Tragedy in the Renaissance*. Urbana: University of Illinois Press, 1965. Pp. viii + 315. $6.75.

HOLLAND, NORMAN N. *Psychoanalysis and Shakespeare*. New York: McGraw-Hill, 1964. Pp. xiii + 413. $9.95.

HONIGMANN, E. A. J. *The Stability of Shakespeare's Text*. Lincoln: University of Nebraska Press, 1965. Pp. xi + 212. $5.50.

HOROWITZ, DAVID. *Shakespeare: An Existential View*. New York: Hill and Wang, 1965. Pp. x + 134. $4.00.

HUNTER, ROBERT GRAMS. *Shakespeare and the Comedy of Forgiveness*. New York: Columbia University Press, 1965. Pp. ix + 272. $7.50.

Italian Plays, 1500–1700, in the University of Illinois Library, comp. MARVIN T. HERRICK. Urbana: University of Illinois Press, 1966. Pp. v + 92. $5.75.

JONES, ELDRED. *Othello's Countrymen: The African in English Renaissance Drama*. London: Oxford University Press, 1965. Pp. xii + 158. $3.40.

JONSON, BEN. *The Alchemist,* ed. DOUGLAS BROWN. New Mermaid Dramabook. New York: Hill and Wang, 1966. Pp. xxvi + 150. $1.25 (paper).

———. *Epicoene or The Silent Woman,* ed. L. A. BEAURLINE. Regents Renaissance Drama. Lincoln: University of Nebraska Press, 1966. Pp. xxiii + 159. $3.00. ($1.00, paper.)

KIRSCH, JAMES. *Shakespeare's Royal Self*. New York: G. P. Putnam for C. G. Jung Foundation, 1966. Pp. xix + 422. $7.95.

KNIGHT, G. WILSON. *The Crown of Life: Essays in Interpretation of Shakespeare's Final Plays*. New York: Barnes & Noble, 1966. Pp. 336. $2.95 (paper). (Orig. publ. 1948.)

———. *The Imperial Theme: Further Interpretations of Shakespeare's Tragedies Including the Roman Plays*. London: Methuen & Co., 1965. Pp. xv + 367. $2.95 (paper). (Orig. publ. 1931.)

KOLVE, V. A. *The Play Called Corpus Christi*. Stanford: Stanford University Press, 1966. Pp. xi + 337. $8.50.

KOZINTSEV, GRIGORI. *Shakespeare: Time and Conscience*. New York: Hill and Wang, 1966. Pp. vii + 276. $5.95.

LUCKI, EMIL. *History of the Renaissance, Book IV: Literature and Art*. Salt Lake City: University of Utah Press, 1965. Pp. xv + 281. $1.95 (paper).

MCDONALD, CHARLES OSBORNE. *The Rhetoric of Tragedy: Form in Stuart Drama*. Amherst: University of Massachusetts Press, 1966. Pp. vii + 360. $7.50.

McFARLAND, THOMAS. *Tragic Meanings in Shakespeare.* New York: Random House, 1966. Pp. ix + 179. $1.95 (paper).

MACK, MAYNARD. King Lear *in Our Time.* Berkeley: University of California Press, 1965. Pp. ix + 126. $3.75.

MARLOWE, CHRISTOPHER. *Doctor Faustus,* ed. ROMA GILL. New Mermaid Dramabook. New York: Hill and Wang, 1966. Pp. xxviii + 100. $1.25 (paper).

MELLERS, WILFRID. *Harmonious Meeting: A Study of the Relationship between English Music, Poetry and Theatre, c. 1600–1900.* London: Dobson Books, 1965. Pp. 317. $7.00.

MIDDLETON, THOMAS, and WILLIAM ROWLEY. *The Changeling,* ed. GEORGE W. WILLIAMS. Regents Renaissance Drama. Lincoln: University of Nebraska Press, 1966. Pp. xxiv + 112. $1.00 (paper).

MOULTON, RICHARD G. *Shakespeare as a Dramatic Artist.* New York: Dover Publications, 1966. Pp. xix + 443. $2.00 (paper). (3rd ed. orig. publ. 1893.)

MYRICK, KENNETH. *Sir Philip Sidney as a Literary Craftsman.* Lincoln: University of Nebraska Press, 1965. Pp. ix + 362. $1.85 (paper). (Orig. publ. 1935.)

NOSWORTHY, J. M. *Shakespeare's Occasional Plays: Their Origin and Transmission.* New York: Barnes & Noble, 1965. Pp. vii + 238. $7.50.

ORGEL, STEPHEN. *The Jonsonian Masque.* Cambridge, Mass.: Harvard University Press, 1965. Pp. x + 216. $4.95.

SAINTSBURY, GEORGE. *Historical Manual of English Prosody.* New York: Schocken Books, 1966. Pp. xxix + 347. $2.45 (paper). (Orig. publ. 1910.)

SCHANZER, ERNEST. *The Problem Plays of Shakespeare.* New York: Schocken Books, 1965. Pp. x + 196. $1.95 (paper). (Orig. publ. 1963.)

SEN GUPTA, S. C. *Shakespeare's Historical Plays.* London: Oxford University Press, 1964. Pp. ix + 172. $5.60.

SHAKESPEARE, WILLIAM. *The Comedy of Errors,* ed. GEORGE LYMAN KITTREDGE, rev. IRVING RIBNER. The Kittredge Shakespeares. Waltham: Blaisdell Publishing, 1966. Pp. xix + 71. $.65 (paper). (Previous ed. 1936.)

———. *The First Part of King Henry the Fourth,* ed. GEORGE LYMAN KITTREDGE, rev. IRVING RIBNER. The Kittredge Shakespeares. Waltham: Blaisdell Publishing, 1966. Pp. xxi + 117. $.65 (paper). (Previous ed. 1940.)

———. *The Second Part of King Henry the Fourth,* ed. A. R. HUMPHREYS. Arden Shakespeare. London: Methuen & Co.; Cambridge, Mass.: Harvard University Press, 1966. Pp. xci + 242. $4.50.

———. *The Second Part of King Henry the Fourth,* ed. GEORGE LYMAN KITTREDGE, rev. IRVING RIBNER. The Kittredge Shakespeares. Waltham: Blaisdell Publishing, 1966. Pp. xviii + 123. $.65 (paper).

———. *Twelfth Night or What You Will*, ed. GEORGE LYMAN KITTREDGE, rev. IRVING RIBNER. The Kittredge Shakespeares. Waltham: Blaisdell Publishing, 1966. Pp. xxi + 104. $.65 (paper). (Previous ed. 1941.)

Shakespeare Celebrated: Anniversary Lectures Delivered at the Folger Library, ed. LOUIS B. WRIGHT. Ithaca: Cornell University Press for The Folger Shakespeare Library, 1966. Pp. ix + 176. $5.00.

Shakespeare Studies 1, ed. J. LEEDS BARROLL. Cincinnati: Shakespeare Studies, 1965. Pp. 374. $8.00.

Shakespeare Then Till Now. Shakespeare Survey 18, ed. ALLARDYCE NICOLL. Cambridge: Cambridge University Press, 1965. Pp. x + 205. $8.50.

Shakespeare: The Tragedies. A Collection of Critical Essays, ed. CLIFFORD LEECH. Chicago: University of Chicago Press, 1965. Pp. xxxii + 256. $2.45 (paper).

Shakespeare's Plutarch, ed. T. J. B. SPENCER. Baltimore: Penguin Books, 1964. Pp. 365. $1.95 (paper).

STAUFFER, DONALD A. *Shakespeare's World of Images: The Development of His Moral Ideas*. Bloomington: Indiana University Press, 1966. Pp. 393. $2.95 (paper). (Orig. publ. 1949.)

STROUP, THOMAS B. *Microcosmos: The Shape of the Elizabethan Play*. Lexington: University of Kentucky Press, 1965. Pp. xi + 235. $6.00.

THALER, ALWIN. *Shakespeare and Our World*. Knoxville: University of Tennessee Press, 1966. Pp. ix + 235. $5.95.

Tudor Plays: An Anthology of Early English Drama, ed. EDMUND CREETH. Garden City: Doubleday & Co., 1966. Pp. xlvii + 569. $2.95 (paper).

WEBSTER, JOHN. *The Duchess of Malfi*, ed. ELIZABETH M. BRENNAN. New Mermaid Dramabook. New York: Hill and Wang, 1966. Pp. xxx + 129. $1.25 (paper).

WILLIAMS, DAVID RHYS. *Shakespeare Thy Name Is Marlowe*. New York: Philosophical Library, 1966. Pp. 94. $3.00.

WRIGHT, LOUIS B. *Shakespeare for Everyman*. New York: Washington Square Press, 1965. Pp. xvi + 223. $4.95.